Nations and Identities: Classic Readings

KEYWORKS IN CULTURAL STUDIES

As cultural studies powers ahead to new intellectual horizons, it becomes increasingly important to chart the discipline's controversial history. This is the object of an exciting new series, KeyWorks in Cultural Studies. By showcasing the best that has been thought and written on the leading themes and topics constituting the discipline, KeyWorks in Cultural Studies provides an invaluable genealogy for students striving to better understand the contested space in which cultural studies takes place and is practiced.

Nations and Identities
Classic Readings

Edited by

Vincent P. Pecora

Copyright © Blackwell Publishers Ltd 2001; editorial matter and organization copyright © Vincent P. Pecora 2001

First published 2001

2 4 6 8 10 9 7 5 3 1

Blackwell Publishers Inc.
350 Main Street
Malden, Massachusetts 02148
USA

Blackwell Publishers Ltd
108 Cowley Road
Oxford OX4 1JF
UK

Library of Congress Cataloging-in-Publication Data

Nations and identities: classic readings / edited by Vincent P. Pecora.
p. cm.—(KeyWorks in cultural studies)
Includes bibliographical references and index.
ISBN 0-631-22208-1 (alk. paper)—ISBN 0-631-22209-X (pbk. : alk.paper)
1. Nationalism—History—20th century. 2. History—Philosophy—History—20th century. 3. Intellectual life—History—20th century. 4. World politics—20th century.
I. Pecora, Vincent P., 1953–II. Series.
D421 .N38 2001
320.1′1—dc21   00–025861

British Library Cataloguing in Publication Data
A CIP catalogue record for this book is available from the British Library.

Typeset in Galliard 10 on 12pt
by Kolam Information Services Pvt. Ltd. Pondicherry, India
Printed in Great Britain by T.J. International, Padstow, Cornwall

This book is printed on acid-free paper.

Contents

Acknowledgments

An anthology of this sort is more than just a gathering of documents. It is also an archive of the counsel and assistance offered by colleagues, students, friends, and editors. This collection had its beginnings in a conversation with Blackwell's Andrew McNeillie, whose good idea sparked the project; it was nurtured by the intelligence and enthusiasm of Jayne Fargnoli, who guided the book to its completion. I am especially indebted to Beth Wightman's research skills and often brilliant suggestions, and Mary Holland's fine editorial assistance. And I must express my deep gratitude to the following individuals for their insights and advice along the way: Perry Anderson, Houston Baker, A. R. Braunmuller, Marshall Brown, King-Kok Cheung, Michael Colacurcio, Robert Hill, H. A. Kelly, Efrain Kristal, Robert Maniquis, Anne Mellor, Donka Minkova, Joseph Nagy, Jonathan Post, Ken Reinhard, Jenny Sharpe, Debora Shuger, Nancy Struever, Peter Wollen, and Michael Wood. Most of all, I want to thank Karen McCauley for her unflagging support and uncommon wisdom. Responsibility for the volume's shortcomings is, of course, mine alone.

Introduction

FLUELLEN: *Captain MacMorris, I think, look you, under your correction, there is not many of your nation –*
MACMORRIS: *Of my nation? What ish my nation? Ish a villain and a bastard and a knave and a rascal? What ish my nation? Who talks of my nation?*
(Shakespeare, Henry V *[1599])[1]*

—But do you know what a nation means? says John Wyse.
—Yes, says Bloom.
—What is it? says John Wyse.
—A nation? says Bloom. A nation is the same people living in the same place.
—By God, then, says Ned, laughing, if that's so I'm a nation for I'm living in the same place for the past five years.
    So of course everyone had the laugh at Bloom and says he, trying to muck out of it:
—Or also living in different places.
—That covers my case, says Joe.
—What is your nation if I may ask? says the citizen.
—Ireland, says Bloom. I was born here. Ireland.
(James Joyce, Ulysses *[1922])[2]*

"What is a nation?" is a famous question, but it has proven no easier to answer than the parallel and equally famous query about time posed by Augustine. "If no one asks me, I know; if I want to explain it to someone who does ask me, I do not know."[3] Most scholars today would say the nation is very much a part of what Giambattista Vico called human, rather than divine, history – that is, history that human beings can understand, because they have made it (even if Vico himself saw the rise and fall of nations as part of a divinely ordained cyclical plan). But while the nation may be a human invention, one that has played an enormous historical role in the last two centuries, it remains a piece of human history that has resisted firm definitions.

Whatever its origins, the nation has involved a complex and rarely consistent mixture of geography, language, custom, law, religion, economy, race, and collective will. The end of the twentieth century has been scarred by so-called "ethnic cleansing" in Bosnia and Kosovo, by the resurgence of nationalist sentiment and attempts to repress it in Turkey and Iraq, in Chechnya and East Timor, and by the horrors of sectarian violence in relatively new, postcolonial nations like Rwanda, Somalia, and Sri Lanka. But it is also true that the nation, in one form or another, has been for some time now a powerful and effective way of responding to both objective social needs and subjective feelings of collective solidarity. The main purpose of this anthology is to illustrate the history of national identity as expressed by some of the major documents that have articulated it. In this preface, I will briefly outline a few of the main issues that have come to shape the contemporary discussion of nations and national identity, including related notions such as nationalism and imperialism. In doing so, I will also try to provide some sense of the pre-history of the national idea and a rationale of sorts for the selections that have been included in this volume.

Nations and States

For many contemporary scholars there are good reasons to restrict the meanings of the words "nation" and especially "nationalism" to a fairly recent, and all too human, phenomenon: the nation-state as it arose in the West. With beginnings in the eighteenth century, the nation-state came to be constituted by internationally recognized sovereignty within a system of similar states; control over a definite geographical territory of some size (that is, larger than a city); an independent, domestically generated, and relatively centralized administrative apparatus; a distinct political structure, legal code, economy, currency, division of labor, and educational system; and a culture, defined by language, arts, customs, religion and/or race, that may be enormously varied by region and ethnicity but that generally has a dominant, hegemonic strain adopted by urban elites. But this list of attributes may soon be transformed. The coming of a unified European Union and the imminent (though still problematic) displacement of national currencies by the Euro may make economic and monetary autonomy less essential in defining a sovereign state, if not spell the end of national sovereignty in Europe as it has previously existed. The EU is beginning to test the degree to which particular nation-state identities can universalize themselves in a transnational, non-imperial political order.[4] It is a task made all the more difficult by enmity toward working-class immigrants from North Africa and Eastern Europe that has fueled resurgent nationalist sentiment in France, Germany, Italy, Spain, and Belgium. The EU's strong opposition in early 2000 to the electorally sanctioned inclusion of Joerg Haider's far right Freedom Party in a new Austrian government already directly challenges the principle of national self-determination.

At the same time, the use of the word "nation" and its cognates in other languages is clearly much older than the nation-state, to the extent that asking about the ultimate origins of nations is a bit like asking about the origins of language or race. One of the earliest accounts of the beginnings of differentiated human community, Genesis of the Hebrew Bible, makes the link between land, language, and kinship explicit with the dispersion of Noah's sons after the flood. For example, in the King James version we read: "These are the sons of Shem, after their families, after their tongues, in their lands, after their nations" (Genesis 10: 31). The word "nations" here is a now misleading but perfectly acceptable sixteenth-century (or even nine-teenth-century) translation of *goyim*, or peoples, a word used in Genesis for both heathen and Israelite. Yet the King James phrasing also captures something important about the uses to which origin myths such as that of Genesis would be put (and *were* put, for example, during the English Revolution), in that modern nationalism often invokes a similarly mythic conjunction of land, language, and kinship (or race). The nation, as the word is commonly used today – that is, to mean a recognized nation-state – may thus be considered a recent invention, but it carries much historical baggage and has appeared with many variations. It consists of geographically bound populations united by widely varying degrees and modes of social solidarity, held together by the machinery of markets, media, and political will backed by force. But it is also haunted by echoes of the past, both ethnic and civic, that are not easy to ignore.

The modern nation-state, with all its peculiar and artificial rituals of identification and enforced solidarity (for example, treating flags with sacred respect, or inculcating official accounts of national history in the young through state-sponsored schools), has both elevated and deeply troubled modern experience in ways that social structure, cultural habits, and govern-mental policy can only begin to explain. A nation-state can assign itself a mission, for example, and pursue it, perhaps to the point of self-destruction. Nation-states answer a deeply felt human need for freedom from domina-tion, but they can also ruthlessly dominate. At the same time, the modern nation, as embodied in a sense, or multiple senses, of nationality, may not be exactly equivalent to the state apparatus that governs it or, quite often, some part of it. Few have been willing to die on a battlefield to extend the political life of a state bureaucracy; but, at least since Homer, duty to one's *patria* or homeland has been as powerful a motive for sacrifice in war as the word of God, fealty to a king, or posthumous personal glory. In Italy, Japan, and Germany during the Second World War, by contrast, nation and state so perfectly coincided that one was routinely substituted for the other in political rhetoric. In Benito Mussolini's words: "It is not the nation which generates the state; that is an antiquated naturalistic concept which afforded a basis for XIXth century publicity in favor of national governments. Rather, it is the state which creates the nation, conferring volition and therefore real life on a people made aware of their moral unity."[5] Indeed, Anthony Smith has argued that Nazism and Fascism were not versions of nationalism at all, but statism pure and simple, with origins in the early twentieth-century "integral nationalism" and clerical monarchism of Maurice Barrès and Léon Daudet, and in Charles Maurras's synthesis of nationalism and socialism (all reactions, one should note, to the Dreyfus affair).[6] (As Isaiah Berlin has pointed out, this strain of Fascism really begins with Joseph de Maistre.[7]) In countless nationalist movements, however, duty to an ethnically conceived nation dispersed and fragmented among different state structures has turned out to be more powerful than the obligation of allegiance to one's duly constituted state: the militant Zionism that led to the state of Israel is a good example, but so is the Palestinian struggle against that state in the name of those who were displaced by its creation. Ever since Kemal Atatürk's founding of the Turkish Republic in 1923, minority populations of Kurds in Turkey, Iraq, Iran, and Syria have struggled to create an independent Kurdistan. Walker Connor has argued that, among the 132 entities recognized as states in 1978, "only 12 states (9.1%) can justifiably be described as nation-states," and that "in 39 (29.5%), the largest nation or potential nation accounts for less than half of the population."[8] Connor's may be an extreme way of defining the nation-state, but his data illustrate the scope of the problem.

A comparison to religious community may be instructive here. Maistre, the late eighteenth-century champion of monarchy and state religion, argued that "man cannot bestow rights on himself; he can only defend those which have been granted him by a superior power; and these rights are *good customs*, good because they are not written and because no beginning or author can be assigned to them."[9] This perspective is similar in certain respects to that of Burke in England and Hegel in Germany: for all three, inherited customs, or communally recognized and religiously based norms – which Hegel called *Sittlichkeit* – were an essential element of the positive law, and for Maistre and Burke they were the only true basis of the national state's governing capacity. Throughout much of the nineteenth century, France was still a Roman

Catholic monarchy and England continued to enforce its own state religion, specifically to exclude Roman Catholics. Both Maistre and Burke also denied the authority of Rousseau's "social compact"; and both objected to Robespierre's attempt to invent a new religion of the state *ex nihilo*. But Maistre went farthest in maintaining a variant of the much older "divine right" argument (as in Sir Robert Filmer's *Patriarcha: or The Natural Power of Kings* [1680]), holding that only God supplied the ethical substance embodied by sovereign authority, in the form of a monarch who was almost literally the father of his people, and by resulting cultural traditions.

Versions of Maistre's argument about religion as the only real basis of national authority and community are still around, from Christian fundamentalism in the United States to Islamic fundamentalism in the Middle East, and they can be powerful engines of nationalism. It can be argued that Polish Catholicism, reinvigorated by a Polish pope, and Islamic revolution in Afghanistan were the sparks that led eventually to the collapse of Soviet hegemony. The conflict that dismembered the former Yugoslavia was largely religious in origin, like that which carved out Pakistan from India, continues to divide Cyprus, and has fueled civil war in Sri Lanka since the mid-1980s. Northern Ireland's "troubles" have been thoroughly religious as well, and they are merely a vestige of Ireland's centuries-long struggle for independence, in which religion played a significant role. Despite its nominally secular government, Israel's national identity depends for many of its citizens on a specific religious heritage. Iran and Afghanistan are now overt theocracies, and Algeria has escaped such a fate only through harsh political repression.

Yet Maistre also recognized that the character of modern nationalist allegiance and patriotic sacrifice was, entirely in itself, a religious phenomenon: "Government is a true religion; it has its dogmas, its mysteries, its priests; to submit it to individual discussion is to destroy it; it has life only through the national mind, that is to say, political faith, which is a *creed*."[10] On this latter point, Maistre begins to approach the quite secular perspective of Emile Durkheim's sociology of religion at the beginning of the twentieth century, according to which the group identity provided by social symbolism, from the totem of the primitive clan to the flag of the modern nation-state, could in fact be understood as the basis, or functional equivalent, of religious belief. For Maistre, and later Barrès, the nation-state may need to be founded on religion; but nation-states should also function like religions in themselves, in which individual reason must be submerged in the "national mind." One could claim that it is precisely the latter formula – the nation as religion, rather than the nation based on religion – that has authorized some of the most powerful forms of nationalist sentiment (*pace* Smith) in the twentieth century. As Léon Brunschvicg is reported to have said to Raymond

Aron in reference to the Nazi pageants of the late 1930s, "Nuremburg is religion according to Durkheim, society adoring itself."[11] What Maistre (as advocate) and Durkheim (as sociologist) glimpsed was the degree to which modern national identity, whether already enshrined in a state or still in the process of consolidation, would become the modern secular religion.[12]

I began with Augustine's influential epigram because I believe it captures something crucial about nations and national identities at the present time. It is likely that a higher percentage of the world's population, gathered in the "global village" of mass media and telecommunications, can now consciously claim "national" identity than ever before – and each claimant, one might say, knows through experience (sometimes painful) what a nation is. Yet asking them to provide a definition would produce a fairly large range of responses. Is there in fact any one thing called a nation, or is it a mythical beast, a community not simply "imagined," as Benedict Anderson has argued, but imaginary through and through?[13] Each nation-state now on earth could supply a slightly different meaning for the word "nation," a different official account (perhaps more than one), not only of its own origins and development, but of the idea of national identity that it supposedly embodies. And yet there are undeniable continuities across time and space. In August of 1999, elections were held in East Timor (forcibly annexed in 1976, once the Portuguese abandoned the island after several centuries of colonial rule, by Indonesia, itself newly independent from the Netherlands) to decide its political fate. In the words of José Alexandre Gusmao, East Timor's formerly imprisoned independence leader, "a long chapter in the history of our people's struggle for affirmation of its culture and firm determination to choose its own future is reaching conclusion" – sentiments that echo those of the German nationalist Fichte nearly two centuries before him.[14]

Ethnicity and Modernity

Ethnicity is often used in a bewildering number of ways to describe such situations, and the term may include one or all of the following elements: customs, language, race, and religion. Nationalists frequently assert the ethnic continuity of a given nation in ways that exclude or oppress minority populations and may make little sense to disinterested observers. And many politically excluded minority populations openly embrace ethnicity in turn as a fundamental ingredient of a defensive solidarity. But nationalism can take various shapes, and it often forcefully overrides the power of ethnic distinctions. Indeed, one could claim that *all* nationalisms must do this in the event, wittingly or not, since ethnic homogeneity on a national scale is generally an illusion. With approximately 6,500 languages extant around the globe, for example, it could hardly be otherwise: a world in which every linguistic community was a nation-state would seem unimaginable. The ethnic components of collective identity are arguably as old as human civilization, and they have been central to modern national sentiment at least since Herder. Yet the history of nationalist thought is filled with invented traditions masquerading as ethnic inheritances (as in Macpherson's notorious "translations" from the Gaelic, Sir Walter Scott's tales of the Scottish Highlands, and the creation of clan tartans out of vanished medieval traditions, all of which established a "Celtic" identity that was supposedly ancient in origin), or the resurrection of a past event, often a military defeat or victory, by elites and intellectuals to serve contemporary political ends (as in the recent re-emergence of the Serb loss to Ottoman Muslims in Kosovo in 1389, or Ulster Protestant marches in honor of the victory of William of Orange).[15] Still, it is hard to discount the continuing force of the ethnic idea. As both Clifford Geertz's and Salman Rushdie's contributions to this volume show, postcolonial life is often a bitter contest between further fragmentation into a multitude of real or imagined ethnic communities and the consolidation of a vague consensus about real or imagined national identity.

Anthony Smith has suggested that the distinction Friedrich Meinecke made in 1908 between the *Kulturnation*, "the largely passive cultural community," and the *Staatsnation*, "the active self-determining political nation," may still be of some use.[16] The problem with such distinctions has always been of the chicken-and-egg sort. Is the "passive cultural community" destined in some sense to develop a political self-consciousness and coalesce into a "self-determining political nation," as Romantic nationalism in general believed, or is there no real connection between the two? Certainly Meinecke's dichotomy accurately describes many irredentist forms of nationalism, in which a politically active national state (like Nazi Germany) acts to recover a more passive, and often tendentiously constructed, cultural community and territory outside its existing borders. But is the Romantic, developmental model correct in saying that the ancient Hebrew, Greek, Germanic, and Celtic "cultural communities" finally made themselves into modern political nations in the last two centuries, that the ancient Egyptian and Chinese dynasties evolved naturally and inexorably into the twentieth-century nation-states we know today? Or do the two entities – old cultural community and new nation-state – simply have little to do with one another? Such questions are not merely theoretical: interpreting modern Israel's claim to certain ancient lands, or Taiwan's proper relationship with mainland China, has had far-reaching practical consequences for over half a century. As Efrain Kristal points out, "No one could have predicted how the Spanish viceroyalties would be parceled into the Spanish American states as we know them today."[17] In Latin America and elsewhere, the distinctiveness or singularity of a *Kulturnation* has often depended on the rise of a nationalist imagination that was born with, or even after, independence. The history of nation-building in Africa is even more striking in this regard. The independent nations that after the Second World War succeeded the nineteenth-century imperial partition of Africa were themselves largely reflections of that imperial geography: prior tribal boundaries and allegiances were often in direct conflict with the new state formations, and have routinely disrupted them ever since.

If we look beyond Connor's narrow definitions, there have been many modern nation-states comprising numerous "national" communities, even if one nationality has been dominant. The now defunct USSR contained a number of semi-autonomous "republics," in which some ethnic identities were nurtured and officially recorded on passports and many others were not, while "Russians" retained a favored status.[18] Switzerland is the often-cited example of a successful state built on a federation of three ethnically and geographically distinct national communities. And the United States of America is a multi-ethnic federal state, ruled primarily by a white, Anglo-Saxon, Protestant elite, with relatively autonomous regional administrations having nothing to do with ethnicity. But seemingly older and more homogeneous nation-states, such as England, France, Spain, Portugal, and Holland, are also quite complex. The modern United Kingdom is a multinational state that has tended to privilege English identity as its ethnic heart and soul. But in the 1860s, for example, the question whether English should remain the dominant language of Wales or be replaced by Welsh – an issue motivated by the Celtic Revival – was very much alive. (Matthew Arnold, though fascinated with the Celts, still insisted upon the primacy of the English language throughout Britain.[19]) England, one of the old European nations, has not been a state unto itself for some time, though the formation in 1999 of an autonomous Scottish Parliament may force changes in England as well. But the apparent unity of English identity is a rather modern phenomenon, and in this, England is very similar to other "old" nations. Throughout the nineteenth century, for example, English-ness was for writers like Arnold anything but straightforward, depending on whether one saw English identity in purely Saxon (Teutonic) terms, or as a mixture of Teuton, Dane, Norman, Latin, and Celt.

In France at this time, as Eugen Weber has dramatically shown, the situation was far less coherent. In the early years of the Third Republic (1870–1914), French was a foreign language for perhaps half the citizens of France, most of them peasants and children.[20] Rural regions like Brittany and Alsace and much of the Basque-, Catalan-, Occitan-, and Provençal-speaking center and south had little identification, patriotic or civil, at mid-century with the "national" government in Paris. Indeed, the racist Gobineau claimed in 1854 that "in France, the country where races are mingled more than anywhere else, there are little communities . . . who feel a repugnance to marrying outside their own village."[21] Although most of the peasants of the countryside would have heard of the Revolution, writes Weber, "a lot of Frenchmen did not know that they belonged together until the long didactic campaigns of the later nineteenth century told them they did."[22] We tend to think of the established nations of Western Europe as having a degree of homogeneity far greater than that of many newly independent nations struggling to create unity out of the fragments of colonial rule – but this may be a form of historical amnesia. It may be that the function of nationalism ever since the French Revolution has been precisely to invent a new political reality out of the illusion of a coherent past. Elie Kedourie's deeply skeptical words, reacting to the statist nationalism of Mussolini and Hitler, sharpen the point: "in the modern world . . . it is very often truer to say that national identity is the creation of nationalist doctrine than that nationalist doctrine is the emanation or expression of national identity."[23] But it would also be hard to deny that such a thesis leaves much about the experience of belonging to a nation unexplained. Basque separatists, still speaking a language historically unrelated to any other, continue to dream of carving out their own nation along the borders of France and Spain, within which Basque culture has long remained relatively distinct. The ethnic dimension of nationalist thought has had a persistence that defies Kedourie's logic.

Nations in History

The most recent spur to the national imagination has surely been the collapse of the Soviet empire and its hegemony over Eastern Europe after 1989. The resurgence since then of ethnic and often religiously based nationalism within the tenuous Russian Federation and on its borders, and among the federated republics of Yugoslavia, has been even more striking, and much of it terribly destructive. At the same time, largely as a result of massive foreign investment and stable market conditions, Estonia now flourishes to such an extent that the Russian colonial exiles who remain there show little desire to return to their homeland. On the one hand, the contemporary global economy, with its trade (rather than military) alliances and multinational corporations, its North American Free Trade Agreement and European Union, its "new world order" and United Nations/NATO interventions (as in the bombing of Serbia), may be changing the way "national sovereignty" is understood – perhaps, some might argue, making the concept itself obsolete. On the other hand, this transnational perspective must confront, in places like Bosnia and Kosovo, a strange historical echo of pre-1914 international relations. For many commentators, a "new tribalism" emerged as the Cold War ended.[24]

Yet it would be wrong to see the twentieth century's last decade, or the end of the Cold War, as unusually important where questions of national identity and nation-states are concerned. Historians and political scientists have been discussing an "ethnic revival" for some time – Clifford Geertz and others addressed the issue in the early 1960s – and much of it has occurred outside Europe.[25] The liquidation of many empires after the Second World War – English, Dutch, and French especially – played a major role in the contemporary reassertion of national identity. The decolonization of India, Indonesia, Vietnam, and most of Africa was both the effect of and a spur to nationalism, nation-building, and, all too often, communal conflict. In a number of cases – Northern Ireland and Palestine are the most glaring examples – the retreat of empire has meant a persistent and seemingly irresolvable struggle over national sovereignty lasting several generations. But the resurgence of ethnic forms of identity has found in this period a multitude of expressions even in the absence of any direct link to fading empire. Led by an Afro-centric and separatist black nationalism in the 1960s and early 1970s, other ethnic minority cultures in the United States have elaborated their identities, even if rarely to the point of actual territorial expectations.[26]

Is it then adequate to trace this latest explosion of nationalist feeling only as far back as the birth of an independent India in 1947? Perhaps we should look three decades earlier to Woodrow Wilson's "Fourteen Points" speech of 1918, reflecting the collapse of the Hapsburg, Ottoman, and Russian empires in the First World War and pointing toward a redrawing of the map of Europe. Wilson's statement defined for the first time within international law a right to "autonomous development" among formerly colonized peoples, where the "interests of the populations concerned" should weigh as heavily as the existing imperial governments in the determination of sovereignty – though Wilson did not then define what would constitute a "population" or a "people." (Black nationalism in the United States had its roots in Marcus Garvey's Universal Negro Improvement Association, which, though founded in Jamaica in 1914 and anticipated by earlier back-to-Africa movements, flourished in post-Wilson 1920s Harlem.[27]) Wilson's League of Nations and the Versailles peace conference created independent states in Yugoslavia, Czechoslovakia, Poland, and Hungary, but these were also part of an ongoing process. Preceding Wilson's idealistic policy statement, there was the growing clamor for national self-determination throughout the nineteenth and early twentieth centuries: in response and then resistance to

Napoleon's France, from Haiti to the Middle East; against the Spanish empire throughout Mexico, Central and South America; for the unification of the semi-feudal German principalities; for a united and independent Poland, Greece, Italy, Ireland, China, and so on. The early nineteenth-century struggle for Greek independence from the Turks became among European intellectuals something of a *cause célèbre*, one in which the English poet Byron lost his life. The year 1848, which saw revolutionary uprisings in cities across Europe, turned out to be a political milestone of sorts, both because it represented the powerful conjunction of nationalist and socialist impulses that would play a role in many subsequent nationalist movements, and because it generated so much failure, disillusionment, and repression afterwards. Richard Wagner, for example, fought as a young socialist and nationalist revolutionary in 1848; but he would live to become one of the great inspirations for anti-Semitism and Nazism in the twentieth century.

The nation has served as a political ideal with a rich historical resonance for an educated elite at least since the mid-eighteenth century. The French Revolution is in almost all accounts a watershed event in the rise of the republican nation-state as the preferred means to achieve the modern political ideals of liberty, equality, and fraternity. Article 3 of the Revolution's *Declaration of the Rights of Man and Citizen* (1789) enshrines the principle of popular sovereignty for many subsequent European revolutions, a principle based on the arguments of Rousseau and on the skeptical reason of the French Enlightenment. As Benedict Anderson points out, however, nationalism in the Americas, North and South, predated European nationalism and was primarily a "Creole" movement, guided by wealthy landowners born in the Americas who spoke like and shared the customs of the English, French, Spanish, and Portuguese masters against whom they rebelled. These Creole landowners – Thomas Jefferson is a good example, but so is the great Liberator of South America, Simón Bolívar, both men slave-owners – were simultaneously deeply afraid of the other sort of revolution threatening the New World at this time: the black slave rebellion in Haiti of Toussaint L'Ouverture, which in 1804 produced the Western Hemisphere's second independent republic.[28] It was the United States, in 1776, that successfully inaugurated this sort of anti-colonial rebellion, consolidating even earlier than the French Revolution and Napoleon's subsequent campaigns the ideal of the self-determining nation-state as the enemy of dynastic empire. Some scholars also point to the imperial partitioning of Poland – in 1772, 1793, and 1795 – as a spur to nationalist sentiment across Europe. Rousseau's advice had been solicited in the service of too-late reforms just before the first partition, while both Burke and later Acton condemned the imperial land-grabs as political errors that only fueled nationalist fervor and spelled disaster for existing multinational states. Still others would begin with the European Religious Wars and the English Civil War of the seventeenth century. The former signaled the original fracturing of the Austrian Hapsburg empire in 1648 with the Treaties of Westphalia, which ended the Thirty Years' War – a war that began in Bohemia as a conflict between the Protestant Reformation and Catholic orthodoxy, and concluded as a series of struggles for national sovereignty that effectively destroyed the continental hegemony of Roman Catholicism, the Pope, and the Holy Roman Emperor.

In England, as John Milton's "The Tenure of Kings and Magistrates" (1649) argues, "the liberty and right of free-born men to be governed as seems to them best" – a sentiment almost directly echoed by Jefferson's "Declaration of Independence" (1776) and Wilson's defense of the League of Nations – included the right to remove a crowned head guilty of tyranny.[29] It was a right taken quite literally in the case of Charles I, whose execution Milton's tract two weeks later was designed to justify. Milton derived this right simultaneously from Aristotle and a Protestant reading of scripture, but it had a long pedigree before him. As the "divine right" monarchist Robert Filmer noted, the English Jesuit Parsons and Scotch Calvinist Buchanan had made similar claims; and popular constraints on crowned sovereigns, nominally in the service of the Pope, were elaborated by scholastic theologians of the Middle Ages. Milton vested the right to self-governance in "a free nation," whether "protestant state or kingdom," which was no longer the vague name for the inhabitants of a region or the king's subjects or (as in Martin Luther's "Open Letter to the Christian Nobility of the German Nation" [1520]) a medieval cultural elite, but rather the collective "authority of the people," from which the king's power was derived.[30] The foundational works of the royalist Hobbes and republicans Locke and Rousseau on the modern state elaborate this identification of a people and sovereignty in terms of a contract (Locke replied specifically to Filmer). Kedourie has argued that such notions of popular sovereignty were complemented by the philosophical revolution of Immanuel Kant, in which the moral autonomy of the individual depends on the freedom to make laws and the imperative to think of them in universal terms. In *Perpetual Peace* (1794), for example, Kant extended this secular, anthropocentric rationale for self-determination to political bodies: only a republican state that was an expression of a people's autonomous will would guarantee stability.[31] Yet we must also recognize that many nationalist revolts have not been very "popular" in reality; that many nation-states have not followed the later Milton's Republican advice (in "The Ready and Easy Way to Establish a Free Commonwealth" [1660]) and have remained, or are once again, nominally monarchies (Britain, Spain, Holland, Belgium, Sweden, Denmark, Norway, and Japan today among them); and that self-serving elites have abused the principle for which both Charles and Louis were sacrificed as readily as they have manipulated the complementary notion of ethnic identity.

As Milton's example suggests, it would be hard to overestimate the Reformation as a crucial transformation in European life, without which many of the qualities later attributed to national identity would not have come about, or would have developed rather differently. Once the power of a single, transnational religious hierarchy was broken and Luther's notions of liberty of conscience, scriptural (rather than institutional) authority, and secular vocation were accepted, it was far easier to substitute national affiliations for religious ones. Without that displacement of allegiance, national*ism* would surely have been a less credible doctrine in educated Christian Europe. As the German Romantic poet and philosopher Novalis (Friedrich Leopold von Hardenberg) wrote in his lament for a religiously unified Europe, "Christendom or Europe" (composed in 1799, though not published until after his death): "With the Reformation it was all up with Christendom. . . . For the first time [princes] felt the weight of their physical power on earth, saw the heavenly powers idle as their representatives were insulted, and now sought little by little and without attracting the attention of their subjects, who were still eager adherents of the Papacy, to throw off the burdensome Roman yoke and make themselves independent on earth."[32] Yet many nationalist revolutions of the nineteenth and twentieth centuries continued to base their claims in religious feelings – indeed, for both Mazzini and Martí, in the Roman Catholicism that Novalis saw threatened. Nevertheless, while religious nationalisms of various sorts are still with us, the Reformation's undoing of the Catholic Church's hegemony in Europe must be counted as one of the founding events in the rise of a modern sense of national identity.

There is, however, another more practical consequence of the Reformation, and that is the immense rise in the importance of vernacular languages – especially in print – that occurred with the publication of Luther's German translation of the Bible (complete in 1534, though portions had appeared earlier) and, about the same time, William Tyndale's English translations of the New Testament (1525–6) and Pentateuch (1530), which make some reference to Luther's earlier translations. (A revised version of Tyndale's translation would become the King James, or Authorized Version, in 1611.) While Benedict Anderson's work has once again turned our attention to the rise in importance of vernacular languages with the advent of the printing press and a nation-wide market economy to distribute texts, the issue has been a central one for most of the twentieth century. Carlton Hayes, whose *Essays on Nationalism* (1926) is one of the founding pieces of modern Anglophone scholarship on the nation, noted both humanism's attempt to restore Latin to its ancient complexity, which made it less useful as a medium of philosophy, literature, religion, and statecraft, and the increasing dependence of the elite on vernacular languages. But most important was "the invention of printing, which served to stereotype the common spoken languages, to fix for each a norm of literary usage, and to render possible the dissemination of national literature among the masses."[33] Hayes's argument about print has now been enlarged and refined. But the essential point has remained the same: the wide distribution in print of a single language among the population who spoke it, even with very low rates of literacy, served to provide a sense of collective coherence – or what Anderson calls a "conception of simultaneity" within a bounded social horizon – that would allow a truly national consciousness to develop.[34] Even if we grant that Eugen Weber's analysis of a multilingual and illiterate peasantry in France provides powerful counter-evidence to Hayes and Anderson, it is still plausible that a national consciousness among the cultural and administrative elite of outlying regions depended on what Anderson calls "print capitalism."

Finally, we should recognize that, for some earlier scholars especially, the history of the nation could not be fully understood without beginning in ancient Israel and Greece. In what may be the most comprehensive study of nations and nationalism in the first half of the twentieth century, Hans Kohn starts with the Romantic pairing of the Hellenes and Hebrews of antiquity (a pairing elaborated by eighteenth-century comparative philology, by German Romantics such as Heine, and later by Moses Hess, Matthew Arnold, Ernest Renan, and Friedrich Nietzsche).[35] Hellenes are marked by "artistic serenity," vision, and a strong sense of space; Hebrews by "burning religiosity," aurality, and a powerful understanding of time. Together, these two ancient nations developed the historical consciousness and worldliness that for Kohn would be essential for all later national identities.[36] Few scholars of the nation today accept the terms of Kohn's Hellene–Hebrew pairing, though it was an influential one throughout the nineteenth and early twentieth centuries. Contemporary discussion likewise finds little value in rehearsing the ancient or medieval pre-history of the nation in great detail – Kohn refers often enough to "nationalism," for example, in eras in which the word (or a near relative) itself did not exist. But a long view of the issue such as Kohn's may shed light on the peculiar historical dilemma that the problem of national identity has posed. For example, Milton, Cromwell, and the English Revolution may represent "the first example of modern nationalism, religious, political, and social at the same time, although it was not the secularized nationalism which arose at the end of the eighteenth century."[37] But the revolution modeled itself, at times rather directly, on the Old Testament story of the ancient Israelites, a story that bequeathed to English Puritans the notions of a chosen people, a Covenant, and Messianic hope.

Moreover, between the ancient Hebrews and the Reformation, one finds a long gestation of the national idea in the humanism, etatism, and patriotism of the Renaissance city-state; in Machiavelli's *Prince* (1513) and Claude de Seyssel's *La Grand' Monarchie de France* (1519); and earlier in Petrarch's hymns to the popular, anti-papal revolutionary Cola di Rienzo (such as his "Letter to Cola di Rienzo and the Roman People" [1347]), who was seen as a possible unifier of Italy under the aegis of Rome. (Rienzo's rebellion would be often commemorated amid the nationalist fervor of the nineteenth century, in Byron's *Childe Harold's Pilgrimage* [1812–18], Bulwer Lytton's *Rienzi, the Last of the Tribunes* [1835], and Richard Wagner's *Rienzi* [1841].) In his Latin treatise "On Eloquence in the Vernacular" (1304–9), Dante praises the power of a single vernacular to unite the disparate regions of Italy – Dante hoped to create such a language in his *Commedia*. Even Augustine, perhaps the most important influence on Luther and Calvin, represents in his *City of God* (428) a heavenly state that nevertheless provides a model for righteous earthly kingdoms. For Kohn, while it is primarily "the revival of ancient patriotism" in figures like Rienzo that offers the clearest prefiguration of later nationalism, there is no simple or sudden eruption of the national idea in European history.[38]

Classical Greece and Rome certainly provide a wealth of literature that elaborates a strong awareness of cultural or ethnic difference, xenophobia, and patriotic zeal. Herodotus's account of the Egyptians in his *Histories* (5th century BC) and Tacitus's treatment of the Germans in his *Germania* (AD 98) are both good examples of the elevated consciousness of difference in manners and customs between peoples that is often basic to national identity. But one could also turn to Hecataeus of Miletus, Hippocrates, Aristotle, Julius Caesar, Livy, and Pliny the Elder for similar evidence. At the same time, though almost always in quite separate writings, such as Plato's *Republic*, Aristotle's *Politics*, and Cicero's treatises "On the Commonwealth" and "On the Laws," the rudiments of the centralized, territorial state – both city-state and imperium – are being developed. In Pericles's funeral oration for the Athenians who had died in the first year of the Peloponnesian War, which Thucydides includes in (or invents for) his *History of the Peloponnesian War* (431–413 BC), one finds a fairly complex patriotism that arises from civic pride in both the ethnic identity and the democratic form of government of the Athenian city-state.

Pericles begins with praise for "our ancestors" who, "generation to generation," through their valor preserved and handed down the homeland – though he also acknowledges that, having become an empire, Athens does not "exclude foreigners from any opportunity of learning or observing." Significantly, he praises "the form of government under which our greatness grew" as well as "the national habits out of which it sprang."[39] Neither

Athens nor any other city-state of ancient Greece (or medieval Italy, for that matter) could be considered a nation in the modern sense of the word. The Greeks and later Italians may have had a vague sense of racial or cultural kinship that allowed for sporadic alliances, but political life was very much determined by the limited *polis*. Still, the intimate relationship in Pericles's words between continuous cultural identity (however imaginary, or ethnically open-minded, it may be) and centralized democratic state is perhaps the closest ancient thinking would come to the notions of national identity that have shaped the world since the Reformation.

In the Shadow of Genealogies: Language, Race, and Land

It might seem as if the best way to get to the heart of any notion of the nation is to look at the word itself, especially at its etymology. The English word *nation*, for example, as well as its cognates in the Romance languages (in German and other languages it is a borrowed term), comes from the Latin *natio*, meaning birth, tribe, or people, but also race, species, class, kind, or breed. In these senses, *natio* is at times used interchangeably in classical Latin with *gens* (from which we get genus, generation, and the like), a word that likewise denotes race, species, tribe, or people, but has perhaps stronger connotations of family, clan, and offspring. Both words convey the sense of a people of common origin and territory, like the German *Volk*. And both may also carry the sense of an uncivilized people – the barbarian nations outside the empire, the gentiles – like the Hebrew *goyim*. Another partial synonym is *populus*, which can have a range of meanings, from a simple multitude, to a people, to a defined political community. Tacitus, who in his *Germania* elaborates the virtues of the "indigenous" (*indigenas*) barbarians to the north in order to shame a complacent Roman Empire into greater vigilance, provides an example of the use of all three words in one sentence.[40] He claims "to accept the opinion of those who believe that in the peoples of Germany [*Germaniae populos*] there appears a peculiar, pure, and unique race [*gentem*] untainted by intermarriage with other nations [*nationum*]."[41] The translations I have supplied here could easily be transposed, and have been by other translators; after all, Tacitus may have wanted nothing more than rhetorical variation. But the abundance of Latin words used to describe what would seem to be the same thing, each bearing nuances that may or may not be relevant, testifies to the verbal fuzziness of nations and national identities that remains with us still.

Such fuzziness, however, can have quite specific effects. While Tacitus's descriptions of his northern neighbors' customs may be trustworthy in certain respects, his view of their ethnic purity is today considered baseless.

But, along with his vivid portrayal of the Germans' military valor, sense of honor, love of freedom, disregard for silver and gold, dislike of cities, their marital fidelity and strong blood ties within the family, Tacitus's portrait of racial purity was happily accepted by the *"Blut und Boden"* (blood and soil) ideology of twentieth-century German nationalism, "assiduously taught in German schools and universities and made into a sort of Bible of German patriotism."[42] More directly than in the case of the English Puritans and ancient Israel, the vague pre-history of the German nation came to haunt the *Volk* lore of the modern nation-state. Houston Stewart Chamberlain, for example, quotes the sentence from Tacitus cited above frequently in his discussion of the Teutonic race and nation.[43] Even so, we should recall that Hitler himself considered many *Volkish* thinkers all too respectful of other nations' rights in their vision of a German homeland restored to the frontiers of 1914. Hitler in fact wanted an expanding *Lebensraum*, or living space, for an expanding nation, one which could no longer be restricted to some mythical connection to its natural, delimited territory. "State boundaries are made by man and changed by man," he wrote near the end of *Mein Kampf*.[44] German soil would finally be whatever the German nation needed; territory was a question of might, not right.

Tacitus's sense of the "indigenous" character of the Germans as a "pure" or "unadulterated" (*sinceram*) race, especially when linked to the modern German appropriation of this construction of nationhood, dramatically highlights the fundamental and age-old problem of the relationship between race and territory, ethnic identity and land. Indeed, the most primitive and literal interpretation of this relationship is aboriginality (from the Latin) or (more graphically) autochthony, from the Greek *autokhthōn*, meaning "one sprung from the land itself." Autochthony is the stock in trade of origin myths around the world; it is given to the Western tradition by Hesiod's *Theogony* and by the Hebrew Bible: "And the Lord God formed man of the dust of the ground..." (Genesis 2: 7). Ovid's account, in the *Metamorphoses*, of the story of Cadmus and the founding of Thebes is a good illustration of the belief as it has been used to explain the origins of peoples and nations. Cadmus slays a dragon and on Minerva's advice sows the dragon's teeth in the plains, from which spring armed warriors (the Spartae) who do battle with one another. The five surviving warriors join Cadmus in building Thebes: they become the ancestors of the race that will inhabit the land.[45] Vico, who cites Tacitus's *Germania* throughout his *New Science*, invokes the aboriginal Giants of "poetic wisdom" as the noble founders of the gentile (non-Hebrew) nations.[46] More recently, the anthropologist Claude Lévi-Strauss has argued that the Greek myth of Oedipus, which begins with the story of Cadmus and ends with Antigone burying her brother against state prohibition, is finally about the inability of a culture that believes in autochthony "to find a satisfactory transition between this theory and the knowledge that human beings are actually born from the union of men and women."[47] It is perhaps true that modern nationalists have not taken autochthony literally, though many have invoked the myth. Like Vico's "poetic wisdom," however, the mythic idea points toward the more-than-metaphorical power of terms like "motherland" and "fatherland" for many nationalist movements.

In the eighteenth century, Montesquieu elaborated another way in which the relationship of nation to land could be understood, in terms of the impressive power of the environment, from climate to geography, on the constitution of the peoples who inhabit it. "It is the variety of wants in different climates that first occasioned a difference in the manner of living, and this gave rise to a variety of laws."[48] Thus, children born in India to Europeans lose the "courage" generated by their parents' native climate and take on the "pusillanimous" character of the Indians; and an ancient German nation that migrates to Spain creates new laws in harmony with that region.[49] Montesquieu did not stress climate alone: soil, population size, religion, inherited traditions, all of these played their part in shaping a given people's laws. And the idea that climate influences the physical and mental constitution of peoples is at least as old as Pliny's first-century *Natural History*: black skin has long been attributed to the tropical sun. But Montesquieu's attitude toward the importance of the physical environment in shaping national character remained a powerful, if impressionistic, influence long after him, in Herder, Rousseau, Maistre and beyond, even up to the twentieth-century Italian Marxist Antonio Gramsci. The thesis of environmental influence fell into some disrepute in the modern period, and for obvious reasons: it had long been widely accepted by vulgar racists and imperialists, since it neatly demonstrated why certain forms of government (for example, self-determining or republican) would not be appropriate in certain climates (such as that of tropical colonies). The motif occupies a special place in the literature of empire, where landscape is often destiny. As the "alienist" (or psychiatrist) in Conrad's *Heart of Darkness* (1898) suggests about his measurement of European heads before and (when possible) after colonial service in Africa, "going native" was as much a function of contact with Africa's climate as the result of contact with its people. E. M. Forster's *Passage to India* (1924) is in this sense an extended meditation on Montesquieu's theme: India's earth and sky, its sun and rains, its vast plains and demoralizing caves all hold the key simultaneously to the eternal intransigence of the Indian people and the inevitable failure of the British Raj's ideals. More recently, climatic and geographical factors have once again gained respectability in serious scholarly research, from the work of French historian Emmanuel Le Roy Ladurie to that of American physiologist Jared Diamond.[50]

Beyond an etymological basis in ethnicity and land, however, little else about the usage of the word *nation* through the centuries is straightforward. Elie Kedourie reminds us that some medieval universities, like the University of Paris, divided its students into "nations" that vaguely indicated the students' provenance, but had no relation to fixed political boundaries or to the modern sense of the word.[51] From the fifteenth to the eighteenth century "nation" was used to denote any body that represented, or elected representatives for, a particular territory at Church Councils (as in Luther's "Open Letter"); and often, under the imperial dynasties of the French and the Hapsburgs up through the eighteenth century, the nation would have meant only the barons, nobles, lords, and bishops, rather than the mass of the population of a territory.[52] Eric Hobsbawm points out that the Dictionary of the Royal Spanish Academy "does not use the terminology of state, nation and language in the modern manner before its edition of 1884," and that prior editions simply defined the word *nación* either as "the aggregate of the inhabitants of a province, a country or a kingdom" or as "a foreigner" (as in its ancient Latin usage).[53]

The word *nationalism* is of much more recent origin. Anthony Smith observes that, while the word was used at Leipzig University as early as the fifteenth century to describe professorial allegiances (like those at the University of Paris), it was not used in the modern sense of a doctrine or political movement supporting the right of a nationality to form an autonomous nation until the very end of the eighteenth century, and even then was not used very much in the early nineteenth century.[54] This view of the meaning and relative modernity of the term "nationalism" is widely accepted, along with a second meaning, chauvinistic pride in one's nation and xenophobia toward other nations, which Smith would like to isolate as mere "national sentiment." In either sense, however, the larger significance of nationalism's modernity is still in some dispute, since (like the nation-state itself) the doctrine has been explained as both the cause and the effect of the national culture it would appear to name.

Etymologies rarely settle arguments of this sort, and they can be a spurious way of reasoning about contemporary events, not least when a fair amount of nationalist rhetoric in the twentieth century has appeared in non-European languages. There is, however, another and perhaps more significant role that the science of etymology has played in the historical discussion of nations and identities. The search for the roots of words resembles in certain ways the search for one's true ancestors. Linguists speak of families of languages – the Romance languages, the Germanic, the Slavic, as well as even broader groupings, such as Indo-European and Semitic – and organize them in much the way biologists classify animal life into classes, species, and genera. The eighteenth-century biological emphasis on classification left an obvious mark on racial theories of the nation (like those of Gobineau, Chamberlain, and Heinrich von Treitschke) in the nineteenth and twentieth centuries, especially after Darwin's work on evolution. But the linguist's classification of languages, which also flourished in the eighteenth century, had an equally powerful role to play in defining modern ideas about the nation, especially for many nationalists.

The context that made classifying languages so important was an underlying philosophical assumption about the power of language to shape individual and collective identities, once the origin of language was detached from divine intervention. German Romanticism was especially concerned with the problem: Herder's *Treatise on the Origin of Language* (1772) exerted a powerful influence on the conception of national languages. In Schleiermacher's "On the Different Methods of Translation" (1800), a language appears as a system of interconnected concepts that form an organic whole, in which intellect and imagination are firmly rooted. However much a cosmopolitan education requires a knowledge of other languages, the native national language should not be supplanted: "Just as a man must decide to belong to one country, he must adhere to one language, or he will float without any bearings above an unpleasant middle ground."[55] But it was William Jones's demonstration, in India in 1786, of the deeper kinship linking Greek and Latin to an even more ancient Hindu Sanskrit that became the crucial touchstone for later comparative philology. The subsequent projection of an ancestral ur-language for this linguistic family – Indo-European, or Indo-Germanic – provided the basis on which scholars could construct coherent genealogies of subsequent languages, cultures, races, and nations. This conjunction of factors was then mapped in both evolutionary and geographical terms: migratory patterns of ethnically homogeneous "peoples" were traceable, in effect, by philological research, which supposedly illustrated how seemingly unrelated populations in different territories shared a certain kinship dispersed over time. Following the work of figures like Barthold Niebuhr, the larger vicissitudes of European, and even world, history would be explained in such terms. The consequence was that the nation as a continuous ethnic and cultural community was given a secular and pseudo-scientific foundation in language that it had never had before.

Few scholars today would treat the national significance of language the way eighteenth- and nineteenth-century intellectuals did. Ernest Renan easily deflated many of the assumptions of comparative philology about language as the key to the history of races and nations: "Languages are historical formations, which give but little indication of the blood of those who speak them."[56] What remained was a longstanding recognition of the pragmatic power of a single national language to unify the nation-state. In his speech addressing "The Question of a National Language" (1917), Gandhi supplies two credible reasons for supporting Hindi as a solution to the problem of multilingual India: that it is not English, the language of the colonizer, and that it is the speech of the majority of the population. Gandhi's practical logic nevertheless met with stiff resistance. As Clifford Geertz notes (in "The Integrative Revolution"), the Indian National Congress had already accepted at this time "the principle of linguistic determination of state boundaries within India," and Nehru was still facing the possibility of linguistic factionalism a year after independence. Like India, many decolonized African nations were (and are) divided by a wealth of tribal languages; some, such as Kenya, continued to use the colonial language (English) as the best mechanism of unifying the state after independence. Like the example of linguistic separatists in India, however, the case of Kenyan writer Ngũgĩ Wa Thiong'o (formerly, James Ngũgĩ) demonstrates that the desire to express an independent cultural identity once the horrors of foreign domination end can imply the need for an indigenous means to express it, politically convenient or not. After writing for years in English, Ngũgĩ (who would be driven into exile in America after being imprisoned for a play critical of the postcolonial nationalist regime in Kenya) embraced Gĩkũyũ, a tribal language, as an integral part of what, echoing Césaire, he called "decolonising the mind" (though he also translated some of his Gĩkũyũ works into English).[57]

The modern nation-state might seem virtually impossible without a single dominant language, a language of state and law, mass communications, and education. Even the liberal John Stuart Mill, a skeptical precursor to Renan in so many ways, thought that democratic institutions would be impossible in a country made up of different nationalities and languages: "Among a people without fellow-feeling, especially if they read and speak different languages, the united public opinion, necessary to the working of representative government, cannot exist."[58] But many nations with entrenched linguistic communities have found moderate success in forging a single coherent polity, and in at least a few cases – Switzerland, which both Mill and Renan cite, Canada, and Belgium – a high degree of political stability has endured in spite of quite distinct linguistic regionalism and rivalry, even if only through federation or, in the case of Belgium, at the cost of massive bureaucratic duplication, proportional representation, and patronage. Still, language tends to define identity in ways that are as profound as any political allegiance, attachment to the land, or religious belief – as the recently fractious Canada, divided by little *except* language, reminds us. There is no reason, however, to think that language must determine a nation's fate.

Between Necessity and Will

While the selections gathered in this anthology reveal a broad range of responses to the question of national identity, I would like to focus briefly on a central historical and philosophical debate, dating originally from the nineteenth century but reformulated by contemporary scholarly discussion. The debate concerns the opposition between necessity and contingency in the life of nations. Is the nation, including its modern form of the nation-state, an inherent, natural, eternal, and necessary part of human development, both as a particular entity unto itself and as a component in a larger, universal teleology? Or is the nation-state a contingent event, a function of the historical vicissitudes of power, will, desire, and institutions, with no metaphysical significance whatsoever? I will focus here on Johann Gottlieb Fichte and Ernest Renan to represent the two poles of this debate; much nineteenth-century discussion falls somewhere in between.

In his *Addresses to the German Nation* (1808), the German philosopher Fichte described the modern nation as history's creation of a people according to a "spiritual law of nature," a "natural law of divine development."[59] In this view, borrowed in part from Herder and reproduced with variations in Alexander von Humboldt and Hegel, nations are eternal in *spirit*, though their practical continuity depends on the development of a conscious national will in harmony with that spirit. In England, Edmund Burke had challenged the French Revolution's attempt at total political transformation by insisting on a similar organicism: lasting changes could only occur when they evolved out of a fidelity to the past cultural and political life of the nation.[60] Unlike Herder, however, Fichte joined this eternal nation to a civil state, which (as he noted in his *Foundations of Natural Law* [1796]) is itself an organic expression of the civic life of a people. While the state involves "the government of human life," it is "not something which is primary and which exists for its own sake, but is merely the means to the higher purpose of the eternal, regular, and continuous development of what is purely human in this nation."[61] For Fichte, then, the state is finally subordinate to the nation, that is, to "the vision and the love of this eternal development."[62] Fichte's argument allows him to acknowledge that the German nation and the German state had never up to that point been the same – Germany as a single nation-state would not exist for decades after Fichte's *Addresses* – while insisting that the two were divinely destined to coincide. While the nation has been preserved in the biological descent, customs, institutions, and especially the language of the "whole common fatherland" of the German people, the state had so far appeared only in divided kingdoms and principalities.

Such an argument posits what Lord Acton, in reference to the partition of Poland, called "a nation demanding to be unified in a State – a soul, as it were, wandering in search of a body in which to begin life over again," or more precisely, a politically fragmented sense of nationality (or national identity) in search of an organically appropriate and all-inclusive government.[63] In this conception of the nation–state dyad, Fichte articulates what may be the most important formulation of nationalism for the modern period. Love of fatherland (that is, of the unified spiritual ideal of the nation) is the engine driving the search for a politically embodied nation-state, a search that must be cultivated through education. Nationalism may be said to be the doctrine that arises from such education, ranging in intensity from the relatively benign program of *Bildung* (or cultural formation) in Fichte to the virulent chauvinism and xenophobia that have characterized some twentieth-century movements. Like Hegel, Fichte is really propounding a philosophy of world history, in which individual nations are integral parts of the grander development of the human spirit toward freedom. The organic necessity of this world historical vision, however, entails some fairly constraining means. "The new education must consist essentially in this, that it completely destroys freedom of will in the soil which it undertakes to cultivate, and produces, on the contrary, strict necessity in the decisions of the will, the opposite being impossible."[64] When Adolf Hitler refers in *Mein Kampf* to the state as "the organism which enables and preserves [the nation's] life on this earth," and looks to "a national organism: *A Germanic State of the German Nation*" as the instrument that will reverse through a millennial *Reich* the degeneration of the Aryan race caused by the Jews, his final objectives may go far beyond anything Fichte imagined. But Hitler nevertheless uses Fichte's formulas to elaborate the nation–state fusion.[65]

At least since Renan's influential essay "What is a Nation?" near the end of the nineteenth century, Fichte's organic understanding of nation and state has been called into question. (In fact, Lord Acton had challenged Fichte's view – as he considered it reproduced in Mill – twenty years earlier by arguing for the greater value to civilization of enlightened, multinational empire.) For Renan, there were no nations in antiquity: there were loosely held aggregates, such as Egypt and China, led by divine rulers; municipal republics, kingdoms, and confederations that may have generated some patriotism, but no sense of nationality; vaguely defined populations in Gaul, Spain, and Italy with no central institutions; and unwiedly feudal empires. Even the Roman Empire, though more like a nation, was primarily an "association" rather than a "state" in the modern sense of the word – and here Renan's view prefigures many contemporary scholars who insist that the meaning of the nation be restricted to the achieved nation-state.[66] Nations are thus historically circumscribed political forms in Renan's view, dating only from the end of what he calls the "Teutonic invasion" of the fifth to the tenth century, and they were born out of the violence of dynastic conquest and migration rather than the peaceful development of one people in the same territory.[67] There are two consequences for Renan of these observations: first, nations must not be confounded with either biological or linguistic races; and second, one should not attribute to linguistic groups a "sovereignty analogous to really existent peoples" (by which Renan appears to mean, "to really existent nation-states").[68]

In fact, Renan explicitly questions all the primary grounds for national identity in the Romantic model: race, language, religion, economy, and geography. Two factors remained for him, and both of them had already been emphasized by Mill: the collective memory of past glory and past sacrifices made on the nation's behalf; and present will, desire, and need. The nation is in Renan still "a spiritual principle" as well as a material substrate of land. But, in what would seem to be a direct response to Fichte, Renan insists that "nations are not something eternal." Rather, they depend on a constant popular affirmation and re-affirmation: "A nation's existence is...a daily plebiscite."[69] Renan's argument, which predicted European confederation, affected almost all subsequent scholarly accounts of national identity and nationalism, and has more recently been embraced as a herald of the postmodern celebration of cultural hybridity within nation-states.[70] It did not, however, actually challenge nationalism or the rather complicated notion of national "self-determination" at all.

Renan's interest in representative government, an interest with origins in the Abbé Sieyès's emphasis on the Third Estate (the "people" as opposed to the elite) as the basis of sovereignty, would seem to leave little room for Fichte's Romantic marriage of *Kulturnation* and *Staatsnation*, ethnicity and state. But Renan still believed that a spiritual and moral solidarity, akin to what Rousseau had called the "general will," was the essence of a nation; Mussolini even thought Renan had "pre-fascist intuitions."[71] As a number of commentators have pointed out, Renan's approach did not so much refute the German Romantic model as dissolve it into conceptual abstraction.[72] Renan continued to believe that only the French language (not patois) could produce serious philosophy and scholarship. And well after his famous essay on the nation, treatises such as his *Histoire du peuple d'Israel* (1889–93) still reproduced old arguments that Indo-Europeans and Semites were opposed linguistic families with distinct humors and aptitudes: intellectual-military in the former, religious in the latter.[73] (Chamberlain responded, in an argument that would influence both Rosenberg and Hitler, that Renan's critique was based on a false assumption in any case. Purity of origins, Chamberlain claimed, are irrelevant. Rather, the task of the nation-state is something like effective animal husbandry: by enabling sustained inbreeding to follow upon episodes of fortuitous crossing, nation-building is in fact the mechanism, rather than the mythical consequence, of the creation of races.[74]) Then there is Renan's invocation of "memories" of past glory and humiliation. Are such "memories" not already essential ingredients of racial, religious, and linguistic forms of ethnic consciousness? Are not present-day political needs and desires stimulated as much by such feelings of ethnic continuity, whether true or false, as by some more immediate concern? Renan's "spiritual principle" has been putatively evacuated of all racial content, but it also grounds the national will in what Durkheim called the "collective consciousness" of a given people, one that is still determined by cultural memory.[75]

Primordialists versus Modernists

Contemporary discussion of the nation has largely abandoned Fichte's perspective on the eternity and necessity of the nation, and it has reformulated the terms of Renan's response. The debate in recent decades has been, if anything, far more complex than in the past. Throughout this Introduction I have emphasized one particular thread of that discussion: the conflict between the claim that ethnicity and ethnic history have played significant roles in shaping the modern nation-state and the claim that modern capitalism, industry, and communications have been more or less solely responsible for the nation-state's appearance. It has been called a debate between "primordialists" and "modernists." Over time, the differences between the two positions, at least among the leading voices, has tended to narrow. But the opposition is still exemplified in current scholarship.

In many ways, it is Elie Kedourie's skeptical treatment of his topic in *Nationalism* (1960) that inaugurates the contemporary era of scholarship on the nation. Kedourie writes very much with the horrors of German Nazism in mind, and he locates many of the most significant contributions to nationalist theory in German Romantic philosophy. For Kedourie, nationalism is largely an illusory set of "eternal" truths based in Romantic metaphysics, a nineteenth-century invention driven by a messianic contempt for things as they are and directed at other-worldly objectives. Nationalist politics are thus "ideological" rather than "constitutional" – that is, based on a quest for idealized social coherence and utopian community rather than on the more mundane social tasks of self-defense, distribution of justice, and enforcement of the law.[76]

Kedourie's emphases on the modernity of the nationalist dream and its imposition of homogeneity were developed with variations by a number of subsequent scholars.[77] Quite opposed to any previous argument, popular or scholarly, that ethnic history and the much older and vaguer *Kulturnation*

have fundamentally shaped the modern nation-state, this school of thought
points to recent and inexorable historical forces that have determined the
way all nation-states, once properly defined, have come into existence.
Whatever a given population may think about its national origin, the modernists argue, there is an analytical reality behind the modern nation's emergence, from the end of the eighteenth century to the present, that depends
on specific social, economic, bureaucratic, and technological innovations.
The nation as we know it is thus largely the creation of a distinctly modernizing, industrial, and capitalist West, a function of markets, education, and
communication in ways that no amount of ideological invention or political
manipulation could account for alone. "It is nationalism which engenders
nations, and not the other way round," writes Ernest Gellner, who became
perhaps the leading proponent of the modernist perspective.[78]

For Gellner, nationalism believes that it "conquers in the name of a
putative folk culture...healthy, pristine, vigorous," and he admits that
such a belief may even have a kernel of truth in cases of decolonization.
But on the whole, nationalism is a "deception and self-deception" involving
"the general imposition of a high culture on society" where "low culture"
had been the norm. It depends on the diffusion through the schools of a
bureaucratic and technological idiom, and establishes in its wake "an anonymous, impersonal society, with mutually substitutable, atomized individuals,
held together by a shared culture of this kind," rather than the complicated
mixture of local folk cultures and idiosyncratic "micro-groups" that had
previously existed.[79] Gellner thus subtly modifies Kedourie's position: "It
is not so much, as Elie Kedourie claims, that nationalism imposes homogeneity; it is rather that a homogeneity imposed by objective, inescapable
imperatives eventually appears on the surface in the form of nationalism."[80]
That imperative is, in essence, the relentless drive toward social rationaliza-
tion elaborated by Durkheim and Max Weber at the end of the nineteenth
century. The division of labor, industrial specialization, and calculating mentality of the marketplace are inevitable historical consequences of the development of civilization. Nationalism in Gellner's terms is simply the
rationalized form of political life falsely robed in Romantic ideals.

Other scholars, however, have sustained the older argument that the
power of ethnicity and ethnic history is crucial in understanding the modern nation-state.[81] These so-called "primordialists" argue that the modern
nation-state would simply be impossible without its ethnic foundations,
though they also admit that such foundations may be greatly idealized or
embellished. Anthony D. Smith is perhaps the leading voice in this group,
and the question he puts to the modernists is a telling one. If, Smith asks, the
nation really is the most important of all "invented traditions," as Hobsbawm and others claim, then "why does this 'invention' so often and in such

different cultural and social settings appear to strike such a deep chord and for so long?...Clearly there is more to the formations of nations than nationalist fabrication, and 'invention' must be understood in its other sense of a novel recombination of existing elements."[82] Smith focuses on the *ethnie*, or pre-modern ethnic community, with its myths of collective descent, shared memories, common culture, and affiliation to a homeland. He identifies two kinds of *ethnie*: the lateral aristocratic *ethnies* that incorporate outlying and lower-class cultures through expanding bureaucracy, as in "old" nations like England, France, and Spain; and the more numerous vertical demotic *ethnies*, which are passive, religiously defined communities mobilized by intellectuals into a political state, as in Ireland, Finland, Switzerland, and most of the "new" nations produced by contemporary decolonization. Smith associates the former lateral type of ethnicity with the civic culture of Western nations, the latter vertical type with a non-Western emphasis on a birth community of common descent.[83]

It is important to recognize that Smith, like a number of others who stress ethnicity, does not actually believe in the "primordial" essence of national communities claimed by ethnic and racial nationalists. He acknowledges that ethnic communities are indeed constructed, and are consolidated by the modern state, but argues that they are built by successive generations of a population out of Renan-like shared memories of the past and shared visions of the future, and further shaped by war, migration, and conversion, rather than invented by intellectual demagogues out of thin air.[84] That is, for Smith, nations are produced from bits and pieces of history that remain lodged in collective life, fragments that are then woven together in new ways by modern nationalists in search of an independent state. Ethnicity, in this view, is important not because it is the authentic cultural continuity invoked by nationalist history, even less because it depends on some racial foundation of the culture, but because it names a loose set of social boundaries and recurrent motifs that limit the degree to which a given cultural identity could be transformed. Ethnicity may thus be mutable and constantly evolving, never static, but it is not for these reasons a fiction.

The modernist thesis, especially Gellner's version with its attention to issues of economic class and social status, has been quite effective in deflating the grander claims of ethnic nationalist rhetoric. In this, it was perhaps a needed blast of cold air on popular political ideals frequently based in myth. But it has been a far too restrictive theory, whether in the form of Kedourie's earlier anti-utopian conservatism or Nairn's and Hobsbawm's Marxism, among many who see the nationalist struggles of often racially distinguished third-world peoples as a deeply *human*, and not just modern or Western, quest for political liberty.[85] On the other hand, the primordialists' emphasis on the ethnic rudiments of nationalist sentiment, especially outside of

Europe, has been a very useful way of thinking about, and taking seriously, anti-colonial (and anti-Western) variants of nationalism. But there is also a risk that distinctions like Smith's, between demotic (largely non-Western) and civic (largely Western) forms of ethnic coherence, could be employed to justify the popular Western perception of non-Western nationalism as an irrational and uncivil sort of politics, driven by racial, tribal, and religious-communal zealotry and little else. The Western media's uncomprehending response to massacres in former European colonies (such as Indonesia in 1965 and, more recently, Rwanda) thus complements what Clifford Geertz has called "the recalcitrance of primordial issues" in the new states.[86] Ever since Thomas Macauley's famous "Minute on Indian Education" (1835), this "recalcitrance" has been invoked by imperial powers to explain the need for Western tutelary rule, lest sectarian "blood-baths" erupt among populations divided by ethnic essentialism.

The point is not that scholars like Smith and Geertz are wrong to empha-size ethnic and communal passions in non-Western nationalism; rather, for many, it is a question of the way such passions are placed in historical and geographical context. For it is certain that the English Revolution was filled with passionate religious sectarianism, that the French Revolution contained its full share of uncivil violence, and that modern German nationalism's systematic racial madness has made the fervor of all other ethnic nationalisms pale by comparison. When one adds the kind of irrational violence that was often par for the course in colonial regimes, as detailed in texts from Eduard Douwes Dekker's *Max Havelaar, or the Coffee Auctions of the Dutch Trading Company* (an account of colonial Java published under the pseudonym Multatuli in 1859) to Aimé Césaire's *Discourse on Colonialism* (1955), it is easy to understand the non-European scholar's impatience with modernist skepticism and primordialist categorization alike, as in the work of Partha Chatterjee and the *Subaltern Studies* group.[87]

Certain variants of the modernist thesis have responded directly to the problems posed by anti-colonial nationalism. Tom Nairn emphasizes that modern nationalism as a whole is mainly a revolt of oppressed peripheries, which have been shut out of the magic of capitalist development, against the metropolitan societies enjoying the benefits of their dominance.[88] Nairn's center-versus-periphery model finds a parallel of sorts in Benedict Ander-son's modernist thesis of the Western hemisphere's "Creole pioneers" of nationalism, though Anderson has largely replaced the popular masses emphasized by Nairn with disenchanted landowners. But Anderson has also slightly altered Gellner's original thesis by stressing that "imagining" and "creation" may be more appropriate terms than Gellner's "invention" and "fabrication," since there may finally be no community, national or otherwise, early or late, that is *not* imagined, and hence invented, in some sense.[89] For Anderson, the "deep, horizontal comradeship" that is able to generate personal sacrifice for the sake of the nation-state may be quite modern and constructed, and it is certainly different from any earlier religious or dynastic sense of community. But it is no more "invented" than were the ties that bound these earlier communities. Anderson thus fully accepts the modernist perspective that the nation-state is a function of specific socio-economic conditions, like print capitalism; but he then grants the national sense of community that emerges, often with ethnic themes, a rationale that is no less real than any other.[90]

Postcolonial Dilemmas: The West and the Rest

One of the central problems thus raised by the conflicting hypotheses of Western modernists and primordialists is the question of how to treat non-Western nations and nationalism. Most contemporary Western studies of the nation assume that both the nation-state and nationalism are phenomena initially arising in Europe and its colonies. But in itself this hardly means that all non-Western nationalisms had to borrow from the European model, even if many did.[91] Gandhi, for example, wished to develop an entirely non-Western, non-capitalist, and non-industrial model of Indian nationhood, though the nation-state that actually emerged with Jawaharlal Nehru was far closer to the Western type. Recently, Prasenjit Duara has argued that it is precisely the Hegelian idea of the nation as a central component of a universal historical *telos* that became the basis for much modern Chinese scholarship on the history of China.[92] For Duara, even the idea of the nation as an historical theme represents an infusion of Western thought that complicates any attempt to narrate a non-Western history of China, to "decolonize the mind," as it were, of Chinese historicism itself. The question of non-Western attitudes to the nation and national identity has been especially important for "postcolonial" scholarship that has appeared since the 1950s. Building especially on Gandhi's contribution, Chatterjee has indicted the tendency of Western-inspired nationalism to produce an elitism and romantic utopianism among intellectuals at the "moment of departure" for independence, as in late nineteenth-century India.[93] And Ashis Nandy, following on the work of Gandhi and Rabindranath Tagore, has argued that however effective in nurturing "the rebellion against the West on the political plane," Western nationalism also attempted "to mould the Indian concept of the public realm to the requirement of standardized western categories," with unfortunate results.[94]

The development of contemporary postcolonial scholarship might be said to begin with the work of the Martinican-born psychiatrist Frantz Fanon,

whose *Black Skin, White Masks* (1952) and *Wretched of the Earth* (1961) may
also be considered founding texts of sorts for what has now become known
as "cultural studies" in the Anglo-American academy.[95] Fanon had been
strongly influenced by Jean-Paul Sartre, and his approach to the national
question bears many of the marks of Sartre's Hegelian existentialism,
Nietzsche's focus on the will to power and *ressentiment*, and the Marxian
interpretation of Hegel elaborated by Alexandre Kojève in the 1930s.[96] That
existentialism appears both in Fanon's refusal of a racially bound "Negro
mission," and in his commitment to a personal freedom detached from the
burdens of history.[97] But Hegel also shapes Fanon's response to the African
Negritude movement founded by Aimé Césaire, Léopold Senghor, and Léon
Damas, a movement dedicated to the transnational affirmation of African
culture and of diasporic "black civilization." For Fanon, the cultural evolution of national consciousness among the colonized evolves in three stages:
mimetic assimilation, followed by ethnic essentialism, and then by a future-
oriented struggle for freedom. Thus, "you do not show proof of your nation
from its culture, but . . . you substantiate its existence in the fight which the
people wage against the forces of occupation."[98] Fanon was also exceptionally sensitive to what he called the "pitfalls of national consciousness," which
led to the rise of newly oppressive class divisions within the new nation.[99] But
his work is perhaps most significant in that it elaborates a distinctly psychological and cultural account of the racial bases of nationalist thought in the
colonized world. Echoing W. E. B. Du Bois's very influential notion of
"double consciousness" in *The Souls of Black Folk* (1903), Fanon writes of
"an inferiority complex that has been created by the death and burial
of . . . local cultural originality" among colonized peoples.[100] For Fanon,
"culture" is not the sum total of a people's customs and practices adum-
brated by anthropologists and some primordialist scholars of ethnicity.
Rather, it is the aesthetic expression of a given people's spirit, and in this
Fanon again follows Romantic philosophers like Fichte and Hegel, and
literary scholars like Matthew Arnold and Hippolyte Taine. Assuming a
direct connection between the cultural health and the psychological health
of a given racial group, Fanon in effect made the existential value of the
decolonized mind and autonomous cultural expression equally central to the
larger problem of national identity.

There were of course many important treatments of national identity
before Fanon that contributed to the rise of a postcolonial perspective: the
writings of Latin American revolutionaries, from Bolívar and Martí to Amil-
car Cabral; Du Bois's *Souls*; Marcus Garvey's Afro-centric black nationalism;
Gandhi's influential elaboration of an ancient and non-Western conception
of national civilization; Tagore's critique of Western notions of nationalism;
Lenin's *Imperialism as the Last Stage of Capitalism* (1916); Gramsci's *Prison*

Notebooks (especially his treatments of cultural hegemony) and his unfinished study of Italy's "Southern Question"(1927–35); C. L. R. James's *Black Jacobins* (1938); and Césaire's *Discourse on Colonialism* must all be counted among them.[101] In the 1960s and 1970s, scholarship on imperialism and colonialism expanded, leading especially to Edward Said's *Orientalism* (1978). For Said, the fundamental problem of understanding the relationship of European empires to their Eastern colonies lay in the nature and uses of knowledge: imperial power was informed by and enabled scholarly research on the putatively fixed nature of the Orient. Following Anwar Abdel-Malik's emphasis on Orientalism's penchant for fixed typologies, Said claimed that "Orientalism assumed an unchanging Orient, absolutely different (the reasons change from epoch to epoch) from the West."[102] Said then located this typology in what French structuralist historian Michel Foucault called a "discourse," a large archive of written documents unified by a certain implicit logic, from the legal to the literary, that had produced (but also imagined) an Oriental reality and an Oriental consciousness.

Said's emphasis on the archive and its stereotypes has been echoed by a range of other scholars, who have paid increasing attention to the way assumptions about collective identities, in both entrenched empires and nascent nations, have been shaped by a dense and often contradictory archive of texts. Such work is exemplified, for example, by Mary Louise Pratt's investigation of the way imperialist scholarship in Latin America was shaped in turn by those it studied.[103] Moreover, a large body of postcolonial work, influenced by Jacques Derrida's philosophical "deconstruction" of identity (whether linguistic, personal, racial, or national), has come to focus on the imagined, socially and textually constructed character of race, ethnicity, and nationality, as in the writings of Gayatri Spivak, Stuart Hall, and Homi Bhabha.[104] Cultural studies has also assumed that the importance Fanon gave to the role of aesthetic expression in forming national (or anti-colonial) consciousness should be extended to popular or mass culture and media. The study of cinema, television, and popular music in particular has become central to the study of the postcolonial nation.[105]

Since Fanon, then, what has differentiated postcolonial and cultural studies approaches to national identity from that of earlier historians and social scientists is that (1) postcolonial approaches are generally framed by imperialism and by cultural, rather than political or economic, colonization; (2) such study is often a politically engaged one – that is, it is designed to serve the decolonization of the mind, imperialist and nationalist alike; and (3) the debate has depended far less on the historical or sociological interpretation of specific nationalist struggles than on the problem of hegemony – that is, on the process by which new nations and minority cultures within established nations find their own voices in terms of Fanon's dialectic, neither assimilating to the dominant culture, nor reverting to an often illusory pre-colonial authenticity. The hybrid vigor of multicultural expression and interdisciplinary scholarship thus becomes the shibboleth of postcolonial and cultural studies projects alike, which presumably (and perhaps paradoxically) must depend on the continuing vitality of distinct cultural traditions from which to borrow.

As postcolonial scholarship's simultaneous engagement with nationalist decolonization and minority resistance to dominant nationalism suggests, there is a dilemma at the heart of its approach to the nation, one that can perhaps be traced as far back as the internationalist harmony envisioned by nineteenth-century nationalists like Mazzini, outlined in Hobson's *Imperialism: A Study* (a crucial influence on Lenin), addressed by early twentieth-century Austrian Marxists like Otto Bauer, and given liberal expression in Wilson's ill-fated League of Nations. It may be Lenin, however, who is most important here. In his critique of Rosa Luxemburg's rejection of nationalist resistance to imperialism as a diversion from the struggles of a world-wide proletariat, Lenin defines an attitude toward nationalism and empire that finds an echo in contemporary postcolonial discussion. "*Insofar as* the bourgeoisie of the oppressed nation fights the oppressor, we are always, in every case, and more strongly than anyone else, *in favour*, for we are the staunchest and the most consistent enemies of oppression. But insofar as the bourgeoisie of the oppressed nation stands for *its own* bourgeois nationalism, we stand against."[106] Lenin's position, which was adopted in part by Fanon, reappears in various guises in postcolonial studies.

Thus, one finds the paradoxes and ambivalence of Said's three-fold insistence, in *Culture and Imperialism*, that real decolonization simultaneously requires (1) a coherent and vital national culture that "sustains communal memory"; (2) the willingness to break down "the barriers between cultures" and interweave their productions; and (3) the need to "pull away from separatist nationalism toward a more integrative view of human community."[107] Salman Rushdie has articulated a rather similar ambivalence to nationalism and the hegemony of national culture, celebrating the collapse of the Raj and longing for a national unity that would end Indian sectarianism while embracing a cosmopolitan, hybrid perspective, one so threatening to theocratic pretensions that it prompted Iran's Ayatollah Khomeini to call for Rushdie's assassination.[108] Paul Gilroy has argued, against the "conservative impulse" he finds in "Afro-American ethnicists," for the need to recognize a transnational "black Atlantic" culture, implicit in the writings of W. E. B. Du Bois, Ida B. Wells, Richard Wright and many others, and defined by a "desire to transcend both the structures of the nation-state and the constraints of ethnicity and national particularity."[109] In these related ways, postcolonial writing attempts to juxtapose (and often preserve) various sorts of national, ethnic, or racial "communal memory" in relation to a quasi-utopian, internationalist vision of "human community," one that is in turn deeply suspicious of the nation-state itself. It is a vision in essence perhaps not that far from Herder's egalitarian communal anarchism, though much of it has been concerned more with high culture of the Arnoldian sort than with the folk whom Herder championed. Such thinking has abandoned both the old Wilsonian and Leninist paths to internationalism and has instead stressed forms of resistance that balance distinct national-cultural vitality with transnational cultural hybridity. It is a balance that has always been available to, and prized by, a cosmopolitan elite, but it is now also one on which the global market for popular culture has capitalized.

Finally, it is important to note that postcolonial studies has made a fundamental contribution to understanding the role of gender in nation-building. As the selections gathered in this anthology indicate, the intellectual conversation about nations and identities has historically been an overwhelmingly masculine one. The anthologies devoted to contemporary debate are not very different. This is due not simply to the fact that, as in almost all facets of past political and cultural life, women's voices have been muffled by a repressive patriarchy. It is also the result of the concurrent rise of the nationalist and the feminist projects in the nineteenth century. Educated women who were denied equal rights and opportunities within established and prospective national cultures alike often had more pressing problems at hand, as feminism from Mary Wollstonecraft forward demonstrates. Partha Chatterjee analyzes how this tension between the nationalist and the feminist project was addressed (or not addressed) in India in the nineteenth and early twentieth centuries, and demonstrates the extent to which the " 'new' woman . . . was subjected to a *new* patriarchy."[110] In the tense inter-war period of the twentieth century, as the world nervously contemplated German rearmament under Hitler, Virginia Woolf's pacifist response to English anxiety was a stinging rebuke to the patriarchy's utter neglect of women's contributions, except in times of crisis. Her feminist "outsider" would say that "in fact, as a woman, I have no country. As a woman I want no country. As a woman my country is the whole world."[111] More recently, Eavan Boland has articulated her own dilemmas as a writer facing Irish nationalist history, and in particular has emphasized the way nationalism expresses its demands and ideals in symbolically gendered terms.

But a number of other contemporary scholars have stressed that women were also an integral part of nationalist programs. Floya Anthias and Nira Yuval-Davis point out that women were often involved, whether voluntarily or not, in nation-building, though less often as active political participants than as passive reproducers of cultural traditions through child-rearing.[112] Kumari Jayawardena has argued that feminism and nationalism were both enabled, in different but interconnected ways, by capitalist expansion in the nineteenth century.[113] And Sylvia Walby suggests that gender, nationalism, and citizenship be thought in dynamic relationship to one another, since a variety of local conditions must be considered along with the more global context of the struggle for women's rights.[114]

Anthologies and Their Vicissitudes

I want to conclude with a few observations about the genre of the present volume. An anthology is, by its nature, an ironic enterprise: it points, often obliquely, to everything that it is not. The present anthology is no exception to this rule. The covers of a book necessarily limit what can go into it, and no one should assume that the selection made in this one tells the whole story or the only viable summary of it. Much of great relevance has been omitted, among which (to name just a few authors available in English) are the writings of Emmanuel Joseph Sieyès, Immanuel Kant, Madame de Staël, Abraham Lincoln, Moses Hess, George Eliot, Heinrich von Treitschke, Israel Zangwill, Sun Yat-sen, Franz Boas, Max Weber, Adolf Hitler, Joseph Stalin, Benito Mussolini, Léopold Senghor, and Gamal Abdul Nasser.[115] In deciding what to include, I have tried to balance the imperatives of breadth and historical influence with an inevitably subjective judgment about the intrinsic significance, originality, and interest of the selection. There are also many contemporary scholars, beyond those I have already mentioned, who might easily have been included, among them Hugh Seton-Watson, Anthony Giddens, John Hutchinson, and Liah Greenfeld.[116] Moreover, an anthology cannot hope to provide adequate context for the slim extractions it makes from oftentimes voluminous oeuvres. For example, the scholarly elucidation of the national idea cannot in practice always be separated from an interested political purpose. From Macpherson and Fichte to Acton, Chamberlain, and Fanon, it would be impossible to survey the discussion of nations and identities if one tried to distinguish rigorously between disinterested scholarship and political engagement. Mill and Renan seem perfectly scholarly in their approaches, but a fuller survey of their work would reveal how deeply both writers were enmeshed in the presumption of their respective nations' superiority over, and management of, colonized peoples. Even in the more specialized disciplines of the twentieth-century academy, political and scholarly imperatives cannot be completely isolated. Only a far more encyclopedic survey of the problem, with numerous entries by each author, would be able to shed light on the deeper complexity of writing about national identity from a position within a given nation-state.

The explosion in contemporary discussion of the nation has produced many more nuances and debates than the few that are suggested by the excerpts that have been included. I have tried in this Introduction and the head notes to mention some of what has been left out, but even here I have omitted much. I must thus end by urging interested readers to return to the sources, and to explore for themselves the rather remarkable flowering of contemporary scholarship in this area. If this anthology provides a modest incentive to further reading, it will have done its job.

All notes are those of the selections' authors, unless otherwise marked.

Notes

1 William Shakespeare, *Henry V*, ed. Gary Taylor (Oxford: Clarendon Press, 1982), Act 3, Scene 3, ll. 61–65. MacMorris is an Irish captain helping to direct Henry's siege of Harfleur; Fluellen a Welsh captain who has little regard for MacMorris's abilities: "By Cheshu, he is an ass . . ." Fluellen declares earlier in the scene. Gary Taylor notes that "the patriotic infighting" represented in this scene "was common enough to be specifically forbidden, as in Garrard's (1591) law 30: 'there shall no soldiers . . . procure or stir up any quarrel with any stranger, that is of other nation and such as serve under one head and lord with them' " (168–9, notes to ll. 62–75). Taylor's commentary suggests that MacMorris may bristle because he does not think Fluellen has any right to regard the Irish as a nation separate from the Welsh, but also because he "expects to hear Ireland defamed (as it often was)" (169, notes to ll. 63 and 64). Already in 1599, an Irish captain serving an English lord might be distrusted in Ireland and England alike, even if military law wished to suppress specific national affiliations in the interest of *esprit de corps* among the King's men.

2 James Joyce, *Ulysses*, ed. Hans Walter Gabler, with Wolfhard Steppe and Claus Melchior (New York: Vintage Books, 1986), Episode 12, ll. 1419–31. Bloom's mother is Irish; his father is of Hungarian Jewish extraction. Though he does not practice any religious faith and is married to an Irish woman, he feels a vague attachment to his father's heritage and is alternately attracted to and repelled by Zionism. In this episode ("Cyclops"), Bloom's loyalty to Ireland is questioned by the patrons of Barney Kiernan's pub, which is the lair of the Citizen, Joyce's parody of virulent but ineffectual Irish nationalism. The Citizen is modeled after Michael Cusack, the founder of the Gaelic Athletic Association, whose concern for "the preservation and cultivation of the national pastimes of the people" (see Richard Ellmann, *James Joyce*, rev. edn [Oxford: Oxford University Press, 1982], 61n) is a direct echo of Rousseau's eighteenth-century advice to the Polish nation. The episode ends with Bloom fleeing the pub, chased out by the Citizen's curses and hurled biscuit tin.

3 Augustine, *The Confessions of Augustine*, trans. John K. Ryan (Garden City, NY: Doubleday & Co., 1960), 287.

4 See Jürgen Habermas, "Citizenship and National Identity: Some Reflections on the Future of Europe," *Praxis International* 12: 1 (1992), 1–18.

5 Benito Mussolini, "Fundamental Ideas," in Benito Mussolini, *Fascism: Doctrine and Institutions*, trans. anon. (Rome: Ardita Publishers, 1935), 12.

6   Anthony D. Smith, *Theories of Nationalism*, 2nd edn (New York: Holmes and Meier Publishers, 1983), 4–5, 260, 262.

7   "Joseph de Maistre and the Origins of Fascism," in *The Crooked Timber of Humanity: Chapters in the History of Ideas*, ed. Henry Hardy (London: John Murray, 1990), 91–174.

8   Walker Connor, "A Nation is a Nation, is a State, is an Ethnic Group, is a . . .," in *Ethnic and Racial Studies* 1 (1978), 377–400.

9   Joseph de Maistre, *Study on Sovereignty* (composed 1793–8; first published 1884), excerpted in Joseph de Maistre, *The Works of Joseph de Maistre*, ed. and trans. Jack Lively (New York: The Macmillan Co., 1965), 108.

10 Ibid., 108–9.

11 Steven Lukes, *Emile Durkheim: His Life and Work* (New York: Harper and Row, 1972), 339 n. 71.

12 For later and quite different attempts to understand the way symbolic practices produce and shape the national consciousness of a people, see Karl Deutsch, *Nationalism and Social Communication* (Cambridge, MA: MIT Press, 1953); and Clifford Geertz, "After the Revolution: The Fate of Nationalism in the New States," *The Interpretation of Cultures: Selected Essays* (New York: Basic Books, 1973), 234–54.

13 Benedict Anderson, *Imagined Communities* (London: Verso, 1991).

14 *Los Angeles Times*, Aug. 30, 1999, A1.

15 For the invention of Highlands tradition, see Hugh Trevor-Roper, "The Invention of Tradition: The Highland Tradition of Scotland," in Eric Hobsbawm and Terence Ranger, eds, *The Invention of Tradition* (Cambridge: Cambridge University Press, 1983), 15–41.

16 Anthony D. Smith, *National Identity* (London: Penguin, 1991), 8.

17 Efrain Kristal, "The Degree Zero of Spanish American Cultural History and the Role of Native Populations in the Formation of Pre-Independence National Pasts," *Poetics Today* 15: 4 (1994), 588.

18 See Rogers Brubaker, *Nationalism Reframed: Nationhood and the National Question in the New Europe* (Cambridge: Cambridge University Press, 1996).

19 See Matthew Arnold, *On the Study of Celtic Literature* (1867) in Matthew Arnold, *Complete Prose Works*, 11 vols, ed. R. H. Super (Ann Arbor: University of Michigan Press, 1960–77), 3: 291–395. See also Vincent P. Pecora, "Arnoldian Ethnology," *Victorian Studies* 41: 3 (1998), 355–79.

20 Eugen Weber, *Peasants into Frenchmen: The Modernization of Rural France, 1870–1914* (Stanford: Stanford University Press, 1976), 70.

21 Arthur de Gobineau, *The Inequality of Human Races*, trans. Adrian Collins (New York: Howard Fertig, 1967), 29.

22 Weber, *Peasants into Frenchmen*, 113.

23 Elie Kedourie, "Afterword" (1984) to *Nationalism*, 4th, expanded edn (Oxford: Blackwell, 1996; originally published 1960), 141.

24 The quoted phrase comes from Michael Waltzer, "The New Tribalism: Notes on a Difficult Problem," *Dissent* (Spring, 1992), 164–71. See also the anthology of essays, many since 1992, on *New Tribalisms: The Resurgence*

of Race and Ethnicity, ed. Michael W. Hughey (New York: New York University Press, 1998).

25 I borrow the quoted phrase from Anthony D. Smith, *The Ethnic Revival* (Cambridge: Cambridge University Press, 1981). But see also the much earlier essays contained in *Old Societies and New States*, ed. Clifford Geertz (New York: The Free Press, 1963), from which the selection of Geertz's work for the present anthology has been taken.

26 On black nationalism, see Alphonso Pinkney, *Red, Black, and Green: Black Nationalism in the United States* (Cambridge: Cambridge University Press, 1976); see also Malcolm X and Alex Haley, *The Autobiography of Malcolm X* (New York: Ballantine, 1965), esp. 282–96. For a rare example of overtly nationalist sentiment in later minority American literature, see Gloria Anzaldúa, *Borderlands / La Frontera: The New Mestiza* (San Francisco: Spinsters/Aunt Lute, 1987).

27 See Marcus Garvey, *The Philosophy and Opinions of Marcus Garvey*, ed. Amy Jacques-Garvey (New York: Atheneum, 1992); and *African Fundamentalism: A Literary and Cultural Anthology of Garvey's Harlem Renaissance*, ed. Tony Martin (Dover, MA: The Majority Press, 1983).

28 Anderson, *Imagined Communities*, 47–65. See also Toussaint L'Ouverture, *Memoires du Géneral Toussaint L'Ouverture* (Paris: Pagnerre, 1853; reproduced by Les Editions Fardin, 1982).

29 John Milton, "The Tenure of Kings and Magistrates," in *Prose Writings*, ed. K. M. Burton (London: J. M. Dent and Sons, 1958), 194.

30 Ibid., 202. Craig Calhoun discusses Luther's "Letter," and the degree to which it anticipated later usage (such as Fichte's) of the term "nation," in Craig Calhoun, *Nationalism* (Buckingham: Open University Press, 1997), 136 n. 4.

31 Kedourie, *Nationalism*, 13–23.

32 Novalis, "Christendom or Europe," in Novalis, *Philosophical Writings*, trans. and ed. Margaret Mahony Stoljar (Albany, NY: State University of New York Press, 1997), 142.

33 Carlton J. H. Hayes, *Essays on Nationalism* (New York: Macmillan, 1926), 33.

34 Anderson, *Imagined Communities*, 24, 30.

35 See Lionel Gossman, "Philhellenism and Antisemitism: Matthew Arnold and his German Models," *Comparative Literature* 46: 1 (1994), 1–39.

36 Hans Kohn, *The Idea of Nationalism: A Study in its Origins and Background* (New York: Macmillan, 1944), 30–6.

37 Ibid., 166.

38 Ibid., 99. For examples of more recent "new historicist" approaches to the pre-history of the national idea, see *Representations* 47 (1994), a special issue on "National Cultures Before Nationalism," ed. Carla Hesse and Thomas Laqueur.

39 Thucydides, *History of the Peloponnesian War*, trans. Richard Crawley (London: Longmans, Green, 1874), vol. II, 35–46.

40 Cornelius Tacitus, *Dialogus, Agricola, Germania*, with accompanying translation by Maurice Hutton (London: William Heinemann, 1920), 264.

41 Ibid., 268, my English translation.

42 H. Mattingly, Introduction to *Tacitus on Britain and Germany*, trans. H. Mattingly (Baltimore: Penguin Books, 1948), 28.

43 See Houston Stewart Chamberlain, *The Foundations of the Nineteenth Century*, 2 vols, trans. John Lees (New York: Howard Fertig, 1994), 1: 496 ff.

44 Adolf Hitler, *Mein Kampf*, trans. Ralph Manheim (Boston: Houghton Mifflin Co., 1971), 653.

45 Ovid, *Metamorphoses*, trans. Rolfe Humphries (Bloomington, IN: Indiana University Press, 1972), 57–61.

46 Giambattista Vico, *The New Science of Giambattista Vico*, trans. Thomas Goddard Bergin and Max Harold Fisch (Ithaca: Cornell University Press, 1968), esp. 112–15.

47 Claude Lévi-Strauss, *Structural Anthropology*, vol. 1, trans. Claire Jacobson and Brooke Grundfest Schoepf (New York: Basic Books, 1963), 216.

48 Baron de Montesquieu, *The Spirit of the Laws*, 2 vols in 1, trans. Thomas Nugent (New York: Hafner Publishing, 1949), 1: 229.

49 Ibid., 1: 224, 232–3.

50 See Emmanuel Le Roy Ladurie, *Times of Feast, Times of Famine: A History of the Climate Since the Year 1000*, trans. B. Bray (London, 1971); and Jared Diamond, *Guns, Germs and Steel: The Fates of Human Societies* (New York: W. W. Norton, 1997).

51 Kedourie, *Nationalism*, 5–6.

52 Ibid., 6.

53 Eric Hobsbawm, *Nations and Nationalism Since 1780: Program, Myth, Reality* (Cambridge: Cambridge University Press, 1990), 14.

54 Smith, *Theories of Nationalism*, 167, 168. Smith borrows the definition of modern nationalism I refer to here from Robert's *Dictionnaire Alphabétique*.

55 Friedrich Schleiermacher, "On the Different Methods of Translation," trans. Andre Lefevere, in *German Romantic Criticism*, ed. A. Leslie Willson (New York: Continuum, 1982), 23.

56 Ernest Renan, "What is a Nation?" in Ernest Renan, *The Poetry of the Celtic Races, and Other Studies*, trans. William G. Hutchison (London: Walter Scott, 1896), 76.

57 See Ngũgĩ Wa Thiong'o, *Decolonising the Mind: The Politics of Language in African Literature* (London: James Curry, 1986). See also Ngũgĩ Wa Thiong'o, *Devil on the Cross*, trans. by the author from Gĩkũyũ (Oxford: Heinemann Publishers, 1982). For Césaire's use of the phrase, see his interview with René Depestre (1967), included in Aimé Césaire, *Discourse on Colonialism*, trans. Joan Pinkham (New York: Monthly Review Press, 1972), 78.

58 John Stuart Mill, *Considerations on Representative Government*, ed. Currin V. Shields. Indianapolis: Bobbs-Merrill Educational Publishing, 1958), 230.

59 See Johann Gottlieb Fichte, *Addresses to the German Nation*, trans. R. F. Jones and G. H. Turnbull (Westport, CT: Greenwood Press, 1979), 134–5.

60 Edmund Burke, *Reflections on the Revolution in France* (London: J. M. Dent and Sons, 1910), 29.

61 Fichte, *Addresses to the German Nation*, 146–7.

62 Ibid., 147.
63 John Emerich Edward Dalberg-Acton, Lord Acton, "Nationality," in *The History of Freedom and Other Essays* (London: Macmillan and Co., 1909), 275–6.
64 Quoted in Kedourie, *Nationalism*, 78.
65 Hitler, *Mein Kampf*, 328, 329; Hitler's italics.
66 Renan, "What is a Nation?" in Renan, *The Poetry of the Celtic Races and Other Studies*, 63.
67 Ibid., 63, 66.
68 Ibid., 61–2.
69 Ibid., 80–2.
70 An anthology of contemporary "postcolonial" approaches to the problem of national identity, *Nation and Narration*, ed. Homi Bhabha (London: Routledge, 1990), begins with Renan's essay, which is the only non-contemporary treatment of the topic to be included.
71 Benito Mussolini, "Political and Social Doctrine," in *Fascism: Doctrine and Institutions*, 22.
72 See Kedourie, *Nationalism*, 76; Weber, *Peasants into Frenchmen*, 112; Anderson, *Imagined Communities*, 200.
73 Ernest Renan, *Histoire du peuple d'Israel*, 5 vols (Paris: Calmann-Lévy, 1889–93).
74 Chamberlain, *Foundations of the Nineteenth Century*, 1: 296.
75 See Emile Durkheim, *The Division of Labor in Society*, trans. W. D. Halls (New York: Free Press, 1984).
76 Kedourie, *Nationalism*, xiii.
77 See especially Ernest Gellner, *Nations and Nationalism* (Ithaca: Cornell University Press, 1983); John Breuilly, *Nationalism and the State* (Manchester: Manchester University Press, 1982); Tom Nairn, *The Break-up of Britain* (London: New Left Books, 1977); and Eric Hobsbawm, *Nations and Nationalism Since 1780: Program, Myth, Reality.*
78 Gellner, *Nations and Nationalism*, 55.
79 Ibid., 57.
80 Ibid., 39.
81 See especially Anthony D. Smith, *The Ethnic Origins of Nations* (Oxford: Blackwell, 1986); John A. Armstrong, *Nations Before Nationalism* (Chapel Hill: University of North Carolina Press, 1982); and Walker Connor, *Ethnonationalism* (Princeton: Princeton University Press, 1994).
82 Anthony D. Smith, "Nationalism and the Historians," in *Ethnicity and Nationalism*, ed. Anthony D. Smith (Leiden: E. J. Brill, 1992), 72.
83 Smith, *National Identity*, 11.
84 Ibid., 23–8.
85 See, for example, Edward Said's remarks on Kedourie, Gellner, and Hobsbawm, in Edward W. Said, *Culture and Imperialism* (New York: Knopf, 1993), 216.
86 Geertz, "The Integrative Revolution," in *Old Societies and New States*, 129. For further discussion of such issues, see Vincent P. Pecora, "The Limits of Local Knowledge," in *The New Historicism*, ed. H. Aram Veeser (New York: Routledge, 1989), 243–76.

87   See especially Partha Chatterjee's critique of the progressive or Enlightenment
     history underlying both Kedourie and Smith in Partha Chatterjee, *Nationalist
     Thought and the Colonial World: A Derivative Discourse?* (Minneapolis: Uni-
     versity of Minnesota Press, 1986), 7–10. For Chatterjee's account of post-
     colonial Indian nationhood, see esp. Partha Chatterjee, *A Possible India: Essays
     in Political Criticism* (Delhi: Oxford University Press, 1997).

88   See Nairn, *The Break-up of Britain*.

89   Anderson, *Imagined Communities*, 6.

90   For further discussion of Anderson's notion of imagined communities, see the
     dialogue over the relation of capitalism to racism in Etienne Balibar and
     Immanuel Wallerstein, *Race, Nation, Class: Ambiguous Identities*, with trans.
     of Balibar by Chris Turner (London: Verso, 1991).

91   For accounts of the way Asian nationalism has paralleled Western models, see
     Delmer M. Brown, *Nationalism in Japan* (Berkeley: University of California
     Press, 1955); and Wang Gungwu, "Nationalism in Asia," in *Nationalism: The
     Nature and Evolution of an Idea*, ed. Eugene Kamenka (Canberra: Australian
     National University, 1973).

92   Prasenjit Duara, *Rescuing History from the Nation: Questioning Narratives of
     Modern China* (Chicago: University of Chicago Press, 1995), 17–50. Duara's
     argument at times approaches that of Anthony D. Smith, though Duara refers
     only to Gellner and the modernists.

93   Chatterjee, *Nationalist Thought and the Colonial World*, 54–84.

94   Ashis Nandy, *The Illegitimacy of Nationalism: Rabindranath Tagore and the
     Politics of Self* (Delhi: Oxford University Press, 1994), 89.

95   On cultural studies, see the anthologies *Cultural Studies*, eds Lawrence Gross-
     berg, Cary Nelson, and Paula A. Treichler (New York: Routledge, 1992); and
     The Identity in Question, ed. John Rajchman (New York: Routledge, 1995),
     especially the essay by Fredric Jameson, "On Cultural Studies," 251–95.

96   See especially Fanon's discussion of the Master–Slave dialectic in Hegel, in
     Frantz Fanon, *Black Skin, White Masks*, trans. Charles Lam Markmann (New
     York: Grove Weidenfeld, 1967), 216–22.

97   Ibid., 228.

98   Frantz Fanon, *The Wretched of the Earth*, trans. Constance Farrington (New
     York: Grove Press, 1968), 223.

99   Ibid., 148–205.

100 Fanon, *Black Skin, White Masks*, 18.

101 See Simón Bolívar, *The Political Thought of Bolívar*, ed. Gerald E. Fitzgerald
     (The Hague: Martinus Nijhoff, 1971); José Martí, *The America of José Martí:
     Selected Writings of José Martí*, trans. Juan de Onís (New York: Funk and
     Wagnalls, 1954); W. E. B. Du Bois, *The Souls of Black Folk* (New York: Penguin
     Books, 1989); Marcus Garvey, *The Philosophy and Opinions of Marcus Garvey*;
     Mohandas Karamchand Gandhi, *The Penguin Gandhi Reader*, ed. Rudrangshu
     Mukherjee (New York: Penguin Books, 1993); Rabindranath Tagore, *Nation-
     alism* (New York: The Macmillan Company, 1917); V. I. Lenin, *Imperialism,
     the Highest Stage of Capitalism: A Popular Outline*, trans. anon. (New York:

International Publishers, 1939); Antonio Gramsci, *Selections from the Prison Notebooks*, ed. and trans. Quintin Hoare and Geoffrey Nowell Smith (New York: International Publishers, 1971), and "The Southern Question" in Antonio Gramsci, *The Modern Prince and Other Writings*, trans. Louis Marks (New York: International Publishers, 1957, 28–57); C. L. R. James, *The Black Jacobins: Toussaint L'Ouverture and the San Domingo Revolution* (New York: Vintage, 1963); and Aimé Césaire, *Discourse on Colonialism*.

102   Edward W. Said, *Orientalism* (New York: Vintage Books, 1979), 96. See Anwar Abdel-Malik, "Orientalism in Crisis," *Diogenes* 44 (1963), 102–40. Said draws heavily from Raymond Schwab, *The Oriental Renaissance: Europe's Discovery of India and the East, 1680–1880*, trans. G. Patterson-Black and V. Reinking (New York: 1984; originally published 1950). But for an earlier survey of Orientalism that Said does not cite, see David Kopf, *British Orientalism and the Bengal Renaissance* (Berkeley: University of California Press, 1969).

103   Mary Louise Pratt, *Imperial Eyes: Travel Writing and Transculturation* (London: Routledge, 1992).

104   See Stuart Hall, *Identity: The Real Me* (London: ICA, 1987); Gayatri Chakravorty Spivak, *In Other Worlds: Essays in Cultural Politics* (New York: Methuen, 1987); and Homi Bhabha, *The Location of Culture* (London: Routledge, 1994).

105   See especially *Third Cinema Reader*, eds J. Pines and P. Willemen (London: British Film Institute, 1989); and Paul Gilroy, *There Ain't No Black in the Union Jack: The Cultural Politics of Race and Nation* (London: Hutchinson, 1987).

106   V. I. Lenin, "The Right of Nations to Self-Determination" (1914), in V. I. Lenin, *National Liberation, Socialism, and Imperialism: Selected Writings* (New York: International Publishers, 1968), 61–2; Lenin's italics.

107   Said, *Culture and Imperialism*, 215–16.

108   See especially Salman Rushdie, *Imaginary Homelands* (London: Penguin Books, 1991).

109   Paul Gilroy, "Cultural Studies and Ethnic Absolutism," in *Cultural Studies*, 197, 194–5.

110   Partha Chatterjee, "The Nationalist Resolution of the Women's Question" (1987), in *Recasting Women: Essays in Indian Colonial History*, eds Kumkum Sangari and Sudesh Vaid (New Brunswick, NJ: Rutgers University Press, 1990), 244.

111   Virginia Woolf, *Three Guineas* (San Diego: Harcourt Brace & Co., 1966), 109.

112   Floya Anthias and Nira Yuval-Davis, "Introduction," in *Woman-Nation-State*, eds Floya Anthias and Nira Yuval-Davis (London: Macmillan, 1989), 1–15; see also the other essays in the collection, as well as essays in the volume *Crossfires: Nationalism, Racism and Gender in Europe*, eds Helma Lutz, Ann Phoenix, and Nira Yuval-Davis (London: Pluto Press, 1995).

113   Kumari Jayawardena, *Feminism and Nationalism in the Third World* (London: Zed Press, 1986).

114 Sylvia Walby, "Woman and Nation," in *Ethnicity and Nationalism*, ed. Anthony D. Smith, 81–100.

115 See Emmanuel Joseph Sieyès, *What is the Third Estate?*, trans. M. Blondel (New York: Praeger, 1963); Immanuel Kant, *Perpetual Peace*, ed. Lewis White Beck (Indianapolis: The Bobbs-Merrill Co., 1957); Madame de Staël, *Major Writings of Germaine de Staël*, trans. Vivian Folkenflik (New York: Columbia University Press, 1987); Abraham Lincoln, "First Inaugural Address, March 4, 1861," in *The Speeches of Abraham Lincoln* (New York: Lincoln Centenary Association, 1908), 308–19; Moses Hess, *Rome and Jerusalem: A Study in Jewish Nationalism*, trans. Meyer Waxman (New York: Bloch Publishing Co., 1918); George Eliot, "The Modern Hep! Hep! Hep!" in *Miscellaneous Essays* (Boston: Dana Estes and Co., 1883); Heinrich von Treitschke, *Politics*, 2 vols, trans. Arthur James Balfour (London: Constable and Co., Ltd., 1916); Israel Zangwill, *The Principle of Nationalities* (New York: The Macmillan Co., 1917); Sun Yat-sen, "Three Principles of the People," in *Nationalism in Asia and Africa*, ed. Elie Kedourie (New York: Meridian Books, 1970); Franz Boas, "Nationalism," in Franz Boas, *Race and Democratic Society* (New York: J. J. Augustin, 1945); Max Weber, "Nationality and Cultural Prestige," *Economy and Society*, 2 vols, trans. Ephraim Fischoff, Hans Gerth, A. M. Henderson, Ferdinand Kolegar, C. Wright Mills, Talcott Parsons, Max Rheinstein, Guenther Roth, Edward Shils, and Claus Wittich (Berkeley: University of California Press, 1978); Adolf Hitler, *Mein Kampf*; Joseph Stalin, *Marxism and the National and Colonial Question* (New York: International Publishers, 1934); Benito Mussolini, *Fascism: Doctrine and Institutions*; Léopold Senghor, *On African Socialism*, trans. M. Cook (New York: Praeger, 1964); and Gamal Abdul Nasser, *Egypt's Liberation: The Philosophy of the Revolution* (Washington, D.C.: Public Affairs Press, 1955). *The Nationalism Reader*, eds Omar Dahbour and Micheline R. Ishay (Atlantic Highlands, NJ: Humanities Press, 1995) includes excerpts of several of these texts in its historical survey of nationalist statements.

116 Among other works by contemporary scholars, see Hugh Seton-Watson, *Nations and States* (London: Methuen, 1977); Anthony Giddens, *A Contemporary Critique of Historical Materialism, II: The Nation-State and Violence* (Cambridge: Polity Press, 1985); John Hutchinson, *The Dynamics of Cultural Nationalism* (London: Allen and Unwin, 1987); Liah Greenfeld, *Nationalism: Five Roads to Modernity* (Cambridge, MA: Harvard University Press, 1992). Many contemporary scholars are well represented in the following collections: *Nationalism*, ed. John Hutchinson and Anthony D. Smith (Oxford: Oxford University Press, 1994); *Ethnicity and Nationalism*, ed. Anthony D. Smith; *Becoming National: A Reader*, ed. Geoff Eley and Ronald Grigor Suny (New York: Oxford University Press, 1996); and *Nationalism: The Nature and Evolution of an Idea*, ed. Eugene Kamenka.

Part I

Inventing the Modern State

1

Leviathan (1651)

Thomas Hobbes

Thomas Hobbes, ch. XVII, "Of the Causes, Generation, and Definition of a Common-wealth," from *Leviathan* (1651) [source: Thomas Hobbes, *Hobbes: Selections*, ed. Frederick J. E. Woodbridge. New York: Charles Scribner's Sons, 1958, 335–40]

Though he supported the monarchy against a rebellious parliament in the English Civil War, the skeptical and materialist Hobbes (1588–1679) worked a revolution of sorts in political theory by rejecting the widely held Aristotelian assumption behind civil society: that man is by nature a *zoon politikon*, or political animal. Instead, Hobbes based his theory, also rooted in natural law, on the conflicting passions and self-interest of acquisitive individuals, and insisted that they are primarily motivated by fear of one another. To avoid the war of all against all that exists in a state of nature, these individuals make a "covenant" or contract with each other to submit to a sovereign authority, whether monarch (which Hobbes favored) or assembly, for protection of themselves and their property. In either case, the sovereign was absolute and would determine its successor – Hobbes saw no need for periodic referenda afterwards. Hobbes is widely regarded as one of the crucial theorists of modern individualism and of the liberal state designed primarily to adjudicate competing interests.

Part II: Of Commonwealth

Chapter XVII: Of the causes, generation, and definition of a commonwealth

The final cause, end, or design of men, who naturally love liberty, and dominion over others, in the introduction of that restraint upon themselves, in which we see them live in commonwealths, is the foresight of their own preservation, and of a more contented life thereby; that is to say, of getting themselves out from that miserable condition of war, which is necessarily consequent, as hath been shown in chapter xiii, to the natural passions of men, when there is no visible power to keep them in awe, and tie them by fear of punishment to the performance of their covenants, and observation of those laws of nature set down in the fourteenth and fifteenth chapters.

For the laws of nature, as *justice, equity, modesty, mercy,* and, in sum, *doing to others, as we would be done to,* of themselves, without the terror of some power, to cause them to be observed, are contrary to our natural passions, that carry us to partiality, pride, revenge, and the like. And covenants, without the sword, are but words, and of no strength to secure a man at all. Therefore notwithstanding the laws of nature, which every one hath then kept, when he has the will to keep them, when he can do it safely, if there be no power erected, or not great enough for our security; every man will, and may lawfully rely on his own strength and art, for caution against all other men. And in all places, where men have lived by small families, to rob and spoil one another, has been a trade, and so far from being reputed against the law of nature, that the greater spoils they gained, the greater was their honour; and men observed no other laws therein, but the laws of honour; that is, to abstain from cruelty, leaving to men their lives, and instruments of husbandry. And as small families did then; so now do cities and kingdoms which are but greater families, for their own security, enlarge their dominions, upon all pretences of danger, and fear of invasion, or assistance that may be given to invaders, and endeavour as much as they can, to subdue, or weaken their neighbours, by open force, and secret arts, for want of other caution, justly; and are remembered for it in after ages with honour.

Nor is it the joining together of a small number of men, that gives them this security; because in small numbers, small additions on the one side or the other, make the advantage of strength so great, as is sufficient to carry the victory; and therefore gives encouragement to an invasion. The multitude sufficient to confide in for our security, is not determined by any certain number, but by comparison with the enemy we fear; and is then sufficient, when the odds of the enemy is not of so visible and conspicuous moment, to determine the event of war, as to move him to attempt.

And be there never so great a multitude; yet if their actions be directed according to their particular judgments, and particular appetites, they can expect thereby no defence, nor protection, neither against a common enemy, nor against the injuries of one another. For being distracted in opinions concerning the best use and application of their strength, they do not help but hinder one another; and reduce their strength by mutual opposition to nothing: whereby they are easily, not only subdued by a very few that agree together; but also when there is no common enemy, they make war upon each other, for their particular interests. For if we could suppose a great multitude of men to consent in the observation of justice, and other laws of nature, without a common power to keep them all in awe; we might as well suppose all mankind to do the same; and then there neither would be, nor need to be any civil government, or commonwealth at all; because there would be peace without subjection.

Nor is it enough for the security, which men desire should last all the time of their life, that they be governed, and directed by one judgment, for a limited time; as in one battle, or one war. For though they obtain a victory by their unanimous endeavour against a foreign enemy; yet afterwards, when either they have no common enemy, or he that by one part is held for an enemy, is by another part held for a friend, they must needs by the difference of their interests dissolve, and fall again into a war amongst themselves.

It is true, that certain living creatures, as bees, and ants, live sociably one with another, which are therefore by Aristotle numbered amongst political creatures; and yet have no other direction, than their particular judgments and appetites; nor speech, whereby one of them can signify to another, what he thinks expedient for the common benefit: and therefore some man may perhaps desire to know, why mankind cannot do the same. To which I answer,

First, that men are continually in competition for honour and dignity, which these creatures are not; and consequently amongst men there ariseth on that ground, envy and hatred, and finally war; but amongst these not so.

Secondly, that amongst these creatures, the common good differeth not from the private; and being by nature inclined to their private, they procure thereby the common benefit. But man, whose joy consisteth in comparing himself with other men, can relish nothing but what is eminent.

Thirdly, that these creatures, having not, as man, the use of reason, do not see, nor think they see any fault, in the administration of their common business; whereas amongst men, there are very many, that think themselves wiser, and able to govern the public, better than the rest; and these strive to reform and innovate, one this way, another that way; and thereby bring it into distraction and civil war.

Fourthly, that these creatures, though they have some use of voice, in making known to one another their desires, and other affections; yet they want that art of words, by which some men can represent to others, that which is good, in the likeness of evil; and evil, in the likeness of good; and augment, or diminish the apparent greatness of good and evil; discontenting men, and troubling their peace at their pleasure.

Fifthly, irrational creatures cannot distinguish between *injury*, and *damage*; and therefore as long as they be at ease, they are not offended with their fellows: whereas man is then most troublesome, when he is most at ease: for then it is that he loves to shew his wisdom, and control the actions of them that govern the commonwealth.

Lastly, the agreement of these creatures is natural; that of men, is by covenant only, which is artificial: and therefore it is no wonder if there be somewhat else required, besides covenant, to make their agreement constant and lasting; which is a common power, to keep them in awe, and to direct their actions to the common benefit.

The only way to erect such a common power, as may be able to defend them from the invasion of foreigners, and the injuries of one another, and thereby to secure them in such sort, as that by their own industry, and by the fruits of the earth, they may nourish themselves and live contentedly; is, to confer all their power and strength upon one man, or upon one assembly of men, that may reduce all their wills, by plurality of voices, unto one will: which is as much as to say, to appoint one man, or assembly of men, to bear their person; and every one to own, and acknowledge himself to be author of whatsoever he that so beareth their person, shall act, or cause to be acted, in those things which concern the common peace and safety; and therein to submit their wills, every one to his will, and their judgments, to his judgment. This is more than consent, or concord; it is a real unity of them all, in one and the same person, made by covenant of every man with every man, in such manner, as if every man should say to every man, *I authorize and give up my right of governing myself, to this man, or to this assembly of men, on this condition, that thou give up thy right to him, and authorize all his actions in like manner.* This done, the multitude so united in one person, is called a COMMONWEALTH, in Latin CIVITAS. This is the generation of that great LEVIATHAN, or rather, to speak more reverently, of that *mortal god,* to which we owe under the *immortal God,* our peace and defence. For by this authority, given him by every particular man in the commonwealth, he hath the use of so much power and strength conferred on him, that by terror thereof, he is enabled to perform the wills of them all, to peace at home, and mutual aid against their enemies abroad. And in him consisteth the essence of the commonwealth; which, to define it, is *one person, of whose acts a great multitude, by mutual covenants one with another, have made themselves every one the author, to the end he may use the strength and means of them all, as he shall think expedient, for their peace and common defence.*

And he that carrieth this person, is called SOVEREIGN, and said to have *sovereign power;* and every one besides, his SUBJECT.

The attaining to this sovereign power, is by two ways. One, by natural force; as when a man maketh his children, to submit themselves, and their children, to his government, as being able to destroy them if they refuse; or by war subdueth his enemies to his will, giving them their lives on that condition. The other, is when men agree amongst themselves, to submit to some man, or assembly of men, voluntarily, on confidence to be protected by him against all others. This latter, may be called a political commonwealth, or commonwealth by *institution*; and the former, a commonwealth by *acquisition*.

2

Two Treatises of Government (1690)

John Locke

John Locke, selections from *Two Treatises of Government* (1690) [source: John Locke, *Two Treatises of Government*, ed. Peter Laslett. New York: Mentor Books, 1963, 377–82]

Locke (1632–1704) followed Hobbes in locating the origin of government in a "compact" agreed to by a majority of free men that would guarantee the safety of person and property. Unlike Hobbes, however, he argued both that men are naturally free and that political society arose out of peaceful circumstances. He believed an original contract underlay even dynastic authority, like that in the empires of Peru and Mexico, and that people act to form a government by collective consent at the first opportunity. Also unlike Hobbes, Locke is a philosopher of republican sovereignty, and he directly challenges Robert Filmer's "divine right" patriarchy: sovereignty rests with popular assent, and the will of the majority is formulated by elected assembly. Locke's Enlightenment empiricism, for which the mind is like a *tabula rasa*, or blank slate, inscribed only by experience, complemented his republican emphasis on self-determination unfettered by inherited tradition or authority.

Book II: Of Civil Government

99.   Whosoever therefore out of a state of Nature unite into a *Community*, must be understood to give up all the power, necessary to the ends for which they unite into Society, to the *majority* of the Community, unless they expressly agreed in any number greater than the majority. And this is done by barely agreeing to *unite into one Political Society*, which is *all the Compact that* is, or needs be, between the Individuals, that enter into, or make up a *Common-wealth*. And thus that, which begins and actually *constitutes any*

Political Society, is nothing but the consent of any number of Freemen capable of a majority to unite and incorporate into such a Society. And this is that, and that only, which did, or could give *beginning* to any *lawful Government* in the World.

100.   To this I find two Objections made.

First, *That there are no Instances to be found in Story of a Company of Men independent and equal one amongst another, that met together, and in this way began and set up a Government.*

Secondly, *'Tis impossible of right that Men should do so, because all Men being born under Government, they are to submit to that, and are not at liberty to begin a new one.*

101.   To the first there is this to Answer. That it is not at all to be wonder'd, that *History* gives us but a very little account of Men, *that lived together in the State of Nature.* The inconveniencies of that condition, and the love, and want of Society no sooner brought any number of them together, but they presently united and incorporated, if they designed to continue together. And if we may not suppose *Men* ever to have been *in the State of Nature*, because we hear not much of them in such a State, we may as well suppose the Armies of *Salmanasser*, or *Xerxes* were never Children, because we hear little of them, till they were Men, and imbodied in Armies. Government is every where antecedent to Records, and Letters seldome come in amongst a People, till a long continuation of Civil Society has, by other more necessary Arts provided for their Safety, Ease, and Plenty. And then they begin to look after the History of their *Founders*, and search into their *original*, when they have out-lived the memory of it. For 'tis with *Commonwealths* as with particular Persons, they are commonly *ignorant of their own Births* and *Infancies*: And if they know any thing of their *Original*, they are beholding, for it, to the accidental Records, that others have kept of it. And those that we have, of the beginning of any Polities in the World, excepting that of the *Jews*, where God himself immediately interpos'd, and which favours not at all Paternal Dominion, are all either plain instances of such a beginning, as I have mentioned, or at least have manifest footsteps of it.

102.   He must shew a strange inclination to deny evident matter of fact, when it agrees not with his Hypothesis, who will not allow that the *beginning* of *Rome* and *Venice* were by the uniting together of several Men free and independent one of another, amongst whom there was no natural Superiority or Subjection. And if *Josephus Acosta*'s word may be taken, he tells us, that in many parts of *America* there was no Government at all. *There are great and apparent Conjectures*, says he, *that these Men*, speaking of those of *Peru, for a long time had neither Kings nor Common-wealths, but lived in Troops, as they do this day in* Florida, *the*

Cheriquanas, *those of* Bresil, *and many other Nations, which have no certain Kings, but as occasion is offered in Peace or War, they choose their Captains as they please*, 1. I. c. 25. If it be said, that every Man there was born subject to his Father, or the head of his Family. That the subjection due from a Child to a Father, took not away his freedom of uniting into what Political Society he thought fit, has been already proved. But be that as it will, these Men, 'tis evident, were actually *free*; and whatever superiority some Politicians now would place in any of them, they themselves claimed it not; but by consent were all *equal*, till by the same consent they set Rulers over themselves. So that their *Politick Societies* all *began* from a voluntary Union, and the mutual agreement of Men freely acting in the choice of their Governours, and forms of Government.

103. And I hope those who went away from *Sparta* with *Palantus*, mentioned by *Justin l. 3, c.* 4 will be allowed to have been *Freemen independent* one of another, and to have set up a Government over themselves, by their own consent. Thus I have given several Examples out of History, of *People free and in the State of Nature*, that being met together incorporated and *began a Common-wealth*. And if the want of such instances be an argument to prove that *Government* were not, nor could not be so *begun*, I suppose the Contenders for Paternal Empire were better let it alone, than urge it against natural Liberty. For if they can give so many instances out of History, of *Governments begun* upon Paternal Right, I think (though at best an Argument from what has been, to what should of right be, has no great force) one might, without any great danger, yield them the cause. But if I might advise them in the Case, they would do well not to search too much into the *Original of Governments*, as they have begun *de facto*, lest they should find at the foundation of most of them, something very little favourable to the design they promote, and such a power as they contend for.

104. But to conclude, Reason being plain on our side, that Men are naturally free, and the Examples of History shewing, that the *Governments* of the World, that were begun in Peace, had their beginning laid on that foundation, and were *made by the Consent of the People*; There can be little room for doubt, either where the Right is, or what has been the Opinion, or Practice of Mankind, about the *first erecting of Governments*.

105. I will not deny, that if we look back as far as History will direct us, towards the *Original of Commonwealths*, we shall generally find them under the Government and Administration of one Man. And I am also apt to believe, that where a Family was numerous enough to subsist by it self, and continued entire together, without mixing with others, as it often happens, where there is much Land and few People, the Government commonly began in the Father. For the Father having, by the Law of Nature, the same Power with every Man else to punish, as he thought fit, any Offences against that Law, might thereby punish his transgressing Children even when they were Men, and out of their Pupilage; and they were very likely to submit to his punishment, and all joyn with him against the Offender, in their turns, giving him thereby power to Execute his Sentence against any transgression, and so in effect make him the Law-maker, and Governour over all, that remained in Conjunction with his Family. He was fittest to be trusted; Paternal affection secured their Property, and Interest under his Care, and the Custom of obeying him, in their Childhood, made it easier to submit to him, rather than to any other. If therefore they must have one to rule them, as Government is hardly to be avoided amongst Men that live together; who so likely to be the Man, as he that was their common Father; unless Negligence, Cruelty, or any other defect of Mind, or Body made him unfit for it? But when either the Father died, and left his next Heir for want of Age, Wisdom, Courage, or any other Qualities, less fit for Rule: or where several Families met, and consented to continue together: There, 'tis not to be doubted, but they used their natural freedom, to set up him, whom they judged the ablest, and most likely, to Rule well over them. Conformable hereunto we find the People of *America*, who (living out of the reach of the Conquering Swords, and spreading domination of the two great Empires of *Peru* and *Mexico*) enjoy'd their own natural freedom, though, *cæteris paribus*, they commonly prefer the Heir of their deceased King; yet if they find him any way weak, or uncapable, they pass him by and set up the stoutest and bravest Man for their Ruler.

106. Thus, though looking back as far as Records give us any account of Peopling the World, and the History of Nations, we commonly find the *Government* to be in one hand, yet it destroys not that, which I affirm, (*viz.*) That the *beginning of Politick Society* depends upon the consent of the Individuals, to joyn into and make one Society; who, when they are thus incorporated, might set up what form of Government they thought fit. But this having given occasion to Men to mistake, and think, that by Nature Government was Monarchical, and belong'd to the Father, it may not be amiss here to consider, why People in the beginning generally pitch'd upon this form, which though perhaps the Father's Preheminency might in the first institution of some Common-wealths, give a rise to, and place, in the beginning, the Power in one hand; Yet it is plain, that the reason, that continued the Form of *Government in a single Person*, was not any Regard, or Respect to Paternal Authority; since all petty Monarchies, that is, almost all *Monarchies*, near their Original, have been commonly, at least upon occasion, *Elective*.

Part II

From Divine to Human History

3

The New Science (1725; 1744)

Giambattista Vico

Giambattista Vico, selection from "Conclusion of the Work," of *The New Science* (1725; 1744) [source: *The New Science of Giambattista Vico*, rev. trans. of third edition (1744), trans. Thomas Goddard Bergin and Max Harold Fisch. Ithaca: Cornell University Press, 1968, 425–6. Reprinted by permission of Copyright Clearance Center.]

Vico (1668–1744) elaborated a natural law of the *gentes*, by which he meant non-Hebraic peoples and the autonomous development of their civil institutions, and broke with the rational bases of earlier seventeenth-century natural law theorists like Pufendorf, Grotius, and Selden. Vico's belief that the "poetic wisdom" or mythology of the ancients could be interpreted as a clue to the origins of civilization, his sense that civil order is based in inherited custom, and his cyclical philosophy of world history anticipate major Romantic themes half a century later. But Vico's distinction between a human history that can be known, because it is humanly made, and a divine history that cannot has also been seen as an important prefiguration of modern sociology and anthropology. Vico's nations arise from mythical beginnings, progress through three ages (gods, heroes, and men), and are the consequence of a divine plan. But their final, human stage is arguably the most important part of the profane universal history that Vico's science displays.

1108 It is true that men have themselves made this world of nations (and we took this as the first incontestable principle of our Science, since we despaired of finding it from the philosophers and philologists), but this world without doubt has issued from a mind often diverse, at times quite contrary, and always superior to the particular ends that men had proposed to themselves; which narrow ends, made means to serve wider ends, it has always employed to preserve the human race upon this earth. Men mean to gratify their bestial lust and abandon their offspring, and they inaugurate the chastity of marriage from which the families arise. The fathers mean to exercise without restraint their paternal power over their clients, and they subject them to the civil powers from which the cities arise. The reigning orders of nobles mean to abuse their lordly freedom over the plebeians, and they are obliged to submit to the laws which establish popular liberty. The free peoples mean to shake off the yoke of their laws, and they become subject to monarchs. The monarchs mean to strengthen their own positions by debasing their subjects with all the vices of dissoluteness, and they dispose them to endure slavery at the hands of stronger nations. The nations mean to dissolve themselves, and their remnants flee for safety to the wilderness, whence, like the phoenix, they rise again. That which did all this was mind, for men did it with intelligence; it was not fate, for they did it by choice; not chance, for the results of their always so acting are perpetually the same.

1109   Hence Epicurus, who believes in chance, is refuted by the facts, along with his followers Hobbes and Machiavelli; and so are Zeno and Spinoza, who believe in fate. The evidence clearly confirms the contrary position of the political philosophers, whose prince is the divine Plato, who shows that providence directs human institutions. Cicero was therefore right in refusing to discuss laws with Atticus unless the latter would give up his Epicureanism and first concede that providence governed human institutions. Pufendorf implicitly denied this by his hypothesis, Selden took it for granted, and Grotius left it out of account; but the Roman jurisconsults established it as the first principle of the natural law of the gentes. For in this work it has been fully demonstrated that through providence the first governments of the world had as their entire form religion, on which alone the family state was based; and passing thence to the heroic or aristocratic civil governments, religion must have been their principal firm basis. Advancing then to the popular governments, it was again religion that served the peoples as means for attaining them. And coming to rest at last in monarchic governments, this same religion must be the shield of princes. Hence, if religion is lost among the peoples, they have nothing left to enable them to live in society: no shield of defense, nor means of counsel, nor basis of support, nor even a form by which they may exist in the world at all.

1110   Let Bayle consider then whether in fact there can be nations in the world without any knowledge of God! And let Polybius weigh the truth of his statement that if there were philosophers in the world there would be no need in the world of religions! For religions alone can bring the peoples to do virtuous works by appeal to their feelings, which alone move men to perform them; and the reasoned maxims of the philosophers concerning virtue are of use only when employed by a good eloquence for kindling the feelings to do the duties of virtue. There is, however, an essential difference between our Christian religion, which is true, and all the others, which are false. In our religion, divine grace causes virtuous action for the sake of an eternal and infinite good. This good cannot fall under the senses, and it is consequently the mind that, for its sake, moves the senses to virtuous actions. The false religions, on the contrary, have proposed to themselves finite and transitory goods, in this life as in the other (where they expect a beatitude of sensual pleasures), and hence the senses must drive the mind to do virtuous works.

1111   But providence, through the order of civil institutions discussed in this work, makes itself palpable for us in these three feelings: the first, the marvel, the second, the veneration, hitherto felt by all the learned for the matchless wisdom of the ancients, and the third, the ardent desire with which they burned to seek and attain it. These are in fact three lights of the divine providence that aroused in them the aforesaid three beautiful and just sentiments; but these sentiments were later perverted by the conceit of scholars and by the conceit of nations – conceits we have sought throughout this work to discredit. The uncorrupted feelings are that all the learned should admire, venerate, and desire to unite themselves to the infinite wisdom of God.

1112   To sum up, from all that we have set forth in this work, it is to be finally concluded that this Science carries inseparably with it the study of piety, and that he who is not pious cannot be truly wise.

4

The Spirit of the Laws (1748)

Charles Louis de Secondat, Baron de Montesquieu

Charles Louis de Secondat, Baron de Montesquieu, Book XIV, "Of Laws in Relation to the Nature of the Climate," of *The Spirit of the Laws* (1748) [source: Baron de Montesquieu, *The Spirit of the Laws*, 2 vols in 1, trans. Thomas Nugent. New York: Hafner Publishing, 1949, 1: 221–34]

Drawing from the philosophical skepticism of Descartes and Malebranche, influenced by Vico, and following Machiavelli and Montaigne with regard to the imperfect nature of human institutions, Montesquieu (1689–1755) is best known for his elaboration of the theme that civil institutions such as the law are profoundly shaped by the physical circumstances and the inherited traditions of a given people or nation. His mechanistic sense of society as a temporally and spatially structured totality, where positive legislation needed to be in harmony with customary institutions, meant that elements from one nation could not be imported haphazardly into another. His argument was thus central to much eighteenth- and nineteenth-century thinking about the distinct spirit of a nation, from Herder, Burke, Maistre, and Fichte on, though subsequent thinkers often revised his assumptions. Herder, for instance, placed far more emphasis on language and tradition than climate. Montesquieu's perspective could be seen as limiting the universalizing pretensions of some forms of colonialism. But it also meant that certain nations and territories would always be suited to despotic rather than constitutional or republican rule.

Book XIV: Of Laws in Relation to the Nature of the Climate

1 – General Idea

If it be true that the temper of the mind and the passions of the heart are extremely different in different climates, the laws ought to be in relation both to the variety of those passions and to the variety of those tempers.

2 – Of the Difference of Men in different Climates

Cold air constringes the extremities of the external fibres of the body;[1] this increases their elasticity, and favors the return of the blood from the extreme parts to the heart. It contracts[2] those very fibres; consequently it increases also their force. On the contrary, warm air relaxes and lengthens the extremes of the fibres; of course it diminishes their force and elasticity.

People are, therefore, more vigorous in cold climates. Here the action of the heart and the reaction of the extremities of the fibres are better performed, the temperature of the humors is greater, the blood moves more freely towards the heart, and reciprocally the heart has more power. This superiority of strength must produce various effects; for instance, a greater boldness, that is, more courage; a greater sense of superiority, that is, less desire of revenge; a greater opinion of security, that is, more frankness, less suspicion, policy, and cunning. In short, this must be productive of very different tempers. Put a man into a close, warm place, and for the reasons above given he will feel a great faintness. If under this circumstance you propose a bold enterprise to him, I believe you will find him very little disposed towards it; his present weakness will throw him into despondency; he will be afraid of everything, being in a state of total incapacity. The inhabitants of warm countries are, like old men, timorous; the people in cold countries are, like young men, brave. If we reflect on the late wars,[3] which are more recent in our memory, and in which we can better distinguish some particular effects that escape us at a greater distance of time, we shall find that the northern people, transplanted into southern regions,[4] did not perform such exploits as their countrymen, who, fighting in their own climate, possessed their full vigor and courage.

This strength of the fibres in northern nations is the cause that the coarser juices are extracted from their ailments. Hence two things result: one, that the parts of the chyle or lymph are more proper, by reason of their large surface, to be applied to and to nourish the fibres; the other, that they are less proper, from their coarseness, to give a certain subtility to the nervous juice. Those people have, therefore, large bodies and but little vivacity.

The nerves that terminate from all parts in the cutis form each a nervous bundle; generally speaking, the whole nerve is not moved, but a very minute part. In warm climates, where the cutis is relaxed, the ends of the nerves are expanded and laid open to the weakest action of the smallest objects. In cold countries the cutis is constringed and the papillæ compressed: the miliary glands are in some measure paralytic; and the sensation does not reach the brain, except when it is very strong and proceeds from the whole nerve at once. Now, imagination, taste, sensibility, and vivacity depend on an infinite number of small sensations.

I have observed the outermost part of a sheep's tongue, where, to the naked eye, it seems covered with papillæ. On these papillæ I have discerned through a microscope small hairs, or a kind of down; between the papillæ were pyramids shaped towards the ends like pincers. Very likely these pyramids are the principal organ of taste.

I caused the half of this tongue to be frozen, and observing it with the naked eye I found the papillæ considerably diminished: even some rows of them were sunk into their sheath. The outermost part I examined with the microscope, and perceived no pyramids. In proportion as the frost went off, the papillæ seemed to the naked eye to rise, and with the microscope the miliary glands began to appear.

This observation confirms what I have been saying, that in cold countries the nervous glands are less expanded: they sink deeper into their sheaths, or they are sheltered from the action of external objects; consequently they have not such lively sensations.

In cold countries they have very little sensibility for pleasure; in temperate countries, they have more; in warm countries, their sensibility is exquisite. As climates are distinguished by degrees of latitude, we might distinguish them also in some measure by those of sensibility. I have been at the opera in England and in Italy, where I have seen the same pieces and the same performers; and yet the same music produces such different effects on the two nations: one is so cold and phlegmatic, and the other so lively and enraptured, that it seems almost inconceivable.

It is the same with regard to pain, which is excited by the laceration of some fibre of the body. The Author of nature has made it an established rule that this pain should be more acute in proportion as the laceration is greater: now it is evident that the large bodies and coarse fibres of the people of the North are less capable of laceration than the delicate fibres of the inhabitants of warm countries; consequently the soul is there less sensible of pain. You must flay a Muscovite alive to make him feel.

From this delicacy of organs peculiar to warm climates it follows that the soul is most sensibly moved by whatever relates to the union of the two sexes: here everything leads to this object.

In northern climates scarcely has the animal part of love a power of making itself felt. In temperate climates, love, attended by a thousand appendages, endeavors to please by things that have at first the appearance, though not the reality, of this passion. In warmer climates it is liked for its own sake, it is the only cause of happiness, it is life itself.

In southern countries a machine of a delicate frame but strong sensibility resigns itself either to a love which rises and is incessantly laid in a seraglio, or to a passion which leaves women in a greater independence, and is consequently exposed to a thousand inquietudes. In northern regions a machine robust and heavy finds pleasure in whatever is apt to throw the spirits into motion, such as hunting, travelling, war, and wine. If we travel towards the North, we meet with people who have few vices, many virtues, and a great share of frankness and sincerity. If we draw near the South, we fancy ourselves entirely removed from the verge of morality; here the strongest passions are productive of all manner of crimes, each man endeavoring, let the means be what they will, to indulge his inordinate desires. In temperate climates we find the inhabitants inconstant in their manners, as well as in their vices and virtues: the climate has not a quality determinate enough to fix them.

The heat of the climate may be so excessive as to deprive the body of all vigor and strength. Then the faintness is communicated to the mind; there is no curiosity, no enterprise, no generosity of sentiment; the inclinations are all passive; indolence constitutes the utmost happiness; scarcely any punishment is so severe as mental employment; and slavery is more supportable than the force and vigor of mind necessary for human conduct.

3 – Contradiction in the Tempers of some Southern Nations

The Indians[5] are naturally a pusillanimous people; even the children[6] of Europeans born in India lose the courage peculiar to their own climate. But how shall we reconcile this with their customs and penances so full of barbarity? The men voluntarily undergo the greatest hardships, and the women burn themselves: here we find a very odd compound of fortitude and weakness.

Nature, having framed those people of a texture so weak as to fill them with timidity, has formed them at the same time of an imagination so lively that every object makes the strongest impression upon them. That delicacy of organs which renders them apprehensive of death contributes likewise to make them dread a thousand things more than death: the very same sensibility induces them to fly and dare all dangers.

As a good education is more necessary to children than to such as have arrived at maturity of understanding, so the inhabitants of those countries have much greater need than the European nations of a wiser legislator. The greater their sensibility, the more it behooves them to receive proper impressions, to imbibe no prejudices, and to let themselves be directed by reason.

At the time of the Romans the inhabitants of the north of Europe were destitute of arts, education, and almost of laws; and yet the good sense annexed to the gross fibres of those climates enabled them to make an admirable stand against the power of Rome, till the memorable period in which they quitted their woods to subvert that great empire.

4 – Cause of the Immutability of Religion, Manners, Customs, and Laws in the Eastern Countries

If to that delicacy of organs which renders the eastern nations so susceptible of every impression you add likewise a sort of indolence of mind, naturally connected with that of the body, by means of which they grow incapable of any exertion or effort, it is easy to comprehend that when once the soul has received an impression it cannot change it. This is the reason that the laws, manners, and customs,[7] even those which seem quite indifferent, such as their mode of dress, are the same to this very day in eastern countries as they were a thousand years ago.

5 – That those are bad Legislators who favor the Vices of the Climate, and good Legislators who oppose those Vices

The Indians believe that repose and non-existence are the foundation of all things, and the end in which they terminate. Hence they consider entire inaction as the most perfect of all states, and the object of their desires. To the Supreme Being they give the title of immovable. The inhabitants of Siam believe that their utmost happiness consists in not being obliged to animate a machine or to give motion to a body.

In those countries where the excess of heat enervates and exhausts the body, rest is so delicious, and motion so painful, that this system of metaphysics seems natural; and Foe,[8] the legislator of the Indies, was directed by his own sensations when he placed mankind in a state extremely passive; but his doctrine arising from the laziness of the climate favored it also in its turn; which has been the source of an infinite deal of mischief.

The legislators of China were more rational when, considering men not in the peaceful state which they are to enjoy hereafter, but in the situation proper for discharging the several duties of life, they made their religion, philosophy, and laws all practical. The more the physical causes incline mankind to inaction, the more the moral causes should estrange them from it.

6 – Of Agriculture in warm Climates

Agriculture is the principal labor of man. The more the climate inclines him to shun this labor, the more the religion and laws of the country ought to incite him to it. Thus the Indian laws, which give the lands to the prince, and destroy the spirit of property among the subjects, increase the bad effects of the climate, that is, their natural indolence.

7 – Of Monkery

The very same mischiefs result from monkery: it had its rise in the warm countries of the East, where they are less inclined to action than to speculation.

In Asia the number of dervishes or monks seems to increase together with the warmth of the climate. The Indies, where the heat is excessive, are full of them; and the same difference is found in Europe.

In order to surmount the laziness of the climate, the laws ought to endeavor to remove all means of subsisting without labor: but in the southern parts of Europe they act quite the reverse. To those who want to live in a state of indolence, they afford retreats the most proper for a speculative life, and endow them with immense revenues. These men who live in the midst of plenty which they know not how to enjoy, are in the right to give their superfluities away to the common people. The poor are bereft of property; and these men indemnify them by supporting them in idleness, so as to make them even grow fond of their misery.

8 – An excellent Custom of China

The historical relations of China mention a ceremony[9] of opening the ground which the emperor performs every year. The design of this public and solemn act is to excite the people to tillage.[10]

Further, the emperor is every year informed of the husbandman who has distinguished himself most in his profession; and he makes him a mandarin of the eighth order.

Among the ancient Persians the kings quitted their grandeur and pomp on the eighth day of the month, called *Chorrem-ruz*, to eat with the husbandmen. These institutions were admirably calculated for the encouragement of agriculture.

9 – Means of encouraging Industry

We shall show, in the nineteenth book, that lazy nations are generally proud. Now the effect might well be turned against the cause, and laziness be destroyed by pride. In the south of Europe, where people have such a high notion of the point of honor, it would be right to give prizes to husbandmen who had excelled in agriculture; or to artists who had made the greatest improvements in their several professions. This practice has succeeded in our days in Ireland, where it has established one of the most considerable linen manufactures in Europe.

10 – Of the Laws in relation to the Sobriety of the People

In warm countries the aqueous part of the blood loses itself greatly by perspiration;[11] it must, therefore, be supplied by a like liquid. Water is there of admirable use; strong liquors would congeal the globules[12] of blood that remain after the transuding of the aqueous humor.

In cold countries the aqueous part of the blood is very little evacuated by perspiration. They may, therefore, make use of spirituous liquors, without which the blood would congeal. They are full of humors; consequently strong liquors, which give a motion to the blood, are proper for those countries.

The law of Mohammed, which prohibits the drinking of wine, is, therefore, fitted to the climate of Arabia: and, indeed, before Mohammed's time, water was the common drink of the Arabs. The law[13] which forbade the Carthaginians to drink wine was a law of the climate; and, indeed, the climate of those two countries is pretty nearly the same.

Such a law would be improper for cold countries, where the climate seems to force them to a kind of national intemperance, very different from personal ebriety. Drunkenness predominates throughout the world, in proportion to the coldness and humidity of the climate. Go from the equator to the north pole, and you will find this vice increasing together with the degree of latitude. Go from the equator again to the south pole, and you will find the same vice travelling south,[14] exactly in the same proportion.

It is very natural that where wine is contrary to the climate, and consequently to health, the excess of it should be more severely punished than in countries where intoxication produces very few bad effects to the person, fewer to the society, and where it does not make people frantic and wild, but only stupid and heavy. Hence those laws[15] which inflicted a double punishment for crimes committed in drunkenness were applicable only to a personal, and not to a national, ebriety. A German drinks through custom, and a Spaniard by choice.

In warm countries the relaxing of the fibres produces a great evacuation of the liquids, but the solid parts are less transpired. The fibres, which act but faintly, and have very little elasticity, are not much impaired; and a small quantity of nutritious juice is sufficient to repair them; for which reason they eat very little.

It is the variety of wants in different climates that first occasioned a difference in the manner of living, and this gave rise to a variety of laws. Where people are very communicative there must be particular laws, and others where there is but little communication.

11 – Of the Laws in relation to the Distempers of the Climate

Herodotus informs us that the Jewish laws concerning the leprosy were borrowed from the practice of the Egyptians. And, indeed, the same distemper required the same remedies. The Greeks and the primitive Romans were strangers to these laws, as well as to the disease. The climate of Egypt and Palestine rendered them necessary; and the facility with which this disease is spread is sufficient to make us sensible of the wisdom and sagacity of those laws.

Even we ourselves have felt the effects of them. The Crusades brought the leprosy amongst us; but the wise regulations made at that time hindered it from infecting the mass of the people.

We find by the law of the Lombards that this disease was spread in Italy before the Crusades, and merited the attention of the legislature. Rotharis ordained that a leper should be expelled from his house, banished to a particular place, and rendered incapable of disposing of his property; because from the very moment he had been turned out of his house he was reckoned dead in the eye of the law. In order to prevent all communication with lepers, they were rendered incapable of civil acts.

I am apt to think that this disease was brought into Italy by the conquests of the Greek emperors, in whose armies there might be some soldiers from Palestine or Egypt. Be that as it may, the progress of it was stopped till the time of the Crusades.

It is related that Pompey's soldiers returning from Syria brought a distemper home with them not unlike the leprosy. We have no account of any regulation made at that time; but it is highly probable that some such step was taken, since the distemper was checked till the time of the Lombards.

It is now two centuries since a disease unknown to our ancestors was first transplanted from the new world to ours, and came to attack human nature even in the very source of life and pleasure. Most of the principal families in the south of Europe were seen to perish by a distemper that had grown too common to be ignominious, and was considered in no other light than in that of its being fatal. It was the thirst of gold that propagated this disease; the Europeans went continually to America, and always brought back a new leaven of it.

Reasons drawn from religion seemed to require that this punishment of guilt should be permitted to continue; but the infection had reached the bosom of matrimony, and given the vicious taint even to guiltless infants.

As it is the business of legislators to watch over the health of the citizens, it would have been a wise part in them to have stopped this communication by laws made on the plan of those of Moses.

The plague is a disease whose infectious progress is much more rapid. Egypt is its principal seat, whence it spreads over the whole globe. Most countries in Europe have made exceedingly good regulations to prevent this infection, and in our times an admirable method has been contrived to stop it; this is by forming a line of troops round the infected country, which cuts off all manner of communication.

The Turks, who have no such regulations, see the Christians escape this infection in the same town, and none but themselves perish; they buy the clothes of the infected, wear them, and proceed in their old way, as if nothing had happened. The doctrine of a rigid fate, which directs their whole conduct, renders the magistrate a quiet spectator; he thinks that everything comes from the hand of God, and that man has nothing more to do than to submit.

12 – Of the Laws against Suicides

We do not find in history that the Romans ever killed themselves without a cause; but the English are apt to commit suicide most unaccountably; they destroy themselves even in the bosom of happiness. This action among the Romans was the effect of education, being connected with their principles and customs; among the English it is the consequence of a distemper,[16] being connected with the physical state of the machine, and independent of every other cause.

In all probability it is a defect of the filtration of the nervous juice: the machine, whose motive faculties are often unexerted, is weary of itself; the soul feels no pain, but a certain uneasiness in existing. Pain is a local sensation, which leads us to the desire of seeing an end of it; the burden of life, which prompts us to the desire of ceasing to exist, is an evil confined to no particular part.

It is evident that the civil laws of some countries may have reasons for branding suicide with infamy: but in England it cannot be punished without punishing the effects of madness.

13 – Effects arising from the Climate of England

In a nation so distempered by the climate as to have a disrelish of everything, nay, even of life, it is plain that the government most suitable to the inhabitants is that in which they cannot lay their uneasiness to any single person's charge, and in which, being under the direction rather of the laws than of the prince, it is impossible for them to change the government without subverting the laws themselves.

And if this nation has likewise derived from the climate a certain impatience of temper, which renders them incapable of bearing the same train of things for any long continuance, it is obvious that the government above mentioned is the fittest for them.

This impatience of temper is not very considerable of itself; but it may become so when joined with courage.

It is quite a different thing from levity, which makes people undertake or drop a project without cause; it borders more upon obstinacy, because it proceeds from so lively a sense of misery that it is not weakened even by the habit of suffering.

This temper in a free nation is extremely proper for disconcerting the projects of tyranny,[17] which is always slow and feeble in its commencement, as in the end it is active and lively; which at first only stretches out a hand to assist, and exerts afterwards a multitude of arms to oppress.

Slavery is ever preceded by sleep. But a people who find no rest in any situation, who continually explore every part, and feel nothing but pain, can hardly be lulled to sleep.

Politics are a smooth file, which cuts gradually, and attains its end by a slow progression. Now the people of whom we have been speaking are incapable of bearing the delays, the details, and the coolness of negotiations: in these they are more unlikely to succeed than any other nation; hence they are apt to lose by treaties what they obtain by their arms.

14 – Other Effects of the Climate

Our ancestors, the ancient Germans, lived in a climate where the passions were extremely calm. Their laws decided only in such cases where the injury was visible to the eye, and went no farther. And as they judged of the outrages done to men from the greatness of the wound, they acted with no other delicacy in respect to the injuries done to women. The law of the Alemans on this subject is very extraordinary. If a person uncovers a woman's head, he pays a fine of fifty sous; if he uncovers her leg up to the knee, he pays the same; and double from the knee upwards. One would think that the law measured the insults offered to women as we measure a figure in geometry; it did not punish the crime of the imagination, but that of the eye. But upon the migration of a German nation into Spain, the climate soon found a necessity for different laws. The law of the Visigoths inhibited the surgeons to bleed a free woman, except either her father, mother, brother, son, or uncle was present. As the imagination of the people grew warm, so did that of the legislators; the law suspected everything when the people had become suspicious.

These laws had, therefore, a particular regard for the two sexes. But in their punishments they seem rather to humor the revengeful temper of private persons than to administer public justice. Thus, in most cases, they reduced both the criminals to be slaves to the offended relatives or to the injured husband; a free-born woman who had yielded to the embraces of a married man was delivered up to his wife to dispose of her as she pleased. They obliged the slaves, if they found their master's wife in adultery, to bind her and carry her to her husband; they even permitted her children to be her accusers, and her slaves to be tortured in order to convict her. Thus their laws were far better adapted to refine, even to excess, a certain point of honor than to form a good civil administration. We must not, therefore, be surprised if Count Julian was of opinion that an affront of that kind ought to be expiated by the ruin of his king and country: we must not be surprised if the Moors, with such a conformity of manners, found it so easy to settle and to maintain themselves in Spain, and to retard the fall of their empire.[18]

15 – Of the different Confidence which the Laws have in the People, according to the Difference of Climates

The people of Japan are of so stubborn and perverse a temper that neither their legislators nor magistrates can put any confidence in them: they set nothing before their eyes but judgments, menaces, and chastisements; every step they take is subject to the inquisition of the civil magistrate. Those laws which out of five heads of families establish one as a magistrate over the other four; those laws which punish a family or a whole ward for a single crime; those laws, in fine, which find nobody innocent where one may happen to be guilty, are made with a design to implant in the people a mutual distrust, and to make every man the inspector, witness, and judge of his neighbor's conduct.

On the contrary, the people of India are mild, tender, and compassionate. Hence their legislators repose great confidence in them. They have established very few punishments; these are not severe, nor are they rigorously executed. They have subjected nephews to their uncles, and orphans to their guardians, as in other countries they are subjected to their fathers; they have regulated the succession by the acknowledged merit of the successor. They seem to think that every individual ought to place entire confidence in the good nature of his fellow- subjects.

They enfranchise their slaves without difficulty, they marry them, they treat them as their children.[19] Happy climate which gives birth to innocence, and produces a lenity in the laws!

Notes

1 This appears even in the countenance: in cold weather people look thinner.
2 We know that it shortens iron.
3 Those for the succession to the Spanish monarchy.
4 For instance, in Spain.
5 "One hundred European soldiers," says Tavernier, "would without any great difficulty beat a thousand Indian soldiers."
6 Even the Persians who settle in the Indies contract in the third generation the indolence and cowardice of the Indians.
7 We find by a fragment of Nicolaus Damascenus, collected by Constantine Porphyrogenitus, that it was an ancient custom in the East to send to strangle a Governor who had given any displeasure; it was in the time of the Medes.
8 Foe[i.e. fó, or Buddha: Ed.] endeavored to reduce the heart to a mere vacuum: "We have eyes and ears, but perfection consists in neither seeing nor hearing; a mouth, hands, etc., but perfection requires that these members should be inactive." This is taken from the dialogue of a Chinese philosopher.
9 Several of the kings of India do the same.
10 Venty[i.e. Huángdì: Ed.], the third Emperor of the third dynasty, tilled the lands himself, and made the Empress and his wives employ their time in the silkworks in his palace.
11 Monsieur Bernier, travelling from Lahore to Cashmere, wrote thus: "My body is a sieve; scarcely have I swallowed a pint of water, but I see it transude like dew out of all my limbs, even to my fingers' ends. I drink ten pints a day, and it does me no manner of harm."
12 In the blood there are red globules, fibrous parts, white globules, and water, in which the whole swims.
13 Plato, book II, of "Laws"; Aristotle, of the care of domestic affairs; Eusebius's "Evangelical Preparation," book XII, chap. xvii.
14 This is seen in the Hottentots, and the inhabitants of the most southern part of Chili.
15 As Pittacus did, according to Aristotle, "Polit." lib. I, cap. iii. He lived in a climate where drunkenness is not a national vice.
16 It may be complicated with the scurvy, which, in some countries especially, renders a man whimsical and unsupportable to himself.

17   Here I take this word for the design of subverting the established power, and especially that of democracy; this is the signification in which it was understood by the Greeks and Romans.

18   [According to legend, a Count Julian aided the Moors invading Spain because his daughter was raped by Rodrigo, the last of Spain's Visigoth Kings. Ed.]

19   I had once thought that the lenity of slavery in India had made Diodorus say that there was neither master nor slave in that country; but Diodorus has attributed to the whole continent of India what, according to Strabo, belonged only to a particular nation.

5

The Social Contract; The Origin of Inequality; and The Government of Poland (1754–72)

Jean-Jacques Rousseau

Jean-Jacques Rousseau, Book I, ch. VI, of *The Social Contract* (1762); selections from "Discourse on the Origin and Basis of Inequality Among Men" (1754) and from *The Government of Poland* (1772) [source: Jean-Jacques Rousseau, *The Social Contract and Discourses*, trans. C. D. H. Cole. London: J. M. Dent, 1993, 190–3, 102–3; and Rousseau, *The Government of Poland*, trans. Willmoore Kendall. Indianapolis, IN: Bobbs-Merrill Co., 1972, 10–14, 19–20]

Rousseau (1712–78) is considered one of the fathers of republican nationalism. Like Milton and Locke, he advanced a notion of popular sovereignty based on collective assent rather than communal history. Rousseau's famous pronouncement in the first chapter of the *Social Contract* – "Man is born free; and everywhere he is in chains" – epitomized the sentiment of republican revolution, and its universality implied more a civic than an ethnic ideal. Rousseau's republicanism derived less from natural law, though this still played a role, or from scripture, as had Milton's, but from the "general will" of the people. His notion of an original social contract, in which each gives himself without reserve to all, and thus to no one in particular, founded government on principles both negative (defense of person and property, individual freedom) and positive (a harmonious union of all in all). But his "general will" was also a moral and spiritual communal identity – Acton called it "ethnological" – rather than a majority opinion. Rousseau denied the legitimacy of elected representation and argued that only small, simple states, in which no conflicts of interest or political intrigue occurred, could achieve true popular sovereignty. He further agreed with Montesquieu "that all forms of government do not suit all countries" or climates (*Social Contract*, Book III, ch. 8). In 1771, a Polish Convention turned to Rousseau (among other French political theorists) for advice on writing a constitution once Poland achieved independence. Rousseau's response to the Convention – recommending a patriotism instilled from birth; an educational system that transmitted the nation's heritage, from literature to law; and national sports and ceremonies – arrived the following year. But by then, Poland was being devoured by the first of the imperial Partitions.

The Social Contract

Chapter 6: The Social Compact

I suppose men to have reached the point at which the obstacles in the way of their preservation in the state of nature show their power of resistance to be greater than the resources at the disposal of each individual for his maintenance in that state. That primitive condition can then subsist no longer; and the human race would perish unless it changed its manner of existence.

But, as men cannot engender new forces, but only unite and direct existing ones, they have no other means of preserving themselves than the formation, by aggregation, of a sum of forces great enough to overcome the resistance. These they have to bring into play by means of a single motive power, and cause to act in concert.

This sum of forces can arise only where several persons come together: but, as the force and liberty of each man are the chief instruments of his self-preservation, how can he pledge them without harming his own interests, and neglecting the care he owes to himself? This difficulty, in its bearing on my present subject, may be stated in the following terms:

"The problem is to find a form of association which will defend and protect with the whole common force the person and goods of each associate, and in which each, while uniting himself with all, may still obey himself alone, and remain as free as before." This is the fundamental problem of which the social contract provides the solution.

The clauses of this contract are so determined by the nature of the act that the slightest modification would make them vain and ineffective; so that, although they have perhaps never been formally set forth, they are everywhere the same and everywhere tacitly admitted and recognized, until, on the violation of the social compact, each regains his original rights and resumes his natural liberty, while losing the conventional liberty in favour of which he renounced it.

These clauses, properly understood, may be reduced to one – the total alienation of each associate, together with all his rights, to the whole community; for, in the first place, as each gives himself absolutely, the conditions are the same for all; and, this being so, no one has any interest in making them burdensome to others.

Moreover, the alienation being without reserve, the union is as perfect as it can be, and no associate has anything more to demand: for, if the individuals retained certain rights, as there would be no common superior to decide between them and the public, each, being on one point his own judge, would ask to be so on all; the state of nature would thus continue, and the association would necessarily become inoperative or tyrannical.

Finally, each man, in giving himself to all, gives himself to nobody; and as there is no associate over which he does not acquire the same right as he yields others over himself, he gains an equivalent for everything he loses, and an increase of force for the preservation of what he has.

If then we discard from the social compact what is not of its essence, we shall find that it reduces itself to the following terms:

"*Each of us puts his person and all his power in common under the supreme direction of the general will, and, in our corporate capacity, we receive each member as an indivisible part of the whole.*"

At once, in place of the individual personality of each contracting party, this act of association creates a corporate and collective body, composed of as many members as the assembly contains voters, and receiving from this act its unity, its common identity, its life, and its will. This public person, so formed by the union of all other persons, formerly took the name of *city*,[1] and now takes that of *Republic* or *body politic*; it is called by its members *State* when passive, *Sovereign* when active, and *Power* when compared with others like itself. Those who associated in it take collectively the name of *people*, and severally are called *citizens*, as sharing in the sovereign authority, and *subjects*, as being under the laws of the State. But these terms are often confused and taken one for another: it is enough to know how to distinguish them when they are being used with precision.

Discourse on the Origin of Inequality

[...] Politicians indulge in the same sophistry about the love of liberty as philosophers about the state of nature. They judge, by what they see, of very different things, which they have not seen; they attribute to man a natural propensity to servitude, because the slaves within their observation are seen to bear the yoke with patience; they fail to reflect that it is with liberty as with innocence and virtue; the value is known only to those who possess them, and the taste for them is forfeited when they are forfeited themselves. "I know the charms of your country," said Brasidas to a Satrap, who was comparing the life at Sparta with that at Persepolis, "but you cannot know the pleasures of mine."

An unbroken horse erects his mane, paws the ground and starts back impetuously at the sight of the bridle; while one which is properly trained suffers patiently even whip and spur: so savage man will not bend his neck to the yoke to which civilized man submits without a murmur, but prefers the most turbulent state of liberty to the most peaceful slavery. We cannot therefore, from the servility of nations already enslaved, judge of the natural disposition of mankind for or against slavery; we should go by the prodigious efforts of every free people to save itself from oppression. I know that the former are for ever holding forth in praise of the tranquillity they enjoy in their chains, and that they call a state of wretched servitude a state of peace: *miserrimam servitutem pacem appellant.* But when I observe the latter sacrificing pleasure, peace, wealth, power, and life itself to the preservation of that one treasure, which is so disdained by those who have lost it; when I see free-born animals dash their brains out against the bars of their cage, from an innate impatience of captivity; when I behold numbers of naked savages, that despise European pleasures, braving hunger, fire, the sword, and death, to preserve nothing but their independence, I feel that it is not for slaves to argue about liberty.

The Government of Poland

III: The foregoing applied to Poland

Poland is a large state, surrounded by yet larger states whose military discipline and despotic forms of government give them great offensive power. In sharp contrast to them, Poland is weak from anarchy, so that, despite the bravery of its citizens, it must accept any outrages its neighbors choose to inflict upon it. It has no fortified places to prevent their incursions into its territory. It is underpopulated, and is therefore well-nigh incapable of defending itself. It has no proper economic system. It has few troops, or rather none at all. It lacks military discipline. It is disorganized. Its people do not obey. Constantly divided within, constantly threatened from without, it has in itself no stability whatever and is at the mercy of its neighbors' whims.

As matters now stand, I see only one means of giving Poland the stability it lacks, namely, to infuse into the entire nation, so to speak, the spirit of your confederates, and to establish the republic in the Poles' own hearts, so that it will live on in them despite anything your oppressors may do. Those hearts are, to my mind, the republic's only place of refuge: there force can neither destroy it nor even reach it. Of this you have just seen a proof that will be remembered forever; Poland was in Russian irons, but the Poles themselves remained free – a great object lesson, which teaches you how you can defy the power and ambition of your neighbors. You cannot possibly keep them from swallowing you; see to it, at least, that they shall not be able to digest you. Whatever you do, your enemies will crush you a hundred times before you have given Poland what it needs in order to be capable of resisting them. There is one rampart, however, that will always be readied for its defense, and that no army can possibly breach; and that is the virtue of its citizens, their patriotic zeal, in the distinctive cast that national institutions are capable of impressing upon their souls. See to it that every Pole is incapable of becoming a Russian, and I answer for it that Russia will never subjugate Poland.

I repeat: *national* institutions. That is what gives form to the genius, the character, the tastes, and the customs of a people; what causes it to be itself rather than some other people; what arouses in it that ardent love of fatherland that is founded upon habits of mind impossible to uproot; what makes unbearably tedious for its citizens every moment spent away from home – even when they find themselves surrounded by delights that are denied them in their own country. Remember the Spartan at the court of the Great King: they chided him when, sated with sensual pleasures, he hungered for the taste of black broth. "Ah!" he sighed to the satrap, "I know your pleasures; but you do not know ours!"

Say what you like, there is no such thing nowadays as Frenchmen, Germans, Spaniards, or even Englishmen – only Europeans. All have the same tastes, the same passions, the same customs, and for good reason: Not one of them has ever been formed *nationally*, by distinctive legislation. Put them in the same circumstances and, man for man, they will do exactly the same things. They will all tell you how unselfish they are, and act like scoundrels. They will all go on and on about the public good, and think only of themselves. They will all sing the praises of moderation, and each will wish himself a modern Croesus. They all dream only of luxury, and know no passion except the passion for money; sure as they are that money will fetch them everything they fancy, they will all sell themselves to the first man who is willing to pay them. What do they care what master's bidding they do, or what country's laws they obey? Their fatherland is any country where there is money for them to steal and women for them to seduce.

Give a different bent to the passions of the Poles; in doing so, you will shape their minds and hearts in a national pattern that will set them apart from other peoples, that will keep them from being absorbed by other peoples, or finding contentment among them, or allying themselves with them. You will give the Poles a spiritual vigor that will end all this iniquitous bandying-about of idle precepts, and will cause them to do by inclination and passionate choice the things that men motivated by duty or interest never do quite well enough. Upon souls like that, a wisely-conceived legislation will take firm hold. They will obey, not elude, the laws, because the laws will suit them, and will enjoy the inward assent of their own wills. They will love their fatherland; they will serve it zealously and with all their hearts. Where love of fatherland prevails, even a bad legislation would produce good citizens. And nothing except good citizens will ever make the state powerful and prosperous.

I shall describe below a system of administration that, leaving the deeper levels of your laws virtually untouched, seems to me what you need in order to raise the patriotism of the Poles, as also the virtues that invariably accompany patriotism, to their highest possible level of intensity. But whether you adopt that system or not, you must still begin by giving the citizens of Poland a high opinion of themselves and of their fatherland. That opinion, in view of the manner in which they have just shown themselves, will not be unfounded, which is to say: Seize the opportunity afforded by the events of the present moment, and raise souls to the pitch of the souls of the ancients. The Confederation of Bar saved your fatherland at a moment when it was about to expire; so much is certain.[2] Now: the story of that glorious episode should be carved in sacred characters upon each Polish heart. I should like you to erect, to the Confederation's memory, a monument inscribed with the name of every one of its members, including, since so great a deed should wipe out the transgressions of an entire lifetime, even those who may subsequently have betrayed the common cause. I should also like you to establish the custom of celebrating the confederates' deeds every ten years in solemn ceremonies – with the pomp appropriate to a republic: simple and proud rather than ostentatious and vain; and in them, with dignity and in language free from exaggeration, let praise be bestowed upon the virtuous citizens who had the honor to suffer for their country in the toils of the enemy. And finally, I should like some honorific distinction, one that would constantly remind the public of this noble heritage from the past, to be conferred even upon the Confederates' families. During these solemnities I should not, however, like you to permit any invective against the Russians, or even any mention of them. That would be to honor them too much; besides which your silence about them at the very moment of remembering their cruelty, and your praise for the men who resisted them, will say about the Russians all that needs be said. You should despise them too much ever to hate them.

I should like you, by means of honors and public prizes, to shed luster on all the patriotic virtues, to keep the Poles' minds constantly on the fatherland, making it their central preoccupation, and to hold it up constantly before their eyes. This, I admit, would give them less opportunity and leave them less time for getting rich, but they would also have less desire and less need for riches: their hearts would come to know happiness of another kind than that which wealth confers. There you have the secret for ennobling men's souls and for making of their ennoblement an incentive more powerful than gold.

I have not been able, from the brief sketch of Polish customs that M. de Wielhorski has kindly placed in my hands, to form an adequate picture of the Poles' civil and domestic usages. But so large a country, and one that has never had much intercourse with its neighbors, must have developed a great many usages that are its very own but are perhaps being bastardized, day in and day out, in line with the Europe-wide tendency to take on the tastes and customs of the French. You must maintain or revive (as the case may be) your ancient customs and introduce suitable new ones that will also be purely Polish. Let these new customs be neither here nor there as far as good and bad are concerned; let them even have their bad points; they would, unless bad in principle, still afford this advantage: they would endear Poland to its citizens and develop in them an instinctive distaste for mingling with the peoples of other countries. I deem it all to the good, for example, that the Poles have a distinctive mode of dress; you must take care to preserve this asset – by doing precisely what a certain czar, whose praises we often hear, did not do. See to it that your king, your senators, everyone in public life, never wear anything but distinctively Polish clothing, and that no Pole shall dare to present himself at court dressed like a Frenchman.

I recommend numerous public games, where Poland, like a good mother, can take delight in seeing her children at play. Let Poland's mind be on them often, so that their minds will always be on Poland. You should prohibit – even, because of the example, at court – the amusements that one ordinarily finds in courts: gambling, the theater, comedies, operas – everything that makes men unmanly, or distracts them, or isolates them, or causes them to forget their fatherland and their duties, or disposes them to feel content anywhere so long as they are being amused. You must create games, festivities, and ceremonials, all peculiar to your court to such an extent that one will encounter nothing like them in any other. Life in Poland must be more fun than life in any other country, but not the same kind of fun. This is to say: you must turn a certain execrable proverb upside-down, and bring each Pole to say from the bottom of his heart: *Ubi patria, ibi bene.*[3] [...]

IV: Education

Here we have the important topic: it is education that you must count on to shape the souls of the citizens in a national pattern and so to direct their opinions, their likes, and dislikes that they shall be patriotic by inclination, passionately, of necessity.

The newly-born infant, upon first opening his eyes, must gaze upon the fatherland, and until his dying day should behold nothing else. Your true republican is a man who imbibed love of the fatherland, which is to say love of the laws and of liberty, with his mother's milk. That love makes up his entire existence: he has eyes only for the fatherland, lives only for his fatherland; the moment he is alone, he is a mere cipher; the moment he has no fatherland, he is no more; if not dead, he is worse-off than if he were dead.

Truly national education belongs exclusively to men who are free; they and they only enjoy a common existence; they and they only are genuinely bound together by laws. Your Frenchman, your Englishman, your Spaniard, your Italian, your Russian, are all pretty much the same man; and that man emerges from school already well-shaped for license, which is to say for servitude. When the Pole reaches the age of twenty, he must be a Pole, not some other kind of man. I should wish him to learn to read by reading literature written in his own country. I should wish him, at ten, to be familiar with everything Poland has produced; at twelve, to know all its provinces, all its roads, all its towns; at fifteen, to have mastered his country's entire history, and at sixteen, all its laws; let his mind and heart be full of every noble deed, every illustrious man, that ever was in Poland, so that he can tell you about them at a moment's notice. I do not, as that should make clear, favor putting the youngsters through the usual round of studies, directed by foreigners and priests. The content, the sequence, even the method of their studies should be specified by Polish law. They should have only Poles for teachers – all of them married men, if that were possible, all men of distinction, alike for their conduct, their probity, their good sense, and their lights, and all destined, after a certain number of years of creditable service as teachers, to fill not more important posts, for there is none more important, but more prestigious and less-exacting ones. Above all, do not make the mistake of turning teaching into a career. A public servant in Poland should have no permanent status other than that of citizen; each post he fills, especially if it be an important one like that of teacher, should be thought of merely as one further testing-ground, one further rung on a ladder, from which to climb, when he deserves to, yet higher. I urge the Poles to give heed to this principle, upon which I shall often insist; I believe it to be a key with which the state can unlock a great storehouse of energy. [...]

Notes

1 The real meaning of this word has been almost wholly lost in modern times; most people mistake a town for a city, and a townsman for a citizen. They do not know that houses make a town, but citizens a city. The same mistake long ago cost the Carthaginians dear. I have never read of the title of citizens being given to the subjects of any prince, not even the ancient Macedonians or the English of today, though they are nearer liberty than any one else. The French alone everywhere familiarly adopt the name of citizens, because, as can be seen from their dictionaries, they have no idea of its meaning; otherwise they would be guilty in usurping it, of the crime of *lèse-majesté*; among them, the name expresses a virtue, and not a right. When Bodin spoke of our citizens and townsmen, he fell into a bad blunder in taking the one class for the other. M. d'Alembert has avoided the error, and, in his article on Geneva, has clearly distinguished the four orders of men (or even five, counting mere foreigners) who dwell in our town, of which two only compose the Republic. No other French writer, to my knowledge, has understood the real meaning of the word citizen.

2 [The Confederation of Bar (1768) was an anti-Russian association (supported by France) formed to resist Russian and Prussian insistence on equal rights for Greek Orthodox Christians and Protestants in largely Roman Catholic Poland. Ed.]

3 [The "execrable proverb" that Rousseau tells the Poles to turn upside-down is an anonymous Latin saying, "*Ubi bene ibi patria*," usually translated: "Where one is happy, there is one's homeland." It was, among other things, a useful sentiment for a big empire that sent its sons all over the uncivilized map. Rousseau advises the Poles to invert the phrase and its meaning, that is, to say "*Ubi patria, ibi bene*," or: "Where one's homeland is, there one is happy." Ed.]

6

Dissertations on Ossian (1763)

James Macpherson

James Macpherson, selections from "A Dissertation Concerning the æra of Ossian" and "A Dissertation Concerning the Poems of Ossian," from James Macpherson, ed., *The Works of Ossian, the Son of Fingal* (1763) [source: James Macpherson, ed., *The Poems of Ossian*. New York: Edward Kearney, 1846, 53–9]

Though he was an indifferent scholar and writer, Macpherson (1736–96) was perhaps the single biggest influence on the flowering of interest in folk culture as the basis of national life throughout the eighteenth and nineteenth centuries. His putative translations of an epic written by a mythical Celtic bard called Ossian, poetry largely created (as Hugh Trevor-Roper observed) by Macpherson out of Irish ballads he then brazenly dismissed as corrupt modern imitations, were the primary documents in establishing the Highland Scots as a distinct *Kulturvolk* – a civilized race of archaic origins. In part a response to the failed Highland uprisings of 1745, Macpherson's forged epic nevertheless lay the foundation not only for the invention of a supposedly ancient Highlands tradition, complete with clan-based tartans, but also for the nineteenth-century Celtic Revival and Irish Twilight, from which important modern Irish poets such as William Butler Yeats would emerge. Macpherson had a decisive influence on Herder and a large body of antiquarian research in oral and folk cultures for more than a century to follow.

A Dissertation Concerning the Æra of Ossian

[...] When virtue in peace, and bravery in war, are the characteristics of a nation, their actions become interesting, and their fame worthy of immortality. A generous spirit is warmed with noble actions, and becomes ambitious of perpetuating them. This is the true source of that divine inspiration, to which the poets of all ages pretended. When they found their themes inadequate to the warmth of their imaginations, they varnished them over with fables supplied with their own fancy, or furnished by absurd traditions. These fables, however ridiculous, had their abettors; posterity either implicitly believed them, or through a vanity natural to mankind, pretended that they did. They loved to place the founders of their families in the days of fable, when poetry, without the fear of contradiction, could give what character she pleased of her heroes. It is to this vanity that we owe the preservation of what remain of the more ancient poems. Their poetical merit made their heroes famous in a country where heroism was much esteemed and admired. The posterity of these heroes, or those who pretended to be descended from them, heard with pleasure the eulogiums of their ancestors; bards were employed to repeat the poems, and to record the connection of their patrons with chiefs so renowned. Every chief, in process of time, had a bard in his family, and the office became at last hereditary. By the succession of these bards, the poems concerning the ancestors of the family were handed down from generation to generation; they were repeated to the whole clan on solemn occasions, and always alluded to in the new compositions of the bards. This custom came down to near our own times; and after the bards were discontinued, a great number in a clan retained by memory, or committed to writing, their compositions, and founded the antiquity of their families on the authority of their poems.

The use of letters was not known in the north of Europe till long after the institution of the bards: the records of the families of their patrons, their own, and more ancient poems, were handed down by tradition. Their poetical compositions were admirably contrived for that purpose. They were adapted to music; and the most perfect harmony was observed. Each verse was so connected with those which preceded or followed it, that if one line had been remembered in a stanza, it was almost impossible to forget the rest. The cadences followed so natural a gradation, and the words were so adapted to the common turn of the voice, after it is raised to a certain key, that it was almost impossible, from a similarity of sound, to substitute one word for another. This excellence is peculiar to the Celtic tongue, and is perhaps to be met with in no other language. Nor does this choice of words clog the sense, or weaken the expression. The numerous flexions of consonants, and variation in declension, make the language very copious.

The descendants of the Celtæ, who inhabited Britain and its isles, were not singular in this method of preserving the most precious monuments of their nation. The ancient laws of the Greeks were couched in verse, and handed down by tradition. The Spartans, through a long habit, became so fond of this custom, that they would never allow their laws to be committed to writing. The actions of great men, and eulogiums of kings and heroes, were preserved in the same manner. All the historical monuments of the old Germans were comprehended in their ancient songs; which were either hymns to their gods, or elegies in praise of their heroes, and were intended to perpetuate the great events in their nation, which were carefully interwoven with them. This species of composition was not committed to writing, but delivered by oral tradition. The care they took to have the poems taught to their children, the uninterrupted custom of repeating them upon certain occasions, and the happy measure of the verse, served to preserve them for a long time uncorrupted. This oral chronicle of the Germans was not forgot in the eighth century; and it probably would have remained to this day, had not learning, which thinks every thing that is not committed to writing, fabulous, been introduced. It was from poetical traditions that Garcilasso composed his account of the Incas of Peru. The Peruvians had lost all other monuments of their history, and it was from ancient poems, which his mother, a princess of the blood of the Incas, taught him in his youth, that he collected the materials of his history. If other nations, then, that had often been overrun by enemies, and hath sent abroad and received colonies, could for many ages preserve, by oral tradition, their laws and histories uncorrupted, it is much more probable that the ancient Scots, a people so free of intermixture with foreigners, and so strongly attached to the memory of their ancestors, had the works of their bards handed down with great purity.

What is advanced in this short dissertation, it must be confessed, is mere conjecture. Beyond the reach of records is settled a gloom which no ingenuity can penetrate. The manners described in these poems suit the ancient Celtic times, and no other period that is known in history. We must, therefore, place the heroes far back in antiquity; and it matters little, who were their contemporaries in other parts of the world. If we have placed Fingal in his proper period, we do honor to the manners of barbarous times. He exercised every manly virtue in Caledonia, while Heliogabalus disgraced human nature at Rome.

A Dissertation Concerning the Poems of Ossian

The history of those nations who originally possessed the north of Europe, is less known than their manners. Destitute of the use of letters, they themselves had not the means of transmitting their great actions to remote posterity. Foreign writers saw them only at a distance, and described them as they found them. The vanity of the Romans induced them to consider the nations beyond the pale of their empire as barbarians; and, consequently, their history unworthy of being investigated. Their manners and singular character were matters of curiosity, as they committed them to record. Some men otherwise of great merit, among ourselves, give into confined ideas on this subject. Having early imbibed their idea of exalted manners from the Greek and Roman writers, they scarcely ever afterward have the fortitude to allow any dignity of character to any nation destitute of the use of letters.

Without derogating from the fame of Greece and Rome, we may consider antiquity beyond the pale of their empire worthy of some attention. The nobler passions of the mind never shoot forth more free and unrestrained than in the times we call barbarous. That irregular manner of life, and those manly pursuits, from which barbarity takes it name, are highly favorable to a strength of mind unknown in polished times. In advanced society, the characters of men are more uniform and disguised. The human passions lie in some degree concealed behind forms and artificial manners; and the powers of the soul, without an opportunity of exerting them, lose their vigor. The times of regular government, and polished manners, are therefore to be wished for by the feeble and weak in mind. An unsettled state, and those convulsions, which attend it is, the proper field for an exalted character, and the exertion of great parts. Merit there rises always superior; no fortuitous event can raise the timid and mean into power. To those who look upon antiquity in this light, it is an agreeable prospect; and they alone can have real pleasure in tracing nations to their source. The establishment of the Celtic states, in the north of Europe, is beyond the reach of written annals. The traditions and songs to which they trusted their history, were lost, or altogether corrupted, in their revolutions and migrations, which were so frequent and universal, that no kingdom in Europe is now possessed by its original inhabitants. Societies were formed, and kingdoms erected, from a mixture of nations, who, in process of time, lost all knowledge of their own origin. If tradition could be depended upon, it is only among a people, from all time, free from intermixture with foreigners. We are to look for these among the mountains and inaccessible parts of a country: places, on account of their barrenness, uninviting to an enemy, or whose natural strength enabled the natives to repel invasions. Such are the inhabitants of the mountains of Scotland. We, accordingly find that they differ materially from those who possess the low and more fertile parts of the kingdom. Their language is pure and original, and their manners are those of an ancient and unmixed race of men. Conscious of their own antiquity, they long despised others, as a new and mixed people. As they lived in a country only fit for pasture, they were free from that toil and business which engross the attention of a commercial people. Their amusement consisted in hearing or repeating their songs and traditions, and these entirely turned on the antiquity of their nation, and the exploits of their forefathers. It is no wonder, therefore, that there are more remains among them, than among any other people in Europe. Traditions, however, concerning remote periods are only to be regarded, in so far as they coincide with contemporary writers of undoubted credit and veracity.

No writers began their accounts for a more early period than the historians of the Scots nation. Without records, or even tradition itself, they gave a long list of ancient kings, and a detail of their transactions, with a scrupulous exactness. One might naturally suppose, that when they had no authentic annals, they should, at least, have recourse to the traditions of their country, and have reduced them into a regular system of history. Of both they seem to have been equally destitute. Born in the low country, and strangers to the ancient language of their nation, they contented themselves with copying from one another, and retailing the same fictions in a new color and dress. [. . .]

7

Ideas for a Philosophy of History of Mankind (1784–91)

Johann Gottfried von Herder

Johann Gottfried von Herder, selections from Book VIII, ch. II, and Book IX, ch. IV, from *Ideas for a Philosophy of History of Mankind* (1784–91) [source: *J. G. Herder on Social and Political Culture*, trans. and ed. F. M. Barnard. Cambridge: Cambridge University Press, 1969, 299–301, 323–6]

The German Romantic understanding of the nation began on the one hand with Kant and his conception of the individual's moral autonomy, and on the other with Kant's student Herder (1744–1803), a Hellenist who located collective political identity not in popularly sovereign government (as had Rousseau) but in an organic national, or *Volk*, culture. Herder is the main early champion of what Meinecke later called the *Kulturnation*, "an extended family with one national character" existing independent of any political organization. Herder's political philosophy was a cooperative egalitarian anarchism, deeply distrustful of all state sovereignty, even that derived from Rousseau's "general will." Herder's understanding of the *Volk* depends on a common language in a common territory (his "Essay on the Origin of Language" argues the secular point that language is a product of human society, with one common source, differentiated by the internal disposition of kinship groups and nations in its development). The spirit of each nation is further expressed in its inherited myths and traditions. Following Montesquieu, Herder acknowledged that migrations revealed the power of climate to affect character; he was skeptical of European attempts to export their culture to Africa or the East Indies through colonization. But he also believed that language and myth could be used to chart a "physico-geographical history of the descent and diversification of our species." Herder's treatment of the *Volk* may be the most important early formulation of ethnic national identity.

II: The Human Imagination is Subject to Organic and Climatic Factors, but It is Universally Guided by Tradition

Of a thing that lies outside the sphere of our perception we can scarcely form a conception. The story of the Siamese king who considered ice and snow as non-things is in a thousand instances applicable to mankind as a whole. The conceptions of every indigenous people are confined to its own region. If it professes to understand words expressing things utterly foreign to it, we have cause to question the reality of this understanding.

[...] Compare the mythology of Greenland with that of India, the Lapp with the Japanese, the Peruvian with Negro mythology: it will provide you with a complete geography of the inventing mind. If the Voluspa of the Icelander were read and expounded to a Brahmin, he would scarcely be able to form a single conception from it; and to the Icelander the Veda would be equally unintelligible.

Why is this so? Have all the different nations invented their own mythology and thus become attached to it as their own property? By no means. They have not invented it; they *inherited* it. Had they produced them as a result of some deep thought, some further deep thought might well have improved on them. But this has not been so [...]

As I see it, the key to the mystery lies in this: were all notions as clear to us as those which we acquire by sight, and had we no other ideas than those which we derive from visual objects or can compare with them, the source of error and deception would soon be eliminated since it would be easily discoverable. Most national myths are, however, stories that reach our *ears*. The ignorant child listens with curiosity to the tales which flow into his mind like his mother's milk, and seem to explain to him what he has seen [...] Where there is movement in nature, where a thing seems to live and change without the eye being able to discern the laws of this change, the ear hears words which explain to it by something unseen the mystery of what is seen. The power of the imagination is aroused and releases by its own imagining the tension that existed before. The ear is in general the most timid and apprehensive of all the senses. It perceives things with great intensity, yet obscurely; it cannot retain or compare them to render them clear, for they pass by at a bewildering rate. Designed to arouse the mind, it can rarely instruct it with clarity without the aid of the other senses, particularly the eye.

We find that the imagination is particularly vivid among peoples who live in solitude, or inhabit wild regions, the desert, rocky country, the stormy coast, the foot of volcanoes, or other areas full of movement and wonders.

The deserts of Arabia have given birth from earliest times to the most sublime myths and those who cherished them have been for the most part solitary men filled with wonder and amazement. In solitude Mohammed began his Koran. His heated imagination caused him to imagine himself in Heaven where, in his ecstasy, he saw all the angels, saints and worlds [. . .] To what extent has the superstition of shamanism spread! It is true that it has been suppressed in Asian countries by religious and political cultures of a more positivist and sophisticated type; yet where it could appear again, in solitude or among the populace, it did so. The worship of Nature has gone round the globe. It manifested itself in the most diverse fancies according to those local circumstances which occasioned the most intense fear and horror of the powers of nature affecting our human needs. In ancient times it was the worship of almost all the nations on earth.

That the way of life and the genius of each nation have decidedly influenced the emergence and propagation of myths scarcely needs mentioning. The shepherd sees nature with different eyes than the fisherman and hunter. What is more, even these occupations differ with every region and are as divergent in their actual form as the diverse national characters [. . .] In short, the mythology of every people is an expression of their own distinctive way of viewing nature. The extent to which they found good or evil to prevail in nature and, in particular, how they sought to account for the one by means of the other, was essentially determined by their climate and their creative genius. Even in its most fanciful and absurd features, mythology is a philosophical essay of the human mind which dreams before it is awake, and which is readily inclined to revert to its state of infancy.

It is generally maintained that angekkoks [Eskimo conjurers], conjurers, magicians, shamans and priests invented myths to blind the people. By dismissing them as cheats one is inclined to think that one has explained everything. They may well have been cheats in many or most places, but this should not induce us to forget that they themselves were people too, and the dupes of myths older than themselves. They were born and brought up in a tribal setting permeated by traditional beliefs. Their consecration was attended by fasting, solitude, exhaustion of body and mind, and all this helped to excite their imagination. No one became a magician, until the spirit moved him to do for others what he had hitherto been doing in solitude. The work he was to perform for the rest of his life by repeated exaltations of his mind and fatigues of his body had ripened within him earlier. The most sceptical travellers have been amazed by the conjuring tricks they saw because they could not think it possible that the power of the imagination could successfully produce effects which they frequently found wholly inexplicable. Of all the powers of the human mind the imagination has been least explored, probably because it is the most difficult to explore. Being connected with the general structure of the body, and with that of the brain and nerves in particular – as many diseases remarkably reveal – it seems to be not only the basic and connecting link of all the finer mental powers, but, indeed, the knot that ties body and mind together. It is one of the first things that are passed down from parents to children [. . .]

The question of the existence of innate ideas has long been a subject of dispute. As these terms are usually understood, the answer must certainly be in the negative. But if we take them to refer to a predisposition to receive, connect and extend certain ideas and images, there seems a great deal to be said in favour of such a postulate and very little against it . . . The history of nations will show how Providence has employed this organic predisposition, as a result of which man's imagination can be so easily, yet so powerfully, influenced. But it will show also to our horror how deceit or despotism has abused it by rendering the limitless ocean of the human imagination and fancy subservient to its purposes [. . .]

IV: Political Organization Consists of Set Rules and Orders Among Men, Grounded, for the Most Part, in Tradition

[. . .] Let me, finally, make some general observations.

1 The maxim, that "man is an animal that needs a lord when he lives with others of his species, so that he may attain happiness and fulfil his destiny on earth",[1] is both facile and noxious as a fundamental principle of a philosophy of history. The proposition, I feel, ought to be reversed. Man is an animal as long as he needs a master to lord over him; as soon as he attains the status of a human being he no longer needs a master in any real sense. Nature has designated no master to the human species; only brutal vices and passions render one necessary. The wife requires a husband; the untutored child requires the instruction of the parents; the sick need the services of a physician; conflicting parties select an umpire, and the herd a leader. These are natural relations; they are inherent in the very notions themselves. The notion of despot, however, is not inherent in the notion of man. It presupposes man to be weak, under age, and hence incapable of managing his own affairs. As a result he needs a protector and guardian. Or, on the other hand, it presupposes man to be a wild, detestable creature, demanding a tamer or a minister of vengeance. Thus all governments of man arose, and continue to exist, because of some

human deficiency. A father who brings up his children in a manner which keeps them under age for the rest of their lives and hence in need of a tutor and guardian, is rightly considered a bad father. A physician who contrives to keep his patient in a wretched state to the end of his days so that he will not dispense with his services, is hardly a credit to his profession. Let us apply this line of reasoning to the political teachers of mankind, to the fathers of nations and their charges. Either the latter are incapable of improvement, or it is odd that the thousands of years that men have been governed should have shown no more perceptible results or even revealed the aims of the educators.

2 It is nature which educates families: the most natural state is, therefore, *one* nation, an extended family with one national character. This it retains for ages and develops most naturally if the leaders come from the people and are wholly dedicated to it. For a nation is as natural a plant as a family, only with more branches. Nothing, therefore, is more manifestly contrary to the purpose of political government than the unnatural enlargement of states, the wild mixing of various races and nationalities under one sceptre. A human sceptre is far too weak and slender for such incongruous parts to be engrafted upon it. Such states are but patched-up contraptions, fragile machines, appropriately called state-*machines*, for they are wholly devoid of inner life, and their component parts are connected through mechanical contrivances instead of bonds of sentiment. Like Trojan horses these machines are pieced together, guaranteeing one another's immortality; yet since they are bereft of national character, it would only be the curse of Fate which would condemn to immortality these forced unions, these lifeless monstrosities. They were contrived by that kind of politics which plays with men and nations as if they were inanimate particles. But history shows sufficiently that these instruments of human pride are formed of clay, and, like all clay, they will dissolve or crumble to pieces.

3 Mutual assistance and protection are the principal ends of all human associations. For a polity, too, this natural order is the best; it should ensure that each of its members be able to become what nature wanted him to become. As soon as the monarch wants to usurp the position of the Creator and bring into being by his own arbitrary will or passion what God had not intended, he becomes the father of misrule and inevitable ruin. The distinctions of social rank, established by tradition, run counter to the forces of nature, which knows no ranks in the distribution of its gifts. Yet since these distinctions persist, it is not surprising that most nations, having tried various forms of government and incurred the inconveniences of each, finally returned in despair to that which wholly made them into machines: despotic hereditary government [. . .]

O, that another Montesquieu would come and really offer us the spirit of the laws and governments of our globe, instead of a mere classification of governments into three or four empty categories, when in fact no two governments are alike. A classification of states, based on political principles, is also of little avail; for no state is founded on verbal principles, let alone invariably adheres to them at all times or under all circumstances. Least of all are we in need of a scissors and paste approach, where examples are assembled at random from all nations, times, and climates, until we can no longer see the wood for the trees; the genius of our earth as one entity is lost. What we do need is a vivid and philosophical presentation of civil history in which, despite the apparent uniformity, no one scene occurs twice. Not the external constitution as such will reveal the continuous change to which a state and its political institutions are subject, but rather the internal changes in the character and culture of a nation. It is only by tracing the historical process of these inner, and essentially traditional, forces, that we can hope to explain the continuous development of the boldest of man's mechanical works of art.

Note

1   [Immanuel Kant, *Idee zu einer allgemeinen Geschichte in weltbürgerlicher Absicht* (1784), *Kant Schriften*, Preuss. Akademie der Wissenschaften edition (Berlin, 1923), vol. VIII, p. 23. Ed.]

8

Discourse on the Hindus (1786)

Sir William Jones

Sir William Jones, selection from "The Third Anniversary Discourse, on the Hindus, delivered to the Asiatic Society, 2 February 1786" (1786) [source: Sir William Jones, *Selected Poetical and Prose Works*, ed. Michael J. Franklin. Cardiff: University of Wales Press, 1995, 360–7]

Founder of the Asiatic Society of Bengal, linguist, polymath, jurist, poet, and youthful re-inventor of Orientalist scholarship at the end of the eighteenth century, Jones (1746–94) perhaps did more to transform Western understanding of Persian, Arabic, and Hindu cultures than anyone else during what Raymond Schwab called an "Oriental Renaissance" in Europe at this time. Jone's poetry and his scholarship on Hindu philosophy and myth helped to establish the complex depth of ancient Indian civilization, and demonstrated its striking similarity to the philosophy and myth of later Greco-Roman culture. His final work, the *Institutes of Hindu Law; or the Ordinances of Menu*, was a digest of ancient Indian law that Jones thought would restore to modern India its own indigenous legal tradition, though it has also been indicted (by Edward Said, for example) for its codifying, imperialist designs. But it was his linguistic research that may have had the most powerful effect. Jones pointed out the strong affinity of Sanskrit with ancient Greek and Latin and suggested that all three had sprung from a common, no longer extant, source. In his hypothesis of an Indo-European language, which effectively founded modern comparative philology, Jones laid a more empirical groundwork for linking language and race (or nation), and for mapping what Herder would call the "physico-geographical history of the descent and diversification" of nations.

[...] I. It is much to be lamented, that neither the *Greeks*, who attended ALEXANDER into *India*, nor those who were long connected with it under the *Bactrian* Princes, have left us any means of knowing with accuracy, what vernacular langauges they found on their arrival in this Empire. The *Moham-medans*, we know, heard the people of proper *Hindustan*, or *India* on a limited scale, speaking a *Bháshá*, or living tongue of a very singular construction, the purest dialect of which was current in the districts round *Agrà*, and chiefly on the poetical ground of *Mat'hurà* and this is commonly called the idiom of *Vraja*. Five words in six, perhaps, of this language were derived from the *Sanscrit*, in which books of religion and science were composed, and which appears to have been formed by an exquisite grammatical *arrangement*, as the name itself implies, from some unpolished idiom; but the basis of the *Hindustáni*, particularly the inflexions and regimen of verbs, differed as widely from both those tongues, as *Arabick* differs from *Persian*, or *German* from *Greek*. Now the general effect of conquest is to leave the current language of the conquered people unchanged, or very little altered, in its groundwork, but to blend with it a considerable number of exotick names both for things and for actions; as it has happened in every country, that I can recollect, where the conquerors have not preserved their own tongue unmixed with that of the natives, like the *Turks* in *Greece*, and the *Saxons* in *Britain*; and this analogy might induce us to believe, that the pure *Hindì*, whether of *Tartarian* or *Chaldean* origin, was primeval in Upper *India*, into which the *Sanscrit* was introduced by conquerors from other kingdoms in some very remote age; for we cannot doubt that the language of the *Véda's* was used in the great extent of country, which has before been delineated, as long as the religion of *Brahmà* has prevailed in it.

The *Sanscrit* language, whatever be its antiquity, is of a wonderful structure; more perfect than the *Greek*, more copious than the *Latin*, and more exquisitely refined than either, yet bearing to both of them a stronger affinity, both in the roots of verbs and in the forms of grammar, than could possibly have been produced by accident; so strong indeed, that no philologer could examine them all three, without believing them to have sprung from some common source, which, perhaps, no longer exists: there is a similar reason, though not quite so forcible, for supposing that both the *Gothick* and the *Celtick*, though blended with a very different idiom, had the same origin with the *Sanscrit*; and the old *Persian* might be added to the same family, if this were the place for discussing any question concerning the antiquities of *Persia*.

The *characters*, in which the languages of *India* were originally written, are called *Nágarí*, from *Nagara*, a city with the word *Déva* sometimes prefixed, because they are believed to have been taught by the Divinity himself, who prescribed the artificial order of them in a voice from heaven. These letters, with no greater variation in their form by the change of straight lines to curves, or conversely, than the *Cusick* alphabet has received in its way to

India, are still adopted in more than twenty kingdoms and states, from the borders of *Cashgar* and *Khoten*, to *Ráma's* bridge, and from the *Sindhu* to the river of *Siam*; nor can I help believing, although the polished and elegant *Dévanágari* may not be so ancient as the monumental characters in the caverns of *Jarasandha*, that the square *Chaldaick* letters, in which most *Hebrew* books are copied, were originally the same, or derived from the same prototype, both with the *Indian* and *Arabian* characters: that the *Phenician*, from which the *Greek* and *Roman* alphabets were formed by various changes and inversions, had a similar origin, there can be little doubt; and the inscriptions at *Canárah*, of which you now possess a most accurate copy, seem to be compounded of *Nágarí* and *Ethiopick* letters, which bear a close relation to each other, both in the mode of writing from the left hand, and in the singular manner of connecting the vowels with the consonants. These remarks may favour an opinion entertained by many, that all the symbols of *sound*, which at first, probably, were only rude outlines of the different organs of speech, had a common origin: the symbols of *ideas*, now used in *China* and *Japan*, and formerly, perhaps, in *Egypt* and *Mexico*, are quite of a distinct nature; but it is very remarkabale, that the order of *sounds* in the *Chinese* grammars corresponds nearly with that observed in *Tibet*, and hardly differs from that, which the *Hindus* consider as the invention of their Gods.

II. Of the *Indian* Religion and Philosophy, I shall here say but little; because a full account of each would require a separate volume: it will be sufficient in this dissertation to assume, what might be proved beyond controversy, that we now live among the adorers of those very deities, who were worshipped under different names in old *Greece* and *Italy*, and among the professors of those philosophical tenets, which the *Ionick* and *Attick* writers illustrated with all the beauties of their melodious language. On one hand we see the trident of NEPTUNE, the eagle of JUPITER, the satyrs of BACCHUS, the bow of CUPID, and the chariot of the *Sun*; on another we hear the cymbals of RHEA, the songs of the *Muses*, and the pastoral tales of APOLLO NOMIUS. In more retired scenes, in groves, and in seminaries of learning, we may perceive the *Bráhmans* and the *Sarmanes*, mentioned by CLEMENS, disputing in the forms of *logick*, or discoursing on the vanity of human enjoyments, on the immortality of the soul, her emanation from the eternal mind, her debasement, wanderings, and final union with her source. The *six* philosophical schools, whose principles are explained in the *Dersana Sàstra*, comprise all the metaphysicks of the old *Academy*, the *Stoa*, the *Lyceum*; nor is it possible to read the *Védánta*, or the many fine compositions in illustration of it, without believing, that PYTHAGORAS and PLATO derived their sublime theories from the same fountain with the sages of *India*. The *Scythian* and *Hyperborean* doctrines and mythology may also be traced in every part of these eastern regions; nor can we doubt, that WOD or ODEN, whose religion, as the northern historians admit, was introduced into *Scandinavia* by a foreign race, was the same with BUDDH, whose rites were probably imported into *India* nearly at the same time, though received much later by the *Chinese*, who soften his name into Fó.

This may be a proper place to ascertain an important point in the Chronology of the *Hindus*, for the priests of BUDDHA left in *Tibet* and *China* the precise epoch of his appearance, real or imagined, in this Empire; and their information, which had been preserved in writing, was compared by the *Christian* Missionaries and scholars with our own era. COUPLET, DE GUIGNES, GIORGI, and BAILLY, differ a little in their accounts of this epoch, but that of *Couplet* seems the most correct: on taking, however, the medium of the four several dates, we may fix the time of BUDDHA, or the *ninth* great incarnation of VISHNU, in the year one *thousand* and *fourteen* before the birth of CHRIST, or *two thousand seven hundred and ninety-nine* years ago. Now the *Cáshmirians*, who boast of his descent in their kingdom, assert that he appeared on earth about *two* centuries after CRISHNA the *Indian* APOLLO, who took so decided a part in the war of the *Mahábhárat*; and, if an Etymologist were to suppose, that the *Athenians* had embellished their poetical history of PANDION's expulsion and the restoration of ÆGEUS with the *Asiatick* tale of the PÁNDUS and YUDHISHTIR, neither of which words they could have articulated, I should not hastily deride his conjecture: certain it is, that *Pándumandel* is called by the *Greeks* the country of PANDION. We have, therefore, determined another interesting epoch, by fixing the age of CRISHNA near the *three thousandth* year from the present time; and, as the three first *Avatàrs*, or descents of VISHNU, relate no less clearly to *an* Universal Deluge, in which eight persons only were saved, than the *fourth* and *fifth* do to the *punishment of impiety* and the *humiliation* of the *proud*, we may for the present assume, that the *second*, or *silver*, age of the *Hindus* was subsequent to the dispersion from *Babel*; so that we have only a dark interval of about a *thousand* years, which were employed in the settlement of nations, the foundation of states or empires, and the cultivation of civil society. The great incarnate Gods of this intermediate age are both named RÁMA but with different epithets; one of whom bears a wonderful resemblance to the *Indian* BACCHUS, and his wars are the subject of several heroick poems. He is represented as a descendent from SÚRYA, or the SUN, as the husband of SÍTÁ, and the son of a princess named CAÚSELYÁ: it is very remarkable, that the *Peruvians*, whose *Incas* boasted of the same descent, styled their greatest festival *Ramasitoa*; whence we may suppose, that South *America* was peopled by the same race, who imported into the farthest parts of *Asia* the rites and fabulous history of RÁMA. These rites and this history are extremely curious; and, although I cannot believe with NEWTON, that ancient mythology was nothing but historical truth in a poetical dress, nor, with BACON, that it consisted solely of moral and metaphysical allegories, nor with BRYANT, that all the heathen divinities are only different attributes and representations of the Sun or of deceased progenitors, but conceive that the whole system of religious fables rose, like the *Nile*, from several distinct sources, yet I cannot but agree, that one great spring and fountain of all idolatry in the four quarters of the globe was the veneration paid by men to the vast body of fire, which 'looks from his sole dominion like the God of this world;' and another, the immoderate respect shown to the memory of powerful or virtuous ancestors, especially the founders of kingdoms, legislators, and warriors, of whom the *Sun* or the *Moon* were wildly supposed to be the parents.

III. The remains of *architecture* and *sculpture* in *India*, which I mention here as mere monuments of antiquity, not as specimens of ancient art, seem to prove an early connection between this country and *Africa*: the pyramids of *Egypt*, the colossal statues described by PAUSANIAS and others, the sphinx, and the HERMES *Canis*, which last bears a great resemblance to the *Varáh ávatár*, or the incarnation of VISHNU in the form of a *Boar*, indicate the style and mythology of the same indefatigable workmen, who formed the vast excavations of *Cánárah*, the various temples and images of BUDDHA, and the idols, which are continually dug up at *Gayá*, or in its vicinity. The letters on many of those monuments appear, as I have before intimated, partly of *Indian*, and partly of *Abyssinian* or *Ethiopick*, origin; and all these indubitable facts may induce no ill-grounded opinion, that *Ethiopia* and *Hindustán* were peopled or colonized by the same extraordinary race; in confirmation of which, it may be added, that the mountaineers of *Bengal* and *Bahàr* can hardly be distinguished in some of their features, particularly their lips and noses, from the modern *Abyssinians*, whom the *Arabs* call the children of CÚSH: and the ancient *Hindus*, according to STRABO, differed in nothing from the *Africans*, but in the straitness and smoothness of their hair, while that of the others was crisp or woolly; a difference proceeding chiefly, if not entirely, from the respective humidity or dryness of their atmospheres; hence the people who *received the first light of the rising sun*, according to the limited knowledge of the ancients, are said by APULEIUS to be the *Arü* and *Ethiopians*, by which he clearly meant certain nations of *India*; where we frequently see figures of BUDDHA with *curled hair* apparently designed for a representation of it in its natural state.

IV. It is unfortunate, that the *Silpi Sástra*, or *collection of treatises on Arts* and *Manufactures*, which must have contained a treasure of useful information on *dying, painting*, and *metallurgy*, has been so long neglected, that few, if any, traces of it are to be found; but the labours of the *Indian* loom and needle have been universally celebrated; and *fine linen* is not improbably supposed to have been called *Sindon*, from the name of the river near which it was wrought in the highest perfection: the people of *Colchis* were also famed for this manufacture, and the *Egyptians* yet more, as we learn from several passages in scripture, and particularly from a beautiful chapter in EZEKIEL containing the most authentick delineation of ancient commerce, of which *Tyre* had been the principal mart. Silk was fabricated immemorially by the *Indians*, though commonly ascribed to the people of *Serica* or *Tancùt*, among whom probably the word *Sèr*, which the *Greeks* applied to the *silk-worm*, signified gold; a sense, which it now bears in *Tibet*. That the *Hindus* were in early ages a *commercial* people, we have many reasons to believe; and in the first of their sacred law-tracts, which they suppose to have been revealed by MENU many *millions* of years ago, we find a curious passage on the legal *interest* of money, and the limited rate of it in different cases, with an exception in regard to *adventures* at *sea*; an exception, which the sense of mankind approves, and which commerce absolutely requires, though it was not before the reign of CHARLES I. that our own jurisprudence fully admitted it in respect of maritime contracts.

We are told by the *Grecian* writers, that the *Indians* were the wisest of nations; and in moral wisdom, they were certainly eminent: their *Níti Sástra*, or *System of Ethicks*, is yet preserved, and the Fables of VISHNUSERMAN, whom we ridiculously call *Pilpay*, are the most beautiful, if not the most ancient, collection of apologues in the world: they were first translated from the *Sanscrit*, in the *sixth* century, by the order of BUZERCHUMIHR, or *Bright as the Sun*, the chief physician and afterwards *Vézír* of the great ANÚSHIR-EVÁN, and are extant under various names in more than twenty languages; but their original title is *Hitópadésa*, or *Amicable Instruction*; and, as the very existence of ESOP, whom the *Arabs* believe to have been an *Abyssinian*, appears rather doubtful, I am not disinclined to suppose, that the first *moral fables*, which appeared in *Europe*, were of *Indian* or *Ethiopian* origin.

The *Hindus* are said to have boasted of *three* inventions, all of which, indeed, are admirable, the method of instructing by *apologues*, the *decimal scale* adopted now by all civilized nations, and the game of *Chess*, on which they have some curious treatises; but, if their numerous works on Grammar, Logick, Rhetorick, Musick, all which are extant and accessible, were explained in some language generally known, it would be found, that they had yet higher pretensions to the praise of a fertile and inventive genius. Their lighter Poems are lively and elegant; their Epick, magnificent and sublime in the highest degree; their *Purána's* comprise a series of mythological Histories in blank verse from the *Creation* to the supposed incarnation of BUDDHA; and their *Védas*, as far as we can judge from that compendium of them, which is called *Upanishat*, abound with noble speculations in metaphysicks, and fine discourses on the being and attributes of GOD. Their most ancient medical book, entitled *Chereca*, is believed to be the work of SIVA; for each of the divinities in their *Triad* has at least one *sacred* composition ascribed to him; but, as to mere human works on *History* and *Geography*, though they are said to be extant in *Cashmír*, it has not been yet in my power to procure them. What their *astronomical* and *mathematical* writings contain, will not, I trust, remain long a secret: they are easily procured, and their importance cannot be doubted. The Philosopher, whose works are said to include a system of the universe founded on the principle of *Attraction* and the *Central* position of the sun, is named YAVAN ACHÁRYA, because he had travelled, we are told, into *Ionia*: if this be true, he might have been one of those, who conversed with PYTHAGORAS; this at least is undeniable, that a book on astronomy in *Sanscrit* bears the title of *Yavana Jática*, which may signify the *Ionic Sect*; nor is it improbable, that the names of the planets and *Zodiacal* stars, which the *Arabs* borrowed from the *Greeks*, but which we find in the oldest *Indian* records, were originally devised by the same ingenious and enterprising race, from whom both *Greece* and *India* were peopled; the race, who, as DIONYSIUS describes them,

> – 'first assayed the deep,
> And wafted merchandize to coasts unknown,
> Those, who digested first the starry choir,
> Their motions mark'd, and call'd them by their names.'

Of these cursory observations on the *Hindus*, which it would require volumes to expand and illustrate, this is the result: that they had an immemorial affinity with the old *Persians*, *Ethiopians*, and *Egyptians*, the *Phenicians*, *Greeks*, and *Tuscans*, the *Scythians* or *Goths*, and *Celts*, the *Chinese*, *Japanese*, and *Peruvians*; whence, as no reason appears for believing, that they were a colony from any one of those nations, or any of those nations from them, we may fairly conclude that they all proceeded from some *central* country, to investigate which will be the object of my future Discourses [. . .]

9

Reflections on the Revolution in France (1790)

Edmund Burke

Edmund Burke, selection from *Reflections on the Revolution in France* (1790) [source:
Edmund Burke, *Reflections on the Revolution in France*. London: J. M. Dent and Sons,
1910, 29–33]

Son of an Irish Protestant father and Catholic mother, Burke (1729–97) found a political ancestor in Montesquieu and an antithesis in Rousseau. Burke also rejected the sensationalism of Locke and Hume, but agreed with Hume that moral order derived from customs and habit, not reason. Burke thus insisted that individual reason was meaningless without a tradition to guide it. The state was a reflection of the organic development of the nation's history and its leading institutions of Church, monarchy, and aristocracy; in this, he was closer to Maistre than to Herder. Burke's conservatism thus grounded political rights neither in natural law nor in immediate experience, but in an inherited constitutional order (dating in England to the Magna Carta), and any alterations must come from within it. Overthrowing that order for a radically new one – as in the French Revolution – would produce anarchy rather than viable and lasting change. Burke's *Reflections*, written in response to Noncomformist support for the Revolution, were composed before the Terror; he felt vindicated afterwards, and only grew more intolerant with age. But he had begun his political career in a more liberal vein, supporting a stronger House of Commons, liberty (though not independence) for the American colonies, free trade and parliamentary autonomy for Ireland, the emancipation of Irish Catholics, and the abolition of the slave trade. His work cast a long shadow in English culture, from Carlyle and Lord Acton to Matthew Arnold and T. S. Eliot.

[...] The third head of right, asserted by the pulpit of the Old Jewry, namely, the "right to form a government for ourselves," has, at least, as little countenance from anything done at the [English] Revolution [of 1688], either in precedent or principle, as the two first of their claims.[1] The Revolution was made to preserve our *ancient* indisputable laws and liberties, and that *ancient* constitution of government which is our only security for law and liberty. If you are desirous of knowing the spirit of our constitution, and the policy which predominated in that great period which has secured it to this hour, pray look for both in our histories, in our records, in our acts of parliament, and journals of parliament, and not in the sermons of the Old Jewry, and the after-dinner toasts of the Revolution Society. In the former you will find other ideas and another language. Such a claim is as ill-suited to our temper and wishes as it is unsupported by any appearance of authority. The very idea of the fabrication of a new government is enough to fill us with disgust and horror. We wished at the period of the Revolution, and do now wish, to derive all we possess as *an inheritance from our forefathers.* Upon that body and stock of inheritance we have taken care not to inoculate any scion alien to the nature of the original plant. All the reformations we have hitherto made have proceeded upon the principle of reverence to antiquity; and I hope, nay I am persuaded, that all those which possibly may be made hereafter, will be carefully formed upon analogical precedent, authority, and example.

Our oldest reformation is that of Magna Charta. You will see that Sir Edward Coke, that great oracle of our law, and indeed all the great men who follow him, to Blackstone, are industrious to prove the pedigree of our liberties. They endeavour to prove, that the ancient charter, the Magna Charta of King John, was connected with another positive charter from Henry I., and that both the one and the other were nothing more than a reaffirmance of the still more ancient standing law of the kingdom. In the matter of fact, for the greater part, these authors appear to be in the right; perhaps not always; but if the lawyers mistake in some particulars, it proves my position still the more strongly; because it demonstrates the powerful prepossession towards antiquity, with which the minds of all our lawyers and legislators, and of all the people whom they wish to influence, have been always filled; and the stationary policy of this kingdom in considering their most sacred rights and franchises as an *inheritance.*

In the famous law of the 3rd of Charles I., called the *Petition of Right*, the parliament says to the king, "Your subjects have *inherited* this freedom," claiming their franchises not on abstract principles "as the rights of men," but as the rights of Englishmen, and as a patrimony derived from their forefathers. Selden, and the other profoundly learned men, who drew this Petition of Right, were as well acquainted, at least, with all the general theories concerning the "rights of men," as any of the discoursers in our pulpits, or on your tribune; full as well as Dr. Price, or as the Abbé Sieyes. But, for reasons worthy of that practical wisdom which superseded their

theoretic science, they preferred this positive, recorded, *hereditary* title to all
which can be dear to the man and the citizen, to that vague speculative right,
which exposed their sure inheritance to be scrambled for and torn to pieces
by every wild, litigious spirit.

The same policy pervades all the laws which have since been made for the
preservation of our liberties. In the Ist of William and Mary, in the famous
statute, called the Declaration of Right, the two Houses utter not a syllable of
"a right to frame a government for themselves." You will see, that their whole
care was to secure the religion, laws, and liberties, that had been long
possessed, and had been lately endangered. "Taking into their most serious
consideration the *best* means for making such an establishment, that their
religion, laws, and liberties might not be in danger of being again subverted,"
they auspicate all their proceedings, by stating as some of those *best* means,
"in the *first place*" to do "as their *ancestors in like cases have usually* done for
vindicating their *ancient* rights and liberties, to *declare*"; – and then they pray
the king and queen, "that it may be *declared* and enacted, that *all and
singular* the rights and liberties *asserted and declared*, are the true *ancient*
and indubitable rights and liberties of the people of this kingdom."

You will observe, that from Magna Charta to the Declaration of Right, it
has been the uniform policy of our constitution to claim and assert our
liberties, as an *entailed inheritance* derived to us from our forefathers, and
to be transmitted to our posterity; as an estate specially belonging to the
people of this kingdom, without any reference whatever to any other more
general or prior right. By this means our constitution preserves a unity in so
great a diversity of its parts. We have an inheritable crown; an inheritable
peerage; and a House of Commons and a people inheriting privileges,
franchises, and liberties, from a long line of ancestors.

This policy appears to me to be the result of profound reflection; or rather
the happy effect of following nature, which is wisdom without reflection, and
above it. A spirit of innovation is generally the result of a selfish temper and
confined views. People will not look forward to posterity, who never look
backward to their ancestors. Besides, the people of England well know, that
the idea of inheritance furnishes a sure principle of conservation and a sure
principle of transmission; without at all excluding a principle of improvement. It leaves acquisition free; but it secures what it acquires. Whatever
advantages are obtained by a state proceeding on these maxims, are locked
fast as in a sort of family settlement; grasped as in a kind of mortmain for
ever. By a constitutional policy, working after the pattern of nature, we
receive, we hold, we transmit our government and our privileges, in
the same manner in which we enjoy and transmit our property and our
lives. The institutions of policy, the goods of fortune, the gifts of providence,
are handed down to us, and from us, in the same course and order. Our

political system is placed in a just correspondence and symmetry with the order of the world, and with the mode of existence decreed to a permanent body composed of transitory parts; wherein, by the disposition of a stupendous wisdom, moulding together the great mysterious incorporation of the human race, the whole, at one time, is never old, or middle-aged, or young, but, in a condition of unchangeable constancy, moves on through the varied tenor of perpetual decay, fall, renovation, and progression. Thus, by preserving the method of nature in the conduct of the state, in what we improve, we are never wholly new; in what we retain, we are never wholly obsolete. By adhering in this manner and on those principles to our forefathers, we are guided not by the superstition of antiquarians, but by the spirit of philosophic analogy. In this choice of inheritance we have given to our frame of polity the image of a relation in blood; binding up the constitution of our country with our dearest domestic ties; adopting our fundamental laws into the bosom of our family affections; keeping inseparable, and cherishing with the warmth of all their combined and mutually reflected charities, our state, our hearths, our sepulchres, and our altars.

Through the same plan of a conformity to nature in our artificial institutions, and by calling in the aid of her unerring and powerful instincts, to fortify the fallible and feeble contrivances of our reason, we have derived several other, and those no small benefits, from considering our liberties in the light of an inheritance. Always acting as if in the presence of canonized forefathers, the spirit of freedom, leading in itself to misrule and excess, is tempered with an awful gravity. This idea of a liberal descent inspires us with a sense of habitual native dignity, which prevents that upstart insolence almost inevitably adhering to and disgracing those who are the first acquirers of any distinction. By this means our liberty becomes a noble freedom. It carries an imposing and majestic aspect. It has a pedigree and illustrating ancestors. It has its bearings, and its ensigns armorial. It has its gallery of portraits; its monumental inscriptions; its records, evidences, and titles. We procure reverence to our civil institutions on the principle upon which nature teaches us to revere individual men; on account of their age, and on account of those from whom they are descended. All your sophisters cannot produce anything better adapted to preserve a rational and manly freedom [. . .]

Note

1. [Burke is refuting Richard Price, a Unitarian minister who preached a sermon in London's "Old Jewry" district claiming that the English Revolution (like the French Revolution) confirmed three rights: "to choose our own governors," "to cashier then for misconduct," and "to frame a government for ourselves." Ed.]

Part III

The Spirit of a People

10

Study on Sovereignty (composed 1793–8; first published 1884)

Joseph de Maistre

Joseph de Maistre, selections from Book One, "On the Origins of Sovereignty," from *Study on Sovereignty* (first published 1884; composed 1793–8) [source: *The Works of Joseph de Maistre*, selected and trans. Jack Lively. New York: The Macmillan Company, 1965, 98–101, 108–11]

A native of Savoy, Maistre (1753–1821) supported the French Revolution until the new Republic invaded his homeland in 1792, upon which he rejected its ideals and blamed its excesses on the Enlightenment's faith in reason. Steeped in Catholicism and a mystical Freemasonry, the reactionary Maistre denied the claims of Bacon's seventeenth-century scientific revolution, the rationalism of Voltaire, Helvétius, and d'Holbach, and Rousseau's social contract, all of which he saw as products of atheism. Like Burke, Maistre distrusted individual judgment and self-legislated rights, and held that instinctive passions, ignorance, and pride could be overcome only through a moral order established by absolute, patriarchal authority. Sovereignty for Maistre thus cannot flow from the people, since it is the sovereign that gives the people, and the nation, its identity. Like Montesquieu, Maistre emphasized cultural tradition and environment over rational (or universally applicable) systems of government. But he then argued that God was directly responsible for the course of human history and for a particular nation's "good customs," on which the moral and civil order of the state rested. For France, the Catholic Church, the Papacy, and the Crown – the union of throne and altar – were the basis of that order. Yet Maistre also referred to a political faith, or religion of the state: individual reason must lose itself in the "national mind," a claim also found in the more liberal Fichte. For commentators like Isaiah Berlin, Maistre was on this last point a crucial prefiguration of Fascism.

On the Origins of Sovereignty

Chapter III: Sovereignty in general

If sovereignty is not anterior to the *people*, at least these two ideas are collateral, since a sovereign is necessary to make a *people*. It is as impossible to imagine a human society, a people, without a sovereign as a hive and bees without a queen: for, by virtue of the eternal laws of nature, a swarm of bees exists in this way or it does not exist at all. Society and sovereignty are thus born together; it is impossible to separate these two ideas. Imagine an isolated man: there is no question of laws or government, since he is not a whole man and society does not yet exist. Put this man in contact with his fellowmen: from this moment you suppose a sovereign. The first man was king over his children; each isolated family was governed in the same way. But once these families joined, a sovereign was needed, and this *sovereign* made a *people* of them by giving them laws, since society exists only through the sovereign. Everyone knows the famous line,

> *The first king was a fortunate soldier.*

This is perhaps one of the falsest claims that has ever been made. Quite the opposite could be said, that

> *The first soldier was paid by a king.*

There was a *people*, some sort of civilization, and a sovereign as soon as men came into contact. The word *people* is a relative term that has no meaning divorced from the idea of sovereignty: for the idea of a *people* involves that of an aggregation around a common center, and without sovereignty there can be no political unity or cohesion. [...]

Chapter IV: Particular sovereignties and nations

The same power that has decreed social order and sovereignty has also decreed different modifications of sovereignty according to the different character of nations.

Nations are born and die like individuals. Nations have *fathers*, in a very literal sense, and *teachers* commonly more famous than their fathers, although the greatest merit of these teachers is to penetrate the character of the infant nation and to create for it circumstances in which it can develop all its capacities.

Nations have a general *soul* and a true moral unity which makes them what they are. This unity is evidenced above all by language.

The Creator has traced on the globe the limits of nations. [...] These boundaries are obvious and each nation can still be seen straining to fill entirely one of the areas within these boundaries. Sometimes invincible circumstances thrust two nations together and force them to mingle. Then their constituent principles penetrate each other and produce a *hybrid* nation which can be either more or less powerful and famous than if it was a *pure* race.

But several national elements thrown together into the same receptacle can be harmful. These seeds squeeze and stifle each other. The men who compose them, condemned to a certain moral and political mediocrity, will never attract the eyes of the world in spite of a large number of individual virtues, until some great shock, starting one of these seeds growing, allows it to engulf the other and to assimilate them into its own substance. *Italiam! Italiam!*

Sometimes a nation lives in the midst of another much more numerous, refuses to integrate because there is not sufficient affinity between them, and preserves its moral unity. [...]

When one talks of the *spirit* of a nation, the expression is not so metaphorical as is believed.

From these different national characteristics are born the different modifications of governments. One can say that each government has its separate character, for even those which belong to the same group and carry the same name reveal subtle differences to the observer.

The same laws cannot suit different provinces which have different customs, live in opposite climates, and cannot accept the same form of government.

The general objects of every good institution must be modified in each country by the relationships which spring as much from the local situation as from the character of the inhabitants. It is on the basis of these relationships that each people should be assigned a particular institutional system, which is the best, not perhaps in itself, but for the state for which it is intended.

There is only one good government for a particular state; yet not only can different governments be suitable for different peoples; they can also be suitable for the same people at different times, since a thousand events can change the inner relationships of a people.

There has always been a great deal of discussion on the best form of government without consideration of the fact that each can be the best in some instances and the worst in others!

Therefore it should not be said that *every form of government is appropriate to every country: for example, liberty, since it will not grow under every climate, is not open to every nation.* The more one thinks about this principle laid down by Montesquieu, the more one feels its force. The more it is contested, the more strongly it is established by new proofs.

Thus the absolute question, What is the best form of government? is as insoluble as it is indefinite; or, to put it another way, it has as many correct solutions as there are possible combinations in the relative and absolute positions of nations.

From these incontestable principles springs a no less incontestable consequence, that the social contract is a chimera. For, if there are as many different governments as there are different peoples, if the forms of these governments are laid down absolutely by the power that has given to each nation its particular moral, physical, geographical, and economic features, it is no longer permissible to talk of a *compact.* Each method of exercising sovereignty is the immediate result of the will of the Creator, like sovereignty in general. For one nation, despotism is as natural and as legitimate as democracy for another. If a man himself worked out these unshakable principles[1] in a book designed to establish that "*it is always necessary to go back to a convention,*"[2] if he wrote in one chapter that "man was born free"[3] and in another that "liberty, since it will not grow under every climate, is not open to every nation,"[4] his utter folly could not be contested.

As no nation has been able to give itself the character and position that fit it to a particular government, all have been agreed not only in accepting this truth in the abstract but also in believing that the Divinity had intervened directly in the institution of their particular sovereignties. [. . .]

These are fables, it will be said. In truth, I do not know; but the fables of every nation, even modern nations, cover many realities. [. . .] It is complete folly to imagine that this universal prejudice is the work of sovereigns. Individual interest might well make bad use of a general belief, but it cannot create it. If that which I am talking about had not been based on the previous consent of nations, not only could a sovereign not have made them accept it; he would have been unable to conceive such a fraud. In general, every universal idea is natural. [. . .]

Chapter X: The national soul

Human reason left to its own resources is completely incapable *not only of creating but also of conserving any religious or political association,* because it can only give rise to disputes and because, to conduct himself well, man needs beliefs, not problems. His cradle should be surrounded by dogmas; and, when his reason awakes, all his opinions should be given, at least all those relating to his conduct. Nothing is more vital to him than *prejudices*. Let us not take this word in bad part. It does not necessarily signify false ideas, but only, in the strict sense of the word, any opinions adopted without examination. Now, these kinds of opinion are essential to man; they are the real basis of his happiness and the palladium of empires. Without them, there can be neither religion, morality, nor government. There should be a state religion just as there is a state political system; or rather, religion and political dogmas, mingled and merged together, should together form a *general* or *national mind* sufficiently strong to repress the aberrations of the individual reason which is, of its nature, the mortal enemy of any association whatever because it gives birth only to divergent opinions.

All known nations have been happy and powerful to the degree that they have faithfully obeyed this national mind, which is nothing other than the destruction of individual dogmas and the absolute and general rule of national dogmas, that is to say, useful prejudices. Once let everyone rely on his individual reason in religion, and you will see immediately the rise of anarchy of belief or the annihilation of religious sovereignty. Likewise, if each man makes himself the judge of the principles of government you will see immediately the rise of civil anarchy or the annihilation of political sovereignty. Government is a true religion; it has its dogmas, its mysteries, its priests; to submit it to individual discussion is to destroy it; it has life only through the national mind, that is to say, political faith, which is a *creed*. Man's primary need is that his nascent reason should be curbed under a double yoke; it should be frustrated, and it should lose itself in the national mind, so that it changes its individual existence for another communal existence, just as a river which flows into the ocean still exists in the mass of water, but without name and distinct reality.

What is patriotism? It is this national mind of which I am speaking; it is individual *abnegation*. Faith and patriotism are the two great thaumaturges of the world. Both are divine. All their actions are miracles. Do not talk to them of scrutiny, choice, discussion, for they will say that you blaspheme. They know only two words, *submission* and *belief*; with these two levers, they raise the world. Their very errors are sublime. These two infants of Heaven prove their origin to all by creating and conserving; and if they unite, join their forces and together take possession of a nation, they exalt it, make it divine and increase its power a hundredfold. [. . .]

But can you, insignificant man, light this sacred fire that inflames nations? Can you give a common soul to several million men? Unite them under your laws? Range them closely around a common center? Shape the mind of men yet unborn? Make future generations obey you and create those age-old customs, those conserving *prejudices*, which are the father of the laws and stronger than them? What nonsense! [...]

Chapter XII: Application of the preceding principles to a particular case – continuation

There is no doubt that, in a certain sense, reason is good for nothing. We have the scientific knowledge necessary for the maintenance of society; we have made conquests in mathematics and what is called natural science; but, once we leave the circle of our needs, our knowledge becomes either useless or doubtful. The human mind, ever restless, proliferates constantly succeeding theories. They are born, flourish, wither, and fall like leaves from the trees; the only difference is that their year is longer.

And in the whole of the moral and political world, what do we know, and what are we able to do? We *know* the morality handed down to us by our fathers, as a collection of dogmas or useful prejudices adopted by the national mind. But on this point we owe nothing to any man's individual reason. On the contrary, every time this reason has interfered, it has perverted morality.

In politics, we *know* that it is necessary to respect those powers established we know not how or by whom. When time leads to abuses capable of altering the root principle of a government, we *know* that it is necessary to remove these abuses, but without touching the principle itself, an act of delicate surgery; and we *are able* to carry through these salutary reforms until the time when the principle of life is totally vitiated and the death of the body politic is inevitable. [...]

Wherever the individual reason dominates, there can be nothing great, for everything great rests on a belief, and the clash of individual opinions left to themselves produces only skepticism which is destructive of everything. General and individual morality, religion, laws, revered customs, useful prejudices, nothing is left standing, everything falls before it; it is the universal dissolvent.

Let us return again to basic ideas. Any *institution* is only a political edifice. In the physical and the moral order, the laws are the same; you cannot build a great edifice on narrow foundations or a durable one on a moving or transient base. Likewise, in the political order, to build high and to build for centuries, it is necessary to rely on an opinion or a belief broad and deep: for if the opinion does not hold the majority of minds and is not deeply rooted, it will provide only a narrow and transient base.

Now, if you seek the great and solid bases of all possible institutions of the first and second order, you will always find religion and patriotism.

And if you reflect still further, you will find that these two things are identical, for there is no true patriotism without religion. You will see it shine out only in the ages of belief, and it always fades and dies with it. Once man divorces himself from the divinity, he corrupts himself and everything he touches. His actions are misguided and end only in destruction. As this powerful binding force weakens in the state, so all the conserving virtues weaken in proportion. Men's characters become degraded, and even good actions are paltry. A murderous selfishness relentlessly presses on public spirit and makes it fall back before it, like those enormous glaciers of the high Alps that can be seen advancing slowly but frighteningly on the area of living things and crushing the useful vegetation in their path.

But once the idea of the divinity is the source of human action, this action is fruitful, creative, and invincible. An unknown force makes itself felt on all sides, and animates, warms, vivifies all things. However much human ignorance and corruption have soiled this great idea with errors and crimes, it no less preserves its incredible influence. [...]

Notes

1 *Social Contract*, Book ii, chap. ix; Book iii, chaps. i, iii, viii.
2 Ibid., Book i, chap. v.
3 Ibid., Book i, chap. i.
4 Ibid., Book iii, chap. viii.

11

Addresses to the German Nation (1808)

Johann Gottlieb Fichte

Johann Gottlieb Fichte, "Eighth Address: What is a People in the Higher Meaning of the Word, and What is Love of Fatherland?", from *Addresses to the German Nation* (1808) [source: Johann Gottlieb Fichte, *Addresses to the German Nation*, trans. R. F. Jones and G.H. Turnbull. Westport, CT: Greenwood Press, 1979, 130–51]

Inheritor of Descartes's rationalism and student of Kant, Fichte (1762–1814) overcame Kant's dualistic antithesis of subjective phenomena and objective noumena (or "things-in-themselves") by insisting that the thinking mind was the only, monistic, reality. Fichte carried Romantic metaphysical egoism about as far as it would go: the ego, or subject, defined itself by creating its opposite – experience – through which it would exercise its freedom. Fichte's later work expanded subjective reality into the divine idea behind all experience. His influential *Addresses* complemented this later conception. Fichte derived the nation from a "spiritual law of nature" that was both divine in origin and eternal. Like Herder, he situated it in the language, customs, institutions, and racial descent of the "whole common fatherland" of the German people, but unlike Herder he joined this idea of the nation to a liberal conception of the civil state that remained subordinate to the "higher purpose" of the nation's development. Fichte's stress on education, which he saw as a way of subordinating the individual to the national will through *Bildung*, or cultural formation, would be central to many subsequent national movements, not least that of modern Germany. He had a profound influence on Hegel, whose phenomenology of mind (or spirit), philosophy of right, and philosophy of history all follow Fichte's lead. And he appears to be one of the principal targets of Renan's later insistence that nations are neither racially homogeneous, nor eternal.

Eighth Address: What is a People in the Higher Meaning of the Word, and What is Love of Fatherland?

110. The last four addresses have answered the question: What is the German as contrasted with other peoples of Teutonic descent? The proof to be adduced by all this for our investigation as a whole is completed when we examine the further question: What is a people? This latter question is similar to another, and when it is answered the other is answered too. The other question, which is often raised and the answers to which are very different, is this: What is love of fatherland, or, to express it more correctly, what is the love of the individual for his nation?

If we have hitherto proceeded correctly in the course of our investigation, it must here be obvious at once that only the German – the original man, who has not become dead in an arbitrary organization – really has a people and is entitled to count on one, and that he alone is capable of real and rational love for his nation.

The problem having been thus stated, we prepare the way for its solution by the following observation, which seems at first to have no connection with what has preceded it.

111.   Religion, as we have already remarked in our third address, is able to transcend all time and the whole of this present sensuous life, without thereby causing the slightest detriment to the righteousness, morality, and holiness of the life that is permeated by this belief. Even if one is firmly persuaded that all our effort on this earth will not leave the slightest trace behind it nor yield the slightest fruit, nay more, that the divine effort will even be perverted and become an instrument of evil and of still deeper moral corruption, one can none the less continue the effort, solely in order to maintain the divine life that has manifested itself in us, and with a view to a higher order of things in a future world, in which no deed that is of divine origin is lost. Thus the apostles, for example, and the primitive Christians in general, because of their belief in heaven had their hearts entirely set on things above the earth even in their lifetime; and earthly affairs – the State, their earthly fatherland, and nation – were abandoned by them so entirely that they no longer deemed them worthy of attention. Possible though this is, and to faith not difficult, and joyfully though one must resign one's self, once it is the unalterable will of God, to having an earthly fatherland no longer and to being serfs and exiles here below, nevertheless it is not the natural condition nor the rule of the universe; on the contrary, it is a rare exception. It is a gross misuse of religion, a misuse of which Christianity among other religions has frequently been guilty, to make a point of recommending, on principle and without regard to existing circumstances, such a withdrawal from the affairs of the State and the nation as the mark of a true religious disposition. In such a condition of things, if it is true and real and not merely the product of fitful religious zeal, temporal life loses all independent existence and becomes merely a forecourt of true life and a period of severe trial which is endured only out of obedience and resignation to the will of God. Then it is true that immortal souls, as many have imagined, are housed in earthly bodies, as in prisons, for their punishment. But, on the other hand, in the regular order of things this earthly life itself is intended to be truly life, of which we may be glad and which we may enjoy in gratitude, while, of course, looking forward to a higher life. Although it is true that religion is, for one thing, the consolation of the unjustly oppressed slave, yet this above all is the mark of a religious disposition, viz., to fight against slavery and, as far as possible, to prevent religion from sinking into a mere consolation for captives. No doubt it suits the tyrant well to preach religious resignation and to bid those look to heaven to whom he allows not the smallest place on earth. But we for our part must be in less haste to adopt this view of religion that he recommends; and we must, if we can, prevent earth from being made into a hell in order to arouse a greater longing for heaven.

112. The natural impulse of man, which should be abandoned only in case of real necessity, is to find heaven on this earth, and to endow his daily work on earth with permanence and eternity; to plant and to cultivate the eternal in the temporal – not merely in an incomprehensible fashion or in a connection with the eternal that seems to mortal eye an impenetrable gulf, but in a fashion visible to the mortal eye itself.

Let me begin with an example that everyone will understand. What man of noble mind is there who does not earnestly wish to relive his own life in a new and better way in his children and his children's children, and to continue to live on this earth, ennobled and perfected in their lives, long after he is dead? Does he not wish to snatch from the jaws of death the spirit, the mind, and the moral sense by virtue of which, perchance, he was in the days of his life a terror to wrong doing and corruption, and by which he supported righteousness, aroused men from indolence, and lifted them out of their depression? Does he not wish to deposit these qualities, as his best legacy to posterity, in the souls of those he leaves behind, so that they too, in their turn, may some day hand them on again, increased and made more beautiful? What man of noble mind is there who does not want to scatter, by action or thought, a grain of seed for the unending progress in perfection of his race, to fling something new and unprecedented into time, that it may remain there and become the inexhaustible source of new creations? Does he not wish to pay for his place on this earth and the short span of time allotted to him with something that even here below will endure for ever, so that he, the individual, although unnamed in history (for the thirst for posthumous fame is contemptible vanity), may yet in his own consciousness and his faith leave behind him unmistakable memories that he, too, was a dweller on the earth? What man of noble mind is there, I said, who does not want this? But only according to the needs of noble-minded men is the world to be regarded and arranged; as they are, so all men ought to be, and for their sake alone does a world exist. They are its kernel, and those of other mind exist only for their sake, being themselves only a part of the transitory world so long as they are of that mind. Such men must conform to the wishes of the noble-minded until they have become like them.

113. Now, what is it that could warrant this challenge and this faith of the noble-minded man in the permanence and eternity of his work? Obviously nothing but an order of things which he can acknowledge as in itself eternal and capable of taking up into itself that which is eternal. Such an order of things, however, is the special spiritual nature of human environment which, although indeed it is not to be comprehended in any conception, nevertheless truly exists, and from which he himself, with all his thoughts and deeds and with his belief in their eternity, has proceeded – the people, from which he is descended and among which he was educated and grew up to be what he now is. For, though it is true beyond dispute that his work, if he rightly claims it to be eternal, is in no wise the mere result of the spiritual law of nature of his nation or absolutely the same thing as this result, but on the contrary is something more than that and in so far streams forth directly from original and divine life; it is, nevertheless, equally true that this 'something more,' immediately on its first embodiment in a visible form, submitted itself to that special spiritual law of nature and found sensuous expression for itself only according to that law. So long as this people exists, every further revelation of the divine will appear and take shape in that people in accordance with the same natural law. But this law itself is further determined by the fact that this man existed and worked as he did, and his influence has become a permanent part of this law. Hence, everything that follows will be bound to submit itself to, and connect itself with, that law. So he is sure that the improvement achieved by him remains in his people so long as the people itself remains, and that it becomes a permanent determining factor in the evolution of his people.

114. This, then, is a people in the higher meaning of the word, when viewed from the standpoint of a spiritual world: the totality of men continuing to live in society with each other and continually creating themselves naturally and spiritually out of themselves, a totality that arises together out of the divine under a certain special law of divine development. It is the subjection in common to this special law that unites this mass in the eternal

world, and therefore in the temporal also, to a natural totality permeated by itself. The significance of this law itself can indeed be comprehended as a whole, as we have comprehended it by the instance of the Germans as an original people; it can even be better understood in many of its further provisions by considering the manifestations of such a people; but it can never be completely grasped by the mind of anyone, for everyone continually remains under its influence unknown to himself, although, in general, it can be clearly seen that such a law exists. This law is a "something more" of the world of images, that coalesces absolutely in the phenomenal world with the "something more" of the world of originality that cannot be imaged; hence, in the phenomenal world neither can be separated again from the other. That law determines entirely and completes what has been called the national character of a people – that law of the development of the original and divine. From this it is clear that men who, as is the case with what we have described as the foreign spirit, do not believe at all in something original nor in its continuous development, but only in an eternal recurrence of apparent life, and who by their belief become what they believe, are in the higher sense not a people at all. As they in fact, properly speaking, do not exist, they are just as little capable of having a national character.

115.   The noble-minded man's belief in the eternal continuance of his influence even on this earth is thus founded on the hope of the eternal continuance of the people from which he has developed, and on the characteristic of that people as indicated in the hidden law of which we have spoken, without admixture of, or corruption by, any alien element which does not belong to the totality of the functions of that law. This characteristic is the eternal thing to which he entrusts the eternity of himself and of his continuing influence, the eternal order of things in which he places his portion of eternity; he must will its continuance, for it alone is to him the means by which the short span of his life here below is extended into continuous life here below. His belief and his struggle to plant what is permanent, his conception in which he comprehends his own life as an eternal life, is the bond which unites first his own nation, and then, through his nation, the whole human race, in a most intimate fashion with himself, and brings all their needs within his widened sympathy until the end of time. This is his love for his people, respecting, trusting, and rejoicing in it, and feeling honoured by descent from it. The divine has appeared in it, and that which is original has deemed this people worthy to be made its vesture and its means of directly influencing the world; for this reason there will be further manifestations of the divine in it. Hence, the noble-minded man will be active and effective, and will sacrifice himself for his people. Life merely as such, the mere continuance of changing existence, has in any case never had any value for him; he has wished for it only as the source of what is

permanent. But this permanence is promised to him only by the continuous and independent existence of his nation. In order to save his nation he must be ready even to die that it may live, and that he may live in it the only life for which he has ever wished.

116. So it is. Love that is truly love, and not a mere transitory lust, never clings to what is transient; only in the eternal does it awaken and become kindled, and there alone does it rest. Man is not able to love even himself unless he conceives himself as eternal; apart from that he cannot even respect, much less approve of, himself. Still less can he love anything outside himself without taking it up into the eternity of his faith and of his soul and binding it thereto. He who does not first regard himself as eternal has in him no love of any kind, and, moreover, cannot love a fatherland, a thing which for him does not exist. He who regards his invisible life as eternal, but not his visible life as similarly eternal, may perhaps have a heaven and therein a fatherland, but here below he has no fatherland, for this, too, is regarded only in the image of eternity – eternity visible and made sensuous – and for this reason also he is unable to love his fatherland. If none has been handed down to such a man, he is to be pitied. But he to whom a fatherland has been handed down, and in whose soul heaven and earth, visible and invisible meet and mingle, and thus, and only thus, create a true and enduring heaven – such a man fights to the last drop of his blood to hand on the precious possession unimpaired to his posterity.

So it always has been, although it has not always been expressed in such general terms and so clearly as we express it here. What inspired the men of noble mind among the Romans, whose frame of mind and way of thinking still live and breathe among us in their works of art, to struggles and sacrifices, to patience and endurance for the fatherland? They themselves express it often and distinctly. It was their firm belief in the eternal continuance of their Roma, and their confident expectation that they themselves would eternally continue to live in this eternity in the stream of time. In so far as this belief was well founded, and they themselves would have comprehended it if they had been entirely clear in their own minds, it did not deceive them. To this very day there still lives in our midst what was truly eternal in their eternal Roma; they themselves live with it, and its consequences will continue to live to the very end of time.

117. People and fatherland in this sense, as a support and guarantee of eternity on earth and as that which can be eternal here below, far transcend the State in the ordinary sense of the word, viz., the social order as comprehended by mere intellectual conception and as established and maintained under the guidance of this conception. The aim of the State is positive law, internal peace, and a condition of affairs in which everyone may by diligence earn his daily bread and satisfy the needs of his material existence, so long as

God permits him to live. All this is only a means, a condition, and a framework for what love of fatherland really wants, viz., that the eternal and the
divine may blossom in the world and never cease to become more and more
pure, perfect, and excellent. That is why this love of fatherland must itself
govern the State and be the supreme, final, and absolute authority. Its first
exercise of this authority will be to limit the State's choice of means to secure
its immediate object – internal peace. To attain this object, the natural
freedom of the individual must, of course, be limited in many ways. If the
only consideration and intention in regard to individuals were to secure
internal peace, it would be well to limit that liberty as much as possible, to
bring all their activities under a uniform rule, and to keep them under
unceasing supervision. Even supposing such strictness were unnecessary, it
could at any rate do no harm, if this were the sole object. It is only the higher
view of the human race and of peoples which extends this narrow calculation.
Freedom, including freedom in the activities of external life, is the soil in
which higher culture germinates; a legislation which keeps the higher culture
in view will allow to freedom as wide a field as possible, even at the risk of
securing a smaller degree of uniform peace and quietness, and of making the
work of government a little harder and more troublesome.

118. To illustrate this by an example. It has happened that nations have
been told to their face that they do not need so much freedom as many other
nations do. It may even be that the form in which the opinion is expressed is
considerate and mild, if what is really meant is that the particular nation
would be quite unable to stand so much freedom, and that nothing but
extreme severity could prevent its members from destroying each other. But,
when the words are taken as meaning what they say, they are true only on the
supposition that such a nation is thoroughly incapable of having original life
or even the impulse towards it. Such a nation – if a nation could exist in
which there were not even a few men of noble mind to make an exception to
the general rule – would in fact need no freedom at all, for this is needed only
for the higher purposes that transcend the State. It needs only to be tamed
and trained, so that the individuals may live peaceably with each other and
that the whole may be made into an efficient instrument for arbitrary
purposes in which the nation as such has no part. Whether this can be said
with truth of any nation at all we may leave undecided; this much is clear, that
an original people needs freedom, that this is the security for its continuance
as an original people, and that, as it goes on, it is able to stand an ever-
increasing degree of freedom without the slightest danger. This is the first
matter in respect of which love of fatherland must govern the State itself.

119. Then, too, it must be love of fatherland that governs the State by
placing before it a higher object than the usual one of maintaining internal
peace, property, personal freedom, and the life and well-being of all. For this

higher object alone, and with no other intention, does the State assemble an armed force. When the question arises of making use of this, when the call comes to stake everything that the State, in the narrow conception of the word, sets before itself as object, viz., property, personal freedom, life, and well-being, nay, even the continued existence of the State itself; when the call comes to make an original decision with responsibility to God alone, and without a clear and reasonable idea that what is intended will surely be attained – for this is never possible in such matters – then, and then only, does there live at the helm of the State a truly original and primary life, and at this point, and not before, the true sovereign rights of government enter, like God, to hazard the lower life for the sake of the higher. In the maintenance of the traditional constitution, the laws, and civil prosperity there is absolutely no real true life and no original decision. Conditions and circumstances, and legislators perhaps long since dead, have created these things; succeeding ages go on faithfully in the paths marked out, and so in fact they have no public life of their own; they merely repeat a life that once existed. In such times there is no need of any real government. But, when this regular course is endangered, and it is a question of making decisions in new and unprecedented cases, then there is need of a life that lives of itself. What spirit is it that in such cases may place itself at the helm, that can make its own decisions with sureness and certainty, untroubled by any hesitation? What spirit has an undisputed right to summon and to order everyone concerned, whether he himself be willing or not, and to compel anyone who resists, to risk everything including his life? Not the spirit of the peaceful citizen's love for the constitution and the laws, but the devouring flame of higher patriotism, which embraces the nation as the vesture of the eternal, for which the noble-minded man joyfully sacrifices himself, and the ignoble man, who only exists for the sake of the other, must likewise sacrifice himself. It is not that love of the citizen for the constitution; that love is quite unable to achieve this, so long as it remains on the level of the understanding. Whatever turn events may take, since it pays to govern they will always have a ruler over them. Suppose the new ruler even wants to introduce slavery (and what is slavery if not the disregard for, and suppression of, the characteristic of an original people? – but to that way of thinking such qualities do not exist), suppose he wants to introduce slavery. Then, since it is profitable to preserve the life of slaves, to maintain their numbers and even their well-being, slavery under him will turn out to be bearable if he is anything of a calculator. Their life and their keep, at any rate, they will always find. Then what is there left that they should fight for? After those two things it is peace which they value more than anything. But peace will only be disturbed by the continuance of the struggle. They will, therefore, do anything just to put an end to the fighting, and the sooner the better; they will submit, they will yield; and why should they not? All they have ever been concerned about, and all they have ever hoped from life, has been the continuation of the habit of existing under tolerable conditions. The promise of a life here on earth extending beyond the period of life here on earth – that alone it is which can inspire men even unto death for the fatherland.

120. So it has been hitherto. Wherever there has been true government, wherever bitter struggles have been endured, wherever victory has been won in the face of mighty opposition, there it has been that promise of eternal life which governed and struggled and won the victory. Believing in that promise the German Protestants, already mentioned in these addresses, entered upon the struggle. Do you think they did not know that peoples could be governed by that old belief too, and held together in law and order, and that under the old belief men could procure a comfortable existence? Why, then, did their princes decide upon armed resistance, and why did the peoples enthusiastically make such resistance? It was for heaven and for eternal bliss that they willingly poured out their blood. But what earthly power could have penetrated to the Holy of holies in their souls and rooted out their belief – a belief which had been revealed to them once for all, and on which alone they based their hope of bliss? Thus it was not their own bliss for which they fought; this was already assured to them; it was the bliss of their children and of their grandchildren as yet unborn and of all posterity as yet unborn. These, too, should be brought up in that same doctrine, which had appeared to them as the only means of salvation. These, too, should partake of the salvation that had dawned for them. This hope alone it was that was threatened by the enemy. For it, for an order of things that long after their death should blossom on their graves, they so joyfully shed their blood. Let us admit that they were not entirely clear in their own minds, that they made mistakes in their choice of words to denote the noblest that was in them, and with their lips did injustice to their souls; let us willingly confess that their confession of faith was not the sole and exclusive means of becoming a partaker of the heaven beyond the grave; none the less it is eternally true that more heaven on this side of the grave, a braver and more joyful look from earth upwards, and a freer stirring of the spirit have entered by their sacrifice into the whole life of succeeding ages. To this very day the descendants of their opponents, just as much as we ourselves, their own descendants, enjoy the fruits of their labours.

121. In this belief our earliest common forefathers, the original stock of the new culture, the Germans, as the Romans called them, bravely resisted the on-coming world-dominion of the Romans. Did they not have before their eyes the greater brilliance of the Roman provinces next to them and the more refined enjoyments in those provinces, to say nothing of laws and judges' seats and lictors' axes and rods in superfluity? Were not the Romans willing enough to let them share in all these blessings? In the case of several of their own princes, who did no more than intimate that war against such benefactors of mankind was rebellion, did they not experience proofs of the belauded Roman clemency? To those who submitted the Romans gave marks of distinction in the form of kingly titles, high commands in their armies, and Roman fillets; and if they were driven out by their countrymen, did not the Romans provide for them a place of refuge and a means of subsistence in their colonies? Had they no appreciation of the advantages of Roman civilization, *e.g.*, of the superior organization of their armies, in which even an Arminius did not disdain to learn the trade of war? They cannot be charged with ignorance or lack of consideration of any one of these things. Their descendants, as soon as they could do so without losing their freedom, even assimilated Roman culture, so far as this was possible without losing their individuality. Why, then, did they fight for several generations in bloody wars, that broke out again and again with ever renewed force? A Roman writer puts the following expression into the mouth of their leaders: "What was left for them to do, except to maintain their freedom or else to die before they became slaves." Freedom to them meant just this: remaining Germans and continuing to settle their own affairs independently and in accordance with the original spirit of their race, going on with their development in accordance with the same spirit, and propagating this independence in their posterity. All those blessings which the Romans offered them meant slavery to them, because then they would have to become something that was not German, they would have to become half Roman. They assumed as a matter of course that every man would rather die than become half a Roman, and that a true German could only want to live in order to be, and to remain, just a German and to bring up his children as Germans.

They did not all die; they did not see slavery; they bequeathed freedom to their children. It is their unyielding resistance which the whole modern world has to thank for being what it now is. Had the Romans succeeded in bringing them also under the yoke and in destroying them as a nation, which the Roman did in every case, the whole development of the human race would have taken a different course, a course that one cannot think would have been more satisfactory. It is they whom we must thank – we, the immediate heirs of their soil, their language, and their way of thinking – for being Germans still, for being still borne along on the stream of original and independent life. It is they whom we must thank for everything that we have been as a nation since those days, and to them we shall be indebted for everything that we shall be in the future, unless things have come to an end with us now and the last drop of blood inherited from them has dried up in our veins. To them the other branches of the race, whom we now look upon as foreigners, but who by descent from them are our brothers, are indebted for their very existence. When our ancestors triumphed over Roma the eternal, not one of all these peoples was in existence, but the possibility of their existence in the future was won for them in the same fight.

122. These men, and all others of like mind in the history of the world, won the victory because eternity inspired them, and this inspiration always does, and always must, defeat him who is not so inspired. It is neither the strong right arm nor the efficient weapon that wins victories, but only the power of the soul. He who sets a limit to his sacrifices, and has no wish to venture beyond a certain point, ceases to resist as soon as he finds himself in danger at this point, even though it be one which is vital to him and which ought not to be surrendered. He who sets no limit whatever for himself, but on the contrary stakes everything he has, including the most precious possession granted to dwellers here below, namely, life itself, never ceases to resist, and will undoubtedly win the victory over an opponent whose goal is more limited. A people that is capable of firmly beholding the countenance of that vision from the spiritual world, independence, even though it be only its highest representatives and leaders who are capable of perceiving it – a people capable of being possessed by love of this vision, as our earliest forefathers were, will undoubtedly win the victory over a people that is used, as were the Roman armies, only as the tool of foreign ambition to bring independent people under the yoke; for the former have everything to lose, and the latter merely something to gain. But the way of thinking which regards war as a game of chance, where the stakes are temporal gain or loss, and which fixes the amount to be staked on the cards even before it begins the game – such a way of thinking is defeated even by a whim. Think, for example, of a Mahomet – not the Mahomet of history, about whom I confess I have no opinion, but the Mahomet of a well-known French poet. He takes it firmly into his head once for all that he is one of those exceptional beings who are called to lead the obscure and common folk of the earth, and in accordance with this preliminary assumption all his notions, no matter how mean and limited they may be in reality, of necessity seem to him, just because they are his own, great and sublime ideas full of blessings for mankind; all who set themselves against these notions seem to him obscure and common people, enemies of their own good, evil-minded, and hateful. Then, in order to justify this conceit of himself as a divine call, he lets this thought absorb his whole life; he must stake everything on it, and cannot rest until he has trodden underfoot all who refuse to think as highly of him as he does of himself, and until he sees his own belief in his divine mission reflected in the whole contemporary world. I will not say what would happen to him if a spiritual vision, true and clear to itself, entered the lists against him, but he is sure to be victorious over those gamesters with limited stakes, for he stakes everything against them and they do not stake everything. No spirit drives them, but he is driven by a spirit, though it be but a raving one, the violent and powerful spirit of his own conceit.

123. From all this it follows that the State, merely as the government of human life in its progress along the ordinary peaceful path, is not something which is primary and which exists for its own sake, but is merely the means to the higher purpose of the eternal, regular, and continuous development of what is purely human in this nation. It follows, too, that the vision and the love of this eternal development, and nothing else, should have the higher supervision of State administration at all times, not excluding periods of peace, and that this alone is able to save the people's independence when it is endangered. In the case of the Germans, among whom as an original people this love of fatherland was possible and, as we firmly believe, did actually exist up to the present time, it has been able up to now to reckon with great confidence on the security of what was most vital to it. As was the case with the ancient Greeks alone, with the Germans the State and the nation were actually separated from each other, and each was represented for itself, the former in the separate German realms and principalities, the latter represented visibly in the imperial connection and invisibly – by virtue of a law, not written, but living and valid in the minds of all, a law whose results struck the eye everywhere – in a mass of customs and institutions. Wherever the German language was spoken, everyone who had first seen the light of day in its domain could consider himself as in a double sense a citizen, on the one hand, of the State where he was born and to whose care he was in the first instance commended, and, on the other hand, of the whole common fatherland of the German nation. To everyone it was permitted to seek out for himself in the whole length and breadth of this fatherland the culture most congenial to him or the sphere of action to which his spirit was best adapted; and talent did not root itself like a tree in the place where it first grew up, but was allowed to seek out its own place. Anyone who, because of the turn taken by his own development, became out of harmony with his immediate environment, easily found a willing reception elsewhere, found new friends in place of those he had lost, found time and leisure to make his meaning plainer and perhaps to win over and to reconcile even those who were offended with him, and so to unite the whole. No German-born prince ever took upon himself to mark out for his subjects as their fatherland, with mountains or rivers as boundaries, the territory over which he ruled, and to regard his subjects as bound to the soil. A truth not permitted to find expression in one place might find expression in another, where it might happen that those truths were forbidden which were permitted in the first. So, in spite of the many instances of one-sidedness and narrowness of heart in the separate States, there was nevertheless in Germany, considered as a whole, the greatest freedom of investigation and publication that any people has ever possessed. Everywhere the higher culture was, and continued to be, the result of the interaction of the citizens of all German States: and then this higher culture gradually worked its way down in this form to the people at large, which thus never ceased, broadly speaking, to educate itself by itself. This essential security for the continuance of a German nation was, as we have said, not impaired by any man of German spirit seated at the helm of government; and though with respect to other original decisions things may not always have happened as the higher German love of fatherland could not but wish, at any rate there has been no act in direct opposition to its interests; there has been no attempt to undermine that love or to extirpate it and put a love of the opposite kind in its place.

124. But what if the original guidance of that higher culture, as well as of the national power which may not be used except to serve that culture and its continuance, the utilization of German property and blood – what if this should pass from the control of the German spirit to that of another? What would then be the inevitable results?

This is the place where there is special need of the disposition which we invoked in our first address – the disposition not to deceive ourselves wilfully about our own affairs, and the courage to be willing to behold the truth and confess it to ourselves. Moreover, it is still permitted to us, so far as I know, to speak to each other in the German language about the fatherland, or at least to sigh over it, and, in my opinion, we should not do well if we anticipated of our own accord such a prohibition, or if we were ready to restrain our courage, which without doubt will already have taken counsel with itself as to the risk to be run, with the chains forged by the timidity of some individuals.

Picture to yourselves, then, the new power, which we are presupposing, as well-disposed and as benevolent as ever you may wish; make it as good as God Himself; will you be able to impart to it divine understanding as well? Even though it wish in all earnestness the greatest happiness and well-being of everyone, do you suppose that the greatest well-being it is able to conceive will be the same thing as German well-being? In regard to the main point which I have put before you to-day, I hope I have been thoroughly well understood by you; I hope that several, while they listened to me, thought and felt that I was only expressing in plain words what has always lain in their minds; I hope that the other Germans who will some day read this will have the same feeling – indeed, several Germans have said practically the same thing before I did, and the unconscious basis of the resistance that has been repeatedly manifested to a purely mechanical constitution and policy of the State has been the view of things which I have presented to you. Now, I challenge all those who are acquainted with the modern literature of foreign countries to show me one of their poets or legislators who in recent times has ever betrayed a glimmering of anything similar to the view that regards the human race as eternally progressing, and that refers all its activities in this world solely to this eternal progress. Even in the period of their boldest flights of political creation, was there a single one who demanded more from the State than the abolition of inequalities, the maintenance of peace within their borders and of national reputation without, or, in the extremest case, domestic bliss? If, as we must conclude from all these indications, this is their highest good, they will not attribute to us any higher needs or any higher demands on life. Assuming they always display that beneficent disposition towards us and are free from any selfishness or desire to be greater than we are, they will think they have provided splendidly for us if we are given everything that they themselves know to be desirable. But the thing for which alone the nobler men among us wish to live is then blotted out of public life; and as soon as the people, which has always shown itself responsive to the stirrings of the noble mind and which we were entitled to hope might be elevated in a body to that nobility, is treated as those to whom we are referring want to be treated, it is degraded and dishonoured, and, by its confluence with a people of a lower species, it is blotted out of the universe.

125. But he, in whom those higher demands on life remain alive and powerful and who has a feeling that their right is divine, feels himself set back, much against his will, into those early days of Christianity, when it was said: "Resist not evil; but whosoever shall smite thee on the right cheek, turn to him the other also; and if any man will take away thy coat, let him have thy cloke also." The latter is well said, for, so long as he sees that thou still hast a cloke, he seeks to pick a quarrel with thee so as to take this from thee also, and only when thou art quite naked wilt thou escape his attention and be left in peace. To such a man the earth becomes a hell and a place of horror, just because of his higher mind, which does him honour. He wishes he had never been born; he wishes that his eyes may be closed to the light of day, and the sooner the better; his days are filled with everlasting sorrow until he descends to the grave, and for those whom he loves he can wish no greater boon than a dull and contented mind, so that with less suffering they may live for an eternal life beyond the grave.

These addresses lay before you the sole remaining means, now that the others have been tried in vain, of preventing this annihilation of every nobler impulse that may break out among us in the future, and of preventing this degradation of our whole nation. They propose that you establish deeply and indelibly in the hearts of all, by means of education, the true and all- powerful love of fatherland, the conception of our people as an eternal people and as the security for our own eternity. What kind of education can do this, and how it is to be done, we shall see in the following addresses.

12

The Philosophy of History
(1830–1)

G. W. F. Hegel

G. W. F. Hegel, selection from the Introduction to *The Philosophy of History* (1830–1) [source: G. W. F. Hegel, *The Philosophy of History*, trans. J. Sibree. New York: Dover Publications, 1956, 52–3]

Hegel (1770–1831) may be the most important and influential German philosopher of the nineteenth century. Like Fichte, Hegel rejected Kant's epistemological dualism in favor of a unified view of reality, in which subjective perception and the objective world were dialectical moments in the unfolding of absolute knowledge, rather than irrevocably cut off from one another. Hegel's view of morality, civil society, and political order is similarly unified, in that the private, autonomous individual is neither completely distinct from public ethics, nor absorbed by the national mind (as in Maistre and Fichte), but appears as an element in the development of consciousness toward an organic state. Hegel's state, with its consititutional balance (borrowed from the English model) of bourgeois, market-driven commons, landed aristocracy, and monarchy, reflects this development. His philosophy of history embodied the unfolding of consciousness in national identities, rooted simultaneously in a nation's laws, geography, natural resources, property, and the memory of ancestral accomplishments. In Hegel's universal history, each nation represents one animating spirit or collective individual in a development that follows the sun's trajectory, from the despotism of the East, where consciousness is simple and undifferentiated, to the flowering of the World Spirit in Western religion, art, science, and philosophy. The fully developed state is then the return of the unconscious harmony of paradise before the fall, on the higher plane of perfect, complete, and consciously willed political freedom.

[...] Summing up what has been said of the State, we find that we have been led to call its vital principle, as actuating the individuals who compose it – Morality. The State, its laws, its arrangements, constitute the rights of its members; its natural features, its mountains, air, and waters, are *their* country, their fatherland, their outward material property; the history of this State, *their* deeds; what their ancestors have produced, belongs to them and lives in their memory. All is their possession, just as they are possessed by it; for it constitutes their existence, their being.

Their imagination is occupied with the ideas thus presented, while the adoption of these laws, and of a fatherland so conditioned is the expression of their will. It is this matured totality which thus constitutes *one* Being, the spirit of *one* People. To it the individual members belong; each unit is the Son of his Nation, and at the same time – in as far as the State to which he belongs is undergoing development – the Son of his Age. None remains behind it, still less advances beyond it. This spiritual Being (the Spirit of his Time) is his; he is a representative of it; it is that in which he originated, and in which he lives. Among the Athenians the word Athens had a double import; suggesting primarily, a complex of political institutions, but no less, in the second place, that Goddess who represented the Spirit of the People and its unity.

This Spirit of a People is a *determinate* and particular Spirit, and is, as just stated, further modified by the degree of its historical development. This Spirit, then, constitutes the basis and substance of those other forms of a nation's consciousness, which have been noticed. For Spirit in its self-consciousness must become an object of contemplation to itself, and objectivity involves, in the first instance, the rise of differences which make up a total of distinct spheres of objective spirit; in the same way as the Soul exists only as the complex of its faculties, which in their form of concentration in a simple unity produce that Soul. It is thus *One Individuality* which, presented in its essence as God, is honored and enjoyed in *Religion*; which is exhibited as an object of sensuous contemplation in *Art*; and is apprehended as an intellectual conception, in *Philosophy*. In virtue of the original identity of their essence, purport, and object, these various forms are inseparably united with the Spirit of the State. Only in connection with this particular religion, can this particular political constitution exist; just as in such or such a State, such or such a Philosophy or order of Art.

The remark next in order is, that each particular National genius is to be treated as only One Individual in the process of Universal History. For that history is the exhibition of the divine, absolute development of Spirit in its highest forms – that gradation by which it attains its truth and consciousness of itself. The forms which these grades of progress assume are the characteristic "National Spirits" of History; the peculiar tenor of their moral life, of their Government, their Art, Religion, and Science. To realize these grades is the boundless impulse of the World-Spirit – the goal of its irresistible urging, for this division into organic members, and the full development of each, is its Idea. – Universal History is exclusively occupied with showing how Spirit comes to a recognition and adoption of the Truth: the dawn of knowledge appears; it begins to discover salient principles, and at last it arrives at full consciousness. [. . .]

13

The Inequality of Human Races (1854)

Arthur de Gobineau

Arthur de Gobineau, ch. IV, vol. I, of *The Inequality of Human Races* (1854) [source: Arthur de Gobineau, *The Inequality of Human Races*, trans. Adrian Collins. New York: Howard Fertig, 1967, 23–35]

Arguably the most important theorist of race in the nineteenth century, the fame of Gobineau (1816–82) rests on his study of degeneration. Unlike earlier treatments of this theme, from Plato's to Gibbon's, which attributed the decline of societies to moral corruption caused by various excesses of appetite, consumption, and pride, Gobineau discounted such forces in favor of one overriding concern: the mixing of distinct races. For Gobineau, races and their nations were shaped neither by civic institutions (as in Rousseau) nor by environment (as in Montesquieu), but were differentiated by nature and essentially unequal in character and status. Members of different races thus had an inborn affinity with their own kind and a "secret repulsion from the crossing of blood." Gobineau may have been the most radical racist of his time. But he was also a critic of colonization, since the conquering (and *de facto* stronger) nations, like those of the white or Aryan race, would inevitably mix their blood with the conquered (and thus weaker) ones. The more numerous the conquests, the more inevitable the degeneration in the conquering stock. Gobineau found examples in the Hindu, Persian, Greek, and Roman empires. He also predicted that, since India had been dominated but not racially assimilated by the English, the Raj would collapse and "India will again live publicly, as she already does privately, under her own laws." Gobineau's views on degeneration gained widespread recognition; they influenced Lombroso, Chamberlain, Nietzsche, and Nordau, and held a prominent place in Nazi ideology.

Chapter IV: The Meaning of the Word "Degeneration"; the Mixture of Racial Elements; how Societies are Formed and Broken Up

However little the spirit of the foregoing pages may have been understood, no one will conclude from them that I attach no importance to the maladies of the social organism, and that, for me, bad government, fanaticism, and irreligion are mere unmeaning accidents. On the contrary I quite agree with the ordinary view, that it is a lamentable thing to see a society being gradually undermined by these fell diseases, and that no amount of care and trouble would be wasted if a remedy could only be found. I merely add that if these poisonous blossoms of disunion are not grafted on a stronger principle of destruction, if they are not the consequences of a hidden plague more terrible still, we may rest assured that their ravages will not be fatal and that after a time of suffering more or less drawn out, the society will emerge from their toils, perhaps with strength and youth renewed.

The examples I have brought forward seem to me conclusive, though their number might be indefinitely increased. Through some such reasoning as this the ordinary opinions of men have at last come to contain an instinctive perception of the truth. It is being dimly seen that one ought not to have given such a preponderant importance to evils which were after all merely derivative, and that the true causes of the life and death of peoples should have been sought elsewhere, and been drawn from a deeper well. Men have begun to look at the inner constitution of a society, by itself, quite apart from all circumstances of health or disease. They have shown themselves ready to admit that no external cause could lay the hand of death on any society, so long as a certain destructive principle, inherent in it from the first, born from its womb and nourished on its entrails, had not reached its full maturity; on the other hand, so soon as this destructive principle had come into existence, the society was doomed to certain death, even though it had the best of all possible governments – in exactly the same way as a spent horse will fall dead on a concrete road.

A great step in advance was made, I admit, when the question was considered from this point of view, which was anyhow much more philosophic than the one taken up before. Bichat, as we know, did not seek to discover the great mystery of existence by studying the human subject from the outside; the key to the riddle, he saw, lay within. Those who followed the same method, in our own subject, were travelling on the only road that really led to discoveries. Unfortunately, this excellent idea of theirs was the result of mere instinct; its logical implications were not carried very far, and it was shattered on the first difficulty. "Yes," they cried, "the cause of destruction lies hidden in the very vitals of the social organism; but what *is* this cause?" "*Degeneration,*" was the answer; "nations die when they are composed of elements that have *degenerated.*" The answer was excellent, etymologically and otherwise. It only remained to define the meaning of "nation that has degenerated." This was the rock on which they foundered; a *degenerate people* meant, they said, "A people which through bad government, misuse of wealth, fanaticism, or irreligion, had lost the characteristic virtues of its ancestors." What a fall is there! Thus a people dies of its endemic diseases because it is degenerate, and is degenerate because it dies. This circular argument merely proves that the science of social anatomy is in its infancy. I quite agree that societies perish because they are degenerate, and for no other reason. This is the evil condition that makes them wholly unable to withstand the shock of the disasters that close in upon them; and when they can no longer endure the blows of adverse fortune, and have no power to raise their heads when the scourge has passed, then we have the sublime spectacle of a nation in agony. If it perish, it is because it has no longer the same vigour as it had of old in battling with the dangers of life; in a word, because it is *degenerate.* I repeat, the term is excellent; but we must explain it a little better, and give it a definite meaning. How and why is a nation's vigour lost? How does it degenerate? These are the questions which we must try to answer. Up to the present, men have been content with finding the word, without unveiling the reality that lies behind. This further step I shall now attempt to take.

The word *degenerate,* when applied to a people, means (as it ought to mean) that the people has no longer the same intrinsic value as it had before, because it has no longer the same blood in its veins, continual adulterations having gradually affected the quality of that blood. In other words, though the nation bears the name given by its founders, the name no longer connotes the same race; in fact, the man of a decadent time, the *degenerate* man properly so called, is a different being, from the racial point of view, from the heroes of the great ages. I agree that he still keeps something of their essence; but the more he degenerates the more attenuated does this "something" become. The heterogeneous elements that henceforth prevail in him give him quite a different nationality – a very original one, no doubt, but such originality is not to be envied. He is only a very distant kinsman of those he still calls his ancestors. He, and his civilization with him, will certainly die on the day when the primordial race-unit is so broken up and swamped by the influx of foreign elements, that its effective qualities have no longer a sufficient freedom of action. It will not, of course, absolutely disappear, but it will in practice be so beaten down and enfeebled, that its power will be felt less and less as time goes on. It is at this point that all the results of degeneration will appear, and the process may be considered complete.

If I manage to prove this proposition, I shall have given a meaning to the word "degeneration." By showing how the essential quality of a nation gradually alters, I shift the responsibility for its decadence, which thus becomes, in a way, less shameful, for it weighs no longer on the sons, but on the nephews, then on the cousins, then on collaterals more or less removed. And when I have shown by examples that great peoples, at the moment of their death, have only a very small and insignificant share in the blood of the founders, into whose inheritance they come, I shall thereby have explained clearly enough how it is possible for civilizations to fall – the reason being that they are no longer in the same hands. At the same time I shall be touching on a problem which is much more dangerous than that which I have tried to solve in the preceding chapters. This problem is: "Are there serious and ultimate differences of value between human races; and can these differences be estimated?"

I will begin at once to develop the series of arguments that touch the first point; they will indirectly settle the second also.

To put my ideas into a clearer and more easily intelligible form I may compare a nation to a human body, which, according to the physiologists, is constantly renewing all its parts; the work of transformation that goes on is incessant, and after a certain number of years the body retains hardly any of its former elements. Thus, in the old man, there are no traces of the man of middle age, in the adult no traces of the youth, nor in the youth of the child; the personal identity in all these stages is kept purely by the succession of inner and outer forms, each an imperfect copy of the last. Yet I will admit one difference between a nation and a human body; in the former there is no question of the "forms" being preserved, for these are destroyed and disappear with enormous rapidity. I will take a people, or better, a tribe, at the moment when, yielding to a definite vital instinct, it provides itself with laws and begins to play a part in the world. By the mere fact of its wants and powers increasing, it inevitably finds itself in contact with other similar associations, and by war or peaceful measures succeeds in incorporating them with itself.

Not all human families can reach this first step; but it is a step that every tribe must take if it is to rank one day as a nation. Even if a certain number of races, themselves perhaps not very far advanced on the ladder of civilization, have passed through this stage, we cannot properly regard this as a general rule.

Indeed, the human species seems to have a very great difficulty in raising itself above a rudimentary type of organization; the transition to a more complex state is made only by those groups of tribes, that are eminently gifted. I may cite, in support of this, the actual condition of a large number of communities spread throughout the world. These backward tribes, especially the Polynesian negroes, the Samoyedes and others in the far north, and the majority of the African races, have never been able to shake themselves free from their impotence; they live side by side in complete independence of each other. The stronger massacre the weaker, the weaker try to move as far away as possible from the stronger. This sums up the political ideas of these embryo societies, which have lived on in their imperfect state, without possibility of improvement, as long as the human race itself. It may be said that these miserable savages are a very small part of the earth's population. Granted; but we must take account of all the similar peoples who have lived and disappeared. Their number is incalculable, and certainly includes the vast majority of the pure-blooded yellow and black races.

If then we are driven to admit that for a very large number of human beings it has been, and always will be, impossible to take even the first step towards civilization; if, again, we consider that these peoples are scattered over the whole face of the earth under the most varying conditions of climate and environment, that they live indifferently in the tropics, in the temperate zones, and in the Arctic circle, by sea, lake, and river, in the depths of the forest, in the grassy plains, in the arid deserts, we must conclude that a part of mankind, is in its own nature stricken with a paralysis, which makes it for ever unable to take even the first step towards civilization, since it cannot overcome the natural repugnance, felt by men and animals alike, to a crossing of blood.

Leaving these tribes, that are incapable of civilization, on one side, we come, in our journey upwards, to those which understand that if they wish to increase their power and prosperity, they are absolutely compelled, either by war or peaceful measures, to draw their neighbours within their sphere of influence. War is undoubtedly the simpler way of doing this. Accordingly, they go to war. But when the campaign is finished, and the craving for destruction is satisfied, some prisoners are left over; these prisoners become slaves, and as slaves, work for their masters. We have class distinctions at once, and an industrial system: the tribe has become a little people. This is a higher rung on the ladder of civilization, and is not necessarily passed by all the tribes which have been able to reach it; many remain at this stage in cheerful stagnation.

But there are others, more imaginative and energetic, whose ideas soar beyond mere brigandage. They manage to conquer a great territory, and assume rights of ownership not only over the inhabitants, but also over their land. From this moment a real nation has been formed. The two races often continue for a time to live side by side without mingling; and yet, as they become indispensable to each other, as a community of work and interest is gradually built up, as the pride and rancour of conquest begin to ebb away, as those below naturally tend to rise to the level of their masters, while the masters have a thousand reasons for allowing, or even for promoting, such a tendency, the mixture of blood finally takes place, the two races cease to be associated with distinct tribes, and become more and more fused into a single whole.

The spirit of isolation is, however, so innate in the human race, that even those who have reached this advanced stage of crossing refuse in many cases to take a step further. There are some peoples who are, as we know positively, of mixed origin, but who keep their feeling for the clan to an extraordinary degree. The Arabs, for example, do more than merely spring from different branches of the Semitic stock; they belong at one and the same time to the so-called families of Shem and Ham, not to speak of a vast number of local strains that are intermingled with these. Nevertheless, their attachment to the tribe, as a separate unit, is one of the most striking features of their national character and their political history. In fact, it has been thought possible to attribute their expulsion from Spain not only to the actual break-ing up of their power there, but also, to a large extent, to their being continually divided into smaller and mutually antagonistic groups, in the struggles for promotion among the Arab families at the petty courts of Valentia, Toledo, Cordova, and Grenada.[1]

We may say the same about the majority of such peoples. Further, where the tribal separation has broken down, a national feeling takes its place, and acts with a similar vigour, which a community of religion is not enough to destroy. This is the case among the Arabs and the Turks, the Persians and the Jews, the Parsees and the Hindus, the Nestorians of Syria and the Kurds. We find it also in European Turkey, and can trace its course in Hungary, among the Magyars, the Saxons, the Wallachians, and the Croats. I know, from what I have seen with my own eyes, that in certain parts of France, the country where races are mingled more than perhaps anywhere else, there are little communities to be found to this day, who feel a repugnance to marrying outside their own village.

I think I am right in concluding from these examples, which cover all countries and ages, including our own, that the human race in all its branches has a secret repulsion from the crossing of blood, a repulsion which in many of the branches is invincible, and in others is only conquered to a slight extent. Even those who most completely shake off the yoke of this idea cannot get rid of the few last traces of it; yet such peoples are the only members of our species who can be civilized at all.

Thus mankind lives in obedience to two laws, one of repulsion, the other of attraction; these act with different force on different peoples. The first is fully respected only by those races which can never raise themselves above the elementary completeness of the tribal life, while the power of the second, on the contrary, is the more absolute, as the racial units on which it is exercised are more capable of development.

Here especially I must be concrete. I have just taken the example of a people in embryo, whose state is like that of a single family. I have given them the qualities which will allow them to pass into the state of a nation. Well, suppose they have become a nation. History does not tell me what the elements were that constituted the original group; all I know is that these elements fitted it for the transformation which I have made it undergo. Now that it has grown, it has only two possibilities. One or other of two destinies is inevitable. It will either conquer or be conquered.

I will give it the better part, and assume that it will conquer. It will at the same time rule, administer, and civilize. It will not go through its provinces, sowing a useless harvest of fire and massacre. Monuments, customs, and institutions will be alike sacred. It will change what it can usefully modify, and replace it by something better. Weakness in its hands will become strength. It will behave in such a way that, in the words of Scripture, it will be magnified in the sight of men.

I do not know if the same thought has already struck the reader; but in the picture which I am presenting – and which in certain features is that of the Hindus, the Egyptians, the Persians and the Macedonians – two facts appear to me to stand out. The first is that a nation, which itself lacks vigour and power, is suddenly called upon to share a new and a better destiny – that of the strong masters into whose hands it has fallen; this was the case with the Anglo-Saxons, when they had been subdued by the Normans. The second fact is that a picked race of men, a sovereign people, with the usual strong propensities of such a people to cross its blood with another's, finds itself henceforth in close contact with a race whose inferiority is shown, not only by defeat, but also by the lack of the attributes that may be seen in the conquerors. From the very day when the conquest is accomplished and the fusion begins, there appears a noticeable change of quality in the blood of the masters. If there were no other modifying influence at the work, then – at the end of a number of years, which would vary according to the number of peoples that composed the original stock – we should be confronted with a new race, less powerful certainly than the better of its two ancestors, but still of considerable strength. It would have developed special qualities resulting from the actual mixture, and unknown to the communities from which it sprang. But the case is not generally so simple as this, and the intermingling of blood is not confined for long to the two constituent peoples.

The empire I have just been imagining is a powerful one; and its power is used to control its neighbours. I assume that there will be new conquests;

and, every time, a current of fresh blood will be mingled with the main stream. Henceforth, as the nation grows, whether by war or treaty, its racial character changes more and more. It is rich, commercial, and civilized. The needs and the pleasures of other peoples find ample satisfaction in its capitals, its great towns, and its ports; while its myriad attractions cause many foreigners to make it their home. After a short time, we might truly say that a distinction of castes takes the place of the original distinction of races.

I am willing to grant that the people of whom I am speaking is strengthened in its exclusive notions by the most formal commands of religion, and that some dreadful penalty lurks in the background, to awe the disobedient. But since the people is civilized, its character is soft and tolerant, even to the contempt of its faith. Its oracles will speak in vain; there will be births outside the caste-limits. Every day new distinctions will have to be drawn, new classifications invented; the number of social grades will be increased, and it will be almost impossible to know where one is, amid the infinite variety of the subdivisions, that change from province to province, from canton to canton, from village to village. In fact, the condition will be that of the Hindu countries. It is only, however, the Brahman who has shown himself so tenacious of his ideas of separation; the foreign peoples he civilized have never fastened these cramping fetters on their shoulders, or any rate have long since shaken them off. In all the States that have made any advance in intellectual culture, the process has not been checked for a single moment by those desperate shifts to which the law-givers of the Aryavarta were put, in their desire to reconcile the prescriptions of the Code of Manu with the irresistible march of events. In every other place where there were really any castes at all, they ceased to exist at the moment when the chance of making a fortune, and of becoming famous by useful discoveries or social talents, became open to the whole world, without distinction of origin. But also, from that same day, the nation that was originally the active, conquering, and civilizing power began to disappear; its blood became merged in that of all the tributaries which it had attracted to its own stream.

Generally the dominating peoples begin by being far fewer in number than those they conquer; while, on the other hand, certain races that form the basis of the population in immense districts are extremely prolific – the Celts, for example, and the Slavs. This is yet another reason for the rapid disappearance of the conquering races. Again, their greater activity and the more personal part they take in the affairs of the State make them the chief mark for attack after a disastrous battle, a proscription, or a revolution. Thus, while by their very genius for civilization they collect round them the different elements in which they are to be absorbed, they are the victims, first of their original smallness of number, and then of a host of secondary causes which combine together for their destruction.

It is fairly obvious that the time when the disappearance takes place will vary considerably, according to circumstances. Yet it does finally come to pass, and is everywhere quite complete, long before the end of the civilization which the victorious race is supposed to be animating. A people may often go on living and working, and even growing in power, after the active, generating force of its life and glory has ceased to exist. Does this contradict what I have said above? Not at all; for while the blood of the civilizing race is gradually drained away by being parcelled out among the peoples that are conquered or annexed, the impulse originally given to these peoples still persists. The institutions which the dead master had invented, the laws he had prescribed, the customs he had initiated – all these live after him. No doubt the customs, laws, and institutions have quite forgotten the spirit that informed their youth; they survive in dishonoured old age, every day more sapless and rotten. But so long as even their shadows remain, the building stands, the body seems to have a soul, the pale ghost walks. When the original impulse has worked itself out, the last word has been said. Nothing remains; the civilization is dead.

I think I now have all the data necessary for grappling with the problem of the life and death of nations; and I can say positively that a people will never die, if it remains eternally composed of the same national elements. If the empire of Darius had, at the battle of Arbela, been able to fill its ranks with Persians, that is to say with real Aryans; if the Romans of the later Empire had had a Senate and an army of the same stock as that which existed at the time of the Fabii, their dominion would never have come to an end. So long as they kept the same purity of blood, the Persians and Romans would have lived and reigned. In the long run, it might be said, a conqueror, more irresistible than they, would have appeared on the scene; and they would have fallen under a well-directed attack, or a long siege, or simply by the fortune of a single battle. Yes, a State might be overthrown in this way, but not a civilization or a social organism. Invasion and defeat are but the dark clouds that for a time blot out the day, and then pass over. Many examples might be brought forward in proof of this.

In modern times the Chinese have been twice conquered. They have always forced their conquerors to become assimilated to them, and to respect their customs; they gave much, and took hardly anything in return. They drove out the first invaders, and in time will do the same with the second.

The English are the masters of India, and yet their moral hold over their subjects is almost non-existent. They are themselves influenced in many ways by the local civilization, and cannot succeed in stamping their ideas on a people that fears its conquerors, but is only physically dominated by them. It keeps its soul erect, and its thoughts apart from theirs. The Hindu race has become a stranger to the race that governs it to-day, and its civilization does

not obey the law that gives the battle to the strong. External forms, kingdoms, and empires have changed, and will change again; but the foundations
on which they rest, and from which they spring, do not necessarily change
with them. Though Hyderabad, Lahore, and Delhi are no longer capital
cities, Hindu society none the less persists. A moment will come, in one way
or another, when India will again live publicly, as she already does privately,
under her own laws; and, by the help either of the races actually existing or of
a hybrid proceeding from them, will assume again, in the full sense of the
word, a political personality.

The hazard of war cannot destroy the life of a people. At most, it suspends
its animation for a time, and in some ways shears it of its outward pomp. So
long as the blood and institutions of a nation keep to a sufficient degree the
impress of the original race, that nation exists. Whether, as in the case of the
Chinese, its conqueror has, in a purely material sense, greater energy than
itself; whether, like the Hindu, it is matched, in a long and arduous trial of
patience, against a nation, such as the English, in all points its superior; in
either case the thought of its certain destiny should bring consolation – one
day it will be free. But if, like the Greeks, and the Romans of the later Empire,
the people has been absolutely drained of its original blood, and the qualities
conferred by the blood, then the day of its defeat will be the day of its death.
It has used up the time that heaven granted at its birth, for it has completely
changed its race, and with its race its nature. It is therefore degenerate.

In view of the preceding paragraph, we may regard as settled the vexed
question as to what would have happened if the Carthaginians, instead of
falling before the fortunes of Rome, had become masters of Italy. Inasmuch
as they belonged to the Phœnician stock, a stock inferior in the citizen-
virtues to the races that produced the soldiers of Scipio, a different issue of
the battle of Zama could not have made any change in their destiny. If they
had been lucky on one day, the next would have seen their luck recoil on their
heads; or they might have been merged in the Italian race by victory, as they
were by defeat. In any case the final result would have been exactly the same.
The destiny of civilizations is not a matter of chance; it does not depend on
the toss of a coin. It is only men who are killed by the sword; and when the
most redoubtable, warlike, and successful nations have nothing but valour in
their hearts, military science in their heads, and the laurels of victory in their
hands, without any thought that rises above mere conquest, they always end
merely by learning, and learning badly, from those they have conquered, how
to live in time of peace. The annals of the Celts and the Nomadic hordes of
Asia tell no other tale than this.

I have now given a meaning to the word *degeneration*; and so have been
able to attack the problem of a nation's vitality. I must next proceed to prove
what for the sake of clearness I have had to put forward as a mere hypothesis;

namely, that there are real differences in the relative value of human races. The consequences of proving this will be considerable, and cover a wide field. But first I must lay a foundation of fact and argument capable of holding up such a vast building; and the foundation cannot be too complete. The question with which I have just been dealing was only the gateway of the temple.

Note

1   This attachment of the Arab tribes to their racial unity shows itself sometimes in a very curious manner. A traveller (M. Fulgence Fresnel, I think) says that at Djiddah, where morals are very lax, the same Bedouin girl who will sell her favours for the smallest piece of money would think herself dishonoured if she contracted a legal marriage with the Turk or European to whom she contemptuously lends herself.

14

Considerations on Representative Government (1861)

John Stuart Mill

John Stuart Mill, ch. XVI, "Of Nationality, as Connected with Representative Government," from *Considerations on Representative Government* (1861) [source: John Stuart Mill, *Considerations on Representative Government*, ed. Currin V. Shields. Indianapolis, IN: Bobbs-Merrill Educational Publishing, 1958, 229–37]

Mill (1806–73) took his utilitarianism from the associationist psychology of his father (James) and from Bentham's calculus of the "greatest good for the greatest number." The former emphasized habituated mental associations, to the extent that virtue pursued for selfish ends could become a desired end in itself; the latter reduced moral and political truth to a quantification of pleasures and pains. Utilitarianism promoted radical reform, though Mill dissented from its sterner doctrines by asserting "that some *kinds* of pleasure are more desirable than others," and by reasserting the eighteenth-century sentimentalism of Shaftesbury and Hutcheson, for whom virtuous, sociable action could be a pleasure in itself. Mill's political philosophy, like his father's, accepted the ideas of popular sovereignty and parliamentary government. But, influenced by Tocqueville, Mill wished to constrain participatory democracy and majority rule through the restriction of legislative and executive power to appointed experts, plural voting for an intellectual and financial elite, and proportional representation. Moreover, government must suit the historically evolved aptitudes of the people: thus, China and India might never progress beyond despotism without Western intervention. Anticipating Renan, Mill favored racial hybrid vigor; a nation rests on "common sympathies" that may or may not be generated by race, language, or religion (though a common language would seem necessary). But "fellow-feeling" demands that "the boundaries of governments should coincide with those of nationalities."

Chapter XVI: Of Nationality, as Connected with Representative Government

A portion of mankind may be said to constitute a nationality if they are united among themselves by common sympathies which do not exist between them and any others – which make them co-operate with each other more willingly than with other people, desire to be under the same government, and desire that it should be government by themselves or a portion of themselves exclusively. This feeling of nationality may have been generated by various causes. Sometimes it is the effect of identity of race and descent. Community of language and community of religion greatly contribute to it. Geographical limits are one of its causes. But the strongest of all is identity of political antecedents: the possession of a national history, and consequent community of recollections; collective pride and humiliation, pleasure and regret, connected with the same incidents in the past. None of these circumstances, however, are either indispensable or necessarily sufficient by themselves. Switzerland has a strong sentiment of nationality, though the cantons are of different races, different languages, and different religions. Sicily has, throughout history, felt itself quite distinct in nationality from Naples, notwithstanding identity of religion, almost identity of language, and a considerable amount of common historical antecedents. The Flemish and the Walloon provinces of Belgium, notwithstanding diversity of race and language, have a much greater feeling of common nationality than the former have with Holland, or the latter with France. Yet in general the national feeling is proportionally weakened by the failure of any of the causes which contribute to it. Identity of language, literature, and, to some extent, of race and recollections have maintained the feeling of nationality in considerable strength among the different portions of the German name, though they have at no time been really united under the same government; but the feeling has never reached to making the separate states desire to get rid of their autonomy. Among Italians an identity, far from complete, of language and literature, combined with a geographical position which separates them by a distinct line from other countries, and, perhaps more than everything else, the possession of a common name, which makes them all glory in the past achievements in arts, arms, politics, religious primacy, science, and literature, of any who share the same designation, give rise to an amount of national feeling in the population which, though still imperfect, has been sufficient to produce the great events now passing before us,

notwithstanding a great mixture of races, and although they have never, in
either ancient or modern history, been under the same government except
while that government extended or was extending itself over the greater part
of the known world.

Where the sentiment of nationality exists in any force, there is a *prima facie*
case for uniting all the members of the nationality under the same government, and a government to themselves apart. This is merely saying that the
question of government ought to be decided by the governed. One hardly
knows what any division of the human race should be free to do if not to
determine with which of the various collective bodies of human beings they
choose to associate themselves. But when a people are ripe for free institutions, there is a still more vital consideration. Free institutions are next to
impossible in a country made up of different nationalities. Among a people
without fellow-feeling, especially if they read and speak different languages,
the united public opinion, necessary to the working of representative government, cannot exist. The influences which form opinions and decide
political acts are different in the different sections of the country. An altogether different set of leaders have the confidence of one part of the country
and of another. The same books, newspapers, pamphlets, speeches do not
reach them. One section does not know what opinions or what instigations
are circulating in another. The same incidents, the same acts, the same system
of government affect them in different ways; and each fears more injury
to itself from the other nationalities than from the common arbiter, the
state. Their mutual antipathies are generally much stronger than jealousy
of the government. That any one of them feels aggrieved by the policy of the
common ruler is sufficient to determine another to support that policy. Even
if all are aggrieved, none feel that they can rely on the others for fidelity in a
joint resistance; the strength of none is sufficient to resist alone, and each
may reasonably think that it consults its own advantage most by bidding for
the favor of the government against the rest. Above all, the grand and only
effectual security in the last resort against the despotism of the government is
in that case wanting: the sympathy of the army with the people. The military
are the part of every community in whom, from the nature of the case, the
distinction between their fellow countrymen and foreigners is the deepest
and strongest. To the rest of the people foreigners are merely strangers; to
the soldier, they are men against whom he may be called, at a week's notice,
to fight for life or death. The difference to him is that between friends and
foes – we may almost say between fellow men and another kind of animals;
for as respects the enemy, the only law is that of force, and the only mitiga-
tion the same as in the case of other animals – that of simple humanity.
Soldiers to whose feelings half or three-fourths of the subjects of the same
government are foreigners will have no more scruple in mowing them down,

and no more desire to ask the reason why, than they would have in doing the same thing against declared enemies. An army composed of various nationalities has no other patriotism than devotion to the flag. Such armies have been the executioners of liberty through the whole duration of modern history. The sole bond which holds them together is their officers and the government which they serve; and their only idea, if they have any, of public duty is obedience to orders. A government thus supported – by keeping its Hungarian regiments in Italy and its Italian in Hungary – can long continue to rule in both places with the iron rod of foreign conquerors.

If it be said that so broadly marked a distinction between what is due to a fellow countryman and what is due merely to a human creature is more worthy of savages than of civilized beings, and ought, with the utmost energy, to be contended against, no one holds that opinion more strongly than myself. But this object, one of the worthiest to which human endeavour can be directed, can never, in the present state of civilization, be promoted by keeping different nationalities of anything like equivalent strength under the same government. In a barbarous state of society the case is sometimes different. The government may then be interested in softening the antipathies of the races that peace may be preserved and the country more easily governed. But when there are either free institutions or a desire for them, in any of the peoples artificially tied together, the interest of the government lies in an exactly opposite direction. It is then interested in keeping up and envenoming their antipathies that they may be prevented from coalescing, and it may be enabled to use some of them as tools for the enslavement of others. The Austrian court has now for a whole generation made these tactics its principal means of government, with what fatal success, at the time of the Vienna insurrection and the Hungarian contest, the world knows too well. Happily there are now signs that improvement is too far advanced to permit this policy to be any longer successful.

For the preceding reasons, it is in general a necessary condition of free institutions that the boundaries of governments should coincide in the main with those of nationalities. But several considerations are liable to conflict in practice with this general principle. In the first place, its application is often precluded by geographical hindrances. There are parts even of Europe in which different nationalities are so locally intermingled that it is not practicable for them to be under separate governments. The population of Hungary is composed of Magyars, Slovaks, Croats, Serbs, Romanians, and in some districts Germans, so mixed up as to be incapable of local separation; and there is no course open to them but to make a virtue of necessity and reconcile themselves to living together under equal rights and laws. The community of servitude, which dates only from the destruction of Hungarian independence in 1849, seems to be ripening and disposing them for such an equal union. The German colony of East Prussia is cut off from Germany by part of the ancient Poland and, being too weak to maintain separate independence, must, if geographical continuity is to be maintained, be either under a non-German government or the intervening Polish territory must be under a German one. Another considerable region in which the dominant element of the population is German, the provinces of Kurland, Estonia, and Livonia, is condemned by its local situation to form part of a Slavonian state. In Eastern Germany itself there is a large Slavonic population: Bohemia is principally Slavonic, Silesia and other districts partially so. The most united country in Europe, France, is far from being homogeneous: independently of the fragments of foreign nationalities at its remote extremities, it consists, as language and history prove, of two portions, one occupied almost exclusively by a Gallo-Roman population, while in the other the Frankish, Burgundian, and other Teutonic races form a considerable ingredient.

When proper allowance has been made for geographical exigencies, another more purely moral and social consideration offers itself. Experience proves that it is possible for one nationality to merge and be absorbed in another; and when it was originally an inferior and more backward portion of the human race the absorption is greatly to its advantage. Nobody can suppose that it is not more beneficial to a Breton, or a Basque of French Navarre, to be brought into the current of the ideas and feelings of a highly civilized and cultivated people – to be a member of the French nationality, admitted on equal terms to all privileges of French citizenship, sharing the advantages of French protection and the dignity and prestige of French power – than to sulk on his own rocks, the half-savage relic of past times, revolving in his own little mental orbit, without participation or interest in the general movement of the world. The same remark applies to the Welshman or the Scottish Highlander as members of the British nation.

Whatever really tends to the admixture of nationalities and the blending of their attributes and peculiarities in a common union is a benefit to the human race. Not by extinguishing types, of which, in these cases, sufficient examples are sure to remain, but by softening their extreme forms and filling up the intervals between them. The united people, like a crossed breed of animals (but in a still greater degree, because the influences in operation are moral as well as physical), inherits the special aptitudes and excellences of all its progenitors, protected by the admixture from being exaggerated into the neighboring vices. But to render this admixture possible, there must be peculiar conditions. The combinations of circumstances which occur, and which affect the result, are various.

The nationalities brought together under the same government may be about equal in numbers and strength, or they may be very unequal. If unequal, the least numerous of the two may either be the superior in civilization, or the inferior. Supposing it to be superior, it may either, through that superiority, be able to acquire ascendancy over the other, or it may be overcome by brute strength and reduced to subjection. This last is a sheer mischief to the human race and one which civilized humanity with one accord should rise in arms to prevent. The absorption of Greece by Macedonia was one of the greatest misfortunes which ever happened to the world; that of any of the principal countries of Europe by Russia would be a similar one.

If the smaller nationality, supposed to be the more advanced in improvement, is able to overcome the greater, as the Macedonians, reinforced by the Greeks, did Asia, and the English India, there is often a gain to civilization; but the conquerors and the conquered cannot in this case live together under the same free institutions. The absorption of the conquerors in the less advanced people would be an evil; these must be governed as subjects, and the state of things is either a benefit or a misfortune, according as the subjugated people have or have not reached the state in which it is an injury not to be under a free government, and according as the conquerors do or do not use their superiority in a manner calculated to fit the conquered for a higher stage of improvement. This topic will be particularly treated of in a subsequent chapter.

When the nationality which succeeds in overpowering the other is both the most numerous and the most improved, and especially if the subdued nationality is small and has no hope of reasserting its independence, then, if it is governed with any tolerable justice and if the members of the more powerful nationality are not made odious by being invested with exclusive privileges, the smaller nationality is gradually reconciled to its position and becomes amalgamated with the larger. No Bas-Breton, nor even any Alsatian, has the smallest wish at the present day to be separated from France. If all Irish men have not yet arrived at the same disposition toward England, it is partly because they are sufficiently numerous to be capable of constituting a respectable nationality by themselves; but principally because, until of late years, they had been so atrociously governed that all their best feelings combined with their bad ones in rousing bitter resentment against the Saxon rule. This disgrace to England, and calamity to the whole empire, has, it may be truly said, completely ceased for nearly a generation. No Irishman is now less free than an Anglo-Saxon, nor has a less share of every benefit either to his country or to his individual fortunes than if he were sprung from any other portion of the British dominions. The only remaining real grievance of Ireland, that of the State Church, is one which half, or nearly half, the people of the larger island have in common with them. There is now next to nothing, except the memory of the past and the difference in the predominant religion, to keep apart two races, perhaps the most fitted of any two in the world to be the completing counterpart of one another. The consciousness of being at last treated not only with equal justice but with equal consideration is making such rapid way in the Irish nation as to be wearing off all feelings that could make them insensible to the benefits which the less numerous and less wealthy people must necessarily derive from being fellow citizens instead of foreigners to those who are not only their nearest neighbors, but the wealthiest and one of the freest as well as most civilized and powerful nations of the earth.

The cases in which the greatest practical obstacles exist to the blending of nationalities are when the nationalities which have been bound together are nearly equal in numbers and in the other elements of power. In such cases each, confiding in its strength and feeling itself capable of maintaining an equal struggle with any of the others, is unwilling to be merged in it; each cultivates with party obstinacy its distinctive peculiarities; obsolete customs, and even declining languages, are revived to deepen the separation; each deems itself tyrannized over if any authority is exercised within itself by functionaries of a rival race; and whatever is given to one of the conflicting nationalities is considered to be taken from all the rest. When nations thus divided are under a despotic government which is a stranger to all of them, or which, though sprung from one, yet feeling greater interest in its own power than in any sympathies of nationality, assigns no privilege to either nation and chooses its instruments indifferently from all, in the course of a few genera-tions identity of situation often produces harmony of feeling and the differ-ent races come to feel toward each other as fellow countrymen, particularly if they are dispersed over the same tract of country. But if the era of aspiration to free government arrives before this fusion has been effected, the oppor-tunity has gone by for effecting it. From that time, if the unreconciled nationalities are geographically separate, and especially if their local position is such that there is no natural fitness or convenience in their being under the same government (as in the case of an Italian province under a French or German yoke), there is not only an obvious propriety, but, if either freedom or concord is cared for, a necessity, for breaking the connection altogether. There may be cases in which the provinces, after separation, might usefully remain united by a federal tie; but it generally happens that if they are willing to forego complete independence and become members of a federation, each of them has other neighbors with whom it would prefer to connect itself, having more sympathies in common if not also greater community of inter-est.

15

Nationality (1862)

John Emerich Edward Dalberg-Acton

John Emerich Edward Dalberg-Acton, Lord Acton, selection from "Nationality" (1862) [source: John Emerich Edward Dalberg-Acton, Lord Acton, *The History of Freedom and Other Essays*. London: Macmillan and Co., 1909, 273–6, 288–91, 297–300]

A Roman Catholic opposed to the doctrine of papal infallibility, Acton (1834–1902) was educated in Paris, Edinburgh, and Munich, served as a Whig MP, and taught modern history at Cambridge. Starting from the premise that the rights of nationalities were neither recognized nor asserted in absolutist Europe before the eighteenth century, he emphasized (following Burke) the imperial partition of Poland in the later eighteenth century as a mistake that "awakened the theory of nationality...converting a dormant right into an aspiration." Acton further agreed with Burke that of the two forms of national liberty – the French of 1789, the English of 1688 – the latter, based on customs and constitutional traditions, was much the preferable. Acton argued, however, that the French model supplanted such traditions not with civic republicanism (as has often been claimed), but with an "ethno-logical" unit of descent, embodied in the general will, wholly distinct from representative government, and superior to the state. Thus, a "notion of abstract nationality" with no regard for political history was born. English liberty, by contrast, aimed to curb the power of the state resulting from despotism and revolution alike. Since each nation had different (and unequal) political customs and histories, Acton argued (contrary to Gobineau) that the multinational state (like the Austrian or British Empires) was a "necessary" condition of civilized life: it was the only arrangement by which "inferior races" were improved by their superiors and older, "exhausted" nations "revived by the contact of a younger vitality."

[. . .] In the old European system, the rights of nationalities were neither recognised by governments nor asserted by the people. The interest of the reigning families, not those of the nations, regulated the frontiers; and the administration was conducted generally without any reference to popular desires. Where all liberties were suppressed, the claims of national independence were necessarily ignored, and a princess, in the words of Fénelon, carried a monarchy in her wedding portion. The eighteenth century acquiesced in this oblivion of corporate rights on the Continent, for the absolutists cared only for the State, and the liberals only for the individual. The Church, the nobles, and the nation had no place in the popular theories of the age; and they devised none in their own defence, for they were not openly attacked. The aristocracy retained its privileges, and the Church her property; and the dynastic interest, which overruled the natural inclination of the nations and destroyed their independence, nevertheless maintained their integrity. The national sentiment was not wounded in its most sensitive part. To dispossess a sovereign of his hereditary crown, and to annex his dominions, would have been held to inflict an injury upon all monarchies, and to furnish their subjects with a dangerous example, by depriving royalty of its inviolable character. In time of war, as there was no national cause at stake, there was no attempt to rouse national feeling. The courtesy of the rulers towards each other was proportionate to the contempt for the lower orders. Compliments passed between the commanders of hostile armies; there was no bitterness, and no excitement; battles were fought with the pomp and pride of a parade. The art of war became a slow and learned game. The monarchies were united not only by a natural community of interests, but by family alliances. A marriage contract sometimes became the signal for an interminable war, whilst family connections often set a barrier to ambition. After the wars of religion came to an end in 1648, the only wars were those which were waged for an inheritance or a dependency, or against countries whose system of government exempted them from the common law of dynastic States, and made them not only unprotected but obnoxious. These countries were England and Holland, until Holland ceased to be a republic, and until, in England, the defeat of the Jacobites in the forty-five [Second Jacobite Rebellion, 1745–6] terminated the struggle for the Crown. There was one country, however, which still continued to be an exception; one monarch whose place was not admitted in the comity of kings.

Poland did not possess those securities for stability which were supplied by dynastic connections and the theory of legitimacy, wherever a crown could be obtained by marriage or inheritance. A monarch without royal blood, a crown bestowed by the nation, were an anomaly and an outrage in that age of dynastic absolutism. The country was excluded from the European system by the nature of its institutions. It excited a cupidity which could not be satisfied. It gave the reigning families of Europe no hope of permanently strengthening themselves by intermarriage with its rulers, or of obtaining it by bequest or by inheritance. The Habsburgs had contested the possession of Spain and the Indies with the French Bourbons, of Italy with the Spanish Bourbons, of the empire with the house of Wittelsbach, of Silesia with the house of Hohenzollern. There had been wars between rival houses for half the territories of Italy and Germany. But none could hope to redeem their losses or increase their power in a country to which marriage and descent gave no claim. Where they could not permanently inherit they endeavoured, by intrigues, to prevail at each election, and after contending in support of candidates who were their partisans, the neighbours at last appointed an instrument for the final demolition of the Polish State. Till then no nation had been deprived of its political existence by the Christian Powers, and whatever disregard had been shown for national interests and sympathies, some care had been taken to conceal the wrong by a hypocritical perversion of law. But the partition of Poland was an act of wanton violence, committed in open defiance not only of popular feeling but of public law. For the first time in modern history a great State was suppressed, and a whole nation divided among its enemies.

This famous measure, the most revolutionary act of the old absolutism, awakened the theory of nationality in Europe, converting a dormant right into an aspiration, and a sentiment into a political claim. "No wise or honest man," wrote Edmund Burke, "can approve of that partition, or can contemplate it without prognosticating great mischief from it to all countries at some future time" ["Observations on the Conduct of the Minority"]. Thenceforward there was a nation demanding to be united in a State, – a soul, as it were, wandering in search of a body in which to begin life over again; and, for the first time, a cry was heard that the arrangement of States was unjust – that their limits were unnatural, and that a whole people was deprived of its right to constitute an independent community. Before that claim could be efficiently asserted against the overwhelming power of its opponents, – before it gained energy, after the last partition, to overcome the influence of long habits of submission, and of the contempt which previous disorders had brought upon Poland, – the ancient European system was in ruins, and a new world was rising in its place. [...]

In pursuing the outward and visible growth of the national theory we are prepared for an examination of its political character and value. The absolutism which has created it denies equally that absolute right of national unity which is a product of democracy, and that claim of national liberty which belongs to the theory of freedom. These two views of nationality, corresponding to the French and to the English systems, are connected in name only, and are in reality the opposite extremes of political thought. In one case, nationality is founded on the perpetual supremacy of the collective will, of which the unity of the nation is the necessary condition, to which every other influence must defer, and against which no obligation enjoys authority, and all resistance is tyrannical. The nation is here an ideal unit founded on the race, in defiance of the modifying action of external causes, of tradition, and of existing rights. It overrules the rights and wishes of the inhabitants, absorbing their divergent interests in a fictitious unity; sacrifices their several inclinations and duties to the higher claim of nationality, and crushes all natural rights and all established liberties for the purpose of vindicating itself. Whenever a single definite object is made the supreme end of the State, be it the advantage of a class, the safety or the power of the country, the greatest happiness of the greatest number, or the support of any speculative idea, the State becomes for the time inevitably absolute. Liberty alone demands for its realisation the limitation of the public authority, for liberty is the only object which benefits all alike, and provokes no sincere opposition. In supporting the claims of national unity, governments must be subverted in whose title there is no flaw, and whose policy is beneficent and equitable, and subjects must be compelled to transfer their allegiance to an authority for which they have no attachment, and which may be practically a foreign domination. Connected with this theory in nothing except in the common enmity of the absolute state, is the theory which represents nationality as an essential, but not a supreme element in determining the forms of the State. It is distinguished from the other, because it tends to diversity and not to uniformity, to harmony and not to unity; because it aims not at an arbitrary change, but at careful respect for the existing conditions of political life, and because it obeys the laws and results of history, not the aspirations of an ideal future. While the theory of unity makes the nation a source of despotism and revolution, the theory of liberty regards it as the bulwark of self-government, and the foremost limit to the excessive power of the State. Private rights, which are sacrificed to the unity, are preserved by the union of nations. No power can so efficiently resist the tendencies of centralisation, of corruption, and of absolutism, as that community which is the vastest that can be included in a State, which imposes on its members a consistent similarity of character, interest, and opinion, and which arrests the action of the sovereign by the influence of a divided patriotism. The presence of different nations under the same sovereignty is similar in its effect to the independence of the Church in the State. It provides against the servility which flourishes under the shadow of a single authority, by balancing interests, multiplying associations, and giving to the subject the restraint and support of a combined opinion. In the same way it promotes independence by forming definite groups of public opinion, and by affording a great source and centre of political sentiments, and of notions of duty not derived from the sovereign will. Liberty provokes diversity, and diversity preserves liberty by supplying the means of organisation. All those portions of law which govern the relations of men with each other, and regulate social life, are the varying result of national custom and the creation of private society. In these things, therefore, the several nations will differ from each other; for they themselves have produced them, and they do not owe them to the State which rules them all. This diversity in the same State is a firm barrier against the intrusion of the government beyond the political sphere which is common to all into the social department which escapes legislation and is ruled by spontaneous laws. This sort of interference is characteristic of an absolute government, and is sure to provoke a reaction, and finally a remedy. That intolerance of social freedom which is natural to absolutism is sure to find a corrective in the national diversities, which no other force could so efficiently provide. The co-existence of several nations under the same State is a test, as well as the best security of its freedom. It is also one of the chief instruments of civilisation; and, as such, it is in the natural and providential order, and indicates a state of greater advancement than the national unity which is the ideal of modern liberalism.

The combination of different nations in one State is as necessary a condition of civilised life as the combination of men in society. Inferior races are raised by living in political union with races intellectually superior. Exhausted and decaying nations are revived by the contact of a younger vitality. Nations in which the elements of organisation and the capacity for government have been lost, either through the demoralising influence of despotism, or the disintegrating action of democracy, are restored and educated anew under the discipline of a stronger and less corrupted race. This fertilising and regenerating process can only be obtained by living under one government. It is in the cauldron of the State that the fusion takes place by which the vigour, the knowledge, and the capacity of one portion of mankind may be communicated to another. Where political and national boundaries coincide, society ceases to advance, and nations relapse into a condition corresponding to that of men who renounce intercourse with their fellow-men. The difference between the two unites mankind not only by the benefits it confers on those who live together, but because it connects society either by a political or a national bond, gives to every people an interest in its neighbours, either because they are under the same government or because they are of the same race, and thus promotes the interests of humanity, of civilisation, and of religion. [...]

The great importance of nationality in the State consists in the fact that it is the basis of political capacity. The character of a nation determines in great measure the form and vitality of the State. Certain political habits and ideas belong to particular nations, and they vary with the course of the national history. A people just emerging from barbarism, a people effete from the excesses of a luxurious civilisation, cannot possess the means of governing itself; a people devoted to equality, or to absolute monarchy, is incapable of producing an aristocracy; a people averse to the institution of private property is without the first element of freedom. Each of these can be converted into efficient members of a free community only by the contact of a superior race, in whose power will lie the future prospects of the State. A system which ignores these things, and does not rely for its support on the character and aptitude of the people, does not intend that they should administer their own affairs, but that they should simply be obedient to the supreme command. The denial of nationality, therefore, implies the denial of political liberty.

The greatest adversary of the rights of nationality is the modern theory of nationality. By making the State and the nation commensurate with each other in theory, it reduces practically to a subject condition all other nationalities that may be within the boundary. It cannot admit them to an equality with the ruling nation which constitutes the State, because the State would then cease to be national, which would be a contradiction of the principle of its existence. According, therefore, to the degree of humanity and civilisation in that dominant body which claims all the rights of the community, the inferior races are exterminated, or reduced to servitude, or outlawed, or put in a condition of dependence.

If we take the establishment of liberty for the realisation of moral duties to be the end of civil society, we must conclude that those states are substantially the most perfect which, like the British and Austrian Empires, include various distinct nationalities without oppressing them. Those in which no mixture of races has occurred are imperfect; and those in which its effects have disappeared are decrepit. A State which is incompetent to satisfy different races condemns itself; a State which labours to neutralise, to absorb, or to expel them, destroys its own vitality; a State which does not include them is destitute of the chief basis of self-government. The theory of nationality, therefore, is a retrograde step in history. It is the most advanced form of the revolution, and must retain its power to the end of the revolutionary period, of which it announces the approach. Its great historical importance depends on two chief causes.

First, it is a chimera. The settlement at which it aims is impossible. As it can never be satisfied and exhausted, and always continues to assert itself, it prevents the government from ever relapsing into the condition which provoked its rise. The danger is too threatening, and the power over men's minds too great, to allow any system to endure which justifies the resistance of nationality. It must contribute, therefore, to obtain that which in theory it condemns, – the liberty of different nationalities as members of one sovereign community. This is a service which no other force could accomplish; for it is a corrective alike of absolute monarchy, of democracy, and of constitutionalism, as well as of the centralisation which is common to all three. Neither the monarchical, nor the revolutionary, nor the parliamentary system can do this; and all the ideas which have excited enthusiasm in past times are impotent for the purpose except nationality alone.

And secondly, the national theory marks the end of the revolutionary doctrine and its logical exhaustion. In proclaiming the supremacy of the rights of nationality, the system of democratic equality goes beyond its own extreme boundary, and falls into contradiction with itself. Between the democratic and the national phase of the revolution, socialism had intervened, and had already carried the consequences of the principle to an absurdity. But that phase was passed. The revolution survived its offspring, and produced another further result. Nationality is more advanced than socialism, because it is a more arbitrary system. The social theory endeavours to provide for the existence of the individual beneath the terrible burdens which modern society heaps upon labour. It is not merely a development of the notion of equality, but a refuge from real misery and starvation. However false the solution, it was a reasonable demand that the poor should be saved from destruction; and if the freedom of the State was sacrificed to the safety of the individual, the more immediate object was, at least in theory, attained. But nationality does not aim either at liberty or prosperity, both of which it sacrifices to the imperative necessity of making the nation the mould and measure of the State. Its course will be marked with material as well as moral ruin, in order that a new invention may prevail over the works of God and the interests of mankind. There is no principle of change, no phase of political speculation conceivable, more comprehensive, more subversive, or more arbitrary than this. It is a confutation of democracy, because it sets limits to the exercise of the popular will, and substitutes for it a higher principle. It prevents not only the division, but the extension of the State, and forbids to terminate war by conquest, and to obtain a security for peace. Thus, after surrendering the individual to the collective will, the revolutionary system makes the collective will subject to conditions which are independent of it, and rejects all law, only to be controlled by an accident.

Although, therefore, the theory of nationality is more absurd and more criminal than the theory of socialism, it has an important mission in the world, and marks the final conflict, and therefore the end, of two forces which are the worst enemies of civil freedom, – the absolute monarchy and the revolution.

16

To the Italians (1871)

Giuseppe Mazzini

Giuseppe Mazzini, selection from "To the Italians" (1871) [source: Giuseppe Mazzini, *The Duties of Man and Other Essays*, trans. Thomas Okey. London: J. M. Dent, 1907, 234–41]

Born in Genoa, Mazzini (1805–72) was the most important theorist of nineteenth-century Italian nationalism, and he became a symbol of the nationalist intellectual (along with Garibaldi the soldier) throughout Europe at this time. An admirer of Dante and Byron, Mazzini promoted revolution to establish a unified and republican Italy beginning in the early 1820s. He founded the Young Italy movement, which Garibaldi would join, and spent much time in exile to avoid imprisonment and execution. In 1848, he returned to Milan to join the uprising against Austrian rule, but found only dissension between the republicans he supported and monarchists. The moderate Cavour prevailed and Victor Emmanuel II, son of the Piedmont king Charles Albert, was enthroned, though Mazzini continued to fight for a republic based in Rome until the French intervened. Mazzini's thought is in many ways a synthesis of nationalist ideas in the century before him. He unites Herder's populism and emphasis on tradition, Rousseau's civic republicanism (calling for a "National Contract"), Fichte's idealism ("the Government will be the *mind* of a Nation"), and Hegel's progressive universal history ("Nations are the individuals of Humanity") with a faith in the Christian God as the ultimate source of the unity and equality of humanity. Mazzini rejected the individualist, Protestant, *laissez-faire* character of English nationalism as well as the collective will, Catholicism, and controlled economy of European models in search of an ideal, utopian, republic: *"All things in Liberty and for Association."*

[...] To one who sees in a Nation something more than an aggregation of individuals born to produce and consume corn, the foundations of its life are, fraternity of faith, consciousness of a common *ideal*, and the association of all faculties to work in harmony and with success towards that ideal. You cannot make it believe that life and growth are possible in a never-ending dualism between its government and itself; that the temple of its worship can have *privilege* written on its *summit* and *equality* on its base; or that it can live, a useless member of the European family, abdicating every duty, every office, every mission for the good of others, concentrating all its activity on the petty interests of the individuals that compose it, without debasing its moral sense, its intelligence, the exercise of its faculties, or compassing its own destruction in loss of confidence, and apathy, and doubt. And we see the symptoms of this growing only too fast. The Italy of to-day is no longer the Italy of 1860. The masses, cheated of the vast hopes they entertained at one time of the benefits of Unity, are fast losing the national political sense, and lending an eager ear to the fatal whisperings of a federalist school that was dumb ten years ago. The middle class is becoming – as its abstention from the elections proves – more and more indifferent to the exercise of its political rights. The Chamber, part of it blindly subservient to government influence, part of it tied by the narrow formula which the Deputies swear, though they know it to be false and hurtful, has parted with its initiative, and is every day losing the importance that should belong to it. A feeling of torpor, the feeling of a man who sees no remedy for recurring dangers, infects men's minds with scepticism, and entices them from the public arena to the exclusive care of their own private concerns. What between the examples given in high places, and the logical consequences of the spread of materialism, which is partly the result of the Government's false tactics towards a dying religion, morality is losing its hold on the public mind. This is how Nations die, not how they are born.

It is high time to leave a policy of expedients, of opportunism, of entanglements and crooked ways, of parliamentary hypocrisy, concealment, and compromise, that characterises the languid life of worn-out nations, and return to the virgin, loyal, simple, logical policy that derives directly from a moral standard, that is the consequences of a ruling *principle* that has always inaugurated the young life of peoples that are called to high destinies.

The first condition of this life is the solemn declaration, made with the unanimous and free consent of our greatest in wisdom and virtue, that Italy, feeling the times to be ripe, rises with one spontaneous impulse, in the name of the Duty and Right inherent in a people, to constitute itself a Nation of free and equal brothers, and demand that rank which by right belongs to it among the Nations that are already formed. The next condition is the declaration of the body of religious, moral, and political *principles* in which the Italian people believes at the present day, of the common ideal to which it is striving, of the *special* mission that distinguishes it from other peoples and to which it intends to consecrate itself for its own benefit and for the benefit of Humanity. And the final condition is to determine the methods to be employed, and the men to whom the country should delegate the function of developing the national conception of life, and the application of its practical consequences to the manifold branches of social activity.

Without this, a *country* may exist, stumbling along from insurrection to insurrection, from revolution to revolution; but there cannot exist a NATION.

And these three conditions can only be fulfilled by a NATIONAL CON-TRACT, dictated in Rome by a constituent assembly elected by direct or indirect suffrage, and by all the citizens that Italy contains.

The National Contract is the inauguration, the baptism of the nation. It is the *initiative* that determines the normal life, the successive and peaceful development of the forces and faculties of the country. Without that initiative, which gives life to the exercise of the vote, and directs it to the common *ideal* under the guidance of a *principle* and a *moral* doctrine, even popular suffrage is at the mercy of arbitrary influence, or the passions of the day, or the false suggestions of ambitious agitators. Plebiscites taken under circumstances like these, the perverted and unenlightened expression of mere brute numbers, have, within the space of a few years, led, and will lead again, to a republic, a limited monarchy, and the despotism of a Bonaparte. Until a people is educated to uniformity and brotherhood, the initiative determines in every place and time the character of the solemn acts to which the masses are called.

Every one knows what is the form of government that we believe to be the logical deduction from the principles in which we believe, and from the national Italian tradition: we define it as *the development and application of a Nation's ideal, duly entrusted by the chosen of the Country to men of recognised capacity and proven virtue.* We hope to show in our publication how it is only by adopting this formula of government that Italy can escape an indefinite series of more or less fatal crises, and fulfil her destinies, great, prosperous, educated to virtue. Quite recently it was said to us by partisans of the government: "Write and discuss with us. Every way of public propaganda is open to you. Why is that not enough? We have a right to combat conspiracies and attempts at insurrection; but we will all respect the peaceful and philosophical expression of ideas." We reply once again to the invitation, and write. We have often attempted it, but the Government did not keep faith with its interpreters, and answered our statements, even when they only repeated the pages of History, by sequestrating our property, and prosecuting us, without any one protesting against its action.

Nevertheless, we make another attempt, if only to see whether the Government can ever learn wisdom, or if the men who gave this invitation will join us to protect liberty of thought. Our publication is frankly Republican, but it will not call to arms, or teach the people to rise, or provoke rebellions.

When Italians are once convinced they will act for themselves. We, who are ever ready to follow them by any means, or any paths that may lead, without crime, to the *ideal*, will use the present to meet the errors and prejudices which are constantly turning many minds from the idea that is the basis of our mission. When we undertake to discuss in theory the present and future condition of Italy, Italians will be able to gauge from the attitude of the Government towards us the measure of its conscientiousness and moral strength.

And we will, above all, meet the errors that proceed from our own camp, and degrade, and warp, or lessen the purity of our Ideal. Many of the accusations that come from the opposite camp do not merit any lengthy refutation. Those who even now speak of anarchy and feebleness as inseparable from republican institutions, we can meet with the miracles of progress and power recently performed by the United States, and the steady peace which reigns by the side of liberty in the valleys of Switzerland. Those who are not ashamed to cast in our teeth their childish suspicions of popular tyranny, or terrorism, or spoliation, we can answer with the names of Venice and Rome, and all that we have done or written during the last forty years. But the materialism that shatters the unity of human nature, and while it supplies us with an object, suppresses all the noble impulses, all the sacred beliefs that stimulate us to fulfil it, – the false philosophies that lead, consciously or unconsciously, to the worship of accomplished *facts*, and success, and Force, – the schools of politics and of economics that select a single instance from among the manifold integral terms of the social problem, and deduce from it the solution of all secondary problems, – the blind, servile copying of the old French Revolution, still rooted only too deeply in most of our hearts, that fetters us with theoretical formulas of *individual rights* which are but the summary expression of a dead age which we have abandoned for the *initiative* of the future age, – the excessive tendency to mete out the same blame, the same suspicion, so often unjust, to many who, like us, love the Fatherland, but are intellectually at fault as to method, that we mete to the few selfish schemers who, through thirst of lucre and power, consciously defile and betray the National Italian Revolution, – the narrow-mindedness that anathematises a grand and fruitful past out of hatred to a poor and feeble *present*, that falsifies History, that tries to deprive us of our glories, and denies the tradition which is the very life of Humanity, – all these deserve, and we will give them, an attentive and thorough examination. It is these and other errors brought to our Democracy from foreign schools of thought that have made the Italian intellect stray from the right path.

It is time to call it back from barren criticism to the National School, with its constructive methods, its tendencies to correlate and harmonise; from a materialism that presumes to understand, explain, determine motion while it destroys the motive power, to the old ever-present doctrine of the Spirit that harmonises motion and motor. As far as our powers permit we will try to accomplish this.

Only on this condition can our National Revolution be achieved. Blind revolts lead only to victories of a day. Simple negations can overthrow an old worn-out edifice; they never lay the foundations of a new one; they never win a people to organised and effective action, or build the Temple of the Nation.

Our party is faithful to the ideal of our country's Traditions, but ready to harmonise them with the Traditions of Humanity and the inspirations of conscience; it is tolerant and moral, and it must therefore now confute, without attacking or misconstruing motives. We need not fear that we are forging weapons for the enemy, if we declare the religions of the world to be successive expressions of a series of ages that have educated the human race; if we recognise the religious faculty as eternal in the human soul, eternal, too, the bond between heaven and earth. We can admire in Gregory VII. the gigantic energy of will, the sublime moral effort that could not be realised with the instrument that Christianity could lend, and, at the same time, in the name of the progress we have made, declare the Papacy to be for ever dead. We can recognise the Mission which Aristocracy and Monarchy had for other peoples in the past, and yet proclaim, for all of us, the duty and the right to outstrip those worn-out forms. We may, without denying the reverence due to Authority – for that is the real object of all our efforts – claim the task of attacking every Authority that is not based on two conditions – the free and enlightened consent of the governed, and the power of directing the national life and making it fruitful.

We believe in God.

In a providential Law given by Him to life.

In a Law, not of the *Atonement*, not of the *Fall*, and *Redemption* by the *grace* of past or present mediators between God and *man*, but of PROGRESS, unlimited Progress, founded on, and measured by, our works.

In the *Unity* of Life, misunderstood, as we believe, by the Philosophy of the last two centuries.

In the *Unity* of the Law through both the manifestations of Life, *collective* and *individual*.

In the immortality of the *Ego*, which is nothing but the application of the Law of PROGRESS, revealed beyond doubt now and for ever by Historical Tradition, by Science, by the aspirations of the soul, to the Life that is manifested in the individual.

In Liberty, by which alone exists responsibility, the consciousness and price of *progress*.

In the successive and increasing *association* of all human faculties and powers, as the sole normal means of *progress*, at once collective and individual.

In the *Unity* of the human race, and in the moral *equality* of all the children of God, without distinction of sex, colour, or condition, to be forfeited by *crime* alone.

And hence we believe in the holy, inexorable, dominating idea of DUTY, the sole standard of Life. *Duty* that embraces in each one, according to the sphere in which he moves and the means that he possesses, Family, Fatherland, Humanity. Family the altar of the Fatherland; Fatherland the sanctuary of Humanity; Humanity a part of the Universe, and a temple built to God, who created the Universe, that it might draw near to Him. *Duty*, that bids us promote the progress of others that our own may be effected, and of ourselves that it may profit that of others. *Duty*, without which no *right* exists, that creates the virtue of self-sacrifice, in truth the only pure virtue, holy and mighty in power, the noblest jewel that crowns and hallows the human soul.

And finally, we believe, not in the doctrines of the present day, but in a great religious manifestation founded upon these principles, that sooner or later will arise from the initiative of a people of freemen and believers – perhaps from Rome if Rome knows her mission – and which, while it includes that chapter of Truth that former religions won, will reveal yet another chapter, and will open the road to future progress, destroying in their germ all privilege and intolerance of caste. [. . .]

17

What is a Nation? (1882)

Ernest Renan

Ernest Renan, "What is a Nation?" (1882) [source: Ernest Renan, *The Poetry of the Celtic Races, and Other Studies*, trans. William G. Hutchison. London: Walter Scott, 1896, 61–83]

Breton by birth, philologist and historian, Renan (1823–92) wrote influential studies on the origins of Christianity, following German critical biblical scholarship, and on Orientalist themes, such as his histories of the Semitic languages and the people of Israel. His writing was marked by the distinction between the inorganic and inferior Semitic tongues and the organic, regenerative Indo-European languages inherited from earlier comparative philologists like Jones, Friedrich Schlegel, and Bopp, as well as by Romantic views (from Herder to Hess) that differentiated rational Hellenes from spiritual Hebrews. Such oppositions dominated Renan's early work: the Semites appeared (like their language) to be simple and narrow-minded. But even his late work on the history of the Jews argued that Indo-European civilization excelled intellectually, politically, and militarily – and was hence obligated to guide and revitalize inferior or degenerate races – while Semitic culture developed religious belief. Renan distinguished, however, between his philological use of the word "race," meaning nothing more than a linguistic group, and the anthropologist's usage, which denoted blood relationship and descent. In "What is a Nation?" he challenged the assumption that physiological race is represented by a single language, and separated both biological and linguistic notions of race (along with religion, economy, and geography) from the idea of a nation. Stressing cultural memory and will alone, Renan helped shape the modern scholarly discussion of the nation-state.

I propose to analyse with you an idea, simple in appearance, but capable of the most dangerous misunderstanding. The forms of human society are of the most varied types. Great conglomerations of people, as in the case of China, of Egypt, of ancient Babylon; the tribe, as in the case of the Hebrews and the Arabs; the city, as in the case of Athens and Sparta; unions of different countries, in the fashion of the Empire of Achæmenes, the Roman Empire, or the Carlovingian Empire; communities of no country, held together by the bond of religion, like the Israelites or the Parsees; nations like France, England, and the majority of modern European autonomies; confederations, as in the case of Switzerland and America; relationships similar to those which race and, in a greater degree, language establish between the different branches of the Teutonic family, the different branches of the Slavs; – these are modes of grouping which all exist, or at least have existed, and which cannot be confounded, the one with the other, without the most serious inconvenience. At the time of the French Revolution there was a belief that the institutions of small independent towns, such as Sparta and Rome, could be applied to our great nations of thirty or forty millions of souls. In our own day a still graver error is committed: the race is confounded with the nation, and to racial, or rather to linguistic groups, is attributed a sovereignty analogous to that of really existent peoples. Let us attempt to arrive at some precision in these difficult questions, where the least confusion in the sense of words, at the beginning of the discussion, may produce in the end the most fatal errors. What we are about to undertake is a delicate task; it is almost vivisection. We are to deal with living men, as, under ordinary circumstances, the dead alone are treated. In doing so we shall use coolness, and the most absolute impartiality.

I

Since the end of the Roman Empire, or rather since the disruption of the Empire of Charlemagne, Western Europe appears to us divided into nations, of which some, at certain epochs, have sought to exercise a supremacy over others, without any lasting success. What Charles V., Louis XIV., and Napoleon I. were unable to do in the past, is hardly likely to be achieved by any one in the future. The establishment of a new Roman Empire, or a new Carlovingian Empire, has become an impossibility. Europe is too deeply divided for an attempt at universal dominion not to provoke, and that quickly, a coalition which would force the ambitious nation to retire within its natural bounds. A species of equilibrium has long been in existence. France, England, Germany, and Russia will still be, in centuries to come, and in spite of the vicissitudes they will have gone through, historic individualities, essential pieces of a chess-board, the squares of which vary unceasingly in importance and greatness, but are never altogether confused.

Nations, understood in this way, are a new feature in history. Antiquity knew them not; Egypt, China, ancient Chaldea, were to no extent nations. There were flocks led by a son of the Sun, or a son of Heaven. There were no Egyptian citizens, as there are no Chinese citizens. Classical antiquity had republics, and municipal kingdoms, confederations of neighbouring republics, and empires; it scarcely had the nation, in the sense in which we understand it. Athens, Sparta, Sidon, and Tyre were little centres of admirable patriotism; but they were cities with a comparatively restricted territory. Gaul, Spain, and Italy, before their absorption in the Roman Empire, were clusters of peoples, often in league with one another, but unpossessed of central institutions or dynasties. Nor were even the Assyrian Empire, the Persian Empire, or that of Alexander, nations. There were never Assyrian patriots; the Persian Empire was one vast feudality. Not a single nation traces its origin to the colossal enterprise of Alexander, which was nevertheless so pregnant with consequences for the general history of civilisation.

The Roman Empire was much nearer to being a nation. In return for the immense boon of the cessation of wars, the Roman dominion, at first so painful, was very quickly loved. It was a great association, synonymous with order, peace, and civilisation. In the later days of the Empire there was among the greater minds, among enlightened bishops, and among the lettered, a genuine feeling for "the Roman Peace," as opposed to the menacing chaos of barbarism. But an Empire twelve times greater in extent than the France of the present day could not form a state in the modern acceptance of the term. The severance of East and West was inevitable. The attempts at a Gaulish Empire in the third century were unsuccessful. It was the Teutonic invasion that introduced into the world the principle which, later, served as a basis to the existence of nationalities.

What, in fact, were those Teutonic peoples doing, from their great invasions of the fifth century to the last Norman conquests in the tenth? They changed the essential character of races only slightly; but they imposed dynasties and a military aristocracy upon more or less considerable portions of the former Empire of the West, which took the name of their invaders. Thence arose a France, a Burgundy, a Lombardy – later still, a Normandy. The rapid preponderance assumed by the Frankish Empire revived for a moment the unity of the West; but that Empire was shattered irremediably towards the middle of the ninth century, the treaty of Verdun traced divisions immutable in principle; and thenceforward France, Germany, England, Italy, and Spain journeyed by ways, often circuitous, and through a thousand vicissitudes, to their full national existence, such as we see flourishing to-day.

What, then, is the characteristic feature of these different states? It consists in the fusion of the populations which compose them. In the countries that we have just enumerated, there is nothing analogous to what you will find in

Turkey, where the Turk, the Slav, the Greek, the Armenian, the Arab, the Syrian, and the Kurd are as distinct now as on the day of their conquest. Two essential circumstances contributed to bring this result to pass. First of all is the fact, that the Teutonic tribes adopted Christianity as soon as they had had relations of some little duration with the Greek and Latin peoples. When conqueror and conquered are of the same religion, or rather when the conqueror adopts the religion of the conquered, the Turkish system, the absolute distinction of men according to their respective faiths, can no longer be possible. The second circumstance was the conquerors' forgetfulness of their own language. The grandsons of Clovis, of Alaric, of Gondebaud, of Alboin, and of Rollo were already speaking Romance. This fact was itself the consequence of another important peculiarity, namely, that the Franks, the Burgundians, the Goths, the Lombards, and the Normans had very few women of their own race with them. For several generations the chiefs espoused only Teutonic women; but their concubines were Latin, the nurses of their children were Latin; the whole tribe married Latin women. And so it was that the *Lingua Francica* and the *Lingua Gothica* had a very short existence, after the settlement of the Franks and Goths in Roman territories. The same was not the case in England, for there can be no doubt that the Anglo-Saxon invaders had women with them; the ancient British population took to flight; and, moreover, Latin was no longer dominant in Britain, indeed it had never been so. Even if Gaulish had been generally spoken in Gaul in the fifth century, Clovis and his followers would not have abandoned Teutonic for it.

From this ensues the important fact, that in spite of the extreme violence of the manners of the Teutonic invaders, the mould that they imposed became, in the course of centuries, the very mould of the nation. France, very legitimately, came to be the name of a country into which only an imperceptible minority of Franks had entered. In the tenth century, in the earliest *Chansons de Geste*, which are such a perfect mirror of the spirit of the age, all the inhabitants of France are Frenchmen. The idea of a difference of races in the population of France, that is so apparent in Gregory of Tours, is not present to any extent in the French writers and poets, posterior to Hugh Capet.

The difference between noble and serf is as accentuated as it well can be; but in no respect is the difference an ethnical one; it is a difference in courage, in habits, and in hereditarily transmitted education. The idea, that the beginning of it all may be a conquest, does not occur to anybody. The fictitious theories, according to which nobility owed its origin to a privilege, conferred by the king for great services rendered to the state, to such an extent that all nobility is an acquisition, were established as a dogma in the thirteenth century. The same thing was the sequel of nearly all the Norman conquests. At the end of one or two generations, the Norman invaders were no longer to be distinguished from the rest of the population. Their influence had not been the less profound; to the conquered land they had given a nobility, warlike habits, and a patriotism hitherto unexistent.

Forgetfulness, and I shall even say historical error, form an essential factor in the creation of a nation; and thus it is that the progress of historical studies may often be dangerous to the nationality. Historical research, in fact, brings back to light the deeds of violence that have taken place at the commencement of all political formations, even of those the consequences of which have been most beneficial. Unity is ever achieved by brutality. The union of Northern and Southern France was the result of an extermination, and of a reign of terror that lasted for nearly a hundred years. The king of France who was, if I may say so, the ideal type of a secular crystalliser, the king of France who made the most perfect national unity in existence, lost his prestige when seen at too close a distance. The nation that he had formed cursed him; and to-day the knowledge of what he was worth, and what he did, belongs only to the cultured.

It is by contrast that these great laws of the history of Western Europe become apparent. In the undertaking which the King of France, in part by his tyranny, in part by his justice, achieved so admirably, many countries came to disaster. Under the crown of St. Stephen, Magyars and Slavs have remained as distinct as they were eight hundred years ago. Far from combining the different elements in its dominions, the house of Hapsburg has held them apart, and often opposed to one another. In Bohemia the Czech element and the German element are superimposed like oil and water in a glass. The Turkish policy of separation of nationalities according to religion has had much graver results. It has brought about the ruin of the East. Take a town like Smyrna or Salonica; you will find there five or six communities, each with its own memories, and possessing among them scarcely anything in common. But the essence of a nation is, that all its individual members should have many things in common; and also, that all of them should hold many things in oblivion. No French citizen knows whether he is a Burgundian, an Alan, or a Visigoth; every French citizen ought to have forgotten St. Bartholomew, and the massacres of the South in the thirteenth century. There are not ten families in France able to furnish proof of a French origin; and yet, even if such a proof were given, it would be essentially defective, in consequence of a thousand unknown crosses, capable of deranging all genealogical systems.

The modern nation is then the historical result of a series of events, converging in the same direction. Sometimes unity has been achieved by a dynasty, as in the case of France; sometimes by the direct will of the provinces, as in the case of Holland, Switzerland, and Belgium; sometimes by a general feeling slowly vanquishing the caprices of feudality, as in the case of

Italy and Germany. But a profound *raison d'être* has always governed these formations. The principles in such cases come to light in the most unexpected ways. In our own times we have seen Italy united by her defeats, and Turkey destroyed by her victories. Every defeat advanced the cause of Italy, every victory was a loss to Turkey; for Italy is a nation, Turkey, outside Asia Minor, is not. It is the glory of France to have proclaimed by the French Revolution that a nation exists by itself. We ought not to complain because we find ourselves imitated. Ours is the principle of nations. But what then is a nation? Why is Holland a nation, while Hanover or the Grand Duchy of Parma is not? How does France persist in being a nation, when the principle which created her has disappeared? How is Switzerland, with three languages, two religions, and three or four races, a nation, while Tuscany, for example, which is homogeneous, is not? Why is Austria a state and not a nation? In what respect does the principle of nationality differ from the principle of races? These are the points upon which a reflective mind must be fixed, if it is to find a satisfactory solution. The affairs of the world are scarcely regulated by such reasoning; but serious students wish to carry into such matters a certain amount of reason, and to unravel the confusions in which superficial minds entangle themselves.

II

In the opinion of certain political theorists a nation is, before all else, a dynasty representing an ancient conquest, a conquest first accepted and then forgotten by the mass of the people. According to the politicians of whom I speak, the grouping of provinces effected by a dynasty, by its wars, by its marriages, or by its treaties, comes to an end with the dynasty which has formed it. It is very true that the majority of modern nations owe their existence to a family of feudal origin, which contracted a marriage with the soil, and was in some measure a nucleus of centralisation. There was nothing natural or necessary about the boundaries of France in 1789. The large zone that the house of Capet added to the narrow limits of the Treaty of Verdun, was in every sense the personal acquisition of that house. At the time when the annexations were made, there was no idea of natural frontiers, or of the rights of nations, or of the will of the provinces. The union of England, Ireland, and Scotland was in like manner a dynastic act. The reason for Italy delaying so long in becoming a nation was that no one of her numerous reigning houses, before the present century, made itself the centre of unity. And it is a strange thing that it is from the obscure island of Sardinia, from territory scarcely Italian, that she has taken a royal title. Holland, which created herself by an act of heroic resolution, has nevertheless contracted a marriage with the house of Orange, and would run real dangers on the day of that union's being compromised.

But is such a law as this absolute? Certainly not. Switzerland and the United States, conglomerations formed by successive additions, have no dynastic base. I shall not discuss the question with regard to France. It would be necessary to have the secret of the future. Let us only say that the great royal house of France had been so highly national, that, on the morrow of its fall, the nation was able to stand without its support. And then the eighteenth century had changed everything. Man had returned, after centuries of abasement, to the old spirit, to self-respect, to the idea of his rights. The words "country" and "citizen" had resumed their significance. Thus it was that the boldest operation ever attempted in history was accomplished – an operation which might be compared to what in physiology would be the gift of life and its first identity, to a body from which head and heart had been removed.

It must then be admitted that a nation can exist without a dynastic principle; and even that nations formed by dynasties can separate themselves from them without, for that reason, ceasing to exist. The old principle, which held account of no right but that of princes, can no longer be maintained; above the dynastic right there is the national right. On what foundation shall we build up this national right, by what sign shall we know it, from what tangible fact shall we derive it?

(I) From race, say several with assurance. Artificial divisions resulting from feudality, royal marriages, or diplomatic congresses, are unstable. What does remain firm and fixed is the race of populations. That it is which constitutes right and legitimacy. The Teutonic family, for example, according to this theory, has the right of reclaiming such of its members as are beyond the pale of Teutonism – even when these members do not seek reunion. The right of Teutonism over such a province is greater than the right of the inhabitants of the province over themselves. Thus is created a kind of primordial right, analogous to that of the divine right of kings; for the principle of nations is substituted that of ethnography. This is a very grave error, which, if it became dominant, would cause the ruin of European civilisation. So far as the national principle is just and legitimate, so far is the primordial right of races narrow, and full of danger for true progress.

It may be admitted that, in the tribe and the city of antiquity, the fact of race had an importance of the highest order. But the ancient tribe and city were only extensions of the family. In Sparta and in Athens all the citizens were more or less closely related. It was the same in the Beni-Israel, it is so to this day among the Arab tribes. From Athens, from Sparta, from the Israelite tribe, let us now turn to the Roman Empire. The situation is altogether different. Founded by violence, then maintained by self-interest, this great agglomeration of towns, and altogether diverse provinces, dealt a blow of the gravest kind to the idea of race. Christianity, with its universal and absolute character, tended still more efficiently in the same direction. It entered into a close alliance with the Roman Empire, and the effect of those two incomparable agents of unity was to banish ethnographical reason for centuries from the government of human affairs.

The barbarian invasion was, despite appearances, a step further in the same direction. There was nothing racial in the division of barbaric kingdoms; they were governed by the force or the caprice of the invaders. The race of the populations that they subjugated was, for them, a matter of the greatest indifference. Charlemagne achieved again, in his own way, what Rome had achieved already: a single empire composed of the most diverse races. The authors of the Treaty of Verdun, when they traced imperturbably their two great lines from North to South, had not the slightest care for the race of the peoples on either side. The changes of frontier, which took place later than the Middle Ages, were also free from all racial considerations. If the continuous policy of the house of Capet succeeded in grouping together, under the name of France, almost all the territories of ancient Gaul, we do not have there an effect of the tendencies that those countries should have had, to rejoin their own congeners. The Dauphiny, Bresse, Provence, the Franche-Comté, no longer had memories of a common origin. All Gaulish feeling had perished in the second century of our era; and it is only by the eyes of erudition that, in our own days, the individuality of the Gaulish character has been retrospectively found once more.

Racial considerations have then been for nothing in the constitution of modern nations. France is Celtic, Iberian, Teutonic. Germany is Teutonic, Celtic, and Slavonic. Italy is the country where ethnography is most confused. Gauls, Etruscans, Pelasgians, and Greeks, to say nothing of many other elements, are crossed in an undecipherable medley. The British Isles, as a whole, exhibit a mixture of Celtic and Teutonic blood, the relative proportions of which it is singularly difficult to define.

The truth is that there is no pure race; and that making politics depend upon ethnographical analysis, is allowing it to be borne upon a chimæra. The most noble countries, England, France, Italy, are those where blood is most mingled. Is Germany an exception to this rule? Is she purely Teutonic? What an illusion is this! The whole of the South was once Gaulish. The whole of the East beyond the Elbe is Slavonic. And what, in point of fact, are the parts alleged to be really pure? Here we touch on one of the problems concerning which it is most important to have our ideas clear, and to avoid misunderstandings.

Discussions upon race are interminable, because the word "race" is taken by the philological historians and by physiological anthropologists in two totally different senses. For the anthropologists race has the same meaning as it has in zoology; it indicates a real descent, a relationship by blood. But the study of languages and history does not lead to the same classifications as physiology. The words *Brachycephalus* and *Dolichocephalus* have no place in history or philology. In the human group, that created the Aryan languages and customs, there were already *Brachycephali* and *Dolichocephali*. The same must be said of the primitive group, that created the languages and institutions known as Semitic. In other words, the zoological origins of humanity are enormously anterior to the origins of culture, civilisation, and language. The primitive Aryan, primitive Semitic, and primitive Tauranian groups, had no physiological unity. These groupings are historical facts which took place at a certain epoch – let us say fifteen or twenty thousand years ago – while the zoological origin of man is lost in incalculable mystery. What is philologically and historically called the Teutonic race, is assuredly a very distinct family of the human species. But is it a family in the anthropological sense? Certainly not; the appearance of the Teutonic individuality in history only took place a very few centuries before the Christian era. Apparently the Teutons had not emerged from the earth up to that time. Before it, mingled as they were with the Slavs in the great indistinct mass of the Scythians, they had no individuality of their own. An Englishman is a distinct type in the aggregate of humanity. But the type of what is very improperly called the Anglo-Saxon race[1] is neither the Briton of the time of Cæsar, nor the Anglo-Saxon of Hengist, nor the Dane of Knut, nor the Norman of William the Conqueror; it is the product of them all. The Frenchman is neither a Gaul, nor a Frank, nor a Burgundian. He is that which has come out of the great caldron, where, under the governance of the King of France, the most various elements have fermented together. An inhabitant of Jersey or Guernsey differs in nothing, as regards origin, from the Norman population of the neighbouring coast. In the eleventh century, the most penetrative vision could not have detected the slightest difference between the two sides of the channel. From insignificant circumstances, it happened that Philip Augustus did not take these islands with the rest of Normandy. Separated for nearly seven hundred years, the two populations have become, not only foreign to one another, but unlike in every respect. Race, as we historians understand it, is then something that makes and unmakes itself. The study of race is of capital importance to the student who occupies himself with the history of mankind. It has no application in politics. The instinctive consciousness which presided over the construction of the map of Europe took no account of race; and the greatest European nations are nations of essentially mixed blood.

Racial facts then, important as they are in the beginning, have a constant tendency to lose their importance. Human history is essentially different from zoology. Race is not everything, as it is in the case of the rodents and felines; and we have no right to go about the world feeling the heads of people, then taking them by the throat, and saying, "You are of our blood; you belong to us!" Beyond anthropological characteristics there are reason, justice, truth, and beauty; and these are the same in all. Nay, this ethnographical politics is not even safe. You exploit it to-day on other people; some day you may see it turned against yourselves. Is it certain that the Germans, who have raised the flag of ethnography so high, will not see the Slavs coming to analyse in their turn the names of villages in Saxony and Lusatia, to seek for traces of the Wilzen or the Obotrites, and to ask account of the massacres and slavery which their ancestors suffered at the hands of the Othos? It is good for all to know how to forget. I have a great liking for ethnography; it is a science of rare interest; but because I wish to see it free, I wish it to be without political application. In ethnography, as in all studies, systems change; it is the condition of progress. Should then nations change with the systems also? If so, the frontiers of states would follow the fluctuations of science. Patriotism would depend on a more or less paradoxical dissertation. They would come to the patriot and say, "You are deceived; you have been shedding your blood for such and such a cause; you believed yourself to be a Celt, while, as a matter of fact, you are a Teuton." And then, ten years afterwards, they would come and tell him that he was a Slav. To avoid falsifying science, let us abstain from giving advice upon these problems, in which so many interests are involved. You may be sure that if science is charged with the duty of furnishing the elements of diplomacy, it will be, in many cases, found to be in the gravest error. It has better work to do; let us simply demand of it the truth.

(II) What we have been saying about race must also be said of language. Language invites re-union; it does not force it. The United States and England, Spanish America and Spain, speak the same languages, and do not form single nations. On the contrary, Switzerland, which owes her stability to the fact that she was founded by the assent of her several parts, counts three or four languages. In man there is something superior to language, – will. The will of Switzerland to be united, in spite of the variety of her languages, is a much more important fact than a similarity of language, often obtained by persecution.

It is an honourable fact for France, that she has never sought to procure unity of speech by measures of coercion. Can we not have the same feelings and thoughts, and love the same things in different languages? We were speaking just now of the inconvenience of making international politics depend on ethnography. There would not be less in making politics depend on comparative philology. Let us allow the fullest liberty of discussion to these interesting studies; do not let us mingle them with that which would affect their serenity. The political importance attached to languages results from the way in which they are regarded as signs of race. Nothing can be more incorrect. Prussia, where nothing but German is now spoken, spoke Slavonic a few centuries ago; Wales speaks English; Gaul and Spain speak the primitive idiom of Alba Longa; Egypt speaks Arabic; indeed, examples are innumerable. Even at the beginning similarity of speech did not imply similarity of race. Let us take the proto-Aryan or proto-Semitic tribe; there were to be found slaves accustomed to speak the same language as their masters; but nevertheless the slave was then very often of a different race from that of his master. Let us repeat it; these classifications of the Indo-European, Semitic, and other tongues, created with such admirable sagacity by comparative philology, do not coincide with the classifications of anthropology. Languages are historical formations, which give but little indication of the blood of those who speak them; and, in any case, cannot enchain human liberty, when there is a question of determining the family with which we unite ourselves for life and death.

The exclusive consideration of language has, like the unduly great attention given to race, its dangers and its drawbacks. When we thus exaggerate it, we imprison ourselves in a limited culture, held as being national; we are hemmed in, cooped up. We quit the great atmosphere that we breathe in the vast field of humanity, to shut ourselves up in conventicles of compatriots. Nothing can be worse for the mind, nothing more hurtful to civilisation. Do not let us abandon this fundamental principle, that man is a reasonable and moral being before being allotted to such and such a language, before being a member of such and such a race, an adherent of such and such a culture. Before French culture, German culture, Italian culture, there is human culture. Consider the great men of the Renaissance; they were neither French, nor Italian, nor German. They had found anew, by their intercourse with antiquity, the secret of the true education of the human mind; to it they devoted themselves body and soul; and they did well!

(III) Nor can religion offer a sufficient basis for the establishment of a modern nationality. In the beginning religion was essential to the very existence of the social group. The social group was an extension of the family. Religious rites were family rites. The Athenian religion was the cult of Athens itself, of its mythical founders, of its laws and customs. It implied no dogmatic theology. This religion was in every sense of the term a State religion. If any one refused to practise it, he was no longer an Athenian. In reality it was the worship of the personified Acropolis. To swear on the altar of Agraulos was to take an oath to die for one's country. This religion was the equivalent of what drawing lots for military service, or the cult of the flag, is among us. To refuse to participate in such a worship was like a refusal of military service in our modern societies. It was a declaration that one was not an Athenian.

From another point of view, it is clear that such a religion had no force for any one who was not an Athenian; and thus no proselytism was exercised to compel aliens to accept it. The slaves in Athens did not practise it. The same thing held good in some small mediæval republics. A man was not a good Venetian if he did not swear by St. Mark; he was not a good citizen of Amalfi if he did not place St. Andrew above all the other saints of Paradise. In those small communities tyranny, which in later days meant persecution, was legitimate, and of as little consequence as our own fashion of keeping the birthday of the father of the family, and addressing our good wishes to him on New Year's day.

What was right at Sparta and Athens was already no longer so in the kingdoms that originated in Alexander's conquest; above all, was no longer right in the Roman Empire. The persecutions of Antiochus Epiphanes, for the purpose of forcing the worship of the Olympian Jupiter on the East, those of the Roman Empire for the purpose of keeping up a pseudo-State religion, were a mistake, a crime, a veritable absurdity. In our own days the position is perfectly clear. No longer are there masses of people professing a uniform belief. Every one believes and practises after his own fashion, what he can, as he pleases. The state-religion is a thing of the past. One can be a Frenchman, an Englishman, or a German; and at the same time be a Catholic, a Protestant, or a Jew, or else be of no creed at all. Religion has become a matter for the individual; it affects the individual's conscience alone. The division of nations into Catholic and Protestant no longer exists. Religion, which fifty-two years ago was so considerable an element in the formation of Belgium, retains all its importance in the spiritual jurisdiction of each man; but it has almost completely disappeared from the considerations that trace the limits of peoples.

(IV) Community of interests is assuredly a powerful bond between men. But nevertheless can interests suffice to make a nation? I do not believe it. Community of interests makes commercial treaties. There is a sentimental side to nationality; it is at once body and soul; a *Zollverein* is not a fatherland.

(V) Geography, or what we may call natural frontiers, certainly plays a considerable part in the division of nations. Geography is one of the essential factors of history. Rivers have carried races forward; mountains have checked them. The former have favoured, the latter limited, historic movements. Can it be said, however, that, as certain persons believe, the boundaries of a nation are inscribed upon the map; and that this nation has a right to judge what is necessary, to round off certain contours, to reach some mountain or river, to which a species of *a priori* faculty of limitation is ascribed? I know of no doctrine more arbitrary, or more disastrous. By it all violence is justified. First, let us ask, do mountains or rivers constitute these so-called natural frontiers? It is incontestable that mountains separate; but, on the other hand, rivers unite. And then all mountains cannot cut off states. Which are those that separate, and those that do not separate? From Biarritz to the Tornea there is not a single river-estuary which, more than another, has the character of a boundary. Had history required it, the Loire, the Seine, the Meuse, the Elbe, and the Oder would have, to the same extent as the Rhine, that character of a natural frontier which has caused so many infractions of the fundamental right, – the will of men. Strategical considerations are mooted. Nothing is absolute; it is clear that many concessions must be made to necessity. But these concessions need not go too far. Otherwise the whole world would claim its military conveniences; and there would be war without end. No, it is no more the land than the race that makes a nation. The land provides the *substratum*, the field of battle and work; man provides the soul. Man is everything in the formation of that sacred thing which we call a people. Nothing of a material nature suffices for it. A nation is a spiritual principle, the result of profound historical complications, a spiritual family, not a group determined by the configuration of the soil. We have now seen what do not suffice for the creation of such a spiritual principle; race, language, interests, religious affinity, geography, military necessities. What more, then, is necessary?

III

A nation is a living soul, a spiritual principle. Two things, which in truth are but one, constitute this soul, this spiritual principle. One is in the past, the other in the present. One is the common possession of a rich heritage of memories; the other is the actual consent, the desire to live together, the will to preserve worthily the undivided inheritance which has been handed down. Man does not improvise. The nation, like the individual, is the outcome of a long past of efforts, and sacrifices, and devotion. Ancestor-worship is therefore all the more legitimate; for our ancestors have made us what we are. A heroic past, great men, glory, – I mean glory of the genuine kind, – these form the social capital, upon which a national idea may be founded. To have common glories in the past, a common will in the present; to have done great things together, to will to do the like again, – such are the essential conditions for the making of a people. We love in proportion to the sacrifices we have consented to make, to the sufferings we have endured. We love the house that we have built, and will hand down to our descendants. The Spartan hymn, "We are what you were; we shall be what you are," is in its simplicity the national anthem of every land.

In the past an inheritance of glory and regrets to be shared, in the future a like ideal to be realised; to have suffered, and rejoiced, and hoped together;

all these things are worth more than custom-houses in common, and frontiers in accordance with strategical ideas; all these can be understood in spite of diversities of race and language. I said just now, "to have suffered together," for indeed suffering in common is a greater bond of union than joy. As regards national memories, mournings are worth more than triumphs; for they impose duties, they demand common effort.

A nation is then a great solidarity, constituted by the sentiment of the sacrifices that its citizens have made, and of those that they feel prepared to make once more. It implies a past; but it is summed up in the present by a tangible fact – consent, the clearly expressed desire to live a common life. A nation's existence is – if you will pardon the metaphor – a daily plebiscite, as the individual's existence is a perpetual affirmation of life. I know very well that this is less metaphysical than divine right, less brutal than pseudo-historic right. In the order of ideas that I submit to you, a nation has no more right than a king to say to a province, "Thou art mine; I take thee unto myself." For us, a province means its inhabitants; and if any one has a right to be consulted in such an affair, it is the inhabitants. A nation never favours its true interests when it annexes or retains a country, regardless of the latter's wishes. The will of nations is then the only legitimate criterion; and to it we must always return.

We have banished from politics metaphysical and theological abstractions. What still remains? There remains man, his desires and his needs. Dismemberment, you will tell me, and, in the long run, natural decay, are the consequences of a system that puts those old organisms at the mercy of wills that are often little enlightened. It is clear that, in such a matter, no principle ought to be pushed to excess. Truths of this order are only applicable when taken as a whole, and in a very general way. Human wills change, but is there here on earth anything changeless? The nations are not something eternal. They have had their beginnings, they shall have their end. A European confederation will probably take their place. But such is not the law of the age in which we live. At the present hour, the existence of nations is good, even necessary. Their existence is the guarantee of liberty, which would be lost if the world had but one law and one master.

By their diverse and often antagonistic faculties, the nations take part in the common work of civilisation; each brings a note to that great chorus of humanity, which in sum is the highest ideal reality to which we attain. Isolated, their parts are feeble. I often tell myself that an individual who should have the faults regarded by nations as good qualities, who should feed himself with vain glory, who should be in the same way jealous, egoistical, and quarrelsome, who should be able to bear nothing without drawing the sword, would be the most unsupportable of men. But all these discords of detail disappear in the mass. Poor humanity, how much thou hast suffered!

How many trials await thee still! May the spirit of wisdom be thy guide, and preserve thee from the countless perils with which thy path is sown!

But to resume: man is neither enslaved by his race, nor by his language, nor by his religion, nor by the course of rivers, nor by the direction of mountain ranges. A great aggregation of men, sane of mind, and warm of heart, creates a moral consciousness, which is called a nation. So far as this moral consciousness proves its strength, through the sacrifices exacted by the individual's abdication for the good of the community, it is legitimate and has a right to exist. If doubts arise concerning frontiers, consult the populations in dispute. They have a very good right to have a voice in the matter. This no doubt will bring a smile to the transcendentalists of politics, those infallible beings who pass their lives in self-deception, and from the height of their superior principles look down in pity upon our modest views. "Consult the populations, indeed! What artlessness! These are the pitiful French ideas, which would replace diplomacy and war by an infantine simplicity." Let us wait; let us suffer the reign of the transcendentalists to pass away; let us know how to submit to the disdain of the strong. It may be that after much unfruitful groping the world will return to our modest empirical solutions. At certain times, the way to be right in the future consists in knowing how to resign ourselves to being out of the fashion in the present.

Note

1   The Teutonic element is not much more considerable in the United Kingdom than it was in France, at the time when she possessed Alsace and Metz. The Teutonic tongue dominated in the British Isles, simply because Latin had not entirely supplanted the Celtic idioms, as it had done among the Gauls.

18

Our America (1891)

José Martí

José Martí, "Our America" (1891) [source: *The America of José Martí: Selected Writings of José Martí*, trans. Juan de Onís. New York: Funk and Wagnalls, 1954, 138–51]

Martí (1853–95) was born in Cuba and exiled to Spain (attending university there), lived briefly in Mexico and Guatemala, and settled after 1880 in New York, where he wrote journalism and poetry that would help found Spanish-American *Modernismo*. Martí was killed in a failed expedition to liberate Cuba (not independent until 1902) from Spain, which abandoned its colony in the aftermath of the Spanish-American War. His writing appeared in newspapers from Buenos Aires and Caracas to Mexico City and New York. Like Bolívar, whom he admired, Martí linked national identity to a conception of the entire continent's cultural unity. But unlike his predecessor, Martí had a lively sense of the "mute Indian masses"; he believed that the foreign intellect and "false erudition" of the Creole had been conquered by the "natural men" of the Indian race, and that "the uncultured will govern." In this, Martí is close to Herder and Montesquieu: "The spirit of the government must be the same as that of the country. The form of government must conform to the natural constitution of the country." Even European learning must give way to the history of America, "from the Incas to the present." Martí was also guided by Catholicism: thus, "with the rosary as our guide," and "under the standard of the Virgin," the peoples of Spanish America would enter the community of nations in the spirit of democracy and love. Martí's warnings about the hegemonic ambition of the United States (the "blond nation of the continent") were pointed. As he noted, "the day of the visit is at hand."

The villager fondly believes that the world is contained in his village, and he thinks the universal order good if he can be mayor, humiliate the rival who stole his sweetheart, or add to the savings in his sock – unaware of the giants with seven-league boots who can crush him under foot, or the strife in the heavens between comets, which streak through space, devouring worlds. What remains of the parochial in America must awake. These are not times for sleeping in a nightcap, but rather with weapons for a pillow, like the warriors of Juan de Castellanos: weapons of the mind, which conquer all others. Barricades of ideas are worth more than barricades of stone.

There is no prow that can cleave a cloud-bank of ideas. An energetic idea, unfurled in good season before the world, turns back a squadron of ironsides with the power of the mystic banner of the judgement day. Nations that do not know one another should make haste to do so, as brothers-in-arms. Those who shake their fists at each other, like jealous brothers who covet the same land, or the cottager who envies the squire his manor, should clasp hands until they are one. Those who allege the sanction of a criminal tradition to lop off the lands of their brother, with a sword dipped in his own blood, had best return the lands to the brother punished far beyond his due, if they do not want to be called thieves. The honorable do not seek money in satisfaction of debts of honor, at so much a slap. We can no longer be a people like foliage, living in the air, heavy with blossoms, bursting and fluttering at the whim of light's caress, or buffeted and tossed by the tempest: the trees must form ranks so the giant with seven-league boots shall not pass! It is the hour of muster and the united march. We must advance shoulder-to-shoulder, one solid mass like the silver lodes in the depths of the Andes.

Only the seven-month birthling will lack the courage. Those who do not have faith in their country are seven-month men. They cannot reach the first limb with their puny arms, arms with painted nails and bracelets, arms of Madrid or Paris; and they say the lofty tree cannot be climbed. The ships must be loaded with these destructive insects, who gnaw the marrow of the country that nourishes them. If they are Parisians or Madrilenians, let them stroll along the Prado under the lamplights, or take sherbet at Tortoni's. These carpenter's sons who are ashamed of their father for his trade! These American sons who are ashamed of the mother that loves them because she wears an Indian apron, and disown their sick mother, the scoundrels, abandoning her on her sick bed! Well, who is the man worthy of the name? The one who stays with his mother to nurse her in her sickness, or the one who puts her to work out of the sight of the world and lives off her labors in the decadent lands, affecting fancy cravats, cursing the womb that carried him, displaying the sign of traitor on the back of his paper cassock? These children of our America, which will be saved by its Indians, and goes from less to more, these deserters who take up arms in the armies of North America, which drowns its Indians in blood, and goes from more to less! These delicate beings, who are men but do not want to do the work of men! The Washington who forged this land, did he go to live with the English, to live with them during the years in which he saw them coming against his own country? These *incroyables* of their honor, who trail it through alien lands, like their counterparts in the French Revolution, with their dancing, their affectations, their drawling speech!

For in what lands can a man take greater pride than in our long-suffering republics of America, raised up from among the mute Indian masses by the bleeding arms of a hundred apostles to the sounds of battle between the book and the thurible. Never in history have such advanced and unified nations been forged in less time from such disordered elements. The fool in his pride believes that the earth was created to serve him as a pedestal because words flow easily from his pen, or his speech is colorful, and he charges his native land with being worthless and beyond salvation because its virgin jungles do not provide him with means to travel continually abroad, driving Persian ponies and lavishing champagne, like a tycoon. The incapacity does not lie with the nascent country, which seeks suitable forms and greatness that will serve, but with those who attempt to rule nations of a unique character, and singular, violent composition, with laws that derive from four centuries of operative liberty in the United States, and nineteen centuries of French monarchy. A decree by Hamilton does not halt the charge of the *llanero*'s pony. A phrase of Sieyès does nothing to quicken the stagnant blood of the Indian race. One must see things as they are, to govern well; the good governor in America is not one who knows how government is conducted in France or Germany, but who knows the elements of which his country is composed and how they can be marshaled so that by methods and institutions native to the country the desirable state may be attained wherein every man realizes himself, and all share in the abundance that Nature bestowed for the common benefit on the nation they enrich with their labor and defend with their lives. The government must be the child of the country. The spirit of the government must be the same as that of the country. The form of government must conform to the natural constitution of the country. Good government is nothing more than the true balance between the natural elements of the nation.

For that reason, the foreign book has been conquered in America by the natural man. The natural men have vanquished the artificial, lettered men. The native-born half-breed has vanquished the exotic Creole. The struggle is not between barbarity and civilization, but between false erudition and nature. The natural man is good. He respects and rewards superior intelligence, as long as his submission is not turned against him, or he is not offended by being disregarded, a thing the natural man does not forgive, prepared as he is to regain by force the respect of whoever has wounded his pride or threatened his interests. Tyrants in America have risen to power serving these scorned natural elements, and have fallen the moment they betrayed them. Republics have paid in tyrannies for their inability to recognize the true elements of their countries, to derive from them the proper form of government, and govern accordingly. To be a governor of a new country means to be a creator.

In nations of cultured and uncultured elements, the uncultured will govern, because it is their habit to strike and resolve all doubts by force, whenever the cultured prove incapable in office. The uncultured mass is lazy, and timed in matters of the mind. It asks only to be well-governed. But if the government hurts it, it rebels and governs itself. How can the universities be expected to produce governors, if there is not one university in America that teaches the rudimentary in the art of government, which is the analysis of the elements peculiar to America? Young men go out into the world wearing Yankee or French spectacles, and hope to govern by guesswork a nation they do not know. In the political race, all entries should be scratched who do not demonstrate a knowledge of the political rudiments. The prize in literary contests should go not to the best ode, but to the best study of the political factors in one's country. Newspapers, universities, and schools should foment the study of their country's dynamic factors. They have only to be stated, straightforward and in plain language. For whoever disregards any portion of the truth, whether by ignorance or design, is doomed to fall; the truth he lacked grows in the negligence and brings down whatever was erected without it. It is easier to determine the elements and attack the problem, than to attack the problem without knowing the elements. The natural man arrives, indignant and strong, and topples the authority based on books because he was not governed according to the obvious realities of the country. Knowledge holds the key. To know one's country, and govern it with that knowledge, is the only alternative to tyranny. The European university must give way to the American university. The history of America, from the Incas to the present, must be taught until it is known by heart, even if the Archons of the Greeks go by the board. Our Greece must take priority over the Greece that is not ours: we need it more. Nationalist statesmen must replace cosmopolitan statesmen. Let the world be grafted on our republics; but the trunk must be our own. And let the vanquished pedant hold his tongue: for there are no lands in which a man can take greater pride than in our long-suffering American republics.

With the rosary as our guide, our head white and our body mottled, both Indian and Creole, we intrepidly entered the community of nations. We set out to conquer liberty under the standard of the Virgin. A priest, a handful of lieutenants, and a woman raised the Mexican Republic on the shoulders of the Indians. A few heroic students, instructed in French liberty by a Spanish cleric, raised Central America against Spain under a Spanish general. In the oriflammed habits of monarchy, Venezuelans and Argentinians set out, from north and south, to deliver nations. When the two heroes collided, and the continent almost rocked, one, and not the lesser, turned back. But when the wars ended, heroism, by being less glorious, became rarer; it is easier for men to die with honor than to think with order. It was discovered that it is simpler to govern when sentiments are exalted and united, than in the wake of battle when divisive, arrogant, exotic, and ambitious ideas emerge. The forces routed in the epic conflict sought, with the feline cunning of their species, and utilizing the weight of realities, to undermine the new structure, which embraced at once the rude and singular provinces of our half-breed America, and the cities of silken hose and Parisian frock coat, beneath the unfamiliar flag of reason and liberty, borrowed from nations skilled in the arts of government. The hierarchical constitution of the colonies resisted the democratic organization of the republics. The capitals of stock and collar kept the countryside of horse-hide boots cooling its heels in the vestibule. The cultured leaders did not realize that the revolution had triumphed because their words had unshackled the soul of the nation, and that they had to govern with that soul, and not against it or without it. America began to suffer, and still suffers, from the effort of trying to find an adjustment between the discordant and hostile elements it inherited from a despotic and perverse colonizer, and the imported ideas and forms which have retarded the logical government because of their lack of local reality. The continent, disjointed by three centuries of a rule that denied men the right to use their reason, embarked on a form of government based on reason, without thought or reflection on the unlettered hordes which had helped in its redemption; it was to be the reason of all in matters of general concern, not the reason of the university over the reason of the province. The problem of the Independence was not the change in forms, but the change in spirit.

It was necessary to make common cause with the downtrodden, to secure the new system against the interests and habits of rule of the oppressors. The tiger, frightened off by the powder flash, returns at night to the haunts of his prey. When he dies, it is with flames shooting from his eyes and claws unsheathed. But his step cannot be heard, for he comes on velvet paws. When the prey awakes, the tiger is upon him. The colony lives on in the republic; and our America is saving itself from its grave errors – the arrogance of the capital cities, the blind triumph of the scorned country people, the influx of foreign ideas and formulas, the wicked and unpolitic disdain in which the aboriginal race is held – through the superior virtue, backed by the necessary conviction, of the republic that struggles against the colony. The tiger lurks behind each tree, waiting at every turn. He will die with his claws unsheathed and flames shooting from his eyes.

But "these countries will be saved," as the Argentine Rivadavia announced, whose sin was to be gentlemanly in crude times; a silk scabbard does not become the *machete*, nor can the lance be discarded in a country won by the lance, for it becomes angry, and presents itself at the door of Iturbide's congress demanding that "the blond one be made emperor." These countries will be saved because a genius for moderation, found in Nature's imperturbable harmony, seems to prevail in the continent of light, where there emerges a new realistic man schooled for these realistic times in the critical philosophy, which in Europe has succeeded the literature of sect and opinion in which the previous generation was steeped.

We were a strange sight with the chest of an athlete, the hands of a coxcomb, and the brain of a child. We were a masquerade in English trousers, Parisian vest, North American jacket, and Spanish hat. The Indian circled about us in silent wonder, and went to the mountains to baptize his children. The runaway Negro poured out the music of his heart on the night air, alone and unknown among the rivers and wild beasts. The men of the land, the creators, rose up in blind indignation against the scornful city, against their own child. We were all epaulets and tunics in countries that came into the world with hemp sandals on their feet and headbands for hats. The stroke of genius would have been to couple the headband and tunic with the charity of heart and daring of the founding father; to rescue the Indian; to make a place for the able Negro; to fit liberty to the body of those who rose up and triumphed in its name. We were left with the judge, the general, the scholar and the prebendary. As if caught in the tentacles of an octopus, the angelic young men lunged toward Heaven, only to fall back, crowned with clouds, in sterile glory. The natural people, driven by instinct, swept away the golden staffs of office in blind triumph. The European or Yankee book could not provide the answer to the Hispanic-American enigma. Hate was tried, and the countries wasted away, year by year. Exhausted by the senseless struggle between the book and the lance, of reason against dogma, of the city against the country, of the impossible rule by rival city cliques over the natural nation alternately tempestuous and inert, we begin almost without realizing it to try love. The nations stand up and salute each other. "What are we like?" they ask; and they begin to tell one another what they are like. When a problem arises in Cojimar, they do not send to Danzig for the answer. The frock coat is still French, but thought begins to be American. The youth of America roll up their sleeves and plunge their hands into the dough; it rises with the leavening of their sweat. They understand that there is too much imitation, and that creation holds the key to salvation. "Create" is the password of this generation. The wine is from plantain, and if it proves sour, it is our wine! It is understood that the forms of government must accommodate themselves to the natural elements of the country, that absolute ideas must take relative forms if they are to escape emasculation by the failure of the form, that liberty, if it is to be viable, must be sincere and complete, that the republic which does not open its arms to all, and move ahead with all, must die. The tiger within enters through the fissure, and the tiger from without. The general restrains his cavalry to a pace that suits his infantry, for if the infantry be left behind, the cavalry is surrounded by the enemy. Politics is strategy. Nations should live in continual self-criticism, because criticism is healthy; but always with one heart and one mind. Go down to the unfortunate and take them in your arms! Dissolve what is clotted in America with the fire of the heart! Make the natural blood of the nations course and throb through their veins! Erect, with the happy, sparkling eyes of workingmen, the new Americans salute one another from country to country. The natural statesman appears, schooled in the direct study of Nature. He reads to apply what he reads, not to copy. Economists study the problems at their origin. Orators begin to be lofty. Dramatists bring native characters to the stage. Academies consider practical subjects. Poetry shears off its romantic locks and hangs its red vest on the glorious tree. Prose, lively and discriminating, is charged with ideas. Governors study Indian in republics of Indians.

America is escaping all its dangers. The octopus still sleeps on some republics; but others, in contrast, drain the ocean from their lands with a furious, sublime haste, as if to make up for lost centuries. Some, forgetting that Juárez rode in a mule-drawn coach, hitch their coach to the wind and entrust the reins to a soap-bubble; poisonous luxury, the enemy of liberty, corrupts the frivolous and opens the door to the outlander. In others, where independence is threatened, an epic spirit produces a heightened manliness. Still others spawn a rabble-in-arms in rapacious wars against their neighbors which may yet turn and devour them. But there is yet another danger which does not come from within, but from the difference in origins, methods and interests between the two halves of the continent. The hour is fast approaching when our America will be confronted by an enterprising and energetic nation seeking close relations, but with indifference and scorn for us and our ways. And since strong countries, self-made by the rifle and the law, love, and love only, strong countries; since the hour of recklessness and ambition, of which North America may be freed if that which is purest in her blood predominates, or on which she may be launched by her vengeful and sordid masses, her tradition of expansion or the ambition of some powerful leaders, is not so near at hand, even to the most timorous eye, that there is not time to show the self-possessed and unwavering pride that would confront and dissuade her; since her good name as a republic in the eyes of the world puts on the America of the North a brake which cannot be removed even by the puerile grievances, the pompous arrogance, or parricidal discords of our American nations, the pressing need for our America, is to show herself as she is, one in soul and purpose, swift conqueror of a suffocating tradition, stained only by the blood drawn from hands that struggle to clear away ruins, and the scars left us by our masters. The scorn of our formidable neighbor, who does not know us, is the greatest danger for our America; and it is imperative that our neighbor know us, and know us soon, so she shall not scorn us, for the day of the visit is at hand. Through ignorance, she might go so far as to lay hands on us. From respect, once she came to know us, she would remove her hands. One must have faith in the best in men and distrust the worst. If not, the worst prevails. Nations should have a pillory for whoever fans useless hates; and another for whoever does not tell them the truth in time.

There can be no racial hate, because there are no races. The rachitic thinkers and theorists juggle and warm over the library-shelf races, which the open-minded traveler and well-disposed observer seek in vain in Nature's justice, where the universal identity of man leaps forth from triumphant love and the turbulent lust for life. The soul emanates, equal and eternal, from bodies distinct in shape and color. Whoever foments and propagates antagonism and hate between races, sins against Humanity. But as nations take shape among other different nations, they acquire distinctive and vital characteristics of thought and habit, of expansion and conquest, of vanity and greed, which from the latent state of national preoccupation could be converted in a period of internal unrest, or precipitation of the accumulated character of the nation, into a serious threat to the neighboring countries, isolated and weak, which the strong country declares perishable and inferior. The thought is father to the deed. But it must not be supposed, from a parochial animus, that there is a fatal and ingrained evil in the blond nation of the continent, because it does not speak our tongue, nor see the world as we do, nor resemble us in its political faults, which are of a different order, nor favorably regard the excitable, dark-skinned people, nor look charitably, from its still uncertain eminence, on those less favored by History, who climb the road of republicanism by heroic stages. The self-evident facts of the problem should not be obscured for it can be resolved, to the benefit of peaceful centuries yet to come, by timely study and the tacit, immediate union of the continental soul. The hymn of oneness sounds already; the actual generation carries a purposeful America along the road enriched by their sublime fathers; from the Rio Grande to the straits of Magellan, the Great Semi [pre-Columbian Taíno deity], seated on the flank of the condor, sows the seed of the new America through the romantic nations of the continent and the sorrowful islands of the sea!

19

The Jewish State (1896)

Theodor Herzl

Theodor Herzl, selection from the Introduction to *The Jewish State* (1896) [source: Theodor Herzl, *The Jewish State*, trans. Sylvie d'Avigdor and Jacob Alkow. New York: Dover Publications, 1988, 75–80]

Born in Budapest into a family with assimilationist views, Herzl (1860–1904) attended a Reform temple as a boy, studied law in Vienna, and became a journalist in Paris. Though confronted with rising anti-Semitism in Europe and with anti-Semitic writers like Dühring and Drumont, Herzl initially rejected Zionism as a "childish" wish for a homeland, where Jews would find themselves separated by diverse nationalities and united only by external pressures. He thus first conceived the "Jewish question" to be a social (rather than national, or religious) question, one that could be solved by tolerance and understanding. But the Dreyfus affair in France forced him to recognize the deeper roots of anti-Semitism. Out of that experience came his plan for a Jewish State, now based on the belief that, because true assimilation will always be thwarted, the Jewish question is indeed a national one. His claim that the Jews are "one people" whose "distinctive nationality...neither can, will, nor must be destroyed" was received with enthusiasm among Eastern European Jews, but met with some resistance in Western Europe: assimilationists feared it would only spark new distrust of the Jews, while the religiously orthodox considered it impious. Herzl still maintained that it was the Jews' "external enemies," not race or even religion, that made them into a unified nation. But he now vaguely echoed the views of Moses Hess and treated the Jews as a *Volk* in the German Romantic sense, a people whose spirit was destined to be housed in one territory (he briefly considered Argentina and Uganda as alternatives to Palestine) and governed by one state.

[. . .] The Jewish question still exists. It would be foolish to deny it. It is a remnant of the Middle Ages, which civilized nations do not even yet seem able to shake off, try as they will. They certainly showed a generous desire to do so when they emancipated us. The Jewish question exists wherever Jews live in perceptible numbers. Where it does not exist, it is carried by Jews in the course of their migrations. We naturally move to those places where we are not persecuted, and there our presence produces persecution. This is the case in every country, and will remain so, even in those highly civilized – for instance, France – until the Jewish question finds a solution on a political basis. The unfortunate Jews are now carrying the seeds of Anti-Semitism into England; they have already introduced it into America.

I believe that I understand Anti-Semitism, which is really a highly complex movement. I consider it from a Jewish standpoint, yet without fear or hatred. I believe that I can see what elements there are in it of vulgar sport, of common trade jealousy, of inherited prejudice, of religious intolerance, and also of pretended self-defence. I think the Jewish question is no more a social than a religious one, notwithstanding that it sometimes takes these and other forms. It is a national question, which can only be solved by making it a political world-question to be discussed and settled by the civilized nations of the world in council.

We are a people – one people.

We have honestly endeavored everywhere to merge ourselves in the social life of surrounding communities and to preserve the faith of our fathers. We are not permitted to do so. In vain are we loyal patriots, our loyalty in some places running to extremes; in vain do we make the same sacrifices of life and property as our fellow-citizens; in vain do we strive to increase the fame of our native land in science and art, or her wealth by trade and commerce. In countries where we have lived for centuries we are still cried down as strangers, and often by those whose ancestors were not yet domiciled in the land where Jews had already had experience of suffering. The majority may decide which are the strangers; for this, as indeed every point which arises in the relations between nations, is a question of might. I do not here surrender any portion of our prescriptive right, when I make this statement merely in my own name as an individual. In the world as it now is and for an indefinite period will probably remain, might precedes right. It is useless, therefore, for us to be loyal patriots, as were the Huguenots who were forced to emigrate. If we could only be left in peace. . . .

But I think we shall not be left in peace.

Oppression and persecution cannot exterminate us. No nation on earth has survived such struggles and sufferings as we have gone through. Jew-baiting has merely stripped off our weaklings; the strong among us were invariably true to their race when persecution broke out against them. This attitude was most clearly apparent in the period immediately following the emancipation of the Jews. Those Jews who were advanced intellectually and materially entirely lost the feeling of belonging to their race. Wherever our political well-being has lasted for any length of time, we have assimilated with our surroundings. I think this is not discreditable. Hence, the statesman who would wish to see a Jewish strain in his nation would have to provide for the duration of our political well-being; and even a Bismarck could not do that.

For old prejudices against us still lie deep in the hearts of the people. He who would have proofs of this need only listen to the people where they speak with frankness and simplicity: proverb and fairy-tale are both Anti-Semitic. A nation is everywhere a great child, which can certainly be educated; but its education would, even in most favorable circumstances, occupy such a vast amount of time that we could, as already mentioned, remove our own difficulties by other means long before the process was accomplished.

Assimilation, by which I understood not only external conformity in dress, habits, customs, and language, but also identity of feeling and manner – assimilation of Jews could be effected only by intermarriage. But the need for mixed marriages would have to be felt by the majority; their mere recognition by law would certainly not suffice.

The Hungarian Liberals, who have just given legal sanction to mixed marriages, have made a remarkable mistake which one of the earliest cases clearly illustrates; a baptized Jew married a Jewess. At the same time the struggle to obtain the present form of marriage accentuated distinctions between Jews and Christians, thus hindering rather than aiding the fusion of races.

Those who really wished to see the Jews disappear through intermixture with other nations, can only hope to see it come about in one way. The Jews must previously acquire economic power sufficiently great to overcome the old social prejudice against them. The aristocracy may serve as an example of this, for in its ranks occur the proportionately largest numbers of mixed marriages. The Jewish families which regild the old nobility with their money become gradually absorbed. But what form would this phenomenon assume in the middle classes, where (the Jews being a bourgeois people) the Jewish question is mainly concentrated? A previous acquisition of power could be synonymous with that economic supremacy which Jews are already erroneously declared to possess. And if the power they now possess creates rage and indignation among the Anti-Semites, what outbreaks would such an increase of power create? Hence the first step towards absorption will never be taken, because this step would involve the subjection of the majority to a hitherto scorned minority, possessing neither military nor administrative power of its own. I think, therefore, that the absorption of Jews by means of their prosperity is unlikely to occur. In countries which now are Anti-Semitic my view will be approved. In others, where Jews now feel comfortable, it will probably be violently disputed by them. My happier coreligionists will not believe me till Jew-baiting teaches them the truth; for the longer Anti-Semitism lies in abeyance the more fiercely will it break out. The infiltration of immigrating Jews, attracted to a land by apparent security, and the ascent in the social scale of native Jews, combine powerfully to bring about a revolution. Nothing is plainer than this rational conclusion.

Because I have drawn this conclusion with complete indifference to everything but the quest of truth, I shall probably be contradicted and opposed by Jews who are in easy circumstances. Insofar as private interests alone are held by their anxious or timid possessors to be in danger, they can safely be ignored, for the concerns of the poor and oppressed are of greater importance than theirs. But I wish from the outset to prevent any misconception from arising, particularly the mistaken notion that my project, if realized, would in the least degree injure property now held by Jews. I shall therefore explain everything connected with rights of property very fully. Whereas, if my plan never becomes anything more than a piece of literature, things will merely remain as they are. It might more reasonably be objected that I am giving a handle to Anti-Semitism when I say we are a people – one people; that I am hindering the assimilation of Jews where it is about to be consummated, and endangering it where it is an accomplished fact, insofar as it is possible for a solitary writer to hinder or endanger anything.

This objection will be especially brought forward in France. It will probably also be made in other countries, but I shall answer only the French Jews beforehand, because these afford the most striking example of my point.

However much I may worship personality – powerful individual personality in statesmen, inventors, artists, philosophers, or leaders, as well as the collective personality of a historic group of human beings, which we call a nation – however much I may worship personality, I do not regret its disappearance. Whoever can, will, and must perish, let him perish. But the distinctive nationality of Jews neither can, will, nor must be destroyed. It cannot be destroyed, because external enemies consolidate it. It will not be destroyed; this is shown during two thousand years of appalling suffering. It must not be destroyed, and that, as a descendant of numberless Jews who refused to despair, I am trying once more to prove in this pamphlet. Whole branches of Judaism may wither and fall, but the trunk will remain.

Hence, if all or any of the French Jews protest against this scheme on account of their own "assimilation," my answer is simple: The whole thing does not concern them at all. They are Jewish Frenchmen, well and good! This is a private affair for the Jews alone.

The movement towards the organization of the State I am proposing would, of course, harm Jewish Frenchmen no more than it would harm the "assimilated" of other countries. It would, on the contrary, be distinctly to their advantage. For they would no longer be disturbed in their "chromatic function," as Darwin puts it, but would be able to assimilate in peace, because the present Anti-Semitism would have been stopped for ever. They would certainly be credited with being assimilated to the very depths of their souls, if they stayed where they were after the new Jewish State, with its superior institutions, had become a reality. [. . .]

20

The Conservation of Races (1897)

W. E. B. Du Bois

W. E. B. Du Bois, "The Conservation of Races" (1897) [source: W. E. B. Du Bois, *Writings.* New York: Library of America, 1986, 815–26]

Descended from a white, slave-owning paternal great-grandfather and an enslaved African maternal great-great-grandfather, Du Bois (1868–1963) profoundly influenced both an American and an international readership, including the French-African Negritude movement and West Indian theorists like Fanon. Educated at Harvard and in Germany, Du Bois's work was shaped by Hegelian phenomenology, with its universal historical progress among nations toward self-consciousness. But he also heard the Berlin racial theorist Heinrich von Treitschke declare that "mulattoes are inferior." Du Bois famously argued (in *The Souls of Black Folk*) that "the problem of the twentieth century is the problem of the color line," and his articulation of the American Negro's "double consciousness," which is "no true self-consciousness, but only lets him see himself through the revelation of the other world," would affect almost all subsequent treatments of black identity. His concept of race is both physiological and cultural (or philological), but it is largely derived from a German Romantic concept of national destiny (as in Fichte and Hegel) that Du Bois rewrote in racial terms – "a vast family of human beings, generally of common blood and language, always of common history, traditions and impulses, who are both voluntarily and involuntarily striving together for the accomplishment of certain more or less vividly conceived ideals of life." It was up to a racial elite, Du Bois's "talented tenth," to lead the race toward such ideals.

The American Negro has always felt an intense personal interest in discussions as to the origins and destinies of races: primarily because back of most discussions of race with which he is familiar, have lurked certain assumptions as to his natural abilities, as to his political, intellectual and moral status, which he felt were wrong. He has, consequently, been led to deprecate and minimize race distinctions, to believe intensely that out of one blood God created all nations, and to speak of human brotherhood as though it were the possibility of an already dawning to-morrow.

Nevertheless, in our calmer moments we must acknowledge that human beings are divided into races; that in this country the two most extreme types of the world's races have met, and the resulting problem as to the future relations of these types is not only of intense and living interest to us, but forms an epoch in the history of mankind.

It is necessary, therefore, in planning our movements, in guiding our future development, that at times we rise above the pressing, but smaller questions of separate schools and cars, wage-discrimination and lynch law, to survey the whole question of race in human philosophy and to lay, on a basis of broad knowledge and careful insight, those large lines of policy and higher ideals which may form our guiding lines and boundaries in the practical difficulties of every day. For it is certain that all human striving must recognize the hard limits of natural law, and that any striving, no matter how intense and earnest, which is against the constitution of the world, is vain. The question, then, which we must seriously consider is this: What is the real meaning of Race; what has, in the past, been the law of race development, and what lessons has the past history of race development to teach the rising Negro people?

When we thus come to inquire into the essential difference of races we find it hard to come at once to any definite conclusion. Many criteria of race differences have in the past been proposed, as color, hair, cranial measurements and language. And manifestly, in each of these respects, human beings differ widely. They vary in color, for instance, from the marble-like pallor of the Scandinavian to the rich, dark brown of the Zulu, passing by the creamy Slav, the yellow Chinese, the light brown Sicilian and the brown Egyptian. Men vary, too, in the texture of hair from the obstinately straight hair of the Chinese to the obstinately tufted and frizzled hair of the Bushman. In measurement of heads, again, men vary; from the broad-headed Tartar to the medium-headed European and the narrow-headed Hottentot; or, again in language, from the highly-inflected Roman tongue to the monosyllabic Chinese. All these physical characteristics are patent enough, and if they agreed with each other it would be very easy to classify mankind. Unfortunately for scientists, however, these criteria of race are most exasperatingly intermingled. Color does not agree with texture of hair, for many of the dark races have straight hair; nor does color agree with the breadth of the head, for the yellow Tartar has a broader head than the German; nor, again, has the science of language as yet succeeded in clearing up the relative authority of these various and contradictory criteria. The final word of science, so far, is that we have at least two, perhaps three, great families of human beings – the whites and Negroes, possibly the yellow race. That other races have arisen from the intermingling of the blood of these two. This broad division of the world's races which men like Huxley and Raetzel have introduced as more nearly true than the old five-race scheme of Blumenbach, is nothing more than an acknowledgement that, so far as purely physical characteristics are concerned, the differences between men do not explain all the differences of their history. It declares, as Darwin himself said, that great as is the physical unlikeness of the various races of men their likenesses are greater, and upon this rests the whole scientific doctrine of Human Brotherhood.

Although the wonderful developments of human history teach that the grosser physical differences of color, hair and bone go but a short way toward explaining the different roles which groups of men have played in Human Progress, yet there are differences – subtle, delicate and elusive, though they may be – which have silently but definitely separated men into groups. While these subtle forces have generally followed the natural cleavage of common blood, descent and physical peculiarities, they have at other times swept across and ignored these. At all times, however, they have divided human beings into races, which, while they perhaps transcend scientific definition, nevertheless, are clearly defined to the eye of the Historian and Sociologist.

If this be true, then the history of the world is the history, not of individuals, but of groups, not of nations, but of races, and he who ignores or seeks to override the race idea in human history ignores and overrides the central thought of all history. What, then, is a race? It is a vast family of human beings, generally of common blood and language, always of common history, traditions and impulses, who are both voluntarily and involuntarily striving together for the accomplishment of certain more or less vividly conceived ideals of life.

Turning to real history, there can be no doubt, first, as to the widespread, nay, universal, prevalence of the race idea, the race spirit, the race ideal, and as to its efficiency as the vastest and most ingenious invention for human progress. We, who have been reared and trained under the individualistic philosophy of the Declaration of Independence and the laisser-faire philosophy of Adam Smith, are loath to see and loath to acknowledge this patent fact of human history. We see the Pharaohs, Caesars, Toussaints and Napoleons of history and forget the vast races of which they were but epitomized expressions. We are apt to think in our American impatience, that while it may have been true in the past that closed race groups made history, that here in conglomerate America *nous avons changé tout cela* – we have changed all that, and have no need of this ancient instrument of progress. This assumption of which the Negro people are especially fond, can not be established by a careful consideration of history.

We find upon the world's stage today eight distinctly differentiated races, in the sense in which History tells us the word must be used. They are, the Slavs of eastern Europe, the Teutons of middle Europe, the English of Great Britain and America, the Romance nations of Southern and Western Europe, the Negroes of Africa and America, the Semitic people of Western Asia and Northern Africa, the Hindoos of Central Asia and the Mongolians of Eastern Asia. There are, of course, other minor race groups, as the American Indians, the Esquimaux and the South Sea Islanders; these larger races, too, are far from homogeneous; the Slav includes the Czech, the Magyar, the Pole and the Russian; the Teuton includes the German, the Scandinavian and the Dutch; the English include the Scotch, the Irish and the conglomerate American. Under Romance nations the widely-differing Frenchman, Italian, Sicilian and Spaniard are comprehended. The term Negro is, perhaps, the most indefinite of all, combining the Mulattoes and Zamboes of America and the Egyptians, Bantus and Bushmen of Africa. Among the Hindoos are traces of widely differing nations, while the great Chinese, Tartar, Corean and Japanese families fall under the one designation – Mongolian.

The question now is: What is the real distinction between these nations? Is it the physical differences of blood, color and cranial measurements? Certainly we must all acknowledge that physical differences play a great part, and that, with wide exceptions and qualifications, these eight great races of to-day follow the cleavage of physical race distinctions; the English and Teuton represent the white variety of mankind; the Mongolian, the yellow; the Negroes, the black. Between these are many crosses and mixtures, where Mongolian and Teuton have blended into the Slav, and other mixtures have produced the Romance nations and the Semites. But while race differences have followed mainly physical race lines, yet no mere physical distinctions would really define or explain the deeper differences – the cohesiveness and continuity of these groups. The deeper differences are spiritual, psychical, differences – undoubtedly based on the physical, but infinitely transcending them. The forces that bind together the Teuton nations are, then, first, their race identity and common blood; secondly, and more important, a common history, common laws and religion, similar habits of thought and a conscious striving together for certain ideals of life. The whole process which has brought about these race differentiations has been a growth, and the great characteristic of this growth has been the differentiation of spiritual and mental differences between great races of mankind and the integration of physical differences.

The age of nomadic tribes of closely related individuals represents the maximum of physical differences. They were practically vast families, and there were as many groups as families. As the families, came together to form cities the physical differences lessened, purity of blood was replaced by the requirement of domicile, and all who lived within the city bounds became gradually to be regarded as members of the group; *i.e.*, there was a slight and slow breaking down of physical barriers. This, however, was accompanied by an increase of the spiritual and social differences between cities. This city became husbandmen, this, merchants, another warriors, and so on. The *ideals of life* for which the different cities struggled were different. When at last cities began to coalesce into nations there was another breaking down of barriers which separated groups of men. The larger and broader differences of color, hair and physical proportions were not by any means ignored, but myriads of minor differences disappeared, and the sociological and historical races of men began to approximate the present division of races as indicated by physical researchers. At the same time the spiritual and physical differences of race groups which constituted the nations became deep and decisive. The English nation stood for constitutional liberty and commercial freedom; the German nation for science and philosophy; the Romance nations stood for literature and art, and the other race groups are striving, each in its own way, to develop for civilization its particular message, its particular ideal, which shall help to guide the world nearer and nearer that perfection of human life for which we all long, that

"one far off Divine event."[1]

This has been the function of race differences up to the present time. What shall be its function in the future? Manifestly some of the great races of today – particularly the Negro race – have not as yet given to civilization the full spiritual message which they are capable of giving. I will not say that the Negro race has as yet given no message to the world, for it is still a mooted question among scientists as to just how far Egyptian civilization was Negro in its origin; if it was not wholly Negro, it was certainly very closely allied. Be that as it may, however, the fact still remains that the full, complete Negro message of the whole Negro race has not as yet been given to the world: that the messages and ideal of the yellow race have not been completed, and that the striving of the mighty Slavs has but begun. The question is, then: How shall this message be delivered; how shall these various ideals be realized? The answer is plain: By the development of these race groups, not as individuals, but as races. For the development of Japanese genius, Japanese literature and art, Japanese spirit, only Japanese, bound and welded together, Japanese inspired by one vast ideal, can work out in its fullness the wonderful message which Japan has for the nations of the earth. For the development of Negro genius, of Negro literature and art, of Negro spirit, only Negroes bound and welded together, Negroes inspired by one vast ideal, can work out in its fullness the great message we have for humanity. We cannot reverse history; we are subject to the same natural laws as other races, and if the Negro is ever to be a factor in the world's history – if among the gaily-colored banners that deck the broad ramparts of civilization is to hang one uncompromising black, then it must be placed there by black hands, fashioned by black heads and hallowed by the travail of 200,000,000 black hearts beating in one glad song of jubilee.

For this reason, the advance guard of the Negro people – the 8,000,000 people of Negro blood in the United States of America – must soon come to realize that if they are to take their just place in the van of Pan-Negroism, then their destiny is *not* absorption by the white Americans. That if in America it is to be proven for the first time in the modern world that not only Negroes are capable of evolving individual men like Toussaint, the Saviour, but are a nation stored with wonderful possibilities of culture, then their destiny is not a servile imitation of Anglo-Saxon culture, but a stalwart originality which shall unswervingly follow Negro ideals.

It may, however, be objected here that the situation of our race in America renders this attitude impossible; that our sole hope of salvation lies in our being able to lose our race identity in the commingled blood of the nation; and that any other course would merely increase the friction of races which we call race prejudice, and against which we have so long and so earnestly fought.

Here, then, is the dilemma, and it is a puzzling one, I admit. No Negro who has given earnest thought to the situation of his people in America has failed, at some time in life, to find himself at these cross-roads; has failed to ask himself at some time: What, after all, am I? Am I an American or am I a Negro? Can I be both? Or is it my duty to cease to be a Negro as soon as possible and be an American? If I strive as a Negro, am I not perpetuating the very cleft that threatens and separates Black and White America? Is not my only possible practical aim the subduction of all that is Negro in me to the American? Does my black blood place upon me any more obligation to assert my nationality than German, or Irish or Italian blood would?

It is such incessant self-questioning and the hesitation that arises from it, that is making the present period a time of vacillation and contradiction for the American Negro; combined race action is stifled, race responsibility is shirked, race enterprises languish, and the best blood, the best talent, the best energy of the Negro people cannot be marshalled to do the bidding of the race. They stand back to make room for every rascal and demagogue who chooses to cloak his selfish deviltry under the veil of race pride.

Is this right? Is it rational? Is it good policy? Have we in America a distinct mission as a race – a distinct sphere of action and an opportunity for race development, or is self-obliteration the highest end to which Negro blood dare aspire?

If we carefully consider what race prejudice really is, we find it, historically, to be nothing but the friction between different groups of people; it is the difference in aim, in feeling, in ideals of two different races; if, now, this difference exists touching territory, laws, language, or even religion, it is manifest that these people cannot live in the same territory without fatal collision; but if, on the other hand, there is substantial agreement in laws, language and religion; if there is a satisfactory adjustment of economic life, then there is no reason why, in the same country and on the same street, two or three great national ideals might not thrive and develop, that men of different races might not strive together for their race ideals as well, perhaps even better, than in isolation. Here, it seems to me, is the reading of the riddle that puzzles so many of us. We are Americans, not only by birth and by citizenship, but by our political ideals, our language, our religion. Farther than that, our Americanism does not go. At that point, we are Negroes, members of a vast historic race that from the very dawn of creation has slept, but half awakening in the dark forests of its African fatherland. We are the first fruits of this new nation, the harbinger of that black to-morrow which is yet destined to soften the whiteness of the Teutonic to-day. We are that people whose subtle sense of song has given America its only American music, its only American fairy tales, its only touch of pathos and humor amid its mad money-getting plutocracy. As such, it is our duty to conserve our physical powers, our intellectual endowments, our spiritual ideals; as a race we must strive by race organization, by race solidarity, by race unity to the realization of that broader humanity which freely recognizes differences in men, but sternly deprecates inequality in their opportunities of development.

For the accomplishment of these ends we need race organizations: Negro colleges, Negro newspapers, Negro business organizations, a Negro school of literature and art, and an intellectual clearing house, for all these products of the Negro mind, which we may call a Negro Academy. Not only is all this necessary for positive advance, it is absolutely imperative for negative defense. Let us not deceive ourselves at our situation in this country. Weighted with a heritage of moral iniquity from our past history, hard pressed in the economic world by foreign immigrants and native prejudice, hated here, despised there and pitied everywhere; our one haven of refuge is ourselves, and but one means of advance, our own belief in our great destiny, our own implicit trust in our ability and worth. There is no power under God's high heaven that can stop the advance of eight thousand thousand honest, earnest, inspired and united people. But – and here is the rub – they *must* be honest, fearlessly criticising their own faults, zealously correcting them; they must be *earnest*. No people that laughs at itself, and ridicules itself, and wishes to God it was anything but itself ever wrote its name in history; it *must* be inspired with the Divine faith of our black mothers, that out of the blood and dust of battle will march a victorious host, a mighty nation, a peculiar people, to speak to the nations of earth a Divine truth that shall make them free. And such a people must be united; not merely united for the organized theft of political spoils, not united to disgrace religion with whoremongers and ward-heelers; not united merely to protest and pass resolutions, but united to stop the ravages of consumption among the Negro people, united to keep black boys from loafing, gambling and crime; united to guard the purity of black women and to reduce that vast army of black prostitutes that is today marching to hell; and united in serious organizations, to determine by careful conference and thoughtful inter-change of opinion the broad lines of policy and action for the American Negro.

This, is the reason for being which the American Negro Academy has. It aims at once to be the epitome and expression of the intellect of the black-blooded people of America, the exponent of the race ideals of one of the world's great races. As such, the Academy must, if successful, be

(*a*) Representative in character.
(*b*) Impartial in conduct.
(*c*) Firm in leadership.

It must be representative in character; not in that it represents all interests or all factions, but in that it seeks to comprise something of the *best* thought, the most unselfish striving and the highest ideals. There are scattered in forgotten nooks and corners throughout the land, Negroes of some con-siderable training, of high minds, and high motives, who are unknown to their fellows, who exert far too little influence. These the Negro Academy should strive to bring into touch with each other and to give them a common mouthpiece.

The Academy should be impartial in conduct; while it aims to exalt the people it should aim to do so by truth – not by lies, by honesty – not by flattery. It should continually impress the fact upon the Negro people that they must not expect to have things done for them – they MUST DO FOR THEMSELVES; that they have on their hands a vast work of self-reformation to do, and that a little less complaint and whining, and a little more dogged work and manly striving would do us more credit and benefit than a thou-sand Force or Civil Rights bills.

Finally, the American Negro Academy must point out a practical path of advance to the Negro people; there lie before every Negro today hundreds of questions of policy and right which must be settled and which each one settles now, not in accordance with any rule, but by impulse or individual preference; for instance: What should be the attitude of Negroes toward the educational qualification for voters? What should be our attitude toward separate schools? How should we meet discriminations on railways and in hotels? Such questions need not so much specific answers for each part as a general expression of policy, and nobody should be better fitted to announce such a policy than a representative honest Negro Academy.

All this, however, must come in time after careful organization and long conference. The immediate work before us should be practical and have direct bearing upon the situation of the Negro. The historical work of collecting the laws of the United States and of the various States of the Union with regard to the Negro is a work of such magnitude and importance that no body but one like this could think of undertaking it. If we could accomplish that one task we would justify our existence.

In the field of Sociology an appalling work lies before us. First, we must unflinchingly and bravely face the truth, not with apologies, but with solemn earnestness. The Negro Academy ought to sound a note of warning that would echo in every black cabin in the land: *Unless we conquer our present vices they will conquer us;* we are diseased, we are developing criminal tendencies, and an alarmingly large percentage of our men and women are sexually impure. The Negro Academy should stand and proclaim this over the housetops, crying with Garrison: *I will not equivocate, I will not retreat a single inch, and I will be heard.*[2] The Academy should seek to gather about it the talented, unselfish men, the pure and noble-minded women, to fight an army of devils that disgraces our manhood and our womanhood. There does not stand today upon God's earth a race more capable in muscle, in intellect, in morals, than the American Negro, if he will bend his energies in the right direction; if he will

> Burst his birth's invidious bar
> And grasp the skirts of happy chance,
> And breast the blows of circumstance,
> And grapple with his evil star.[3]

In science and morals, I have indicated two fields of work for the Academy. Finally, in practical policy, I wish to suggest the following *Academy Creed*:

1 We believe that the Negro people, as a race, have a contribution to make to civilization and humanity, which no other race can make.
2 We believe it the duty of the Americans of Negro descent, as a body, to maintain their race identity until this mission of the Negro people is

accomplished, and the ideal of human brotherhood has become a practical possibility.

3   We believe that, unless modern civilization is a failure, it is entirely feasible and practicable for two races in such essential political, economic, and religious harmony as the white and colored people of America, to develop side by side in peace and mutual happiness, the peculiar contribution which each has to make to the culture of their common country.

4   As a means to this end we advocate, not such social equality between these races as would disregard human likes and dislikes, but such a social equilibrium as would, throughout all the complicated relations of life, give due and just consideration to culture, ability, and moral worth, whether they be found under white or black skins.

5   We believe that the first and greatest step toward the settlement of the present friction between the races – commonly called the Negro Problem – lies in the correction of the immorality, crime and laziness among the Negroes themselves, which still remains as a heritage from slavery. We believe that only earnest and long continued efforts on our own part can cure these social ills.

6   We believe that the second great step toward a better adjustment of the relations between the races, should be a more impartial selection of ability in the economic and intellectual world, and a greater respect for personal liberty and worth, regardless of race. We believe that only earnest efforts on the part of the white people of this country will bring much needed reform in these matters.

7   On the basis of the foregoing declaration, and firmly believing in our high destiny, we, as American Negroes, are resolved to strive in every honorable way for the realization of the best and highest aims, for the development of strong manhood and pure womanhood, and for the rearing of a race ideal in America and Africa, to the glory of God and the uplifting of the Negro people.

Notes

1   [Tennyson, *In Memoriam*, Conclusion, stanza xxxvi. Ed.]
2   [Garrison, "Salutatory Address," *The Liberator*, Jan. 1, 1831. Ed.]
3   [Tennyson, *In Memoriam*, lxiv. Ed.]

21

Foundations of the Nineteenth Century (1899)

Houston Stewart Chamberlain

Houston Stewart Chamberlain, "The Nation," from *Foundations of the Nineteenth Century* (1899) [source: Houston Stewart Chamberlain, *Foundations of the Nineteenth Century*, 2 vols, trans. John Lees. Intro. George L. Mosse. New York: Howard Fertig, 1994, vol. I, 292–7]

Born in England, Chamberlain (1855–1927) adopted Germany as his true homeland in 1870. Wagner was an important influence, along with Christian chauvinism (Chamberlain claimed that non- or pre-Christian peoples had no history) and Darwin's evolutionism: he wrote a dissertation on botany, and liberally illustrated his racial theories with examples from animal breeding and anthropometry. He admired Dante (whom he considered German) and Luther, owed much to Gobineau, and accepted the opinion of Tacitus (whose *Germania* he cited frequently) that the Germans are a pure race arising in Europe "as though conjured up out of the soil." He argued that the ancient Germans overcame the earlier racial chaos of the Roman Empire. In fact, Chamberlain rejected the popular wisdom of Renan that civilization developed from highly differentiated primitive races into greater racial simplicity and homogeneity, that is, "from race to racelessness." Instead, a primitive "colourless aggregate" evolved into increasingly differentiated races. Through crossing of closely related racial stems, as in the various Germanic tribes, followed by sustained inbreeding, nation-building became the mechanism, rather than the consequence, of racial identity. The Jews are for Chamberlain the purest, most inbred race (though originally partially Semitic racial hybrids). But their materialism and religious legalism were totally alien to the Christian, Indo-Germanic spirit of Europe, and they needed to be excluded from its culture. Chamberlain provided a widely credited pseudo-scientific basis for Nazi racial ideology.

The Nation

There is one point which I have not expressly formulated, but it is self-evident from all that I have said; the conception of Race has nothing in it unless we take it in the narrowest and not in the widest sense: if we follow the usual custom and use the word to denote far remote hypothetical races, it ends by becoming little more than a colourless synonym for "mankind" – possibly including the long-tailed and short-tailed apes: Race only has a meaning when it relates to the experiences of the past and the events of the present.

Here we begin to understand what nation signifies for race. It is almost always the nation, as a political structure, that creates the conditions for the formation of race or at least leads to the highest and most individual activities of race. Wherever, as in India, nations are not formed, the stock of strength that has been gathered by race decays. But the confusion which prevails with regard to the idea of race hinders even the most learned from understanding this great significance of nations, whereby they are at the same time prevented from understanding the fundamental facts of history. For, in fact, what is it that our historians to-day teach us concerning the relation of race to nation?

I take up any book by chance – Renan's discourse, *What is a Nation?* In hundreds of others we find the same doctrines. The thesis is clearly formulated by Renan: "The fact of race," he writes, "originally of decisive importance, loses significance every day." On what does he base this assertion? By pointing to the fact that the most capable nations of Europe are of mixed blood. What a mass of delusive conclusions this one sentence contains, what incapacity to be taught by what is evident to the eye! Nature and history do not furnish a single example of pre-eminently noble races with individual physiognomies, which were not produced by crossing: and now we are to believe that a nation of such distinct individuality as the English does not represent a race, because it originated from a mixture of Anglo-Saxon, Danish and Norman blood (stems moreover that were closely related)! I am to deny the clearest evidence which shows me that the Englishman is at least as markedly unique a being as the Greek and the Roman of the most brilliant epochs, and that in favour of an arbitrary, eternally indemonstrable abstraction, in favour of the presupposed, original "pure race." Two pages before, Renan himself had stated on the basis of anthropological discoveries that among the oldest Aryans, Semites, Turanians (*les groupes aryen primitif, sémitique primitif, touranien primitif*) one finds men of very different build of body, some with long, others with short skulls, so that they too had possessed no common "physiological unity." What delusions will not arise, as soon as man seeks for supposed "origins"! Again and again I must quote Goethe's great remark: "Animated inquiry into cause does infinite harm." Instead of taking the given fact, the discoverable as it is, and contenting ourselves with the knowledge of the nearest, demonstrable conditions, we ever and again fancy we must start from absolutely hypothetical causes and suppositions lying as far back as possible, and to these we sacrifice without hesitation that which is present and beyond doubt. That is what our "empiricists" are like. That they do not see further than their own noses, we gladly believe from their own confession, but unfortunately they do not see even so far, but run up against solid facts and complain then about the said facts, not about their own shortsightedness. What kind of thing is this originally "physiologically uniform race" of which Renan speaks? Probably a near relation of Haeckel's human apes. And in favour of this hypothetical beast I am to deny that the English people, the Prussians, the Spaniards have a definite and absolutely individual character! Renan misses physiological unity: does he not comprehend that physiological unity is brought about by marriage? Who then tells him that the hypothetical aboriginal Aryans were not also the result of gradual development? We know nothing about it: but what we do know entitles us to suppose it from analogy. There were among them narrow heads and broad ones: who knows but this crossing was necessary to produce one very noble race? The common English horse and the Arabian horse (which doubtless was produced originally by some crossing) were also "physiologically" very different, and yet from their union was produced in the course of time the most physiologically uniform and noblest race of animals in the world, the English thoroughbred. Now the great scholar Renan sees the English human thoroughbred, so to speak, arising before his eyes: the ages of history are before him. What does he deduce therefrom? He says: since the Englishman of to-day is neither the Celt of Cæsar's time nor the Anglo-Saxon of Hengist, nor the Dane of Knut, nor the Norman of the Conqueror, but the outcome of a crossing of all four, one cannot speak of an English race at all. That is to say because the English race, like every other race of which we have any knowledge, has grown historically, because it is something peculiar and absolutely new, therefore it does not exist! In truth, nothing beats the logic of the scholar!

> Was ihr nicht rechnet
> Glaubt ihr, sei nicht wahr.
>
> [What you do not reckon,
> You fancy, is not true.]

Our opinion concerning the importance of nationality in the formation of race must be quite different. The Roman Empire in the imperial period was

the materialisation of the anti-national principle; this principle led to racelessness and simultaneously to intellectual and moral chaos; mankind was
only rescued from this chaos by the more and more decisive development of
the opposite or national principle. Political nationality has not always played
the same *rôle* in the production of individual races as it has in our modern
culture; I need only refer to India, Greece and the Israelites; but the problem
was nowhere solved so beautifully, successfully and as it appears so lastingly,
as by the Teutonic peoples. As though conjured up out of the soil there arose
in this small corner of Europe a number of absolutely new, differentiated
national organisms. Renan is of opinion that race existed only in the old
"polis," because it was only there that the numerical limitation had permitted community of blood; this is absolutely false; one need only reckon
back a few centuries, and every one has a hundred thousand ancestors; what,
therefore, in the narrow circle of Athens took place in a comparatively short
time, namely, the physiological union, took place in our case in the course of
several centuries and is still continued. Race formation, far from decreasing
in our nations, must daily increase. The longer a definite group of countries
remains politically united, the closer does the "physiological unity" which is
demanded become, and the more quickly and thoroughly does it assimilate
strange elements. Our anthropologists and historians simply presuppose that
in their hypothetical primitive races the specific distinguishing characteristics
were highly developed, but that they are now progressively decreasing; there
is consequently, they aver, a movement from original complexity to increasing simplicity. This supposition is contrary to all experience, which rather
teaches us that individualisation is a result of growing differentiation and
separation. The whole science of biology contradicts the supposition that an
organic creature first appears with clearly marked characteristics, which then
gradually disappear; it actually forces us to the very opposite hypothesis that
the early human race was a variable, comparatively colourless aggregate, from
which the individual types have developed with increasing divergence and
increasingly distinct individuality; a hypothesis which all history confirms.
The sound and normal evolution of man is therefore not from race to
racelessness but on the contrary from racelessness to ever clearer distinctness
of race. The enrichment of life by new individualities seems everywhere to be
one of the highest laws of inscrutable nature. Now here in the case of man
the nation plays a most important part, because it almost always brings about
crossing, followed by inbreeding. All Europe proves this. Renan shows how
many Slavs have united with the Teutonic peoples, and asks somewhat
sneeringly whether we have any right to call the Germans of to-day "Teutonic": well, we need not quarrel about names in such a case – what the
Germans are to-day Renan has been able to learn in the year 1870; he has
been taught it too by the German specialists, to whose industry he owes

nine-tenths of his knowledge. That is the valuable result of the creation of race by nation-building. And since race is not a mere word, but an organic living thing, it follows as a matter of course that it never remains stationary; it is ennobled or it degenerates, it develops in this or that direction and lets this or that quality decay. This is a law of all individual life. But the firm national union is the surest protection against going astray: it signifies common memory, common hope, common intellectual nourishment; it fixes firmly the existing bond of blood and impels us to make it ever closer.

Part IV

Nations at the End of Empires

22

Home Rule; Enlightened Anarchy; and National Language (1909–39)

Mohandas Karamchand Gandhi

Mohandas Karamchand Gandhi, selections from chs IX–X, "The Condition of India," and ch. XIII, "What is True Civilization?" from *Hind Swaraj, or Indian Home Rule* (1909); selections from statements on "Independence vs Swaraj" (1928) and "Enlightened Anarchy" (1939); and from a statement on "The Question of a National Language" (1917) [sources: *The Penguin Gandhi Reader*, ed. Rudrangshu Mukherjee, trans. anon. New York: Penguin Books, 1993, 24–7, 29–30, 34–7, 73–5, 79; and M. K. Gandhi, *Thoughts on National Language*, trans. anon. Ahmedabad, India: Navajivan Publishing House, 1956, 3–7, reprinted by permission of Navajivan Trust]

Gandhi (1869–1948) belonged to the Bania, or businessman, caste in India, though his family had produced several generations of Prime Ministers in Western Indian states. He studied law in England and was admitted to the bar in 1891; he traveled to South Africa as a business attorney, where he began his political career by leading "colored" (Indian) residents in their struggle for civil rights. In 1920 he joined the All-India Home Rule League and became its president. Though perhaps the central symbol of India's struggle against British domination, he was, like Tagore, not a nationalist, and little of his philosophy was emboided in the state that emerged under Nehru in 1947. Influenced by Tolstoi, Ruskin, and Edward Carpenter, as well as by Hindu scripture, Gandhi became famous for his doctrine of non-violence (ahimsa) in the performance of civil disobedience, which gained an international following, most notably in Martin Luther King's black civil rights campaign in the United States. Gandhi's Luddite rejection of Western civilization, reason, and technological progress was based on a notion of "self-rule" (or swaraj) guided by the individual's control over bodily needs and desires: "to observe morality is to attain mastery over our mind and our passions. So doing, we know ourselves."

Civilization thus meant "good conduct" derived from tradition, not material prosperity, and implied "enlightened anarchy" free of state authority. For Gandhi, India was an ancient nation that needed to put aside sectarian disputes in pursuit of utopian goals higher than that of political independence.

Chapter IX: The Condition of India (continued): Railways

[...] EDITOR: Good travels at a snail's pace – it can, therefore, have little to do with the railways. Those who want to do good are not selfish, they are not in a hurry, they know that to impregnate people with good requires a long time. But evil has wings. To build a house takes time. Its destruction takes none. So the railways can become a distributing agency for the evil one only. It may be a debatable matter whether railways spread famines, but it is beyond dispute that they propagate evil.

READER: Be that as it may, all the disadvantages of the railways are more than counterbalanced by the fact that it is due to them that we see in India the new spirit of nationalism.

EDITOR: I hold this to be a mistake. The English have taught us that we were not one nation before and that it will require centuries before we become one nation. This is without foundation. We were one nation before they came to India. One thought inspired us. Our mode of life was the same. It was because we were one nation that they were able to establish one kingdom. Subsequently they divided us.

READER: This requires an explanation.

EDITOR: I do not wish to suggest that because we were one nation we had no differences, but it is submitted that our leading men travelled throughout India either on foot or in bullock-carts. They learned one another's languages and there was no aloofness between them. What do you think could have been the intention of those farseeing ancestors of ours who established Setubandha (Rameshwar) in the South, Jagannath in the East and Hardwar in the North as places of pilgrimage? You will admit they were no fools. They knew that worship of God could have been performed just as well at home. They taught us that those whose hearts were aglow with righteousness had the Ganges in their own homes. But they saw that India was one undivided land so made by nature. They, there-fore, argued that it must be one nation. Arguing thus, they established holy places in various parts of India, and fired the people with an idea of nationality in a manner unknown in other parts of the world. And we Indians are one as no two Englishmen are. Only you and I and others who consider ourselves civilized and superior persons imagine that we are many nations. It was after the advent of railways that we began to believe in distinctions, and you are at liberty now to say that it is through the railways that we are beginning to abolish those distinctions. An opium-eater may argue the advantage of opium-eating from the fact that he began to understand the evil of the opium habit after having eaten it. I would ask you to consider well what I had said on the railways.

READER: I will gladly do so, but one question occurs to me even now. You have described to me the India of the pre-Mahomedan period, but now we have Mahomedan, Parsis and Christians. How can they be one nation? Hindus and Mahomedans are old enemies. Our very proverbs prove it. Mahomedans turn to the West for worship, whilst Hindus turn to the East. The former look down on the Hindus as idolaters. The Hindus worship the cow, the Mahomedans kill her. The Hindus believe in the doctrine of non-killing, the Mahomedans do not. We thus meet with differences at every step. How can India be one nation?

Chapter X: The Condition of India (continued): The Hindus & the Mahomedans

EDITOR: Your last question is a serious one and yet, on careful consideration, it will be found to be easy of solution. The question arises because of the presence of the railways, of the lawyers and of the doctors. We shall presently examine the last two. We have already considered the railways. I should, however, like to add that man is so made by nature as to require him to restrict his movements as far as his hands and feet will take him. If we did not rush about from place to place by means of railways and such other maddening conveniences, much of the confusion that arises would be obviated. Our difficulties are of our own creation. God set a limit to man's locomotive ambition in the construction of his body. Man immediately proceeded to discover means of overriding the limit. God gifted man with intellect that he might know his Maker. Man abused it so that he might forget his Maker. I am so constructed that I can only serve my immediate neighbours, but in my conceit I pretend to have discovered that I must with my body serve every individual in the Universe. In thus attempting the impossible, man comes in contact with different natures, different religions, and is utterly confounded. According to this reasoning, it must be apparent to you that railways are a most dangerous institution. Owing to them, man has gone further away from his Maker.

READER: But I am impatient to hear your answer to my question. Has the introduction of Mahomedanism not unmade the nation?

EDITOR: India cannot cease to be one nation because people belonging to different religions live in it. The introduction of foreigners does not necessarily destroy the nation; they merge in it. A country is one nation only when such a condition obtains in it. That country must have a faculty for assimilation. India has ever been such a country. In reality, there are as many religions as there are individuals; but those who are conscious of the spirit of nationality do not interfere with one another's religion. If they do, they are not fit to be considered a nation. If the Hindus believe that India should be peopled only by Hindus, they are living in dreamland. The Hindus, the Mahomedans, the Parsis and the Christians who have made India their country are fellow countrymen, and they will have to live in unity, if only for their own interest. In no part of the world are one nationality and one religion synonymous terms; nor has it ever been so in India.

READER: But what about the inborn enmity between Hindus and Mahomedans?

EDITOR: That phrase has been invented by our mutual enemy. When the Hindus and Mahomedans fought against one another, they certainly spoke in that strain. They have long since ceased to fight. How, then, can there be any inborn enmity? Pray remember this too, that we did not cease to fight only after British occupation. The Hindus flourished under Moslem sovereigns and Moslems under the Hindu. Each party recognized that mutual fighting was suicidal, and that neither party would abandon its religion by force of arms. Both parties, therefore, decided to live in peace. With the English advent quarrels recommenced.

The proverbs you have quoted were coined when both were fighting; to quote them now is obviously harmful. Should we not remember that many Hindus and Mahomedans own the same ancestors and the same blood runs through their veins? Do people become enemies because they change their religion? Is the God of the Mahomedan different from the God of the Hindu? Religions are different roads converging to the same point. What does it matter that we take different roads so long as we reach the same goal? Wherein is the cause for quarrelling?

Moreover, there are deadly proverbs as between the followers of Shiva and those of Vishnu, yet nobody suggests that these two do not belong to the same nation. It is said that the Vedic religion is different from Jainism, but the followers of the respective faiths are not different nations. The fact is that we have become enslaved and, therefore, quarrel and like to have our quarrels decided by a third party. There are Hindu iconoclasts as there are Mahomedan. The more we advance in true knowledge, the better we shall understand that we need not be at war with those whose religion we may not follow. [...]

READER: But will the English ever allow the two bodies to join hands?

EDITOR: This question arises out of your timidity. It betrays our shallowness. If two brothers want to live in peace, is it possible for a third party to separate them? If they were to listen to evil counsels we would consider them to be foolish. Similarly, we Hindus and Mahomedans would have to blame our folly rather than the English, if we allowed them to put us asunder. A clay pot would break through impact, if not with one stone, then with another. The way to save the pot is not to keep it away from the danger point but to bake it so that no stone would break it. We have then to make our hearts of perfectly baked clay. Then we shall be steeled against all danger. This can be easily done by the Hindus. They are superior in numbers; they pretend that they are more educated; they are, therefore, better able to shield themselves from attack on their amicable relations with the Mahomedans.

There is mutual distrust between the two communities. The Mahomedans, therefore, ask for certain concessions from Lord Morley. Why should the Hindus oppose this? If the Hindus desisted, the English would notice it, the Mahomedans would gradually begin to trust the Hindus, and brotherliness would be the outcome. We should be ashamed to take our quarrels to the English. Everyone can find out for himself that the Hindus can lose nothing by desisting. That man who has inspired confidence in another has never lost anything in this world.

I do not suggest that the Hindus and the Mahomedans will never fight. Two brothers living together often do so. We shall sometimes have our heads broken. Such a thing ought not to be necessary, but all men are not equitable. When people are in a rage, they do many foolish things. These we have to put up with. But when we do quarrel, we certainly do not want to engage counsel and resort to English or any law courts. Two men fight; both have their heads broken, or one only. How shall a third party distribute justice amongst them? Those who fight may expect to be injured.

Chapter XIII: What is True Civilization?

READER: You have denounced railways, lawyers and doctors. I can see that you will discard all machinery. What, then, is civilization?

EDITOR: The answer to that question is not difficult. I believe that the civilization India has evolved is not to be beaten in the world. Nothing can equal the seeds sown by our ancestors. Rome went, Greece shared the same fate; the might of the Pharaohs was broken; Japan has become westernized; of China nothing can be said; but India is still, somehow or other, sound at the foundation. The people of Europe learn their lessons from the writings of the men of Greece or Rome, which exist no longer in their former glory. In trying to learn from them, the Europeans imagine that they will avoid the mistakes of Greece and Rome. Such is their pitiable condition. In the midst of all this India remains immovable and that is her glory. It is a charge against India that her people are so uncivilized, ignorant and stolid, that it is not possible to induce them to adopt any changes. It is a charge really against our merit. What we have tested and found true on the anvil of experience, we dare not change. Many thrust their advice upon India, and she remains steady. This is her beauty: it is the sheet-anchor of our hope.

Civilization is that mode of conduct which points out to man the path of duty. Performance of duty and observance of morality are convertible terms. To observe morality is to attain mastery over our mind and our passions. So doing, we know ourselves. The Gujarati equivalent for civilization means "good conduct".

If this definition be correct, then India, as so many writers have shown, has nothing to learn from anybody else, and this is as it should be. We notice that the mind is a restless bird; the more it gets the more it wants, and still remains unsatisfied. The more we indulge our passions, the more unbridled they become. Our ancestors, therefore, set a limit to our indulgences. They saw that happiness was largely a mental condition. A man is not necessarily happy because he is rich, or unhappy because he is poor. The rich are often seen to be unhappy, the poor to be happy. Millions will always remain poor. Observing all this, our ancestors dissuaded us from luxuries and pleasures. We have managed with the same kind of plough as existed thousands of years ago. We have retained the same kind of cottages that we had in former times and our indigenous education remains the same as before. We have had no system of life-corroding competition. Each followed his own occupation or trade and charged a regulation wage. It was not that we did not know how to invent machinery, but our forefathers knew that, if we set our hearts after such things, we would become slaves and lose our moral fibre. They, therefore, after due deliberation decided that we should only do what we could with our hands and feet. They saw that our real happiness and health consisted in a proper use of our hands and feet. They further reasoned that large cities were a snare and a useless encumbrance and that people would not be happy in them, that there would be gangs of thieves and robbers, prostitution and vice flourishing in them and that poor men would be robbed by rich men. They were, therefore, satisfied with small villages. They saw that kings and their swords were inferior to the sword of ethics, and they, therefore, held the sovereigns of the earth to be inferior to the Rishis and the Fakirs. A nation with a constitution like this is fitter to teach others than to learn from others. This nation had courts, lawyers and doctors, but they were all within bounds. Everybody knew that these professions were not particularly superior; more-over, these vakils and vaids did not rob people; they were considered people's dependants, not their masters. Justice was tolerably fair. The ordinary rule was to avoid courts. There were no touts to lure people into them. This evil, too, was noticeable only in and around capitals. There common people lived independently and followed their agricultural occupation. They enjoyed true Home Rule.

And where this cursed modern civilization has not reached, India remains as it was before. The inhabitants of that part of India will very properly laugh at your new-fangled notions. The English do not rule over them, nor will you ever rule over them. Those in whose name we speak we do not know, nor do they know us. I would certainly advise you and those like you who love the motherland to go into the interior that has yet been not polluted by the railways and to live there for six months; you might then be patriotic and speak of Home Rule.

Now you see what I consider to be real civilization. Those who want to change conditions such as I have described are enemies of the country and are sinners.

READER: It would be all right if India were exactly as you have described it, but it is also India where there are hundreds of child widows, where two-year-old babies are married, where twelve-year-old girls are mothers and housewives, where women practise polyandry, where the practice of Niyoga obtains, where, in the name of religion, girls dedicate themselves to prostitution, and in the name of religion sheep and goat are killed. Do you consider these also symbols of the civilization that you have described?

EDITOR: You make a mistake. The defects that you have shown are defects. Nobody mistakes them for ancient civilization. They remain in spite of it. Attempts have always been made and will be made to remove them. We may utilize the new spirit that is born in us for purging ourselves of these evils. But what I have described to you as emblems of modern civilization are accepted as such by its votaries. The Indian civilization, as described by me, has been so described by its votaries. In no part of the world, and under no civilization, have all men attained perfection. The tendency of the Indian civilization is to elevate the moral being, that of the Western civilization is to propagate immorality. The latter is godless, the former is based on a belief in God. So understanding and so believing, it behoves every lover of India to cling to the old Indian civilization even as a child clings to the mother's breast.

Independence vs Swaraj

[...] Let us, therefore, understand what we mean by independence. England, Russia, Spain, Italy, Turkey, Chile, Bhutan have all their independence.

Which independence do we want? I must not be accused of begging the question. For, if I were told that it is Indian independence that is desired, it is possible to show that no two persons will give the same definition. The fact of the matter is that we do not know our distant goal. It will be determined not by our definitions but by our acts, voluntary and involuntary. If we are wise, we will take care of the present and the future will take care of itself. God has given us only a limited sphere of action and a limited vision. Sufficient unto the day is the good thereof.

I submit that swaraj is an all-satisfying goal for all time. We the English-educated Indians often unconsciously make the terrible mistake of thinking that the microscopic minority of English-speaking Indians is the whole of India. I defy anyone to give for independence a common Indian word intelligible to the masses. Our goal at any rate may be known by an indigenous word understood of the three hundred millions. And we have such a word in "swaraj" first used in the name of the nation by Dadabhai Naoroji. It is infinitely greater than and includes independence. It is a vital word. It has been sanctified by the noble sacrifices of thousands of Indians. It is a word which, if it has not penetrated the remotest corner of India, has at least got the largest currency of any similar word. It is a sacrilege to displace that word by a foreign importation of doubtful value. This Independence Resolution is perhaps the final reason for conducting Congress proceedings in Hindustani and that alone. No tragedy like that of the Independence Resolution would then have been possible. The most valiant speakers would then have ornamented the native meaning of the word "swaraj" and attempted all kinds of definitions, glorious and inglorious. Would that the independents would profit by their experience and resolve henceforth to work among the masses for whom they desire freedom and taboo English speech in its entirety in so far as meetings such as the Congress are concerned.

Personally, I crave not for "independence", which I do not understand, but I long for freedom from the English yoke. I would pay any price for it. I would accept chaos in exchange for it. For the English peace is the peace of the grave. Anything would be better than this living death of a whole people. This Satanic rule has well-nigh ruined this fair land materially, morally and spiritually. I daily see its law courts denying justice and murdering truth. I have just come from terrorized Orissa. This rule is using my own countrymen for its sinful sustenance. I have a number of affidavits swearing that, in the district of Khurda, acknowledgments of enhancement of revenue are being forced from the people practically at the point of the bayonet. The unparalleled extravagance of this rule has demented the Rajas and the Maharajas who, unmindful of consequences, ape it and grind their subjects to dust. In order to protect its immoral commerce, this rule regards no means too mean, and in order to keep three hundred millions under the heels of a hundred thousand, it carries a military expenditure which is keeping millions in a state of semi-starvation and polluting thousands of mouths with intoxicating liquor.

But my creed is non-violence under all circumstances. My method is conversion, not coercion; it is self-suffering, not the suffering of the tyrant. I know that method to be infallible. I know that a whole people can adopt it without accepting it as its creed and without understanding its philosophy. People generally do not understand the philosophy of all their acts. My ambition is much higher than independence. Through the deliverance of India, I seek to deliver the so-called weaker races of the earth from the crushing heels of Western exploitation in which England is the greatest partner. If India converts, as it can convert, Englishmen, it can become the predominant partner in a world commonwealth of which England can have the privilege of becoming a partner if she chooses. India has the right, if she only knew, of becoming the predominant partner by reason of her numbers, geographical position and culture inherited for ages. This is big talk, I know. For a fallen India to aspire to move the world and protect weaker races is seemingly an impertinence. But in explaining my strong opposition to this cry for independence, I can no longer hide the light under a bushel. Mine is an ambition worth living for and worth dying for. In no case do I want to reconcile myself to a state lower than the best for fear of consequences. It is, therefore, not out of experience that I oppose independence as my goal. I want India to come to her own and that state cannot be better defined by any single word than "swaraj". Its content will vary with the action that the nation is able to put forth at a given moment. India's coming to her own will mean every nation doing likewise.

Enlightened Anarchy

Political power, in my opinion, cannot be our ultimate aim. It is one of the means used by men for their all-round advancement. The power to control national life through national representatives is called political power. Representatives will become unnecessary if the national life becomes so perfect as to be self-controlled. It will then be a state of enlightened anarchy in which each person will become his own ruler. He will conduct himself in such a way that his behaviour will not hamper the well-being of his neighbours. In an ideal State there will be no political institution and therefore no political power. That is why Thoreau has said in his classic statement that the government is the best which governs the least.

The Question of a National Language

Let us now consider the question of a national language. If English is to become our national language then it must be made a compulsory subject in our schools.

But let us first consider whether English can become our national language. Some of our learned men, who are also good patriots, contend that even to raise the question betrays ignorance. In their opinion it already occupies that place. His Excellency the Viceroy in his recent speech has merely expressed the hope that it will occupy this place. His zeal in this regard does not take him so far as to say that it has already become our national language and that there can now be no question about it. He, however, believes that English will spread in the country day by day, enter our homes and finally attain to the exalted status of a national language. On a superficial consideration, this view appears correct. Looking at the educated section of our society, one is likely to gain the impression that in the absence of English, all our work would come to a stop. But deeper reflection will show that English cannot and ought not to become our national language.

Let us see what should be the requirements of a national language:

1   It should be easy to learn for Government officials.
2   It should be capable of serving as a medium of religious, economic and political intercourse throughout India.
3   It should be the speech of the majority of the inhabitants of India.
4   It should be easy to learn for the whole of the country.
5   In choosing this language considerations of temporary or passing interest should not count.

English does not fulfil any of these requirements.

The first ought to have been placed last but I have purposely given it the first place because it seems as though English fulfilled it. Closer examination will, however, show that even at the present moment it is not for the officials an easy language to learn or to handle. The constitution under which we are being ruled envisages that the number of English officials will progressively decrease until finally only the Viceroy and a few more will be left here. The majority of the people in Government services are even today Indians and their number will increase as time goes on. I think no one will deny that. For them English is more difficult than any other language.

As regards the second requirement: Religious intercourse through English is an impossibility unless our people throughout the land begin to speak

English. Spread of English among the masses to this extent is clearly impossible.

English simply cannot satisfy the third requirement because the majority in India do not speak it.

The fourth also cannot be met by English because it is not an easy language to learn for the whole of India.

Considering the fifth we see that the status which English enjoys today is temporary. The fact is that in India the need for English in national affairs will be, if at all, very little. It will certainly be required for imperial affairs. It will remain the language of diplomacy between different States within the Empire. But that is a different matter. English will be necessary for that purpose. We do not hate English. All that we want is not to allow it to go beyond its proper limits. And because English will remain the imperial language we will compel our Malaviyajis, our Shastris and our Banerjees to learn it and expect them to enhance the glory of our country wherever they go. But English cannot become the national language of India. To give it that place will be like introducing Esperanto into the country. To think that English can become our national language is a sign of weakness and betrays ignorance.

Then which is the language which fulfils all the five requirements? We shall have to admit that it is Hindi.

I call that language Hindi which Hindus and Muslims in the North speak and which is written either in the Devanagari or Urdu script. There has been some objection against this definition.

It is argued that Hindi and Urdu are two different languages. But this is incorrect. Both Hindus and Muslims speak the same language in Northern India. The difference has been created by educated classes. Educated Hindus Sanskritize their Hindi with the result that Muslims cannot follow it. In the same way the Muslims of Lucknow Persianize their Urdu and make it unintelligible to Hindus. To the masses both these languages are foreign and for which they have no use. I have lived in the North and have freely mixed with both Hindus and Muslims, and though my knowledge of Hindi is very limited I have never found any difficulty in holding communication through it with them. Therefore call it Hindi or Urdu, the language which people in Northern India speak is the same. Write it in the Urdu script and you may then call it Urdu; write the same in the Nagari script and it becomes Hindi.

There now remains the question of the script. For the present Muslims will certainly use the Urdu script and Hindus will mostly write in Devanagari. I say "mostly" because thousands of Hindus even today write in the Urdu script and some even do not know the Nagari script. Finally, when there is absolutely no suspicion left between Hindus and Muslims – when all causes for distrust between the two have been removed, the script which has greater power will be more widely used and thus become the national script. In the intervening period Hindus and Muslims who desire to write their petitions in the Urdu script should be free to do so and these should be accepted, at all Government offices.

No other language can compete with Hindi in satisfying these five requirements. Next to Hindi comes Bengali. But the Bengalis themselves make use of Hindi outside Bengal. The Hindi- speaking man speaks Hindi wherever he goes and no one feels surprised at this. The Hindi-speaking Hindu preachers and the Urdu-speaking Maulvis make their religious speeches throughout India in Hindi and Urdu, and even the illiterate masses understand them. Even an unlettered Gujarati when he goes to the North attempts to speak a few Hindi words. But the Northern *bhaiya* who works as gate-keeper to the Bombay *seth*, declines to speak in Gujarati and it is the *seth*, his employer, who is obliged to speak to him in broken Hindi. I have heard Hindi spoken even in far off Southern provinces. It is not correct to say that in Madras one cannot do without English. I have successfully used Hindi there for all my work. In the trains I have heard Madrasi passengers speaking to other passengers in Hindi. Besides, the Muslims of Madras know enough Hindi to use it sufficiently well. It has to be noted that Muslims throughout India speak Urdu and they are found in large numbers in every province.

Thus Hindi has already established itself as the national language of India. We have been using it as such for a long time. The birth of Urdu itself is due to this fact.

Muslim kings could not make Persian or Arabic the national language. They accepted the Hindi grammar; only they used more Persian words in their speech and employed the Urdu script for writing. But they could not carry on intercourse with the masses through a foreign tongue. Similar is the case with the English rulers. Those who have any knowledge of how they deal with the *sipahees* in the army know that for this purpose they have coined Hindi or Urdu terms.

Thus we see that Hindi alone can become the national language. No doubt it presents some difficulty to the educated classes of Madras. But for Maharashtrians, Gujaratis, Sindhis and Bengalis it should be very easy. In a few months they can acquire enough command of Hindi to be able to use it for national purposes. It is not so easy for Tamilians. Tamil and the other languages of the South belong to the Dravidian group. Their structure and grammar are different from those of Sanskrit. The only thing common between these two groups is their Sanskrit vocabulary. But the difficulty is confined to the present educated classes only. We have a right to appeal to their patriotic spirit and expect them to put forth special effort to learn Hindi. If Hindi attains to its due status, then it will be introduced in every school in Madras and Madras will thus be in a position to cultivate acquaintance with other provinces. English has failed to reach the masses. But Hindi will do so in no time. The Telugu people have already started moving in this direction. If this conference can reach a decision on the question as to which language deserves most to become our national language then we may think out ways and means of achieving it. In general, however, the ways which have been suggested for the promotion of the mother tongue may with suitable modifications be applied to the national language. The responsibility of making Gujarati the medium of instruction will have to be shouldered mainly by us but in the movement to popularize the national language the whole country must play its part.

23

The Right of Nations to Self-Determination (1914)

V. I. Lenin

V. I. Lenin, selection from "The Right of Nations to Self-Determination" (1914) [source: V. I. Lenin, *National Liberation, Socialism, and Imperialism: Selected Writings.* New York: International Publishers, 1968, 45–6, 46–7, 49–50, 51–2, 55–6, 57–8, 59–62]

Leader of the Bolsheviks who captured the Russian state in 1917, Lenin (1870–1924) endured imprisonment, political exile, and the execution of a brother who plotted to assassinate Tsar Alexander III. Lenin was a thorough materialist, but came to reject "stupid materialism" in favor of Hegel's "intelligent idealism": the dialectical method, for which seemingly essential contradictions became moments of a dynamic process working toward resolution. Lenin followed Marx's grounding of Hegel's contradictions in material and social reality (the class struggle), and stressed the hastening of history with direct action by a vanguard party, insisting (against the moderates) on a dictatorship of (really, in the name of) a proletariat that excluded the liberal bourgeoisie and conservative peasantry. Early on, Lenin argued against Rosa Luxemburg's claim that revolutionary Marxism should reject nationalism as an abstract, metaphysical invention unrelated to real material conditions. For Lenin, "the historico-economic conditions of the national movements" entailed the "final victory of capitalism over feudalism," in which the bourgeoisie secured home markets through a linguistically unified territory supporting free commerce. Communism in turn depended on the overthrow of fully achieved capitalism. Hence, true communism supported the principle of self-determination "*insofar* as the bourgeoisie of the oppressed nation fights the [imperial] oppressor," and opposes that bourgeoisie once it attempts to consolidate "*its own* bourgeois nationalism."

1 What is Meant by the Self-Determination of Nations?

Naturally, this is the first question that arises when any attempt is made at a Marxist examination of what is known as self-determination. What should be understood by that term? Should the answer be sought in legal definitions deduced from all sorts of "general concepts" of law? Or is it rather to be sought in a historico-economic study of the national movements? [. . .]

A precise formulation of this question, which no Marxist can avoid, would at once destroy nine-tenths of Rosa Luxemburg's arguments.[1] This is not the first time that national movements have arisen in Russia, nor are they peculiar to that country alone. Throughout the world, the period of the final victory of capitalism over feudalism has been linked up with national movements. For the complete victory of commodity production, the bourgeoisie must capture the home market, and there must be politically united territories whose population speak a single language, with all obstacles to the development of that language and to its consolidation in literature eliminated. Therein is the economic foundation of national movements. Language is the most important means of human intercourse. Unity and unimpeded development of language are the most important conditions for genuinely free and extensive commerce on a scale commensurate with modern capitalism, for a free and broad grouping of the population in all its various classes and, lastly, for the establishment of a close connection between the market and each and every proprietor, big or little, and between seller and buyer.

Therefore, the tendency of every national movement is towards the formation of *national states*, under which these requirements of modern capitalism are best satisfied. The most profound economic factors drive towards this goal, and, therefore, for the whole of Western Europe, nay, for the entire civilised world, the national state is *typical* and normal for the capitalist period.

Consequently, if we want to grasp the meaning of self-determination of nations, not by juggling with legal definitions, or "inventing" abstract definitions, but by examining the historico-economic conditions of the national movements, we must inevitably reach the conclusion that the self-determination of nations means the political separation of these nations from alien national bodies, and the formation of an independent national state.

Later on we shall see still other reasons why it would be wrong to interpret the right to self-determination as meaning anything but the right to existence as a separate state. At present, we must deal with Rosa Luxemburg's efforts to "dismiss" the inescapable conclusion that profound economic factors underline the urge towards a national state. [. . .]

After reading such arguments, one cannot help marvelling at the author's ability to misunderstand *the how and the why of things*. To teach Kautsky, with a serious mien, that small states are economically dependent on big ones, that a struggle is raging among the bourgeois states for the predatory suppression of other nations, and that imperialism and colonies exist – all this is a ridiculous and puerile attempt to be clever, for none of this has the slightest bearing on the subject. Not only small states, but even Russia, for example, is entirely dependent, economically, on the power of the imperialist finance capital of the "rich" bourgeois countries. Not only the miniature Balkan states, but even nineteenth-century America was, economically, a colony of Europe, as Marx pointed out in *Capital*. Kautsky, like any Marxist, is, of course, well aware of this, but that has nothing whatever to do with the question of national movements and the national state.

For the question of the political self-determination of nations and their independence as states in bourgeois society, Rosa Luxemburg has substituted the question of their economic independence. This is just as intelligent as if someone, in discussing the programmatic demand for the supremacy of parliament, i.e., the assembly of people's representatives, in a bourgeois state, were to expound the perfectly correct conviction that big capital dominates in a bourgeois country, whatever the regime in it.

There is no doubt that the greater part of Asia, the most densely populated continent, consists either of colonies of the "Great Powers", or of states that are extremely dependent and oppressed as nations. But does this commonly-known circumstance in any way shake the undoubted fact that in Asia itself the conditions for the most complete development of commodity production and the freest, widest and speediest growth of capitalism have been created only in Japan, i.e., only in an independent national state? The latter is a bourgeois state, and for that reason has itself begun to oppress other nations and to enslave colonies. We cannot say whether Asia will have had time to develop into a system of independent national states, like Europe, before the collapse of capitalism, but it remains an undisputed fact that capitalism, having awakened Asia, has called forth national movements everywhere in that continent, too; that the tendency of these movements is towards the creation of national states in Asia; that it is such states that ensure the best conditions for the development of capitalism. The example of Asia speaks *in favour* of Kautsky and *against* Rosa Luxemburg.

The example of the Balkan states likewise contradicts her, for anyone can now see that the best conditions for the development of capitalism in the Balkans are created precisely in proportion to the creation of independent national states in that peninsula.

Therefore, Rosa Luxemburg notwithstanding, the example of the whole of progressive and civilised mankind, the example of the Balkans and that of Asia prove that Kautsky's proposition is absolutely correct: the national state is the rule and the "norm" of capitalism; the multinational state represents backwardness, or is an exception. From the standpoint of national relations, the best conditions for the development of capitalism are undoubtedly provided by the national state. This does not mean, of course, that such a state, which is based on bourgeois relations, can eliminate the exploitation and oppression of nations. It only means that Marxists cannot lose sight of the powerful *economic* factors that give rise to the urge to create national states. It means that "self-determination of nations" in the Marxists' Programme *cannot*, from a historico-economic point of view, have any other meaning than political self-determination, state independence, and the formation of a national state. [. . .]

2 The Historically Concrete Presentation of the Question

The categorical requirement of Marxist theory in investigating any social question is that it be examined within *definite* historical limits, and, if it refers to a particular country (e.g., the national programme for a given country), that account be taken of the specific features distinguishing that country from others in the same historical epoch.

What does this categorical requirement of Marxism imply in its application to the question under discussion?

First of all, it implies that a clear distinction must be drawn between the two periods of capitalism, which differ radically from each other as far as the national movement is concerned. On the one hand, there is the period of the collapse of feudalism and absolutism, the period of the formation of the bourgeois-democratic society and state, when the national movements for the first time become mass movements and in one way or another draw *all* classes of the population into politics through the press, participation in representative institutions, etc. On the other hand, there is the period of fully formed capitalist states with a long-established constitutional regime and a highly developed antagonism between the proletariat and the bourgeoisie – a period that may be called the eve of capitalism's downfall.

The typical features of the first period are: the awakening of national movements and the drawing of the peasants, the most numerous and the most sluggish section of the population, into these movements, in connection with the struggle for political liberty in general, and for the rights of the nation in particular. Typical features of the second period are: the absence of mass bourgeois-democratic movements and the fact that developed capitalism, in bringing closer together nations that have already been fully drawn into commercial intercourse, and causing them to intermingle to an increasing degree, brings the antagonism between internationally united capital and the international working-class movement into the forefront.

Of course, the two periods are not walled off from each other; they are connected by numerous transitional links, the various countries differing from each other in the rapidity of their national development, in the national make-up and distribution of their population, and so on. There can be no question of the Marxists of any country drawing up their national programme without taking into account all these general historical and concrete state conditions. [...]

3 The Concrete Features of the National Question in Russia, and Russia's Bourgeois-Democratic Reformation

[...] A comparison of the political and economic development of various countries, as well as of their Marxist programmes, is of tremendous importance from the standpoint of Marxism, for there can be no doubt that all modern states are of a common capitalist nature and are therefore subject to a common law of development. But such a comparison must be drawn in a sensible way. The elementary condition for comparison is to find out whether the historical periods of development of the countries concerned are at all *comparable*. For instance, only absolute ignoramuses (such as Prince Y. Trubetskoi in *Russkaya Mysl*) are capable of "comparing" the Russian Marxists' agrarian programme with the programmes of Western Europe, since our programme replies to questions that concern the *bourgeois-democratic* agrarian reform, whereas in the Western countries no such question arises.

The same applies to the national question. In most Western countries it was settled long ago. It is ridiculous to seek an answer to non-existent questions in the programmes of Western Europe. In this respect Rosa Luxemburg has lost sight of the most important thing – the difference between countries where bourgeois-democratic reforms have long been completed, and those where they have not.

The crux of the matter lies in this difference. Rosa Luxemburg's complete disregard of it transforms her verbose article into a collection of empty and meaningless platitudes.

The epoch of bourgeois-democratic revolutions in Western, continental Europe embraces a fairly definite period, approximately between 1789 and 1871. This was precisely the period of national movements and the creation of national states. When this period drew to a close, Western Europe had been transformed into a settled system of bourgeois states, which, as a general rule, were nationally uniform states. Therefore, to seek the right to self-determination in the programmes of West-European socialists at this time of day is to betray one's ignorance of the ABC of Marxism.

In Eastern Europe and Asia the period of bourgeois-democratic revolutions did not begin until 1905. The revolutions in Russia, Persia, Turkey and China, the Balkan wars – such is the chain of world events of *our* period in our "Orient". And only a blind man could fail to see in this chain of events the awakening of a *whole series* of bourgeois-democratic national movements which strive to create nationally independent and nationally uniform states. It is precisely and solely because Russia and the neighbouring countries are passing through this period that we must have a clause in our programme on the right of nations to self-determination.[. . .]

The peculiar conditions in Russia with regard to the national question are just the reverse of those we see in Austria. Russia is a state with a single national centre – Great Russia. The Great Russians occupy a vast, unbroken stretch of territory, and number about 70,000,000. The specific features of this national state are: first, that "subject peoples" (which, on the whole, comprise the majority of the entire population – 57 per cent) inhabit the border regions; secondly, the oppression of these subject peoples is much stronger here than in the neighbouring states (and not even in the European states alone); thirdly, in a number of cases the oppressed nationalities inhabiting the border regions have compatriots across the border, who enjoy greater national independence (suffice it to mention the Finns, the Swedes, the Poles, the Ukrainians and the Rumanians along the western and southern frontiers of the state); fourthly, the development of capitalism and the general level of culture are often higher in the non-Russian border regions than in the centre. Lastly, it is in the neighbouring Asian states that we see the beginning of a phase of bourgeois revolutions and national movements which are spreading to some of the kindred nationalities within the borders of Russia.

Thus, it is precisely the special concrete, historical features of the national question in Russia that make the recognition of the right of nations to self-determination in the present period a matter of special urgency in our country. [. . .]

4 "Practicality" in the National Question

Rosa Luxemburg's argument that §9 of our [i.e. Russian Marxists'] Programme contains nothing "practical" has been seized upon by the opportunists. Rosa Luxemburg is so delighted with this argument that in some parts of her article this "slogan" is repeated eight times on a single page.

She writes: §9 "gives no practical lead on the day-by-day policy of the proletariat, no practical solution of national problems".

Let us examine this argument, which elsewhere is formulated in such a way that it makes §9 look quite meaningless, or else commits us to support all national aspirations.

What does the demand for "practicality" in the national question mean?

It means one of three things: support for all national aspirations; the answer "yes" or "no" to the question of secession by any nation; or that national demands are in general immediately "practicable".

Let us examine all three possible meanings of the demand for "practicality".

The bourgeoisie, which naturally assumes the leadership at the start of every national movement, says that support for all national aspirations is practical. However, the proletariat's policy in the national question (as in all others) supports the bourgeoisie only in a certain direction, but it never coincides with the bourgeoisie's policy. The working class supports the bourgeoisie only in order to secure national peace (which the bourgeoisie cannot bring about completely and which can be achieved only with *complete* democracy), in order to secure equal rights and to create the best conditions for the class struggle. Therefore, it is *in opposition to the practicality* of the bourgeoisie that the proletarians advance their *principles* in the national question: they always give the bourgeoisie *only conditional* support. What every bourgeoisie is out for in the national question is either privileges for its *own* nation, or exceptional advantages for it; this is called being "practical". The proletariat is opposed to all privileges, to all exclusiveness. To demand that it should be "practical" means following the lead of the bourgeoisie, falling into opportunism.

The demand for a "yes" or "no" reply to the question of secession in the case of every nation may seem a very "practical" one. In reality it is absurd; it is metaphysical, in theory, while in practice it leads to subordinating the proletariat to the bourgeoisie's policy. The bourgeoisie always places its national demands in the forefront, and does so in categorical fashion. With the proletariat, however, these demands are subordinated to the interests of the class struggle. Theoretically, you cannot say in advance whether the bourgeois-democratic revolution will end in a given nation seceding from another nation, or in its equality with the latter; *in either case*, the important thing for the proletariat is to ensure the development of its class. For the bourgeoisie it is important to hamper this development by pushing the aims of its "own" nation before those of the proletariat. That is why the proletariat confines itself, so to speak, to the negative demand for recognition of the *right* to self-determination, without giving guarantees to any nation, and without undertaking to give *anything at the expense* of another nation.

This may not be "practical", but it is in effect the best guarantee for the achievement of the most democratic of all possible solutions. The proletariat needs *only* such guarantees, whereas the bourgeoisie of every nation requires guarantees for *its own* interest, regardless of the position of (or the possible disadvantages to) other nations.

The bourgeoisie is most of all interested in the "feasibility" of a given demand – hence the invariable policy of coming to terms with the bourgeoisie of other nations, to the detriment of the proletariat. For the proletariat, however, the important thing is to strengthen its class against the bourgeoisie and to educate the masses in the spirit of consistent democracy and socialism.

This may not be "practical" as far as the opportunists are concerned, but it is the only real guarantee, the guarantee of the greater national equality and peace, despite the feudal landlords and the *nationalist* bourgeoisie.

The whole task of the proletarians in the national question is "unpractical" from the standpoint of the *nationalist* bourgeoisie of every nation, because the proletarians, opposed as they are to nationalism of every kind, demand "abstract" equality; they demand, as a matter of principle, that there should be no privileges, however slight. Failing to grasp this, Rosa Luxemburg, by her misguided eulogy of practicality, has opened the door wide for the opportunists, and especially for opportunist concessions to Great-Russian nationalism.

Why Great-Russian? Because the Great Russians in Russia are an oppressor nation, and opportunism in the national question will of course find expression among oppressed nations otherwise than among oppressor nations.

On the plea that its demands are "practical", the bourgeoisie of the oppressed nations will call upon the proletariat to support its aspirations unconditionally. The most practical procedure is to say a plain "yes" in favour of the secession of a *particular* nation rather than in favour of all nations having the *right* to secede!

The proletariat is opposed to such practicality. While recognising equality and equal rights to a national state, it values above all and places foremost the alliance of the proletarians of all nations, and assesses any national demand, any national separation, *from the angle* of the workers' class struggle. This call for practicality is in fact merely a call for uncritical acceptance of bourgeois aspirations.

By supporting the right to secession, we are told, you are supporting the bourgeois nationalism of the oppressed nations. This is what Rosa Luxemburg says, and she is echoed by Semkovsky, the opportunist, who incidentally is the only representative of liquidationist ideas on this question, in the liquidationist newspaper!

Our reply to this is: No, it is to the bourgeoisie that a "practical" solution of this question is important. To the workers the important thing is to distinguish the *principles* of the two trends. *Insofar as* the bourgeoisie of the oppressed nation fights the oppressor, we are always, in every case, and more strongly than anyone else, *in favour*, for we are the staunchest and the most consistent enemies of oppression. But insofar as the bourgeoisie of the oppressed nation stands for *its own* bourgeois nationalism, we stand against. We fight against the privileges and violence of the oppressor nation, and do not in any way condone strivings for privileges on the part of the oppressed nation.

If, in our political agitation, we fail to advance and advocate the slogan of the *right* to secession, we shall play into the hands, not only of the bourgeoisie, but also of the feudal landlords and the absolutism of the *oppressor* nation. Kautsky long ago used this argument against Rosa Luxemburg, and the argument is indisputable. When, in her anxiety not to "assist" the nationalist bourgeoisie of Poland, Rosa Luxemburg rejects the *right* to secession in the programme of the Marxists *in Russia*, she is *in fact* assisting the Great-Russian Black Hundreds. She is in fact assisting opportunist tolerance of the privileges (and worse than privileges) of the Great Russians.

Carried away by the struggle against nationalism in Poland, Rosa Luxemburg has forgotten the nationalism of the Great Russians, although it is *this* nationalism that is the most formidable at the present time. It is a nationalism that is more feudal than bourgeois, and is the principal obstacle to democracy and to the proletarian struggle. The bourgeois nationalism of *any* oppressed nation has a general democratic content that is directed *against* oppression, and it is this content that we *unconditionally* support. At the same time we strictly distinguish it from the tendency towards national exclusiveness; we fight against the tendency of the Polish bourgeois to oppress the Jews, etc., etc.

This is "unpractical" from the standpoint of the bourgeois and the philistine, but it is the only policy in the national question that is practical, based on principles, and really promotes democracy, liberty and proletarian unity. [...]

Note

1 [See Rosa Luxemburg, "The National Question and Autonomy," in *The National Question: Selected Writings by Rosa Luxemburg*, ed. H. B. Davis (New York: Monthly Review Press, 1976. Ed.]

24

Addresses: The Fourteen Points; and The League of Nations (1918, 1919)

Woodrow Wilson

Woodrow Wilson, selections from "Address to a Joint Session of Congress, January 8, 1918" (The Fourteen Points) and "Address Delivered at Columbus, Ohio, September 4, 1919" [source: Woodrow Wilson, *Selected Literary and Political Papers and Addresses of Woodrow Wilson*, 3 vols. New York: Grosset and Dunlap, 1927, 2: 257–9, 355–63]

President of the United States 1913–21, Wilson (1856–1924) founded a League of Nations to provide mutual assistance against aggression and arbitration of disputes among member states as part of the Treaty of Versailles in 1919. Never ratified by the United States, the League was rendered meaningless by the debilitating war reparations the Treaty imposed on Germany. Wilson's "Fourteen Points" of 1918 enshrined national self-determination as a principle of international relations. Earlier Allied demands for peace, rejected by the Axis Powers, had already included the reorganization of Europe on the basis of nationalities – demands aimed primarily against the tottering Austro-Hungarian (Hapsburg) Empire. Out of Versailles emerged Czechoslovakia, Yugoslavia, Poland, and Hungary, along with European-controlled mandates (e.g. Syria and Palestine) carved from the old Turkish (Ottoman) Empire. Wilson argued for an "impartial adjustment of all colonial claims" based on the principle that governmental authority must be balanced by popular will. In fact, he idealistically saw the League as the "redemption of weak nations" and the extension of "the American principle" that people "have a right to live their own lives under the governments which they themselves choose to set up." Recognizing that states would never strictly match ethnic-national territories, he still aimed to "right the history of Europe" through internationally supervised referenda among minority regions to determine national affiliation – prefiguring the post-Cold War era's "new world order."

The Fourteen Points

[...] The program of the world's peace, therefore, is our program; and that program, the only possible program, as we see it, is this:

I. Open covenants of peace, openly arrived at, after which there shall be no private international understandings of any kind but diplomacy shall proceed always frankly and in the public view.

II. Absolute freedom of navigation upon the seas, outside territorial waters, alike in peace and in war, except as the seas may be closed in whole or in part by international action for the enforcement of international covenants.

III. The removal, so far as possible, of all economic barriers and the establishment of an equality of trade conditions among all the nations consenting to the peace and associating themselves for its maintenance.

IV. Adequate guarantees given and taken that national armaments will be reduced to the lowest point consistent with domestic safety.

V. A free, open-minded, and absolutely impartial adjustment of all colonial claims, based upon a strict observance of the principle that in determining all such questions of sovereignty the interests of the populations concerned must have equal weight with the equitable claims of the government whose title is to be determined.

VI. The evacuation of all Russian territory and such a settlement of all questions affecting Russia as will secure the best and freest coöperation of the other nations of the world in obtaining for her an unhampered and unembarrassed opportunity for the independent determination of her own political development and national policy and assure her of a sincere welcome into the society of free nations under institutions of her own choosing; and, more than a welcome, assistance also of every kind that she may need and may herself desire. The treatment accorded Russia by her sister nations in the months to come will be the acid test of their good will, of their comprehension of her needs as distinguished from their own interests, and of their intelligent and unselfish sympathy.

VII. Belgium, the whole world will agree, must be evacuated and restored, without any attempt to limit the sovereignty which she enjoys in common with all other free nations. No other single act will serve as this will serve to restore confidence among the nations in the laws which they have themselves set and determined for the government of their relations with one another. Without this healing act the whole structure and validity of international law is forever impaired.

VIII. All French territory should be freed and the invaded portions restored, and the wrong done to France by Prussia in 1871 in the matter of Alsace-Lorraine, which has unsettled the peace of the world for nearly fifty years, should be righted, in order that peace may once more be made secure in the interest of all.

IX. A readjustment of the frontiers of Italy should be effected along clearly recognizable lines of nationality.

X. The peoples of Austria-Hungary, whose place among the nations we wish to see safeguarded and assured, should be accorded the freest opportunity of autonomous development.

XI. Rumania, Serbia, and Montenegro should be evacuated; occupied territories restored; Serbia accorded free and secure access to the sea; and the relations of the several Balkan states to one another determined by friendly counsel along historically established lines of allegiance and nationality; and international guarantees of the political and economic independence and territorial integrity of the several Balkan states should be entered into.

XII. The Turkish portions of the present Ottoman Empire should be assured a secure sovereignty, but the other nationalities which are now under Turkish rule should be assured an undoubted security of life and an absolutely unmolested opportunity of autonomous development, and the Dardanelles should be permanently opened as a free passage to the ships and commerce of all nations under international guarantees.

XIII. An independent Polish state should be erected which should include the territories inhabited by indisputably Polish populations, which should be assured a free and secure access to the sea, and whose political and economic independence and territorial integrity should be guaranteed by international covenant.

XIV. A general association of nations must be formed under specific covenants for the purpose of affording mutual guarantees of political independence and territorial integrity to great and small states alike. [...]

The League of Nations

[...] This treaty is unique in the history of mankind, because the center of it is the redemption of weak nations. There never was a congress of nations before that considered the rights of those who could not enforce their rights. There never was a congress of nations before that did not seek to effect some balance of power brought about by means of serving the strength and interest of the strongest powers concerned; whereas this treaty builds up nations that never could have won their freedom in any other way; builds them up by gift, by largess, not by obligations; builds them up because of the conviction of the men who wrote the treaty that the rights of people transcend the rights of governments, because of the conviction of the men who wrote that treaty that the fertile source of war is wrong. The Austro-Hungarian Empire, for example, was held together by military force and consisted of peoples who did not want to live together, who did not have the spirit of nationality as towards each other, who were constantly chafing at the bands that held them. Hungary, though a willing partner of Austria, was willing to be a partner because she could share Austria's strength to accomplish her own ambitions, and her own ambitions were to hold under her the Jugo-Slavic peoples that lay to the south of her; Bohemia, an unhappy partner, a partner by duress, beating in all her veins the strongest national impulse that was to be found anywhere in Europe; and north of that, pitiful Poland, a great nation divided up among the great powers of Europe, torn asunder, kinship disregarded, natural ties treated with contempt, and an obligatory division among sovereigns imposed upon her – a part of her given to Russia, a part of her given to Austria, a part of her given to Germany – great bodies of Polish people never permitted to have the normal intercourse with their kinsmen for fear that that fine instinct of the heart should assert itself which binds families together. Poland could never have won her independence. Bohemia never could have broken away from the Austro-Hungarian combination. The Slavic peoples to the south, running down into the great Balkan peninsula, had again and again tried to assert their nationality and independence, and had as often been crushed, not by the immediate power they were fighting, but by the combined power of Europe. The old alliances, the old balances of power, were meant to see to it that no little nation asserted its right to the disturbance of the peace of Europe, and every time an assertion of rights was attempted they were suppressed by combined influence and force.

This treaty tears away all that: says these people have a right to live their own lives under the governments which they themselves choose to set up. That is the American principle, and I was glad to fight for it. When strategic claims were urged, it was matter of common counsel that such considerations were not in our thought. We were not now arranging for future wars. We were giving people what belonged to them. My fellow citizens, I do not think there is any man alive who has a more tender sympathy for the great people of Italy than I have, and a very stern duty was presented to us when we had to consider some of the claims of Italy on the Adriatic, because strategically, from the point of view of future wars, Italy needed a military foothold on the other side of the Adriatic, but her people did not live there except in little spots. It was a Slavic people, and I had to say to my Italian friends, "Everywhere else in this treaty we have given territory to the people who lived on it, and I do not think that it is for the advantage of Italy, and I am sure it is not for the advantage of the world, to give Italy territory where other people live." I felt the force of the argument for what they wanted, and it was the old argument that had always prevailed, namely, that they needed it from a military point of view, and I have no doubt that if there is no league of nations, they will need it from a military point of view; but if there is a league of nations, they will not need it from a military point of view.

If there is no league of nations, the military point of view will prevail in every instance, and peace will be brought into contempt, but if there is a league of nations, Italy need not fear the fact that the shores on the other side of the Adriatic tower above the lower and sandy shores on her side the sea, because there will be no threatening guns there, and the nations of the world will have concerted, not merely to see that the Slavic peoples have their rights, but that the Italian people have their rights as well. I had rather have everybody on my side than be armed to the teeth. Every settlement that is right, every settlement that is based on the principles I have alluded to, is a safe settlement, because the sympathy of mankind will be behind it.

Some gentlemen have feared with regard to the League of Nations that we will be obliged to do things we do not want to do. If the treaty were wrong, that might be so, but if the treaty is right, we will wish to preserve right. I think I know the heart of this great people whom I, for the time being, have the high honor to represent better than some other men that I hear talk. I have been bred, and am proud to have been bred, in the old revolutionary school which set this Government up, when it was set up as the friend of mankind, and I know if they do not that America has never lost that vision or that purpose. But I have not the slightest fear that arms will be necessary if the purpose is there. If I know that my adversary is armed and I am not, I do not press the controversy, and if any nation entertains selfish purposes set against the principles established in this treaty and is told by the rest of the world that it must withdraw its claims, it will not press them.

The heart of this treaty then, my fellow citizens, is not even that it punishes Germany. That is a temporary thing. It is that it rectifies the age-long wrongs which characterized the history of Europe. There were some of us who wished that the scope of the treaty would reach some other age-long wrongs. It was a big job, and I do not say that we wished that it were bigger, but there were other wrongs elsewhere than in Europe and of the same kind which no doubt ought to be righted, and some day will be righted, but which we could not draw into the treaty because we could deal only with the countries whom the war had engulfed and affected. But so far as the scope of our authority went, we rectified the wrongs which have been the fertile source of war in Europe.

Have you ever reflected, my fellow countrymen, on the real source of revolution? Men do not start revolutions in a sudden passion. Do you remember what Thomas Carlyle said about the French Revolution? He was speaking of the so-called Hundred Days Terror which reigned not only in Paris, but throughout France, in the days of the French Revolution, and he reminded his readers that back of that hundred days lay several hundred years of agony and of wrong. The French people had been deeply and consistently wronged by their Government, robbed, their human rights disregarded, and the slow agony of those hundreds of years had after awhile gathered into a hot anger that could not be suppressed. Revolutions do not spring up over-night. Revolutions come from the long suppression of the human spirit. Revolutions come because men know that they have rights and that they are disregarded; and when we think of the future of the world in connection with this treaty we must remember that one of the chief efforts of those who made this treaty was to remove that anger from the heart of great peoples, great peoples who had always been suppressed, who had always been used, and who had always been the tools in the hands of governments, generally alien governments, not their own. The makers of the treaty knew that if these wrongs were not removed, there could be no peace in the world, because, after all, my fellow citizens, war comes from the seed of wrong and not from the seed of right. This treaty is an attempt to right the history of Europe, and, in my humble judgment, it is a measurable success. I say "measurable," my fellow citizens, because you will realize the difficulty of this:

Here are two neighboring peoples. The one people have not stopped at a sharp line, and the settlements of the other people or their migrations have not begun at a sharp line. They have intermingled. There are regions where you cannot draw a national line and say there are Slavs on this side and Italians on that. It cannot be done. You have to approximate the line. You have to come as near to it as you can, and then trust to the processes of history to redistribute, it may be, the people that are on the wrong side of the line. There are many such lines drawn in this treaty and to be drawn in the Austrian treaty, where there are perhaps more lines of that sort than in the German treaty. When we came to draw the line between the Polish people and the German people – not the line between Germany and Poland; there was no Poland, strictly speaking, but the line between the German and the Polish people – we were confronted by such problems as the disposition of districts like the eastern part of Silesia, which is called Upper Silesia because it is mountainous and the other part is not. Upper Silesia is chiefly Polish, and when we came to draw the line of what should be Poland it was necessary to include Upper Silesia if we were really going to play fair and make Poland up of the Polish peoples wherever we found them in sufficiently close neighborhood to one another, but it was not perfectly clear that Upper

Silesia wanted to be part of Poland. At any rate, there were Germans in Upper Silesia who said that it did not, and therefore we did there what we did in many other places. We said, "Very well, then, we will let the people that live there decide. We will have a referendum. Within a certain length of time after the war, under the supervision of an international commission which will have a sufficient armed force behind it to preserve order and see that nobody interferes with the elections, we will have an absolutely free vote and Upper Silesia shall go either to Germany or to Poland, as the people in Upper Silesia prefer." That illustrates many other cases where we provided for a referendum, or a plebiscite, as they chose to call it. We are going to leave it to the people themselves, as we should have done, what Government they shall live under. It is none of my prerogative to allot peoples to this Government or the other. It is nobody's right to do that allotting except the people themselves, and I want to testify that this treaty is shot through with the American principle of the choice of the governed.

Of course, at times it went further than we could make a practical policy of, because various peoples were keen upon getting back portions of their population which were separated from them by many miles of territory, and we could not spot the map over with little pieces of separated States. I even reminded my Italian colleagues that if they were going to claim every place where there was a large Italian population, we would have to cede New York to them, because there are more Italians in New York than in any Italian city. But I hope, I believe, that the Italians in New York City are as glad to stay there as we are to have them. But I would not have you suppose that I am intimating that my Italian colleagues entered any claim for New York City.

We of all peoples in the world, my fellow citizens, ought to be able to understand the questions of this treaty without anybody explaining them to us, for we are made up out of all the peoples of the world. I dare say that in this audience there are representatives of practically all the people dealt with in this treaty. You do not have to have me explain national aspirations to you. You have been brought up on them. You have learned of them since you were children, and it is those national aspirations which we sought to release and give an outlet to in this great treaty. [...]

25

Aims and Objects of Movement for Solution of Negro Problem (1924)

Marcus Garvey

Marcus Garvey, selection from "Aims and Objects of Movement for Solution of Negro Problem" (1924) [source: Marcus Garvey, *Philosophy and Opinions of Marcus Garvey*, ed. Amy Jacques-Garvey. New York: Atheneum, 1992, 37–40. Reprinted with the permission of Scribner, a division of Simon and Schuster; copyright © 1923, 1925 Amy Jacques-Garvey (Introduction copyright © 1992 Macmillan Publishing Company).]

A native of Jamaica, Garvey (1887–1940) founded there the Universal Negro Improvement Association (UNIA) and African Communities' League (ACL) in 1914, on his return from a year in Europe and England, where he was influenced by the rising tide of nationalist sentiment that produced the First World War. During the war, Garvey moved to the United States, where his ideas first gained attention. Harlem, with its "New Negro" consciousness emerging in the 1920s, became the home of the UNIA. Garvey's substantial following saw him as the Moses of his race, until he was imprisoned for mail fraud and subsequently deported to Jamaica. Influenced by earlier nationalist movements, from Herzl's Zionism to Irish Republicanism, and applying Wilson's declaration of an international right to self-determination, Garvey's militant program of "Africa for the Africans" called for a "general uplift of the Negro peoples of the world," the civilization of the "backward tribes" in Africa, and the establishment in Africa of "a central nation for the race." Garvey was convinced that the white race would never allow for the development of the black race in their midst, and that harmony between the races would only occur on the basis of fraternity between nations, that is, only when blacks returned to their "original home, Africa." Garvey taught "pride and purity of race," for whites and blacks alike, and saw integrationist black intellectuals like Du Bois as promoting a "race destroying doctrine" of miscegenation, leading, as in Gobineau, to a "mongrelization" that would harm both races.

Generally the public is kept misinformed of the truth surrounding new movements of reform. Very seldom, if ever, reformers get the truth told about them and their movements. Because of this natural attitude, the Universal Negro Improvement Association has been greatly handicapped in its work, causing thereby one of the most liberal and helpful human movements of the twentieth century to be held up to ridicule by those who take pride in poking fun at anything not already successfully established.

The white man of America has become the natural leader of the world. He, because of his exalted position, is called upon to help in all human efforts. From nations to individuals the appeal is made to him for aid in all things affecting humanity, so, naturally, there can be no great mass movement or change without first acquainting the leader on whose sympathy and advice the world moves.

It is because of this, and more so because of a desire to be Christian friends with the white race, why I explain the aims and objects of the Universal Negro Improvement Association.

The Universal Negro Improvement Association is an organization among Negroes that is seeking to improve the condition of the race, with the view of establishing a nation in Africa where Negroes will be given the opportunity to develop by themselves, without creating the hatred and animosity that now exist in countries of the white race through Negroes rivaling them for the highest and best positions in government, politics, society and industry. The organization believes in the rights of all men, yellow, white and black. To us, the white race has a right to the peaceful possession and occupation of countries of its own and in like manner the yellow and black races have their rights. It is only by an honest and liberal consideration of such rights can the world be blessed with the peace that is sought by Christian teachers and leaders.

The Spiritual Brotherhood of Man

The following preamble to the constitution of the organization speaks for itself:

"The Universal Negro Improvement Association and African Communities' League is a social, friendly, humanitarian, charitable, educational, institutional, constructive, and expansive society, and is founded by persons, desiring to the utmost to work for the general uplift of the Negro peoples of the world. And the members pledge themselves to do all in their power to conserve the rights of their noble race and to respect the rights of all mankind, believing always in the Brotherhood of Man and the Fatherhood of God. The motto of the organization is: One God! One Aim! One Destiny! Therefore, let justice be done to all mankind, realizing that if the strong oppresses the weak confusion and discontent will ever mark the path of man, but with love, faith and charity toward all the reign of peace and plenty will be heralded into the world and the generation of men shall be called Blessed."

The declared objects of the association are:

"To establish a Universal Confraternity among the race; to promote the spirit of pride and love; to reclaim the fallen; to administer to and assist the needy; to assist in civilizing the backward tribes of Africa; to assist in the development of Independent Negro Nations and Communities; to establish a central nation for the race; to establish Commissaries or Agencies in the principal countries and cities of the world for the representation of all Negroes; to promote a conscientious Spiritual workship among the native tribes of Africa; to establish Universities, Colleges, Academies and Schools for the racial education and culture of the people; to work for better conditions among Negroes everywhere."

Supplying a Long-Felt Want

The organization of the Universal Negro Improvement Association has supplied among Negroes a long-felt want. Hitherto the other Negro movements in America, with the exception of the Tuskegee effort of Booker T. Washington, sought to teach the Negro to aspire to social equality with the whites, meaning thereby the right to intermarry and fraternize in every social way. This has been the source of much trouble and still some Negro organizations continue to preach this dangerous "race destroying doctrine" added to a program of political agitation and aggression. The Universal Negro Improvement Association on the other hand believes in and teaches the pride and purity of race. We believe that the white race should uphold its racial pride and perpetuate itself, and that the black race should do likewise. We believe that there is room enough in the world for the various race groups to grow and develop by themselves without seeking to destroy the Creator's plan by the constant introduction of mongrel types.

The unfortunate condition of slavery, as imposed upon the Negro, and which caused the mongrelization of the race, should not be legalized and continued now to the harm and detriment of both races.

The time has really come to give the Negro a chance to develop himself to a moral-standard-man, and it is for such an opportunity that the Universal Negro Improvement Association seeks in the creation of an African nation for Negroes, where the greatest latitude would be given to work out this racial ideal.

There are hundreds of thousands of colored people in America who desire race amalgamation and miscegenation as a solution of the race problem. These people are, therefore, opposed to the race pride ideas of black and white; but the thoughtful of both races will naturally ignore the ravings of such persons and honestly work for the solution of a problem that has been forced upon us.

Liberal white America and race loving Negroes are bound to think at this time and thus evolve a program or plan by which there can be a fair and amicable settlement of the question.

We cannot put off the consideration of the matter, for time is pressing on our hands. The educated Negro is making rightful constitutional demands. The great white majority will never grant them, and thus we march on to danger if we do not now stop and adjust the matter.

The time is opportune to regulate the relationship between both races. Let the Negro have a country of his own. Help him to return to his original home, Africa, and there give him the opportunity to climb from the lowest to the highest positions in a state of his own. If not, then the nation will have to hearken to the demand of the aggressive, "social equality" organization, known as the National Association for the Advancement of Colored People, of which W. E. B. DuBois is leader, which declares vehemently for social and political equality, viz.: Negroes and whites in the same hotels, homes, residential districts, public and private places, a Negro as president, members of the Cabinet, Governors of States, Mayors of cities, and leaders of society in the United States. In this agitation, DuBois is ably supported by the "Chicago Defender," a colored newspaper published in Chicago. This paper advocates Negroes in the Cabinet and Senate. All these, as everybody knows, are the Negroes' constitutional rights, but reason dictates that the masses of the white race will never stand by the ascendency of an opposite minority group to the favored positions in a government, society and industry that exist by the will of the majority, hence the demand of the DuBois group of colored leaders will only lead, ultimately, to further disturbances in riots, lynching and mob rule. The only logical solution therefore, is to supply the Negro with opportunities and environments of his own, and there point him to the fullness of his ambition.

Negroes Who Seek Social Equality

The Negro who seeks the White House in America could find ample play for his ambition in Africa. The Negro who seeks the office of Secretary of State

in America would have a fair chance of demonstrating his diplomacy in
Africa. The Negro who seeks a seat in the Senate or of being governor of a
State in America, would be provided with a glorious chance for statesman-
ship in Africa.

The Negro has a claim on American white sympathy that cannot be
denied. The Negro has labored for 300 years in contributing to America's
greatness. White America will not be unmindful, therefore, of this consideration, but will treat him kindly. Yet it is realized that all human beings have a
limit to their humanity. The humanity of white America, we realize, will seek
self-protection and self-preservation, and that is why the thoughtful and
reasonable Negro sees no hope in America for satisfying the aggressive
program of the National Association for the Advancement of Colored People, but advances the reasonable plan of the Universal Negro Improvement
Association, that of creating in Africa a nation and government for the Negro
race.

This plan when properly undertaken and prosecuted will solve the race
problem in America in fifty years. Africa affords a wonderful opportunity at
the present time for colonization by the Negroes of the Western world.
There is Liberia, already established as an independent Negro government.
Let white America assist Afro-Americans to go there and help develop the
country. Then, there are the late German colonies; let white sentiment force
England and France to turn them over to the American and West Indian
Negroes who fought for the Allies in the World's War. Then, France, England and Belgium owe America billions of dollars which they claim they
cannot afford to repay immediately. Let them compromise by turning over
Sierra Leone and the Ivory Coast on the West Coast of Africa and add them
to Liberia and help make Liberia a state worthy of her history.

The Negroes of Africa and America are one in blood. They have sprung
from the same common stock. They can work and live together and thus
make their own racial contribution to the world. [. . .]

26

The Myth of the Twentieth Century (1930)

Alfred Rosenberg

Alfred Rosenberg, Book Three, chapter VII, "The Essential Unity," of *The Myth of the Twentieth Century* (1930) [source: Alfred Rosenberg, *The Myth of the Twentieth Century*, trans. Vivian Bird. Newport Beach, CA: Noontide Press, 1982, 447–9, 452–4, 460–2]

Born to German parents in Estonia, Rosenberg (1893–1946) studied architecture in Moscow; with the Russian Revolution, he left for Munich and joined the nascent Nazi Party in 1919 as part of its elite inner circle. Editor of the party newspaper, Rosenberg was influenced by Chamberlain's racial theories and by the "Protocols of the Elders of Zion," a forgery brought to Munich by "White Russian" émigrés that outlined a putative Jewish conspiracy for world conquest. In 1941 he became Reichminister for the occupied eastern territories; he was convicted of war crimes at the Nuremberg trials and hanged. His virulently anti-Semitic, anti-Christian, and anti-Communist rhetoric borrowed heavily from German philosophy, providing pseudo-intellectual support for Hitler's views. Rosenberg argued that history was no longer defined by the struggle of class against class, or religious dogma against dogma, but by "the struggle between blood and blood." He combined earlier German Romantic notions of national spirit with biological race: race was the physical expression of a people's soul. The task of the twentieth century was (as Chamberlain had argued) to create a new Nordic man with a new racial *Volk* consciousness. Rosenberg carried the arguments of ethnic revivalists like Macpherson to new extremes: while the old, embodied images of the Nordic gods may have disappeared, their spirit was eternal and had been mystically revived by the sacrifices of German soldiers in the First World War. By contrast, the "Jewish anti-race," spiritually based in lies and deception and without honor, must perish.

VII: The Essential Unity

A people is lost as a people and is dead, if, in surveying its history and in testing its will-to-the-future, it cannot discover unity. No matter what forms the past may have taken in its course, when a nation arrives at the point of truly denying the allegorical images which stem from its first awakening, then it has denied the roots of its being and of its becoming and it has condemned itself to unfruitfulness. For history is not a development from nothing to something, or from something insignificant to something great. It is not even the transformation of an essence into something completely different. Rather, the first racial *Volkish* awakening brought about by heroes, gods and poets is the ultimate achievement for all times. This first great supreme mythical achievement cannot, in essence, be perfected. It can merely take on other new forms. The value breathed into a god or hero is what is eternal in good and evil. Homer represented the highest enhancement of what was Greek and guarded this even in decline. Jehovah is the symbol of unbridled Jewry. The belief in Jehovah is the strength of even the lowest Jewish haggler in Poland.

This unity also holds for German history, for its men, its values, for the very old and new mythos, and for the supporting ideas of German *Volkhood*. One form of Odin is dead, i.e., the Odin who was the highest of the many gods who appeared as the embodiment of a generation still given up to natural symbolisms. But Odin as the eternal mirrored image of the primal spiritual powers of Nordic man lives today as over 5,000 years ago. Hermann Wirth finds traces of decline also in the ancient world of gods and influences of the Eskimo race. This may be so, but does not influence what is actually Germanic. He embodies himself in honor and heroism, in the creation of song and of art, in the protection of law and in the eternal search for wisdom. Odin learned that through the guilt of the gods, through the breaking of the bond to the builders of Valhalla, the race of gods must perish. Despite this decline, he nevertheless commanded Heimdall to summon the Aesir with his horn for the final decisive battle. Dissatisfied, eternally searching, the god wandered through the universe to try to fathom his destiny and the nature of his being. He sacrificed an eye so that he might participate in the deepest wisdom. As an eternal wanderer he is a symbol of the eternally searching and becoming Nordic soul which cannot withdraw self-confidently back to Jehovah and his representatives. The headstrong activity of the will, which, at first, drives so roughly through the Nordic lands in the battle songs about Thor, showed directly at their first appearance the innate, striving, wisdom-seeking, metaphysical side in Odin the Wanderer. But the same spirit is revealed once again with the great, free Ostrogoths and the devout Ulfilas.

It is also revealed, in accordance with the times, in the strengthened Knights Order and in the great Nordic-Western mystics as seen in their greatest spirit, Meister Eckehart. When, in Frederick's Prussia, the soul which once gave birth to Odin was revived at Hohenfriedberg and Leuthen, it was also reborn in the soul of the Thomas church cantor, Bach, and in Goethe. From this viewpoint our assertion will appear deeply justified, that a heroic Nordic saga, a Prussian march, a composition by Bach, a sermon by Eckehart, and a monologue by Faust are only varied experiences of one and the same soul. They are creations of the same will. They are eternal powers which were first united under the name Odin and which later gained form in Frederick the Great and Bismarck. As long as these powers are operative, as long as Nordic blood mixes with a Nordic soul and will, Nordic man will be active and work in mystic union. This is the prerequisite of every true-to-type creation.

Only the Mythos and its forms are truly alive. This is the thing for which men are ready to die. When the Franks had left the groves of their ancient homeland and their bodies and souls had become restless, the strength gradually vanished from them to resist the more firmly structured lives of the inhabitants of Gaul. In vain Theodoric sought to convert the King of the Franks, Clovis, to liberated Arianism. The Arian "heresy" named after its first teacher, Arius, was based on the idea that Christ, having been created by God, was therefore less divine than God the Father. Thus Theodoric tried to establish nationalism over the internationalism of Rome. Unfortunately, he was himself overruled by his hysterical wife. The leader of the militarily strongest Germanic tribe thus made the spiritual move over to the Roman camp. To be sure, neither he nor the other Franks thought of giving up their characteristic heroism. They only placed it alongside Christianity in order to fight under the latter's banner for their fame and power (*In hoc signo vinces*). Conditioned through the first step, the Roman mythos then overgrew the ancient Germanic ideas of the blood, so that it was able to take over leadership of the German soul. All wars now took place under the sign of the cross. And when this cross had triumphed everywhere, the struggle began within the converted world against the heretics. The Protestants, on their side, likewise bore the sign of the cross into the field. Then the mythos of the martyr's cross died. The present day churches strive to conceal that fact in the same way the Teutons once concealed the death of the old gods. Today, it is impossible to lead a North European army to war for the Christian cross, not even a Spanish or Italian army. Today men admittedly die for ideas, but none of these representations bears the sign which overcame the "devout" Theodoric. It no longer fills our lives in such a passionate manner that we are ready to give our lives for it. It is dead, and no power will any longer awaken it to life. In order to be able to work effectively for the cross today, the churches are forced to hide behind the ideas and symbols of our newly awakened mythos. But these are actually the signs of a strength whose destruction "Bonifacius" and Willibald had once planned. The signs of that blood which once created Odin and Baldur, which once produced Meister Eckehart, finally rose to self-consciousness, especially when the words *Altdeutschland* are uttered. Goethe once saw the task of our people in breaking the Roman *Reich* and in founding a new world.[. . .]

The consequences are of the most significant kind. Goethe's aphorism, "What is fruitful, alone is true," signifies the essence of all that is organic. A new measuring rod, which has never been used, has emerged. In recognition of inner truth we will learn that error, even "sin," can be true in the highest degree – if we make fruitful the rationally motivated, intuitive actively-willed man and enhance his strength as the creator, even if he has erred. Upon this rests, for example, the great value also of those natural science hypotheses which later have been revealed as materially incorrect. They have almost always stimulated the researching spirit to new thinking and helped to discover new facts. In short, they have enhanced life. The errors of observation led us to discovery of the diffraction of rays. Here organic truth reaches its hands out anew to the mysticism of Meister Eckehart.

A layman could now conclude from this that free rein is given to lies. This is not at all the case. The lie is vitally connected with a lack of feeling of honor and courage. Even if every man burdens himself with many lies, no lying German will be able to call himself "good" precisely because lies contradict the innermost character values which alone provide us with value and worth. The lie is thus not only actively willed, but is simultaneously an organic sin. It is the worst enemy of the Nordic race. Whoever abandons himself to it unchecked, perishes inwardly. He also separates himself voluntarily outwardly from the Germanic environment. He will by necessity seek association with characterless bastards and Jews. Here we observe an interesting counterpart which can be observed in all other domains.

If the actively-willed organic lie is the death of the Nordic man, then this also signifies the life-element of Jewry. Expressed paradoxically, the constant lie is the "organic" truth of the Jewish anti-race. The fact that the real content of the concept of honor is remote, draws with it a swindle which is often a commandment of religious law. Such is laid down in the Talmud and in the Schulchan-Aruch in a monumentally frank way. That brutal searcher for truth, Schopenhauer, called the Jews the "great masters of lies." Further, they are "a nation of shopkeepers and swindlers," according to Kant. Because this is so, the Jew cannot attain mastery in a state which is supported by enhanced concepts of honor. For exactly the same reason, however, the German cannot really live within the democratic system and be fruitful.

Capitalist democracy is built up upon mass swindling and exploitation in great and small things. Either one overcomes it after being poisoned ideally and materially or he perishes without salvation from sins against his organic truth.

A review of life can be represented in manifold ways. At first it occurs in a mythological-mystical manner. Then the clairvoyantly grasped laws of the world and spiritual commandments appear as personalities which possess eternal significance, as long as the race which created them still lives. Therefore Siegfried's life and death are an eternal vital presence (*Dasein*). Therefore the longing for redemption embodied in the *Twilight of the Gods* is necessary, recognized consequence of the breaking of an agreement, i.e., it was an offense against organic inner truth. An obligation to practice truth is an eternal feature of the Germanic consciousness of responsibility. German folk tales also reveal the same substance of truth. These stories are timeless and only wait upon ripe, awakened souls, to blossom anew. They can at any time be recast into another form of our world interpretation, that is, into what is comprehensible. This does not signify a development in the sense of progress. Thus it is necessary that the mythic content be revealed in terms of the climate of opinion of the era, that is, in the mode of representation of the time concerned. A *Weltanschauung* will thus only be "true" when folk tales, legends, mysticism, art and philosophy are mutually interchanged, when they express the same ideas in different manners and when they share inner values of the same kind.

Here the religious cult and public politics, as mythos represented by man himself, join together. To realize this is the goal of the racial cultured ideal of our times. Once the crucifix was able to effect a sudden magnetizing of thousands of men who looked at this symbol. Consciously and subconsciously all associative factors were added – Jesus Christ, the Sermon on the Mount, Golgotha, Resurrection of the faithful – and these were often welded together as deeds in the service of this symbol. Contemporary decay also possesses its symbol: the red flag. This hideous symbol awakens various responses among millions of men: the world brotherhood of the dispossessed, a proletarian state of the future, etc. Everyone who raises the red flag appears as a leader in this domain of the gutter. The old anti-symbols have fallen. Even the black, white and red banner which once fluttered at the head in a thousand battles has been pulled down. The enemies of Germany know what they have done. That the Marxists were able to do this, has robbed the honored flags of 1914 of their inner mythos. But a new symbol has already been raised and struggles with all others: the Swastika. If this symbol is unrolled, then it is the symbol for an old-new mythos. Those who gaze at it think of *Volk* honor and of living space and of the time when, as a symbol of the Nordic wanderers and warriors, it went ahead to Italy and Greece. Then it still appeared hesitantly in the Wars of Liberation, until, after 1918, it became the symbol of a new generation which finally wishes to become one with itself.

The symbol of organic Germanic truth is, today, without dispute, the black Swastika. [. . .]

This new yet ancient mythos of blood, whose countless falsifications we experience, was threatened. In the back of the isolated nation, dark satanic forces became active. They subverted the victorious armies of 1914. Once again a time came when the Fenris wolf broke his chains. He passed over a world with the stench of decomposition. The Midgard serpent whipped up the ocean. The millions could only be prepared for sacrificial death by one slogan. This slogan was called the honor of the *Volk* and its freedom. The world conflagration came to its end. Nameless sacrifices were demanded and made by all. We soon discovered that the demonic forces had triumphed over the god-like by striking the army in the back. More unrestrained than ever they raged, unleashed through the world. They produced new unrest, new conflagrations and new destruction. But at the same time in the bowed souls of the surviving kin of the dead warriors, that mythos of the blood for which the heroes died was renewed, deepened, comprehended and experienced in its most profound ramifications. Today, this inner voice demands fulfillment of the mythos of blood and the mythos of the soul, race and ego, *Volk* and Personality, blood and honor. These virtues must triumph alone and uncompromisingly. They must carry and determine the whole of life. The mythos of the German people demands that the two million dead heroes have not fallen in vain. It demands a world revolution. It no longer suffers any other supreme values alongside it. The personalities must close around the center of the *Volk* and race soul. They must gather around that mysterious center which has emerged from old which was made fruitful by the rhythm of German being and becoming whenever Germany turned towards it. It is that nobility, that freedom of mystic honor-conscious soul which was a previously unwitnessed stream which passed beyond Germany's frontiers as a sacrifice. It did not demand "representation." The individual soul died for freedom and honor of its own choice and for its *Volk*hood. This sacrifice alone can determine the future life-rhythm of the German people and cultivate the new type of German in hard conscious discipline through those who have taught and lived it. The old yet new mythos already impels and enriches millions of human souls. It speaks today with a thousand tongues. We did not "reach our ultimate development around 1800." We wish, with increased consciousness and fluid will, for the first time as an entire people, to become "one with ourselves" in the manner suggested by Meister Eckehart. Mythos is for hundreds of thousands of souls not something which one notices with learned presumption, as a curiosity in catalogues, but a new awakening of the all-shaping spiritual center. Faust's cry of "Allein, ich will" ("I, alone, will do it!") after passing through the whole of science, is the creed of the new time which wishes a new future and a will which is our destiny. But this will perceives not only the substance of old and new cultures in order to then withdraw. In conscious self-reliance it rejects the supreme values of the cultural-cycles overlaying us. The fact that our researchers remain stationary at the history of forms without themselves being able to shape, shows only that their formative-will is broken. But nothing justifies proclaiming their unfruitfulness as the destiny of the whole. The new mythos and the new type-creating strength which today struggles with us for expression, cannot generally be refuted. They will break a path and create facts.

The present day mythos is exactly as heroic as the figures of the generation living a thousand years ago were. The two million Germans who died all over the world for the idea of *Deutschland* suddenly revealed that they cast aside the entire 19th century. In the hearts of the most simple peasant and the most modest worker the old myth-testing power of the Nordic race soul was just as alive as it was once among the Teutons when they moved over the Alps. In everyday life one overlooks only too often what enormous spiritual strength has become alive in a man when he visualizes himself with a tattered regimental banner. Suddenly, he sees in all the many-hundred-year-old deeds of the regiment a piece of himself and the worlds of his ancestors. The sailor who, standing on the keel of the *Nürnberg*, sank before the eyes of the foe into the sea with the waving German flag in his hand, and the nameless officer of the *Magdeburg* who pocketed the secret code and was drowned with it – these are symbols, myths and types who have been forgotten in the present chaos. Whether we correctly respect the Gothic, the Baroque and the Romantic or not remains irrelevant and unimportant. What is important is not that these were just forms of expression of Nordic blood but that their blood in general is still present and that this ancient blood-will still lives. The field grey German *Volk* army was the proof of the myth-forming readiness for sacrifice. The present day renewal movement is a sign that many still uncounted millions have begun to understand what the two million dead heroes are. They are the martyrs to a new mythos of life, to a new faith absolutely. [. . .]

27

Three Guineas (1938)

Virginia Woolf

Virginia Woolf, selection from *Three Guineas* (1938) [source: Virginia Woolf, *Three Guineas*. San Diego: Harcourt Brace & Co., 1966, 104–9. Reprinted by permission of the Society of Authors.]

Woolf (1882–1941) was born into England's cultural elite; the Stephen family included eminent philosophers, jurists, and historians, and Woolf took advantage of her father's library. Her novels were central to literary modernism, but some of her non-fiction (especially *A Room of One's Own* and *Three Guineas*) became essential feminist reading. The bohemian circle that gathered at her family's Bloomsbury home included prominent intellectuals, such as art critic Roger Frye, writer E. M. Forster, and economist John Maynard Keynes. Woolf was cosmopolitan and pacifist, with socialist leanings. She was also one of the first to address in detail the question of women and nationalism. In *Three Guineas*, she responded to a three-year-old letter from a male correspondent that asked "How in your opinion are we to prevent war?" and invited her to join a society for its prevention. By 1938, the question had only gained in urgency. Woolf's answer was a sustained meditation on the relation of masculinity to war and on the larger political implications of gender difference and women's subjugation. But her words also registered recent changes in women's legal and economic status in England. Woolf argued that women would do better to form their own "Outsiders' Society," maintaining an ironic distance from masculine patriotism and nationalism. In fact, the outsider will say that "as a woman I have no country. As a woman I want no country. As a woman my country is the whole world." Woolf's work influenced almost all future Anglo-American feminism.

[...] To begin with an elementary distinction: a society is a conglomeration of people joined together for certain aims; while you, who write in your own person with your own hand are single. You the individual are a man whom we have reason to respect; a man of the brotherhood, to which, as biography proves, many brothers have belonged. Thus Anne Clough, describing her brother, says: "Arthur is my best friend and adviser. . . . Arthur is the comfort and joy of my life; it is for him, and from him, that I am incited to seek after all that is lovely and of good report." To which William Wordsworth, speaking of his sister but answering the other as if one nightingale called to another in the forests of the past, replies:

> The Blessing of my later years
> Was with me when a Boy:
> She gave me eyes, she gave me ears;
> And humble cares, and delicate fears;
> A heart, the fountain of sweet tears;
> And love, and thought, and joy.
> ["The Sparrow's Nest"]

Such was, such perhaps still is, the relationship of many brothers and sisters in private, as individuals. They respect each other and help each other and have aims in common. Why then, if such can be their private relationship, as biography and poetry prove, should their public relationship, as law and history prove, be so very different? And here, since you are a lawyer, with a lawyer's memory, it is not necessary to remind you of certain decrees of English law from its first records to the year 1919 by way of proving that the public, the society relationship of brother and sister has been very different from the private. The very word "society" sets tolling in memory the dismal bells of a harsh music: shall not, shall not, shall not. You shall not learn; you shall not earn; you shall not own; you shall not – such was the society relationship of brother to sister for many centuries. And though it is possible, and to the optimistic credible, that in time a new society may ring a carillon of splendid harmony, and your letter heralds it, that day is far distant. Inevitably we ask ourselves, is there not something in the conglomeration of people into societies that releases what is most selfish and violent, least rational and humane in the individuals themselves? Inevitably we look upon society, so kind to you, so harsh to us, as an ill-fitting form that distorts the truth; deforms the mind; fetters the will. Inevitably we look upon societies as conspiracies that sink the private brother, whom many of us have reason to respect, and inflate in his stead a monstrous male, loud of voice, hard of fist, childishly intent upon scoring the floor of the earth with chalk marks, within whose mystic boundaries human beings are penned, rigidly, separately, artificially; where, daubed red and gold, decorated like a savage with feathers he goes through mystic rites and enjoys the dubious pleasures of power and dominion while we, "his" women, are locked in the private house without share in the many societies of which his society is composed. For such reasons compact as they are of many memories and emotions – for who shall analyse the complexity of a mind that holds so deep a reservoir of time past within it? – it seems both wrong for us rationally and impossible for us emotionally to fill up your form and join your society. For by so doing we should merge our identity in yours; follow and repeat and score still deeper the old worn ruts in which society, like a gramophone whose needle has stuck, is grinding out with intolerable unanimity "Three hundred millions spent upon arms." We should not give effect to a view which our own experience of "society" should have helped us to envisage. Thus, Sir, while we respect you as a private person and prove it by giving you a guinea to spend as you choose, we believe that we can help you most effectively by refusing to join your society; by working for our common ends – justice and equality and liberty for all men and women – outside your society, not within.

But this, you will say, if it means anything, can only mean that you, the daughters of educated men, who have promised us your positive help, refuse to join our society in order that you may make another of your own. And what sort of society do you propose to found outside ours, but in co-operation with it, so that we may both work together for our common ends? That is a question which you have every right to ask, and which we must try to answer in order to justify our refusal to sign the form you send. Let us then draw rapidly in outline the kind of society which the daughters of educated men found and join outside your society but in co-operation with its ends. In the first place, this new society, you will be relieved to learn, would have no honorary treasurer, for it would need no funds. It would have no office, no committee, no secretary; it would call no meetings; it would hold no conferences. If name it must have, it could be called the Outsiders' Society. That is not a resonant name, but it has the advantage that it squares with facts – the facts of history, of law, of biography; even, it may be, with the still hidden facts of our still unknown psychology. It would consist of educated men's daughters working in their own class – how indeed can they work in any other? – and by their own methods for liberty, equality and peace. Their first duty, to which they would bind themselves not by oath, for oaths and ceremonies have no part in a society which must be anonymous and elastic before everything, would be not to fight with arms. This is easy for them to observe, for in fact, as the papers inform us, "the Army Council have no intention of opening recruiting for any women's corps." The country ensures it. Next they would refuse in the event of war to make munitions or nurse the wounded. Since in the last war both these activities were mainly discharged by the daughters of working men, the pressure upon them here too would be slight, though probably disagreeable. On the other hand the next duty to which they would pledge themselves is one of considerable difficulty, and calls not only for courage and initiative, but for the special knowledge of the educated man's daughter. It is, briefly, not to incite their brothers to fight, or to dissuade them, but to maintain an attitude of complete indifference. But the attitude expressed by the word "indifference" is so complex and of such importance that it needs even here further definition. Indifference in the first place must be given a firm footing upon fact. As it is a fact that she cannot understand what instinct compels him, what glory, what interest, what manly satisfaction fighting provides for him – "without war there would be no outlet for the manly qualities which fighting develops" – as fighting thus is a sex characteristic which she cannot share, the counterpart some claim of the maternal instinct which he cannot share, so is it an instinct which she cannot judge. The outsider therefore must leave him free to deal with this instinct by himself, because liberty of opinion must be respected, especially when it is based upon an instinct which is as foreign to her as centuries of tradition and education can make it. This is a fundamental and instinctive distinction upon which indifference may be based. But the outsider will make it her duty not merely to base her indifference upon instinct, but upon reason. When he says, as history proves that he has said, and may say again, "I am fighting to protect our country" and thus seeks to rouse her patriotic emotion, she will ask herself, "What does 'our country' mean to me an outsider?" To decide this she will analyse the meaning of patriotism in her own case. She will inform herself of the position of her sex and her class in the past. She will inform herself of the amount of land, wealth and property in the possession of her own sex and class in the present – how much of "England" in fact belongs to her. From the same sources she will inform herself of the legal protection which the law has given her in the past and now gives her. And if he adds that he is fighting to protect her body, she will reflect upon the degree of physical protection that she now enjoys when the words "Air Raid Precaution" are written on blank walls. And if he says that he is fighting to protect England from foreign rule, she will reflect that for her there are no "foreigners," since by law she becomes a foreigner if she marries a foreigner. And she will do her best to make this a fact, not by forced fraternity, but by human sympathy. All these facts will convince her reason (to put it in a nutshell) that her sex and class has very little to thank England for in the past; not much to thank England for in the present; while the security of her person in the future is highly dubious. But probably she will have imbibed, even from the governess, some romantic notion that Englishmen, those fathers and grand-fathers whom she sees marching in the picture of history, are "superior" to the men of other countries. This she will consider it her duty to check by comparing French historians with English; German with French; the testimony of the ruled – the Indians or the Irish, say – with the claims made by their rulers. Still some "patriotic" emotion, some ingrained belief in the intellectual superiority of her own country over other countries may remain. Then she will compare English painting with French painting; English music with German music; English literature with Greek literature, for translations abound. When all these comparisons have been faithfully made by the use of reason, the outsider will find herself in possession of very good reasons for her indifference. She will find that she has no good reason to ask her brother to fight on her behalf to protect "our" country. " 'Our country,' " she will say, "throughout the greater part of its history has treated me as a slave; it has denied me education or any share in its possessions. 'Our' country still ceases to be mine if I marry a foreigner. 'Our' country denies me the means of protecting myself, forces me to pay others a very large sum annually to protect me, and is so little able, even so, to protect me that Air Raid precautions are written on the wall. Therefore if you insist upon fighting to protect me, or 'our' country, let it be understood, soberly and rationally between us, that you are fighting to gratify a sex instinct which I cannot share; to procure benefits which I have not shared and probably will not share; but not to gratify my instincts, or to protect myself or my country. For," the outsider will say, "in fact, as a woman, I have no country. As a woman I want no country. As a woman my country is the whole world." And if, when reason has said its say, still some obstinate emotion remains, some love of England dropped into a child's ears by the cawing of rooks in an elm tree, by the splash of waves on a beach, or by English voices murmuring nursery rhymes, this drop of pure, if irrational, emotion she will make serve her to give to England first what she desires of peace and freedom for the whole world.

Such then will be the nature of her "indifference" and from this indifference certain actions must follow. She will bind herself to take no share in patriotic demonstrations; to assent to no form of national self-praise; to make no part of any claque or audience that encourages war; to absent herself from military displays, tournaments, tattoos, prize-givings and all such ceremonies as encourage the desire to impose "our" civilization or "our" dominion upon other people. The psychology of private life, moreover, warrants the belief that this use of indifference by the daughters of educated men would help materially to prevent war. For psychology would seem to show that it is far harder for human beings to take action when other people are indifferent and allow them complete freedom of action, than when their actions are made the centre of excited emotion. The small boy struts and trumpets outside the window: implore him to stop; he goes on; say nothing; he stops. That the daughters of educated men then should give their brothers neither the white feather of cowardice nor the red feather of courage, but no feather at all; that they should shut the bright eyes that rain influence, or let those eyes look elsewhere when war is discussed – that is the duty to which outsiders will train themselves in peace before the threat of death inevitably makes reason powerless. [. . .]

28

Discourse on Colonialism (1955)

Aimé Césaire

Aimé Césaire, selections from *Discourse on Colonialism* (1955) [source: Aimé Césaire, *Discourse on Colonialism*, trans. Joan Pinkham. New York: Monthly Review Press, 1972, 13–25, 57–61]

Born in Martinique, educated in Paris at the Ecole Normale Supérieure, poet and dramatist, Césaire (1913-) also wrote a study of Toussaint L'Ouverture. He is regarded as one of the founders, along with Léopold Senghor and Léon Damas, of the Negritude movement among Franco-phone African intellectuals. Negritude was a transnational affirmation of African culture and diasporic "black civilization" that demanded a "decolonization" and "disalienation" of black consciousness: it meant "that we were black and have a history...that contains certain cultural elements of great value." Though communist in outlook, Césaire also chastised French African Marxists for failing to recognize the "historical peculiarities" of "the Negro question." Césaire argued that pre-colonial, pre-capitalist Africa's "natural economies," its democratic, communal, and fraternal societies, were destroyed by European imperialism, which was as barbaric as Hitler (and he considered American imperialism the worst). Césaire acknowledged that, just as bourgeois Europe invented the abstraction *man* to justify its civilizing mission, so "the nation is a bourgeois phenomenon." But he also felt that the imperialist disruption of indigenous cultures would eventually bring about "the ruin of Europe" unless the colonizers initiated a policy of nation-building among the disinherited. Césaire had a large influence on anti-colonial movements in his time, and on postcolonial thinking after him.

[...] First we must study how colonization works to *decivilize* the colonizer, to *brutalize* him in the true sense of the word, to degrade him, to awaken him to buried instincts, to covetousness, violence, race hatred, and moral relativism; and we must show that each time a head is cut off or an eye put out in Vietnam and in France they accept the fact, each time a little girl is raped and in France they accept the fact, each time a Madagascan is tortured and in France they accept the fact, civilization acquires another dead weight, a universal regression takes place, a gangrene sets in, a center of infection begins to spread; and that at the end of all these treaties that have been violated, all these lies that have been propagated, all these punitive expeditions that have been tolerated, all these prisoners who have been tied up and "interrogated," all these patriots who have been tortured, at the end of all the racial pride that has been encouraged, all the boastfulness that has been displayed, a poison has been instilled into the veins of Europe and, slowly but surely, the continent proceeds toward *savagery.*

And then one fine day the bourgeoisie is awakened by a terrific reverse shock: the gestapos are busy, the prisons fill up, the torturers around the racks invent, refine, discuss.

People are surprised, they become indignant. They say: "How strange! But never mind – it's Nazism, it will pass!" And they wait, and they hope; and they hide the truth from themselves, that it is barbarism, but the supreme barbarism, the crowning barbarism that sums up all the daily barbarisms; that it is Nazism, yes, but that before they were its victims, they were its accomplices; that they tolerated that Nazism before it was inflicted on them, that they absolved it, shut their eyes to it, legitimized it, because, until then, it had been applied only to non-European peoples; that they have cultivated that Nazism, that they are responsible for it, and that before engulfing the whole of Western, Christian civilization in its reddened waters, it oozes, seeps, and trickles from every crack.

Yes, it would be worthwhile to study clinically, in detail, the steps taken by Hitler and Hitlerism and to reveal to the very distinguished, very humanistic, very Christian bourgeois of the twentieth century that without his being aware of it, he has a Hitler inside him, that Hitler *inhabits* him, that Hitler is his *demon*, that if he rails against him, he is being inconsistent and that, at bottom, what he cannot forgive Hitler for is not *crime* in itself, *the crime against man*, it is not *the humiliation of man as such*, it is the crime against the white man, the humiliation of the white man, and the fact that he applied to Europe colonialist procedures which until then had been reserved exclusively for the Arabs of Algeria, the coolies of India, and the blacks of Africa.

And that is the great thing I hold against pseudo-humanism: that for too long it has diminished the rights of man, that its concept of those rights has been – and still is – narrow and fragmentary, incomplete and biased and, all things considered, sordidly racist.

I have talked a good deal about Hitler. Because he deserves it: he makes it possible to see things on a large scale and to grasp the fact that capitalist society, at its present stage, is incapable of establishing a concept of the rights of all men, just as it has proved incapable of establishing a system of individual ethics. Whether one likes it or not, at the end of the blind alley that is Europe, I mean the Europe of Adenauer, Schuman, Bidault, and a few others, there is Hitler. At the end of capitalism, which is eager to outlive its day, there is Hitler. At the end of formal humanism and philosophic renunciation, there is Hitler.

And this being so, I cannot help thinking of one of his statements: "We aspire not to equality but to domination. The country of a foreign race must become once again a country of serfs, of agricultural laborers, or industrial workers. It is not a question of eliminating the inequalities among men but of widening them and making them into a law."

That rings clear, haughty, and brutal and plants us squarely in the middle of howling savagery. But let us come down a step.

Who is speaking? I am ashamed to say it: it is the Western *humanist*, the "idealist" philosopher. That his name is Renan is an accident. That the passage is taken from a book entitled *La Réforme intellectuelle et morale*, that it was written in France just after a war which France had represented as a war of right against might, tells us a great deal about bourgeois morals.

> The regeneration of the inferior or degenerate races by the superior races is part of the providential order of things for humanity. With us, the common man is nearly always a déclassé nobleman, his heavy hand is better suited to handling the sword than the menial tool. Rather than work, he chooses to fight, that is, he returns to his first estate. *Regere imperio populos*, that is our vocation. Pour forth this all-consuming activity onto countries which, like China, are crying aloud for foreign conquest. Turn the adventurers who disturb European society into a *ver sacrum*, a horde like those of the Franks, the Lombards, or the Normans, and every man will be in his right role. Nature has made a race of workers, the Chinese race, who have wonderful manual dexterity and almost no sense of honor; govern them with justice, levying from them, in return for the blessing of such a government, an ample allowance for the conquering race, and they will be satisfied; a race of tillers of the soil, the Negro; treat him with kindness and humanity, and all will be as it should; a race of masters and soldiers, the European race. Reduce this noble race to working in the *ergastulum* like Negroes and Chinese, and they rebel. In Europe, every rebel is, more or less, a soldier who has missed his calling, a creature made for the heroic life, before whom you are setting *a task that is contrary to his race* – a poor worker, too good a soldier. But the life at which our workers rebel would make a Chinese or a fellah happy, as they are not military creatures in the least. *Let each one do what he is made for, and all will be well.*

Hitler? Rosenberg? No, Renan.

But let us come down one step further. And it is the long-winded politician. Who protests? No one, so far as I know, when M. Albert Sarraut, the former governor-general of Indochina, holding forth to the students at the Ecole Coloniale, teaches them that it would be puerile to object to the European colonial enterprises in the name of "an alleged right to possess the land one occupies, and some sort of right to remain in fierce isolation, which would leave unutilized resources to lie forever idle in the hands of incompetents."

And who is roused to indignation when a certain Rev. Barde assures us that if the goods of this world "remained divided up indefinitely, as they would be without colonization, they would answer neither the purposes of God nor the just demands of the human collectivity"?

Since, as his fellow Christian, the Rev. Muller, declares: "Humanity must not, cannot allow the incompetence, negligence, and laziness of the uncivilized peoples to leave idle indefinitely the wealth which God has confided to them, charging them to make it serve the good of all."

No one.

I mean not one established writer, not one academician, not one preacher, not one crusader for the right and for religion, not one "defender of the human person."

And yet, through the mouths of the Sarrauts and the Bardes, the Mullers and the Renans, through the mouths of all those who considered – and consider – it lawful to apply to non-European peoples "a kind of expropriation for public purposes" for the benefit of nations that were stronger and better equipped, it was already Hitler speaking!

What am I driving at? At this idea: that no one colonizes innocently, that no one colonizes with impunity either; that a nation which colonizes, that a civilization which justifies colonization – and therefore force – is already a sick civilization, a civilization that is morally diseased, that irresistibly, progressing from one consequence to another, one repudiation to another, calls for its Hitler, I mean its punishment.

Colonization: bridgehead in a campaign to civilize barbarism, from which there may emerge at any moment the negation of civilization, pure and simple.

Elsewhere I have cited at length a few incidents culled from the history of colonial expeditions.

Unfortunately, this did not find favor with everyone. It seems that I was pulling old skeletons out of the closet. Indeed!

Was there no point in quoting Colonel de Montagnac, one of the conquerors of Algeria: "In order to banish the thoughts that sometimes besiege me, I have some heads cut off, not the heads of artichokes but the heads of men."

Would it have been more advisable to refuse the floor to Count d'Hérisson: "It is true that we are bringing back a whole barrelful of ears collected, pair by pair, from prisoners, friendly or enemy."

Should I have refused Saint-Arnaud the right to profess his barbarous faith: "We lay waste, we burn, we plunder, we destroy the houses and the trees."

Should I have prevented Marshal Bugeaud from systematizing all that in a daring theory and invoking the precedent of famous ancestors: "We must have a great invasion of Africa, like the invasions of the Franks and the Goths."

Lastly, should I have cast back into the shadows of oblivion the memorable feat of arms of General Gérard and kept silent about the capture of Ambike, a city which, to tell the truth, had never dreamed of defending itself: "The native riflemen had orders to kill only the men, but no one restrained them; intoxicated by the smell of blood, they spared not one woman, not one child ... At the end of the afternoon, the heat caused a light mist to arise: it was the blood of the five thousand victims, the ghost of the city, evaporating in the setting sun."

Yes or no, are these things true? And the sadistic pleasures, the nameless delights that send voluptuous shivers and quivers through Loti's carcass when he focuses his field glasses on a good massacre of the Annamese? True or not true?[1] And if these things are true, as no one can deny, will it be said, in order to minimize them, that these corpses don't prove anything?

For my part, if I have recalled a few details of these hideous butcheries, it is by no means because I take a morbid delight in them, but because I think that these heads of men, these collections of ears, these burned houses, these Gothic invasions, this steaming blood, these cities that evaporate at the edge of the sword, are not to be so easily disposed of. They prove that colonization, I repeat, dehumanizes even the most civilized man; that colonial activity, colonial enterprise, colonial conquest, which is based on contempt for the native and justified by that contempt, inevitably tends to change him who undertakes it; that the colonizer, who in order to ease his conscience gets into the habit of seeing the other man as *an animal*, accustoms himself to treating him like an animal, and tends objectively to transform *himself* into an animal. It is this result, this boomerang effect of colonization, that I wanted to point out.

Unfair? No. There was a time when these same facts were a source of pride, and when, sure of the morrow, people did not mince words. One last quotation; it is from a certain Carl Siger, author of an *Essai sur la colonisation* (Paris, 1907):

> The new countries offer a vast field for individual, violent activities which, in the metropolitan countries, would run up against certain prejudices, against a sober and orderly conception of life, and which, in the colonies, have greater

freedom to develop and, consequently, to affirm their worth. Thus to a certain extent the colonies can serve as a safety valve for modern society. Even if this were their only value, it would be immense.

Truly, there are stains that it is beyond the power of man to wipe out and that can never be fully expiated.

But let us speak about the colonized.

I see clearly what colonization has destroyed: the wonderful Indian civilizations – and neither Deterding nor Royal Dutch nor Standard Oil will ever console me for the Aztecs and the Incas.

I see clearly the civilizations, condemned to perish at a future date, into which it has introduced a principle of ruin: the South Sea islands, Nigeria, Nyasaland. I see less clearly the contributions it has made.

Security? Culture? The rule of law? In the meantime, I look around and wherever there are colonizers and colonized face to face, I see force, brutality, cruelty, sadism, conflict, and, in a parody of education, the hasty manufacture of a few thousand subordinate functionaries, "boys," artisans, office clerks, and interpreters necessary for the smooth operation of business.

I spoke of contact.

Between colonizer and colonized there is room only for forced labor, intimidation, pressure, the police, taxation, theft, rape, compulsory crops, contempt, mistrust, arrogance, self-complacency, swinishness, brainless élites, degraded masses.

No human contact, but relations of domination and submission which turn the colonizing man into a classroom monitor, an army sergeant, a prison guard, a slave driver, and the indigenous man into an instrument of production.

My turn to state an equation: colonization = "thingification."

I hear the storm. They talk to me about progress, about "achievements," diseases cured, improved standards of living.

I am talking about societies drained of their essence, cultures trampled underfoot, institutions undermined, lands confiscated, religions smashed, magnificent artistic creations destroyed, extraordinary *possibilities* wiped out.

They throw facts at my head, statistics, mileages of roads, canals, and railroad tracks.

I am talking about thousands of men sacrificed to the Congo-Océan. I am talking about those who, as I write this, are digging the harbor of Abidjan by hand. I am talking about millions of men torn from their gods, their land, their habits, their life – from life, from the dance, from wisdom.

I am talking about millions of men in whom fear has been cunningly instilled, who have been taught to have an inferiority complex, to tremble, kneel, despair, and behave like flunkeys.

They dazzle me with the tonnage of cotton or cocoa that has been exported, the acreage that has been planted with olive trees or grapevines.

I am talking about natural *economies* that have been disrupted – harmonious and viable *economies* adapted to the indigenous population – about food crops destroyed, malnutrition permanently introduced, agricultural development oriented solely toward the benefit of the metropolitan countries, about the looting of products, the looting of raw materials.

They pride themselves on abuses eliminated.

I too talk about abuses, but what I say is that on the old ones – very real – they have superimposed others – very detestable. They talk to me about local tyrants brought to reason; but I note that in general the old tyrants get on very well with the new ones, and that there has been established between them, to the detriment of the people, a circuit of mutual services and complicity.

They talk to me about civilization, I talk about proletarianization and mystification.

For my part, I make a systematic defense of the non-European civilizations.

Every day that passes, every denial of justice, every beating by the police, every demand of the workers that is drowned in blood, every scandal that is hushed up, every punitive expedition, every police van, every gendarme and every militiaman, brings home to us the value of our old societies.

They were communal societies, never societies of the many for the few.

They were societies that were not only ante-capitalist, as has been said, but also *anti-capitalist*.

They were democratic societies, always.

They were cooperative societies, fraternal societies.

I make a systematic defense of the societies destroyed by imperialism.

They were the fact, they did not pretend to be the idea; despite their faults, they were neither to be hated nor condemned. They were content to be. In them, neither the word *failure* nor the word *avatar* had any meaning. They kept hope intact.

Whereas those are the only words that can, in all honesty, be applied to the European enterprises outside Europe. My only consolation is that periods of colonization pass, that nations sleep only for a time, and that peoples remain.

This being said, it seems that in certain circles they pretend to have discovered in me an "enemy of Europe" and a prophet of the return to the ante-European past.

For my part, I search in vain for the place where I could have expressed such views; where I ever underestimated the importance of Europe in the history of human thought; where I ever preached a *return* of any kind; where I ever claimed that there could be a *return*.

The truth is that I have said something very different: to wit, that the great historical tragedy of Africa has been not so much that it was too late in making contact with the rest of the world, as the manner in which that contact was brought about; that Europe began to "propagate" at a time when it had fallen into the hands of the most unscrupulous financiers and captains of industry; that it was our misfortune to encounter that particular Europe on our path, and that Europe is responsible before the human community for the highest heap of corpses in history.

In another connection, in judging colonization, I have added that Europe has gotten on very well indeed with all the local feudal lords who agreed to serve, woven a villainous complicity with them, rendered their tyranny more effective and more efficient, and that it has actually tended to prolong artificially the survival of local pasts in their most pernicious aspects.

I have said – and this is something very different – that colonialist Europe has grafted modern abuse onto ancient injustice, hateful racism onto old inequality.

That if I am attacked on the grounds of intent, I maintain that colonialist Europe is dishonest in trying to justify its colonizing activity *a posteriori* by the obvious material progress that has been achieved in certain fields under the colonial regime – since *sudden change* is always possible, in history as elsewhere; since no one knows at what stage of material development these same countries would have been if Europe had not intervened; since the technical outfitting of Africa and Asia, their administrative reorganization, in a word, their "Europeanization," was (as is proved by the example of Japan) in no way tied to the European *occupation*; since the Europeanization of the non-European continents could have been accomplished otherwise than under the heel of Europe; since this movement of Europeanization *was in progress*; since it was even slowed down; since in any case it was distorted by the European takeover.

The proof is that at present it is the indigenous peoples of Africa and Asia who are demanding schools, and colonialist Europe which refuses them; that it is the African who is asking for ports and roads, and colonialist Europe which is niggardly on this score; that it is the colonized man who wants to move forward, and the colonizer who holds things back. [. . .]

One of the values invented by the bourgeoisie in former times and launched throughout the world was *man* – and we have seen what has become of that. The other was the nation.

It is fact: the *nation* is a bourgeois phenomenon.

Exactly; but if I turn my attention from *man* to *nations,* I note that here too there is great danger; that colonial enterprise is to the modern world what Roman imperialism was to the ancient world: the prelude to Disaster and the forerunner of Catastrophe. Come, now! The Indians massacred, the Moslem world drained of itself, the Chinese world defiled and perverted for a good century; the Negro world disqualified; mighty voices stilled forever; homes scattered to the wind; all this wreckage, all this waste, humanity reduced to a monologue, and you think that all that does not have its price? The truth is that this policy *cannot but bring about the ruin of Europe itself*, and that Europe, if it is not careful, will perish from the void it has created around itself.

They thought they were only slaughtering Indians, or Hindus, or South Sea islanders, or Africans. They have in fact overthrown, one after another, the ramparts behind which European civilization could have developed freely.

I know how fallacious historical parallels are, particularly the one I am about to draw. Nevertheless, permit me to quote a page from Edgar Quinet for the not inconsiderable element of truth which it contains and which is worth pondering. Here it is:

> People ask why barbarism emerged all at once in ancient civilization. I believe I know the answer. It is surprising that so simple a cause is not obvious to everyone. The system of ancient civilization was composed of a certain number of nationalities, of countries which, although they seemed to be enemies, or were even ignorant of each other, protected, supported, and guarded one another. When the expanding Roman empire undertook to conquer and destroy these groups of nations, the dazzled sophists thought they saw at the end of this road humanity triumphant in Rome. They talked about the unity of the human spirit; it was only a dream. It happened that these nationalities were so many bulwarks protecting Rome itself....Thus when Rome, in its alleged triumphal march toward a single civilization, had destroyed, one after the other, Carthage, Egypt, Greece, Judea, Persia, Dacia, and Cisalpine and Trans-alpine Gaul, it came to pass that it had itself swallowed up the dikes that protected it against the human ocean under which it was to perish. The magnanimous Caesar, by crushing the two Gauls, only paved the way for the Teutons. So many societies, so many languages extinguished, so many cities, rights, homes annihilated, created a void around Rome, and in those places which were not invaded by the barbarians, barbarism was born spontaneously. The vanquished Gauls changed into Bagaudes. Thus the violent downfall, the progressive extirpation of individual cities, caused the crumbling of ancient civilization. That social edifice was supported by the various nationalities as by so many different columns of marble or porphyry.
>
> When, to the applause of the wise men of the time, each of these living columns had been demolished, the edifice came crashing down; and the wise men of our day are still trying to understand how such mighty ruins could have been made in a moment's time.[2]

And now I ask: what else has bourgeois Europe done? It has undermined civilizations, destroyed countries, ruined nationalities, extirpated "the root of diversity." No more dikes, no more bulwarks. The hour of the barbarian is at hand. The modern barbarian. The American hour. Violence, excess, waste, mercantilism, bluff, gregariousness, stupidity, vulgarity, disorder.

In 1913, Ambassador Page wrote to Wilson:

"The future of the world belongs to us . . . .Now what are we going to do with the leadership of the world presently when it clearly falls into our hands?"

And in 1914: "What are we going to do with this England and this Empire, presently, when economic forces unmistakably put the leadership of the race in our hands?"

This Empire . . . And the others . . .

And indeed, do you not see how ostentatiously these gentlemen have just unfurled the banner of anti-colonialism?

"*Aid to the disinherited countries*," says Truman. "The time of the old colonialism has passed." That's also Truman.

Which means that American high finance considers that the time has come to raid every colony in the world. So, dear friends, here you have to be careful!

I know that some of you, disgusted with Europe, with all that hideous mess which you did not witness by choice, are turning – oh! in no great numbers – toward America and getting used to looking upon that country as a possible liberator.

"What a godsend!" you think.

"The bulldozers! The massive investments of capital! The roads! The ports!"

"But American racism!"

"So what? European racism in the colonies has inured us to it!"

And there we are, ready to run the great Yankee risk.

So, once again, be careful!

American domination – the only domination from which one never recovers. I mean from which one never recovers unscarred.

And since you are talking about factories and industries, do you not see the tremendous factory hysterically spitting out its cinders in the heart of our forests or deep in the bush, the factory for the production of lackeys; do you not see the prodigious mechanization, the mechanization of man; the gigantic rape of everything intimate, undamaged, undefiled that, despoiled as we are, our human spirit has still managed to preserve; the machine, yes, have you never seen it, the machine for crushing, for grinding, for degrading peoples?

So that the danger is immense.

So that unless, in Africa, in the South Sea islands, in Madagascar (that is, at the gates of South Africa), in the West Indies (that is, at the gates of America), Western Europe undertakes on its own initiative a policy of *nationalities*, a new policy founded on respect for peoples and cultures – nay, more – unless Europe galvanizes the dying cultures or raises up new ones, unless it becomes the awakener of countries and civilizations (this being said without taking into account the admirable resistance of the colonial peoples primarily symbolized at present by Vietnam, but also by the Africa of the Rassemblement Démocratique Africain), Europe will have deprived itself of its last chance and, with its own hands, drawn up over itself the pall of mortal darkness.

Which comes down to saying that the salvation of Europe is not a matter of a revolution in methods. It is a matter of the Revolution – the one which, until such time as there is a classless society, will substitute for the narrow tyranny of a dehumanized bourgeoisie the preponderance of the only class that still has a universal mission, because it suffers in its flesh from all the wrongs of history, from all the universal wrongs: the proletariat.

Notes

1 This is a reference to the account of the taking of Thuan-An which appeared in *Le Figaro* in September 1883 and is quoted in N. Serban's book, *Loti, sa vie, son oeuvre*. "Then the great slaughter had begun. They had fired in double-salvos! and it was a pleasure to see these sprays of bullets, that were so easy to aim, come down on them twice a minute, surely and methodically, on command. . . . We saw some who were quite mad and stood up seized with a dizzy desire to run. . . . They zigzagged, running every which way in this race with death, holding their garments up around their waists in a comical way . . . and then we amused ourselves counting the dead, etc."

2 [Césaire is quoting here from Edgar Quinet's *Les Roumains*: see Edgar Quinet, *Oeuvres Complétes* (Paris: Pagnarre, 1857), vol. 6, 127–8. Ed.]

29

On National Culture (1959)

Frantz Fanon

Frantz Fanon, selection from "On National Culture" (1959), from *The Wretched of the Earth* (1961) [source: Frantz Fanon, *The Wretched of the Earth*, trans. Constance Farrington. New York: Grove Press, 1968, 222–5, 236–48]

Born in Martinique, Fanon (1925–61) studied medicine and psychiatry in France. His work has been fundamental in the rise of postcolonial studies. Influenced by Sartre's existentialism, Nietzsche's will to power and critique of *ressentiment*, and the Marxian interpretation of Hegel elaborated by Alexandre Kojève in the 1930s, Fanon early on refused a racially bound "Negro mission" and committed himself to a personal freedom detached from the burdens of history. But his response to African Negritude, which championed African culture and "black civilization," was more complicated. For Fanon, national consciousness among the colonized evolved in three stages: mimetic assimilation, ethnic essentialism, and a future-oriented struggle for national freedom. Fanon warned, however, against the "pitfalls of national consciousness," marked by oppressive class divisions within the new nation. His work was significant in its distinctly psychological and cultural account of the racial effects of colonization. Echoing Du Bois's idea of "double consciousness," Fanon's *Black Skin, White Masks* (1952) refers to "an inferiority complex that has been created by the death and burial of . . . local cultural originality." He understands "culture" to be the aesthetic expression of a given people's spirit, thus following Romantic philosophers like Fichte and Hegel. Fanon made autonomous cultural expression and the psychological, existential health of the decolonized mind equally central to the larger problem of postcolonial national identity.

[...] If we wanted to trace in the works of native writers the different phases which characterize this evolution [of national culture] we would find spread out before us a panorama on three levels. In the first phase, the native intellectual gives proof that he has assimilated the culture of the occupying power. His writings correspond point by point with those of his opposite numbers in the mother country. His inspiration is European and we can easily link up these works with definite trends in the literature of the mother country. This is the period of unqualified assimilation. We find in this literature coming from the colonies the Parnassians, the Symbolists, and the Surrealists.

In the second phase we find the native is disturbed; he decides to remember what he is. This period of creative work approximately corresponds to that immersion which we have just described. But since the native is not a part of his people, since he only has exterior relations with his people, he is content to recall their life only. Past happenings of the byegone days of his childhood will be brought up out of the depths of his memory; old legends will be reinterpreted in the light of a borrowed estheticism and of a conception of the world which was discovered under other skies.

Sometimes this literature of just-before-the-battle is dominated by humor and by allegory; but often too it is symptomatic of a period of distress and difficulty, where death is experienced, and disgust too. We spew ourselves up; but already underneath laughter can be heard.

Finally in the third phase, which is called the fighting phase, the native, after having tried to lose himself in the people and with the people, will on the contrary shake the people. Instead of according the people's lethargy an honored place in his esteem, he turns himself into an awakener of the people; hence comes a fighting literature, a revolutionary literature, and a national literature. During this phase a great many men and women who up till then would never have thought of producing a literary work, now that they find themselves in exceptional circumstances – in prison, with the Maquis, or on the eve of their execution – feel the need to speak to their nation, to compose the sentence which expresses the heart of the people, and to become the mouthpiece of a new reality in action.

The native intellectual nevertheless sooner or later will realize that you do not show proof of your nation from its culture but that you substantiate its existence in the fight which the people wage against the forces of occupation. No colonial system draws its justification from the fact that the territories it dominates are culturally non-existent. You will never make colonialism blush for shame by spreading out little-known cultural treasures under its eyes. At the very moment when the native intellectual is anxiously trying to create a cultural work he fails to realize that he is utilizing techniques and language which are borrowed from the stranger in his country. He contents himself with stamping these instruments with a hallmark which he wishes to be national, but which is strangely reminiscent of exoticism. The native intellectual who comes back to his people by way of cultural achievements behaves in fact like a foreigner. Sometimes he has no hesitation in using a dialect in order to show his will to be as near as possible to the people; but the ideas that he expresses and the preoccupations he is taken up with have no common yardstick to measure the real situation which the men and the women of his country know. The culture that the intellectual leans toward is often no more than a stock of particularisms. He wishes to attach himself to the people; but instead he only catches hold of their outer garments. And these outer garments are merely the reflection of a hidden life, teeming and perpetually in motion. That extremely obvious objectivity which seems to characterize a people is in fact only the inert, already forsaken result of frequent, and not always very coherent, adaptations of a much more fundamental substance which itself is continually being renewed. The man of culture, instead of setting out to find this substance, will let himself be hypnotized by these mummified fragments which because they are static are in fact symbols of negation and outworn contrivances. Culture has never the translucidity of custom; it abhors all simplification. In its essence it is opposed to custom, for custom is always the deterioration of culture. The desire to attach oneself to tradition or bring abandoned traditions to life again does not only mean going against the current of history but also opposing one's own people. When a people undertakes an armed struggle or even a political struggle against a relentless colonialism, the significance of tradition changes. All that has made up the technique of passive resistance in the past may, during this phase, be radically condemned. In an underdeveloped country during the period of struggle traditions are fundamentally unstable and are shot through by centrifugal tendencies. This is why the intellectual often runs the risk of being out of date. The peoples who have carried on the struggle are more and more impervious to demagogy; and those who wish to follow them reveal themselves as nothing more than common opportunists, in other words, latecomers.

In the sphere of plastic arts, for example, the native artist who wishes at whatever cost to create a national work of art shuts himself up in a stereotyped reproduction of details. These artists who have nevertheless thoroughly studied modern techniques and who have taken part in the main trends of contemporary painting and architecture, turn their backs on foreign culture, deny it, and set out to look for a true national culture, setting great store on what they consider to be the constant principles of national art. But these people forget that the forms of thought and what it feeds on, together with modern techniques of information, language, and dress have dialectically reorganized the people's intelligences and that the constant principles which acted as safeguards during the colonial period are now undergoing extremely radical changes.

The artist who has decided to illustrate the truths of the nation turns paradoxically toward the past and away from actual events. What he ultimately intends to embrace are in fact the castoffs of thought, its shells and corpses, a knowledge which has been stabilized once and for all. But the native intellectual who wishes to create an authentic work of art must realize that the truths of a nation are in the first place its realities. He must go on until he has found the seething pot out of which the learning of the future will emerge.

Before independence, the native painter was insensible to the national scene. He set a high value on non-figurative art, or more often specialized in still lifes. After independence his anxiety to rejoin his people will confine him to the most detailed representation of reality. This is representative art which has no internal rhythms, an art which is serene and immobile, evocative not of life but of death. Enlightened circles are in ecstasies when confronted with this "inner truth" which is so well expressed; but we have the right to ask if this truth is in fact a reality, and if it is not already outworn and denied, called in question by the epoch through which the people are treading out their path toward history. [...]

Reciprocal Bases of National Culture and the Fight for Freedom

Colonial domination, because it is total and tends to oversimplify, very soon manages to disrupt in spectacular fashion the cultural life of a conquered people. This cultural obliteration is made possible by the negation of national reality, by new legal relations introduced by the occupying power, by the banishment of the natives and their customs to outlying districts by colonial society, by expropriation, and by the systematic enslaving of men and women.

Three years ago at our first congress[1] I showed that, in the colonial situation, dynamism is replaced fairly quickly by a substantification of the attitudes of the colonizing power. The area of culture is then marked off by fences and signposts. These are in fact so many defense mechanisms of the most elementary type, comparable for more than one good reason to the simple instinct for preservation. The interest of this period for us is that the oppressor does not manage to convince himself of the objective non-existence of the oppressed nation and its culture. Every effort is made to bring the colonized person to admit the inferiority of his culture which has been transformed into instinctive patterns of behavior, to recognize the unreality of his "nation," and, in the last extreme, the confused and imperfect character of his own biological structure.

Vis-à-vis this state of affairs, the native's reactions are not unanimous. While the mass of the people maintain intact traditions which are completely different from those of the colonial situation, and the artisanal style solidifies into a formalism which is more and more stereotyped, the intellectual throws himself in frenzied fashion into the frantic acquisition of the culture of the occupying power and takes every opportunity of unfavorably criticizing his own national culture, or else takes refuge in setting out and substantiating the claims of that culture in a way that is passionate but rapidly becomes unproductive.

The common nature of these two reactions lies in the fact that they both lead to impossible contradictions. Whether a turncoat or a substantialist, the native is ineffectual precisely because the analysis of the colonial situation is not carried out on strict lines. The colonial situation calls a halt to national culture in almost every field. Within the framework of colonial domination there is not and there will never be such phenomena as new cultural departures or changes in the national culture. Here and there valiant attempts are sometimes made to reanimate the cultural dynamic and to give fresh impulses to its themes, its forms, and its tonalities. The immediate, palpable, and obvious interest of such leaps ahead is nil. But if we follow up the consequences to the very end we see that preparations are being thus made to brush the cobwebs off national consciousness, to question oppression, and to open up the struggle for freedom.

A national culture under colonial domination is a contested culture whose destruction is sought in systematic fashion. It very quickly becomes a culture condemned to secrecy. This idea of a clandestine culture is immediately seen in the reactions of the occupying power which interprets attachment to traditions as faithfulness to the spirit of the nation and as a refusal to submit. This persistence in following forms of cultures which are already condemned to extinction is already a demonstration of nationality; but it is a demonstration which is a throwback to the laws of inertia. There is no taking of the offensive and no redefining of relationships. There is simply a concentration on a hard core of culture which is becoming more and more shrivelled up, inert, and empty.

By the time a century or two of exploitation has passed there comes about a veritable emaciation of the stock of national culture. It becomes a set of automatic habits, some traditions of dress, and a few broken-down institutions. Little movement can be discerned in such remnants of culture; there is no real creativity and no overflowing life. The poverty of the people, national oppression, and the inhibition of culture are one and the same thing. After a century of colonial domination we find a culture which is rigid in the extreme, or rather what we find are the dregs of culture, its mineral strata. The withering away of the reality of the nation and the death pangs of the national culture are linked to each other in mutual dependence. This is why it is of capital importance to follow the evolution of these relations during the struggle for national freedom. The negation of the native's culture, the contempt for any manifestation of culture whether active or emotional, and the placing outside the pale of all specialized branches of organization contribute to breed aggressive patterns of conduct in the native. But these patterns of conduct are of the reflexive type; they are poorly differentiated, anarchic, and ineffective. Colonial exploitation, poverty, and endemic famine drive the native more and more to open, organized revolt. The necessity for an open and decisive breach is formed progressively and imperceptibly, and comes to be felt by the great majority of the people. Those tensions which hitherto were non-existent come into being. International events, the collapse of whole sections of colonial empires and the contradictions inherent in the colonial system strengthen and uphold the native's combativity while promoting and giving support to national consciousness.

These new-found tensions which are present at all stages in the real nature of colonialism have their repercussions on the cultural plane. In literature, for example, there is relative overproduction. From being a reply on a minor scale to the dominating power, the literature produced by natives becomes differentiated and makes itself into a will to particularism. The intelligentsia, which during the period of repression was essentially a consuming public, now themselves become producers. This literature at first chooses to confine itself to the tragic and poetic style; but later on novels, short stories, and essays are attempted. It is as if a kind of internal organization or law of expression existed which wills that poetic expression become less frequent in proportion as the objectives and the methods of the struggle for liberation become more precise. Themes are completely altered; in fact, we find less and less of bitter, hopeless recrimination and less also of that violent, resounding, florid writing which on the whole serves to reassure the occupying power. The colonialists have in former times encouraged these modes of expression and made their existence possible. Stinging denunciations, the exposing of distressing conditions and passions which find their outlet in expression are in fact assimilated by the occupying power in a cathartic process. To aid such processes is in a certain sense to avoid their dramatization and to clear the atmosphere.

But such a situation can only be transitory. In fact, the progress of national consciousness among the people modifies and gives precision to the literary utterances of the native intellectual. The continued cohesion of the people constitutes for the intellectual an invitation to go further than his cry of protest. The lament first makes the indictment; and then it makes an appeal. In the period that follows, the words of command are heard. The crystallization of the national consciousness will both disrupt literary styles and themes, and also create a completely new public. While at the beginning the native intellectual used to produce his work to be read exclusively by the oppressor, whether with the intention of charming him or of denouncing him through ethnic or subjectivist means, now the native writer progressively takes on the habit of addressing his own people.

It is only from that moment that we can speak of a national literature. Here there is, at the level of literary creation, the taking up and clarification of themes which are typically nationalist. This may be properly called a literature of combat, in the sense that it calls on the whole people to fight for their existence as a nation. It is a literature of combat, because it molds the national consciousness, giving it form and contours and flinging open before it new and boundless horizons; it is a literature of combat because it assumes responsibility, and because it is the will to liberty expressed in terms of time and space.

On another level, the oral tradition – stories, epics, and songs of the people – which formerly were filed away as set pieces are now beginning to change. The storytellers who used to relate inert episodes now bring them alive and introduce into them modifications which are increasingly fundamental. There is a tendency to bring conflicts up to date and to modernize the kinds of struggle which the stories evoke, together with the names of heroes and the types of weapons. The method of allusion is more and more widely used. The formula "This all happened long ago" is substituted with that of "What we are going to speak of happened somewhere else, but it might well have happened here today, and it might happen tomorrow." The example of Algeria is significant in this context. From 1952–53 on, the storytellers, who were before that time stereotyped and tedious to listen to, completely over-turned their traditional methods of storytelling and the contents of their tales. Their public, which was formerly scattered, became compact. The epic, with its typified categories, reappeared; it became an authentic form of entertainment which took on once more a cultural value. Colonialism made no mistake when from 1955 on it proceeded to arrest these storytellers systematically.

The contact of the people with the new movement gives rise to a new rhythm of life and to forgotten muscular tensions, and develops the imagination. Every time the storyteller relates a fresh episode to his public, he presides over a real invocation. The existence of a new type of man is revealed to the public. The present is no longer turned in upon itself but spread out for all to see. The storyteller once more gives free rein to his imagination; he makes innovations and he creates a work of art. It even happens that the characters, which are barely ready for such a transformation – highway robbers or more or less anti-social vagabonds – are taken up and remodeled. The emergence of the imagination and of the creative urge in the songs and

epic stories of a colonized country is worth following. The storyteller replies
to the expectant people by successive approximations, and makes his way,
apparently alone but in fact helped on by his public, toward the seeking out
of new patterns, that is to say national patterns. Comedy and farce disappear,
or lose their attraction. As for dramatization, it is no longer placed on the
plane of the troubled intellectual and his tormented conscience. By losing its
characteristics of despair and revolt, the drama becomes part of the common
lot of the people and forms part of an action in preparation or already in
progress.

Where handicrafts are concerned, the forms of expression which formerly
were the dregs of art, surviving as if in a daze, now begin to reach out.
Woodwork, for example, which formerly turned out certain faces and attitudes by the million, begins to be differentiated. The inexpressive or over-
wrought mask comes to life and the arms tend to be raised from the body as
if to sketch an action. Compositions containing two, three, or five figures
appear. The traditional schools are led on to creative efforts by the rising
avalanche of amateurs or of critics. This new vigor in this sector of cultural
life very often passes unseen; and yet its contribution to the national effort is
of capital importance. By carving figures and faces which are full of life, and
by taking as his theme a group fixed on the same pedestal, the artist invites
participation in an organized movement.

If we study the repercussions of the awakening of national consciousness in
the domains of ceramics and pottery-making, the same observations may be
drawn. Formalism is abandoned in the craftsman's work. Jugs, jars, and trays
are modified, at first imperceptibly, then almost savagely. The colors, of
which formerly there were but few and which obeyed the traditional rules
of harmony, increase in number and are influenced by the repercussion of the
rising revolution. Certain ochres and blues, which seemed forbidden to all
eternity in a given cultural area, now assert themselves without giving rise to
scandal. In the same way the stylization of the human face, which according
to sociologists is typical of very clearly defined regions, becomes suddenly
completely relative. The specialist coming from the home country and the
ethnologist are quick to note these changes. On the whole such changes are
condemned in the name of a rigid code of artistic style and of a cultural life
which grows up at the heart of the colonial system. The colonialist specialists
do not recognize these new forms and rush to the help of the traditions of
the indigenous society. It is the colonialists who become the defenders of the
native style. We remember perfectly, and the example took on a certain
measure of importance since the real nature of colonialism was not involved,
the reactions of the white jazz specialists when after the Second World War
new styles such as the be-bop took definite shape. The fact is that in their eyes
jazz should only be the despairing, broken-down nostalgia of an old Negro

who is trapped between five glasses of whiskey, the curse of his race, and the racial hatred of the white men. As soon as the Negro comes to an understanding of himself, and understands the rest of the world differently, when he gives birth to hope and forces back the racist universe, it is clear that his trumpet sounds more clearly and his voice less hoarsely. The new fashions in jazz are not simply born of economic competition. We must without any doubt see in them one of the consequences of the defeat, slow but sure, of the southern world of the United States. And it is not utopian to suppose that in fifty years' time the type of jazz howl hiccuped by a poor misfortunate Negro will be upheld only by the whites who believe in it as an expression of negritude, and who are faithful to this arrested image of a type of relationship.

We might in the same way seek and find in dancing, singing, and traditional rites and ceremonies the same upward-springing trend, and make out the same changes and the same impatience in this field. Well before the political or fighting phase of the national movement, an attentive spectator can thus feel and see the manifestation of new vigor and feel the approaching conflict. He will note unusual forms of expression and themes which are fresh and imbued with a power which is no longer that of invocation but rather of the assembling of the people, a summoning together for a precise purpose. Everything works together to awaken the native's sensibility and to make unreal and inacceptable the contemplative attitude, or the acceptance of defeat. The native rebuilds his perceptions because he renews the purpose and dynamism of the craftsmen, of dancing and music, and of literature and the oral tradition. His world comes to lose its accursed character. The conditions necessary for the inevitable conflict are brought together.

We have noted the appearance of the movement in cultural forms and we have seen that this movement and these new forms are linked to the state of maturity of the national consciousness. Now, this movement tends more and more to express itself objectively, in institutions. From thence comes the need for a national existence, whatever the cost.

A frequent mistake, and one which is moreover hardly justifiable, is to try to find cultural expressions for and to give new values to native culture within the framework of colonial domination. This is why we arrive at a proposition which at first sight seems paradoxical: the fact that in a colonized country the most elementary, most savage, and the most undifferentiated nationalism is the most fervent and efficient means of defending national culture. For culture is first the expression of a nation, the expression of its preferences, of its taboos and of its patterns. It is at every stage of the whole of society that other taboos, values, and patterns are formed. A national culture is the sum total of all these appraisals; it is the result of internal and external tensions exerted over society as a whole and also at every level of that society. In the colonial situation, culture, which is doubly deprived of the support of the nation and of the state, falls away and dies. The condition for its existence is therefore national liberation and the renaissance of the state.

The nation is not only the condition of culture, its fruitfulness, its continuous renewal, and its deepening. It is also a necessity. It is the fight for national existence which sets culture moving and opens to it the doors of creation. Later on it is the nation which will ensure the conditions and framework necessary to culture. The nation gathers together the various indispensable elements necessary for the creation of a culture, those elements which alone can give it credibility, validity, life, and creative power. In the same way it is its national character that will make such a culture open to other cultures and which will enable it to influence and permeate other cultures. A non-existent culture can hardly be expected to have bearing on reality, or to influence reality. The first necessity is the re-establishment of the nation in order to give life to national culture in the strictly biological sense of the phrase.

Thus we have followed the breakup of the old strata of culture, a shattering which becomes increasingly fundamental; and we have noticed, on the eve of the decisive conflict for national freedom, the renewing of forms of expression and the rebirth of the imagination. There remains one essential question: what are the relations between the struggle – whether political or military – and culture? Is there a suspension of culture during the conflict? Is the national struggle an expression of a culture? Finally, ought one to say that the battle for freedom however fertile *a posteriori* with regard to culture is in itself a negation of culture? In short, is the struggle for liberation a cultural phenomenon or not?

We believe that the conscious and organized undertaking by a colonized people to re-establish the sovereignty of that nation constitutes the most complete and obvious cultural manifestation that exists. It is not alone the success of the struggle which afterward gives validity and vigor to culture; culture is not put into cold storage during the conflict. The struggle itself in its development and in its internal progression sends culture along different paths and traces out entirely new ones for it. The struggle for freedom does not give back to the national culture its former value and shapes; this struggle which aims at a fundamentally different set of relations between men cannot leave intact either the form or the content of the people's culture. After the conflict there is not only the disappearance of colonialism but also the disappearance of the colonized man.

This new humanity cannot do otherwise than define a new humanism both for itself and for others. It is prefigured in the objectives and methods of the conflict. A struggle which mobilizes all classes of the people and which expresses their aims and their impatience, which is not afraid to count almost exclusively on the people's support, will of necessity triumph. The value of this type of conflict is that it supplies the maximum of conditions necessary for the development and aims of culture. After national freedom has been obtained in these conditions, there is no such painful cultural indecision which is found in certain countries which are newly independent, because the nation by its manner of coming into being and in the terms of its existence exerts a fundamental influence over culture. A nation which is born of the people's concerted action and which embodies the real aspirations of the people while changing the state cannot exist save in the expression of exceptionally rich forms of culture.

The natives who are anxious for the culture of their country and who wish to give to it a universal dimension ought not therefore to place their confidence in the single principle of inevitable, undifferentiated independence written into the consciousness of the people in order to achieve their task. The liberation of the nation is one thing; the methods and popular content of the fight are another. It seems to us that the future of national culture and its riches are equally also part and parcel of the values which have ordained the struggle for freedom.

And now it is time to denounce certain pharisees. National claims, it is here and there stated, are a phase that humanity has left behind. It is the day of great concerted actions, and retarded nationalists ought in consequence to set their mistakes aright. We however consider that the mistake, which may have very serious consequences, lies in wishing to skip the national period. If culture is the expression of national consciousness, I will not hesitate to affirm that in the case with which we are dealing it is the national consciousness which is the most elaborate form of culture.

The consciousness of self is not the closing of a door to communication. Philosophic thought teaches us, on the contrary, that it is its guarantee. National consciousness, which is not nationalism, is the only thing that will give us an international dimension. This problem of national consciousness and of national culture takes on in Africa a special dimension. The birth of national consciousness in Africa has a strictly contemporaneous connection with the African consciousness. The responsibility of the African as regards national culture is also a responsibility with regard to African Negro culture. This joint responsibility is not the fact of a metaphysical principle but the awareness of a simple rule which wills that every independent nation in an Africa where colonialism is still entrenched is an encircled nation, a nation which is fragile and in permanent danger.

If man is known by his acts, then we will say that the most urgent thing today for the intellectual is to build up his nation. If this building up is true, that is to say if it interprets the manifest will of the people and reveals the eager African peoples, then the building of a nation is of necessity accompanied by the discovery and encouragement of universalizing values. Far from keeping aloof from other nations, therefore, it is national liberation which leads the nation to play its part on the stage of history. It is at the heart of national consciousness that international consciousness lives and grows. And this two-fold emerging is ultimately only the source of all culture.

Note

1 [Fanon's essay was originally a statement made at the Second Congress of Black Artists and Writers, Rome, 1959. Ed.]

Part V

Contemporary Perspectives

30

The Integrative Revolution: Primordial Sentiments and Civil Politics in the New States (1963)

Clifford Geertz

Clifford Geertz, "The Integrative Revolution: Primordial Sentiments and Civil Politics in the New States" (1963) [source: *Old Societies and New States: The Quest for Modernity in Asia and Africa*, ed. Clifford Geertz. New York: Free Press, 1963, 105–19]

Geertz is best known for developing an "interpretive" model of cultural anthropology, in which the anthropologist's main goal is understanding what the group being observed imagines it is doing. He was also among the first contemporary scholars to examine the power of "primordial" (or ethnic) concerns in the new nations being created out of collapsing European empires. Geertz's best-known publication is *The Interpretation of Cultures* (1973).

I

In 1948, scarcely a year after Independence, Pandit Nehru found himself in the always unsettling position for an opposition politician finally come to power of being obliged to place in practice a policy he had long espoused but never liked. With Patel and Sitaramayya, he was appointed to the Linguistic Provinces Committee.

The Congress had supported the principle of linguistic determination of state boundaries within India almost since its founding, arguing, ironically enough, that British maintenance of "arbitrary" – that is, nonlinguistic – administrative units was part of a divide-and-rule policy. In 1920 it had actually reorganized its own regional chapters along linguistic lines so as better to secure its popular appeal. But with the echoes of partition perhaps still ringing in his ears, Nehru was deeply shaken by his experience on the Linguistic Committee, and with the candor that makes him virtually unique among the leaders of the new states, he admitted it:

> [This inquiry] has been in some ways an eye-opener for us. The work of 60 years of the Indian National Congress was standing before us, face to face with centuries-old India of narrow loyalties, petty jealousies and ignorant prejudices engaged in mortal conflict and we were simply horrified to see how thin was the ice upon which we were skating. Some of the ablest men in the country came before us and confidently and emphatically stated that language in this country stood for and represented culture, race, history, individuality, and finally a sub-nation.[1]

But, horrified or not, Nehru, Patel, and Sitaramayya in the end were forced to endorse the claims of Andhra as a Telugu-speaking state, and the thin ice was broken. Within the decade India had been almost entirely reorganized along linguistic lines, and a wide range of observers, both domestic and foreign, were wondering aloud whether the country's political unity would survive this wholesale concession to "narrow loyalties, petty jealousies, and ignorant prejudices."[2]

The problem that opened Nehru's eyes in such wide astonishment is phrased in linguistic terms, but the same problems phrased in a wide variety of terms is, of course, literally pandemic to the new states, as the countless references to "dual" or "plural" or "multiple" societies, to "mosaic" or "composite" social structures, to "states" that are not "nations" and "nations" that are not "states," to "tribalism," "parochialism," and "communalism," as well as to pan-national movements of various sorts demonstrate.

When we speak of communalism in India we refer to religious contrasts; when we speak of it in Malaya we are mainly concerned with racial ones, and in the Congo with tribal ones. But the grouping under a common rubric is not simply adventitious; the phenomena referred to are in some way similar. Regionalism has been the main theme in Indonesian disaffection, differences in custom in Moroccan. The Tamil minority in Ceylon is set off from the Sinhalese majority by religion, language, race, region, and social custom; the Shiite minority in Iraq is set off from the dominant Sunnis virtually by an intra-Islamic sectarian difference alone. Pan-national movements in Africa are largely based on race, in Kurdistan, on tribalism; in Laos, the Shan States, and Thailand, on language. Yet all these phenomena, too, are in some sense of a piece. They form a definable field of investigation.

That is, they would, could we but define it. The stultifying aura of conceptual ambiguity that surrounds the terms "nation," "nationality," and "nationalism" has been extensively discussed and thoroughly deplored in almost every work that has been concerned to attack the relationship between communal and political loyalties.[3] But as the preferred remedy has been to adopt a theoretical eclecticism that, in its attempt to do justice to the multifaceted nature of the problems involved, tends to confuse political, psychological, cultural, and demographic factors, actual reduction of that ambiguity has not proceeded very far. Thus a recent symposium on the Middle East refers indiscriminately to the efforts of the Arab League to destroy existing nation-state boundaries, those of the Sudan Government to unify a somewhat arbitrary and accidentally demarcated sovereign state, and those of the Azerin Turks to separate from Iran and join the Soviet Republic of Azerbaijan as "nationalism."[4] Operating with a similarly omnibus concept, Coleman[5] sees Nigerians (or some of them) as displaying five different sorts of nationalism at once – "African," "Nigerian," "Regional," "Group," and "Cultural." And Emerson[6] defines a nation as a "terminal community – the largest community that, when the chips are down, effectively commands men's loyalty, overriding the claims both of the lesser communities within it and those that cut across it or potentially enfold it within a still greater society...," which simply shifts the ambiguity from the term "nation" to the term "loyalty," as well as seeming to leave such questions as whether India, Indonesia, or Nigeria are nations to the determination of some future, unspecified historical crisis.

Some of this conceptual haze is burned away, however, if it is realized that the peoples of the new states are simultaneously animated by two powerful, thoroughly interdependent, yet distinct and often actually opposed motives – the desire to be recognized as responsible agents whose wishes, acts, hopes, and opinions "matter," and the desire to build an efficient, dynamic modern state. The one aim is to be noticed: it is a search for an identity, and a demand that that identity be publicly acknowledged as having import, a social assertion of the self as "being somebody in the world."[7] The other aim is practical: it is a demand for progress, for a rising standard of living, more effective political order, greater social justice, and beyond that of "playing a part in the larger arena of world politics," of "exercising influence among the nations."[8] The two motives are, again, most intimately related, because citizenship in a truly modern state has more and more become the most broadly negotiable claim to personal significance, and because what Mazzini called the demand to exist and have a name is to such a great extent fired by a humiliating sense of exclusion from the important centers of power in world society. But they are not the same thing. They stem from different sources and respond to different pressures. It is, in fact, the tension between them that is one of the central driving forces in the national evolution of the new states; as it is, at the same time, one of the greatest obstacles to such evolution.

This tension takes a peculiarly severe and chronic form in the new states, both because of the great extent to which their peoples' sense of self remains bound up in the gross actualities of blood, race, language, locality, religion, or tradition, and because of the steadily accelerating importance in this century of the sovereign state as a positive instrument for the realization of collective aims. Multiethnic, usually multilinguistic, and sometimes multiracial, the populations of the new states tend to regard the immediate, concrete, and to them inherently meaningful sorting implicit in such "natural" diversity as the substantial content of their individuality. To subordinate these specific and familiar identifications in favor of a generalized commitment to an overarching and somewhat alien civil order is to risk a loss of definition as an autonomous person, either through absorption into a culturally undifferentiated mass or, what is even worse, through domination by some other rival ethnic, racial, or linguistic community that is able to imbue that order with the temper of its own personality. But at the same time, all but the most unenlightened members of such societies are at least dimly aware – and their leaders are acutely aware – that the possibilities for social reform and material progress they so intensely desire and are so determined to achieve rest with increasing weight on their being enclosed in a reasonably large, independent, powerful, well-ordered polity. The insistence on recognition as someone who is visible and matters and the will to be modern and dynamic thus tend to diverge, and much of the political process in the new states pivots around an heroic effort to keep them aligned.

II

A more exact phrasing of the nature of the problem involved here is that, considered as societies, the new states are abnormally susceptible to serious disaffection based on primordial attachments.[9] By a primordial attachment is meant one that stems from the "givens" – or, more precisely, as culture is inevitably involved in such matters, the assumed "givens" – of social existence: immediate contiguity and kin connection mainly, but beyond them the givenness that stems from being born into a particular religious community, speaking a particular language, or even a dialect of a language, and following particular social practices. These congruities of blood, speech, custom, and so on, are seen to have an ineffable, and at times overpowering, coerciveness in and of themselves. One is bound to one's kinsman, one's neighbor, one's fellow believer, *ipso facto*; as the result not merely of personal affection, practical necessity, common interest, or incurred obligation, but at least in great part by virtue of some unaccountable absolute import attributed to the very tie itself. The general strength of such primordial bonds, and the types of them that are important, differ from person to person, from society to society, and from time to time. But for virtually every person, in every society, at almost all times, some attachments seem to flow more from a sense of natural – some would say spiritual – affinity than from social interaction.

In modern societies the lifting of such ties to the level of political supremacy – though it has, of course, occurred and may again occur – has more and more come to be deplored as pathological. To an increasing degree national unity is maintained not by calls to blood and land but by a vague, intermittent, and routine allegiance to a civil state, supplemented to a greater or lesser extent by governmental use of police powers and ideological exhortation. The havoc wreaked, both upon themselves and others, by those modern (or semimodern) states that did passionately seek to become primordial rather than civil political communities, as well as a growing realization of the practical advantages of a wider-ranging pattern of social integration than primordial ties can usually produce or even permit, have only strengthened the reluctance publicly to advance race, language, religion, and the like as bases for the definition of a terminal community. But in modernizing societies, where the tradition of civil politics is weak and where the technical requirements for an effective welfare government are poorly understood, primordial attachments tend, as Nehru discovered, to be repeatedly, in some cases almost continually, proposed and widely acclaimed as preferred bases for the demarcation of autonomous political units. And the thesis that truly legitimate authority flows only from the inherent coerciveness such attachments are conceived somehow to possess is frankly, energetically, and artlessly defended:

> The reasons why a unilingual state is stable and a multilingual state unstable are quite obvious. A state is built on fellow feeling. What is this fellow feeling? To state briefly it is a feeling of a corporate sentiment of oneness which makes those who are charged with it feel that they are kith and kin. This feeling is a double-edged feeling. It is at once a feeling of "consciousness of kind" which, on the one hand, binds together those who have it so strongly that it overrides all differences arising out of economic conflicts or social gradations and, on the other, severs them from those who are not of their kind. It is a longing not to belong to any other group. The existence of this fellow feeling is the foundation of a stable and democratic state.[10]

It is this crystallization of a direct conflict between primordial and civil sentiments – this "longing not to belong to any other group" – that gives to the problem variously called tribalism, parochialism, communalism, and so on, a more ominous and deeply threatening quality than most of the other, also very serious and intractable problems the new states face. Here we have not just competing loyalties, but competing loyalties of the same general order, on the same level of integration. There are many other competing loyalties in the new states, as in any state – ties to class, party, business, union, profession, or whatever. But groups formed of such ties are virtually never considered as possible self-standing, maximal social units, as candidates for nationhood. Conflicts among them occur only within a more or less fully accepted terminal community whose political integrity they do not, as a rule, put into question. No matter how severe they become they do not threaten, at least not intentionally, its existence as such. They threaten governments, or even forms of government, but they rarely at best – and then usually when they have become infused with primordial sentiments – threaten to undermine the nation itself, because they do not involve alternative definitions of what the nation is, of what its scope of reference is. Economic or class or intellectual disaffection threatens revolution, but disaffection based on race, language, or culture threatens partition, irredentism, or merger, a redrawing of the very limits of the state, a new definition of its domain. Civil discontent finds its natural outlet in the seizing, legally or illegally, of the state apparatus. Primordial discontent strives more deeply and is satisfied less easily. If severe enough, it wants not just Sukarno's or Nehru's or Moulay Hasan's head, it wants Indonesia's or India's or Morocco's.

The actual foci around which such discontent tends to crystallize are various, and in any given case several are usually involved concurrently, sometimes at cross-purposes with one another. On a merely descriptive level they are, nevertheless, fairly readily enumerable:[11]

(1) *Assumed Blood Ties.* Here the defining element is quasi-kinship. "Quasi" because kin units formed around known biological relationship (extended families, lineages, and so on) are too small for even the most tradition-bound to regard them as having more than limited significance, and the referent is, consequently, to a notion of untraceable but yet sociologically real kinship, as in a tribe. Nigeria, the Congo, and the greater part of sub-Saharan Africa are characterized by a prominence of this sort of primordialism. But so also are the nomads or seminomads of the Middle East – the Kurds, Baluchis, Pathans, and so on; the Nagas, Mundas, Santals, and so on, of India; and most of the so-called "hill tribes" of Southeast Asia.

(2) *Race.* Clearly, race is similar to assumed kinship, in that it involves an ethnobiological theory. But it is not quite the same thing. Here, the reference is to phenotypical physical features – especially, of course, skin color, but also facial form, stature, hair type, and so on – rather than any very definite

sense of common descent as such. The communal problems of Malaya in large part focus around these sorts of differences, between, in fact, two phenotypically very similar Mongoloid peoples. "Negritude" clearly draws much, though perhaps not all, of its force from the notion of race as a significant primordial property, and the pariah commercial minorities – like the Chinese in Southeast Asia or the Indians and Lebanese in Africa – are similarly demarcated.

(3) *Language*. Linguism – for some yet to be adequately explained reasons – is particularly intense in the Indian subcontinent, has been something of an issue in Malaya, and has appeared sporadically elsewhere. But as language has sometimes been held to be the altogether essential axis of nationality conflicts, it is worth stressing that linguism is not an inevitable outcome of linguistic diversity. As indeed kinship, race, and the other factors to be listed below, language differences need not in themselves be particularly divisive: they have not been so for the most part in Tanganyika, Iran (not a new state in the strict sense, perhaps), the Philippines, or even in Indonesia, where despite a great confusion of tongues linguistic conflict seems to be the one social problem the country has somehow omitted to demonstrate in extreme form. Furthermore, primordial conflicts can occur where no marked linguistic differences are involved, as in Lebanon, among the various sorts of Batak-speakers in Indonesia, and to a lesser extent perhaps between the Fulani and Hausa in northern Nigeria.

(4) *Region*. Although a factor nearly everywhere, regionalism naturally tends to be especially troublesome in geographically heterogeneous areas. Tonkin, Annam, and Cochin in prepartitioned Vietnam, the two baskets on the long pole, were opposed almost purely in regional terms, sharing language, culture, race, etc. The tension between East and West Pakistan involves differences in language and culture too, but the geographic element is of great prominence owing to the territorial discontinuity of the country. Java versus the Outer Islands in archipelagic Indonesia; the Northeast versus the West Coast in mountain-bisected Malaya, are perhaps other examples in which regionalism has been an important primordial factor in national politics.

(5) *Religion*. Indian partition is the outstanding case of the operation of this type of attachment. But Lebanon, the Karens and the Moslem Arakenese in Burma, the Toba Bataks, Ambonese, and Minahassans in Indonesia, the Moros in the Philippines, the Sikhs in Indian Punjab and the Ahmadiyas in Pakistani, and the Hausa in Nigeria are other well-known examples of its force in undermining or inhibiting a comprehensive civil sense.

(6) *Custom*. Again, differences in custom form a basis for a certain amount of national disunity almost everywhere, and are of especial prominence in those cases in which an intellectually and/or artistically rather sophisticated group sees itself as the bearer of a "civilization" amid a largely barbarian

population that would be well advised to model itself upon it: the Bengalis in India, the Javanese in Indonesia, the Arabs (as against the Berbers) in Morocco, the Amhara in – another "old" new state – Ethiopia, etc. But it is important also to point out that even vitally opposed groups may differ rather little in their general style of life: Hindu Gujeratis and Maharashtrians in India; Baganda and Bunyoro in Uganda; Javanese and Sundanese in Indonesia. And the reverse holds also: the Balinese have far and away the most divergent pattern of customs in Indonesia, but they have been, so far, notable for the absence of any sense of primordial discontent at all.

But beyond such a mere listing of the sorts of primordial ties that tend, in one place or another, to become politicized it is necessary to go further and attempt also to classify, or somehow order, the concrete patterns of primordial diversity and conflict that in fact exist in the various new states and of which these ties are the components.

This seemingly routine exercise in political ethnography is a rather more delicate task than at first appears, however, not only because those communalistic challenges to the integrity of the civil state that are at the moment being openly pressed must be discerned, but also because those that are latent, lying concealed in the enduring structure of primordial identifications, ready to take explicit political form given only the proper sorts of social conditions must be revealed. The fact that the Indian minority in Malaya has not so far posed a very serious threat to the viability of the state does not mean that it might not do so if something odd happened to the world price of rubber or if Nehru's hands-off policy toward overseas Indians should be replaced by one more like that of Mao toward the overseas Chinese. The Moro problem, which provided postgraduate field training for select members of several generations of West Pointers, now merely simmers in the Philippines, but it may not do so forever. The Free Thai movement seems dead at the moment, but it could revive with a change in Thailand's foreign policy or even with Pathet success in Laos. Iraq's Kurds, whom General Kassem had ostensibly mollified, now show signs of restlessness again. And so on. Primordially based political solidarities have a deeply abiding strength in most of the new states, but it is not always an active and immediately apparent one.

Initially, a useful analytic distinction can be made with respect to this matter of classification between those allegiances that operate more or less wholly within the confines of a single civil state and those that do not but which run across them. Or, put somewhat differently, one can contrast those cases in which the racial, tribal, linguistic, and so on, reference group that is charged with a "corporate sentiment of oneness" is smaller than the existing civil state, and those where it is larger, or at least transgresses its borders in some fashion. In the first instance primordial discontent arises from a sense of political suffocation; in the second, from a sense of political dismemberment. Karen separatism in Burma, Ashanti in Ghana, or Baganda in Uganda are examples of the former; pan-Arabism, greater Somaliism, pan-Africanism, of the latter.

Many of the new states are plagued by both these sorts of problems at once. In the first place, most interstate primordial movements do not involve entire separate countries, as the pan-movements at least tend to do, but rather minorities scattered through several, for example: the Kurdistan movement to unite Kurds in Iran, Syria, Turkey, and the Soviet Union, perhaps the most unlikely-to-succeed political movement of all time; the Abako movement of Kasuvubu and his Republic of The Congo and Angola allies; the Dravidistan movement, in so far as it comes to see itself as extending across Palk Strait from South India into Ceylon; the movement – or perhaps it is so far only a formless sentiment – for a unified and sovereign Bengal independent of both India and Pakistan. And there are even a few classical irredentist-type problems scattered among the new states – the Malays in South Thailand, the Pushtu speakers along the Afghan border of Pakistan, and so on; and when political boundaries become more firmly established in sub-Saharan Africa there will be a great many more of them. In all these cases, there is – or there may develop – both a desire to escape the established civil state and a longing to reunite a politically divided primordial community.[12]

In the second place, interstate and intrastate primordial attachments often cross-cut one another in a complex network of balanced – if most precariously balanced – commitments. In Malaya one of the more effective binding forces that has, so far at least, held Chinese and Malays together in a single state despite the tremendous centrifugal tendencies the racial and cultural difference generates is the fear on the part of either group that should the Federation dissolve they may become a clearly submerged minority in some other political framework: the Malays through the turn of the Chinese to Singapore and China; the Chinese through the turn of the Malays to Indonesia. In a similar way, in Ceylon both the Tamils and Sinhalese manage to see themselves as minorities: the Tamils because 70 per cent of the Ceylonese are Sinhalese; the Sinhalese because the eight million of them in Ceylon are all there are, while in addition to the two million Tamils on the island there are 28 million more in South India. In Morocco, there has tended to be both a within-state split between Arab and Berber, and an extra-state split between partisans of Nasser's pan-Arabism and of Bourguiba's and Balafrej's *regroupement maghrebin*. And Nasser himself, until the Syrian debacle perhaps the new states' most accomplished virtuoso in the primordial arts, is absorbed in juggling pan-Arabist, pan-Islamic, and pan-African sentiments in the interests of Egyptian hegemony among the Bandung powers.

But whether the relevant attachments outrun state boundaries or not, most of the major primordial battles are for the moment being fought within them. A certain amount of international conflict focusing around, or at least animated by, primordial issues does exist among the new states. The hostility between Israel and her Arab neighbors and the quarrel of India and Pakistan over Kashmir are the most prominent cases, of course. But the embroilment of two older states, Greece and Turkey, over Cyprus is another; the impending clash between Somalia and Ethiopia concerning an essentially irredentist problem a third; the Indonesian difficulties vis-à-vis Peking with respect to the issue of "dual citizenship" for Chinese residents of Indonesia a mild fourth, and so on. As the new states solidify politically, such disputes may well grow both more frequent and more intense. But as of now they have not yet become – with the exception of the Israeli-Arab conflict and, sporadically, the Kashmir problem – paramount political issues, and the immediate significance of primordial differences is almost everywhere primarily domestic, though this is not to say that they are therefore without important international implications.[13]

The construction of a typology of the concrete patterns of primordial diversity that are found within the various new states is severely hampered, however, by the simple lack of detailed and reliable information in the overwhelming majority of the cases. But, again, a gross and merely empirical classification can nonetheless fairly easily be devised, and should prove useful as a rough-and-ready guide to a wilderness otherwise uncharted, and facilitate a more incisive analysis of the role of primordial sentiments in civil politics than is possible in terms of "pluralism," "tribalism," "parochialism," "communalism," and the other clichés of commonsense sociology:

(1) One common and, relatively speaking, simple pattern seems to be that of a single dominant and usually, though not inevitably, larger group set over against a single strong and chronically troublesome minority: Cyprus with Greeks and Turks; Ceylon with Sinhalese and Tamils; Jordan with Jordanians and Palestinians, though in this last case the dominant group is the smaller.

(2) Similar in some ways to this first pattern, but more complex, is that of one central – often enough in a geographic sense as well as a political – group and several mediumly large and at least somewhat opposed peripheral groups: the Javanese versus the Outer Island peoples in Indonesia; the Irrawaddy Valley Burmese versus the various hill tribes and upland valley peoples in Burma; the central plateau Persians and the various tribes in Iran (though, again, this is not strictly a new state); the Atlantic Plain Arabs encircled by the diverse Berber tribes of the Rif, the Atlas, and the Sous; the Mekong Lao and the tribal peoples in Laos; and so on. How far such a pattern is to be found in black Africa is unclear. The one case where it might

have crystallized, with the Ashanti in Ghana, the power of the central group seems to have, at least temporarily, been broken. And whether in a new state the Baganda will be able to maintain their dominant position vis-à-vis the other Uganda groups through their greater education, political sophistication, and so on, and despite their comprising but about a fifth of the population, remains to be seen.

(3) Another pattern that forms an internally even less homogeneous type is a bipolar one of two nearly evenly balanced major groups: Malays and Chinese in Malaya (though there is also a smaller Indian group); or Christians and Moslems in Lebanon (though here both groups are actually aggregates of smaller sects); or Sunnis and Shiis in Iraq. Perhaps the two regions of Pakistan, although the Western region is far from wholly homogeneous within itself, gives that state a somewhat bipolar primordial pattern. Vietnam before partition tended to take this form – Tonkin versus Cochin – this problem now having been solved with the assistance of the great powers. Even Libya, which has scarcely enough people to develop decent group conflicts, has something of this pattern with the Cyrenecia–Tripolitania contrast.

(4) Next, there is the pattern of a relatively even gradation of groups in importance, from several large ones through several medium-sized ones to a number of small ones, with no clearly dominant ones and no sharp cut-off points. India, the Philippines, Nigeria, Kenya are perhaps examples.

(5) Finally, there is simple ethnic fragmentation, as Wallerstein has called it, with multiple small groups, into which somewhat residual category it is necessary to toss much of Africa, at least until more is known about it.[14] One proposal, issuing from the nothing if not experimental Leopoldville Government, suggesting a grouping of the Congo Republic's estimated 250 or so separate tribal-linguistic groups into eighty autonomous tribal regions, which would then be organized into twelve federated states, gives something of an indication of the extent to which such fragmentation can go, and the complexity of primordial allegiances it may involve.

The world of personal identity collectively ratified and publicly expressed is thus an ordered world. The patterns of primordial identification and cleavage within the existing new states are not fluid, shapeless, and infinitely various, but are definitely demarcated and vary in systematic ways. And as they vary, the nature of the individual's problem of social self-assertion varies with them, as it does also according to his position within any one type of pattern. The task of securing recognition as someone who is somebody to whom attention must be paid appears in a different form and light to a Sinhalese in Ceylon than it does to a Javanese in Indonesia or a Malay in Malaya, because to be a member of a major group set over against one minor one is a quite different matter than to be a member of such a group over against a plurality of minor ones or another major one. But it appears also in a different form and light to a Turk in Cyprus than to a Greek, to a Karen in Burma than to a Burmese, to a Tiv in Nigeria than to a Hausa, because membership in a minor group places one in a different position than does membership in a major one, even within a single system.[15] The so-called pariah communities of "foreign" traders that are found in so many of the new states – the Lebanese in West Africa, the Indians in East Africa, the Chinese in Southeast Asia and, in a somewhat different way, the Marwaris in South India – live in an altogether different social universe, so far as the problem of the maintenance of a recognized identity is concerned, than do the settled agricultural groups, no matter how small and insignificant, in the same societies. The network of primordial alliance and opposition is a dense, intricate, but yet precisely articulated one, the product, in most cases, of centuries of gradual crystall-ization. The unfamiliar civil state, born yesterday from the meager remains of an exhausted colonial regime, is superimposed upon this fine-spun and lovingly conserved texture of pride and suspicion and must somehow con-trive to weave it into the fabric of modern politics. [. . .]

Notes

1   Quoted in S. Harrison, "The Challenge to Indian Nationalism," *Foreign Affairs*, 34: 3, April 1956.
2   For a very dim view, see S. Harrison, *India: The Most Dangerous Decades*, Prince-ton, NJ, Princeton University Press, 1960. For a lively Indian view that sees the "scheme of dividing India in the name of Linguistic States" as "full of poison" but yet necessary "to make easy the way to democracy and to remove racial and cultural tension," see B. R. Ambedkar, *Thoughts on Linguistic States*, Delhi, B. R. Ambedkar, ca. 1955.
3   See, for example, K. Deutsch, *Nationalism and Social Communication*, New York, Wiley, 1953, pp. 1–14; R. Emerson, *From Empire to Nation*, Cambridge, Mass., Harvard University Press, 1960; J. Coleman, *Nigeria: Background to Nationalism*, Berkeley, University of California Press, 1958, pp. 419ff; F. Hertz, *Nationalism in History and Politics*, New York, Oxford University Press, 1944, pp. 11–15.
4   Walter Z. Laqueur (ed.), *The Middle East in Transition: Studies in Contemporary History*, New York, Praeger, 1958.
5   *Op. cit.*, pp. 425–6.
6   *Op. cit.*, pp. 95–6.
7   I. Berlin, *Two Concepts of Liberty*, New York, Oxford University Press, 1958, p. 42.
8   E. Shils, "Political Development in the New States," *Comparative Studies in Society and History*, 2: 265–92; 379–411, 1960.

9   E. Shils, "Primordial, Personal, Sacred and Civil Ties," *British Journal of Sociology*, June 1957.

10 Ambedkar, *op. cit.*, p. 11. Noting that the modern bilingual states of Canada, Switzerland, and (white) South Africa might be quoted against him, Ambedkar adds: "It must not be forgotten that the genius of India is quite different than the genius of Canada, Switzerland, and South Africa. The genius of India is to divide – the genius of Switzerland, South Africa and Canada to unite."

11 For a similar but rather differently conceived and organized listing, see Emerson, *op. cit.*, chapters 6, 7, and 8.

12 The intensity, prevalence, or even the reality of such desires in each case is another matter, about which nothing is being asserted here. How much, if any, feeling in favor of assimilation to Malaya exists among the South Thailand Malays, the actual strength of the Abako idea, or the attitudes of Tamils in Ceylon toward the Dravidian separatists of Madras are matters for empirical research.

13 Nor does the interstate significance of primordial sentiments lie wholly in their divisive power. Pan-American attitudes, weak and ill-defined as they may be, have provided a useful context of mild solidarity for the confrontation of leaders of major African countries – Arab and Negro alike – as at Casablanca in January, 1961. Burma's strenuous (and expensive) efforts to strengthen and revitalize international Buddhism, as in the Sixth Great Council at Yegu in 1954, have served to link her more effectively with the other Theravada countries – Ceylon, Thailand, Laos, and Cambodia. And a vague, mainly racial, feeling of common "Malayness" has played a positive role in the relations between Malaya and Indonesia and Malaya and the Philippines (though not, as yet, between Indonesia and the Philippines).

14 I. Wallerstein, "The Emergence of Two West African Nations: Ghana and the Ivory Coast," unpublished Ph.D. thesis, Columbia University, 1959.

15 For a brief discussion of this problem with respect to Indonesia, see C. Geertz, "The Javanese Village," in G. W. Skinner (ed.), *Local, Ethnic and National Loyalties in Village Indonesia*, Yale University, Southeast Asia Studies, Cultural Report Series, No. 8, 1959, pp. 34–41.

31

Nations and Nationalism (1983)

Ernest Gellner

Ernest Gellner, selection from *Nations and Nationalism* (1983) [source: Ernest Gellner, *Nations and Nationalism*. Ithaca: Cornell University Press, 1983, 39–58. Reprinted by permission of Peters, Fraser & Dunlop, London.]

Gellner was for some time the leading voice among those who adopted a "modernist" perspective on the nation, arguing (as had Lenin) that it is a function of economic, technological, and industrial forces emerging in Europe at the end of the eighteenth century, and that the ethnic-national traditions often invoked to establish the modern nation-state are largely imaginary constructions after the fact. His most influential work has been *Nations and Nationalism*.

The Transition to an Age of Nationalism

The most important steps in the argument have now been made. Mankind is irreversibly committed to industrial society, and therefore to a society whose productive system is based on cumulative science and technology. This alone can sustain anything like the present and anticipated number of inhabitants of the planet, and give them a prospect of the kind of standard of living which man now takes for granted, or aspires to take for granted. Agrarian society is no longer an option, for its restoration would simply condemn the great majority of mankind to death by starvation, not to mention dire and unacceptable poverty for the minority of survivors. Hence there is no point in discussing, for any practical purpose, the charms and the horrors of the cultural and political accompaniments of the agrarian age: they are simply not available. We do not properly understand the range of options available to industrial society, and perhaps we never shall; but we understand some of its essential concomitants. The kind of cultural homogeneity demanded by nationalism is one of them, and we had better make our peace with it. It is not the case, as Elie Kedourie claims,[1] that nationalism imposes homogeneity; it is rather that a homogeneity imposed by objective, inescapable imperative eventually appears on the surface in the form of nationalism.

Most of mankind enters the industrial age from the agrarian stage. (The tiny minority which enters it directly from the pre-agrarian condition does not affect the argument, and the same points apply to it.) The social organization of agrarian society, however, is not at all favourable to the nationalist principle, to the convergence of political and cultural units, and to the homogeneity and school-transmitted nature of culture within each political unit. On the contrary, as in medieval Europe, it generates political units which are either smaller or much larger than cultural boundaries would indicate; only very occasionally, by accident, it produced a dynastic state which corresponded, more or less, with a language and a culture, as eventually happened on Europe's Atlantic seaboard. (The fit was never very close. Culture in agrarian society is much more pluralistic than its empires, and generally much broader than its small participatory social units.)

All this being so, the age of transition to industrialism was bound, according to our model, also to be an age of nationalism, a period of turbulent readjustment, in which either political boundaries, or cultural ones, or both, were being modified, so as to satisfy the new nationalist imperative which now, for the first time, was making itself felt. Because rulers do not surrender territory gladly (and every change of a political boundary must make someone a loser), because changing one's culture is very frequently a most painful experience, and moreover, because there were rival cultures struggling to capture the souls of men, just as there were rival centres of political authority striving to suborn men and capture territory: given all this, it immediately follows from our model that this period of transition was bound to be violent and conflict-ridden. Actual historical facts fully confirm these expectations.

Nevertheless, it would not be correct to proceed by simply working out the implications of the implementation of the nationalist imperative for agrarian society. Industrial society did not arrive on the scene by divine fiat. It was itself the fruit of developments within one particular agrarian society, and these developments were not devoid of their own turbulence. When it then conquered the rest of the world, neither this global colonization, nor the abandonment of empire by those who had been carried forward on the wave of industrial supremacy but eventually lost their monopoly of it, were peaceful developments. All this means that in actual history the effects of nationalism tend to be conflated with the other consequences of industrialism.

Though nationalism is indeed an effect of industrial social organization, it is not the *only* effect of the imposition of this new social form, and hence it is necessary to disentangle it from those other developments.

The problem is illustrated by the fascinating relationship between the Reformation and nationalism. The stress of the Reformation on literacy and scripturalism, its onslaught on a monopolistic priesthood (or, as Weber clearly saw, its universalization rather than abolition of priesthood), its individualism and links with mobile urban populations, all make it a kind of harbinger of social features and attitudes which, according to our model, produce the nationalist age. The role of Protestantism in helping to bring about the industrial world is an enormous, complex and contentious topic; and there is not much point in doing more than cursorily alluding to it here. But in parts of the globe in which both industrialism and nationalism came later and under external impact, the full relationship of Protestant-type attitudes and nationalism is yet to be properly explored.

This relationship is perhaps the most conspicuous in Islam. The cultural history of the Arab world and of many other Muslim lands during the past hundred years is largely the story of the advance and victory of Reformism, a kind of Islamic Protestantism with a heavy stress on scripturalism and above all a sustained hostility to spiritual brokerage, to the local middlemen between man and God (and, in practice, between diverse groups of men), who had become so very prominent in pre-modern Islam. The history of this movement and that of modern Arab (and other) nationalisms can hardly be separated from each other. Islam always had an in-built proclivity or potential for this kind of "reformed" version of the faith, and had been seduced away from it, presumably, by the social need of autonomous rural groups for the incarnated, personalized location of sanctity which is invaluable for local mediation purposes. Under modern conditions its capacity to be a more abstract faith, presiding over an anonymous community of equal believers, could reassert itself.

But even religions which might be thought to have had little inherent potential for such "protestant" interpretation, could nonetheless be turned in that direction during the age when the drives to industrialism and to nationalism were making their impact. Formally speaking, one would not expect Shintoism to have any marked resemblance to, say, English noncon-formity. Nevertheless, during the Japanese modernization drive, it was the sober, orderly, as it were Quaker elements in it (which evidently can be found or imposed anywhere if one tries hard enough) which were stressed to the detriment of any ecstatic elements and any undue private familiarity with the sacred.[2] Had ancient Greece survived into the modern age, Dionysiac cults might have assumed a more sober garb as Hellas lurched forward along the path of development.

Apart from the links between the Protestant and nationalist ethos, there are the direct consequences of industrialization itself. The general and pervasive consequences of an established industrial order have already been discussed, in connection with our general model linking the industrial division of labour with the implementation of the nationalist principle. But certain specific consequences of early industrialization which do not generally persist later nevertheless have a significant role to play. Early industrialism means population explosion, rapid urbanization, labour migration, and also the economic and political penetration of previously more or less inward-turned communities, by a global economy and a centralizing polity. It means that the at least relatively stable and insulated Babel system of traditional agrarian communities, each inward-turned, kept separate by geography sideways, and by an enormous social distance upwards, is replaced by quite a new kind of Babel, with new cultural boundaries that are not stable but in constant and dramatic movement, and which are seldom hallowed by any kind of custom.

There is also a link between nationalism and the processes of colonialism, imperialism and de-colonization. The emergence of industrial society in Western Europe had as its consequence the virtual conquest of the entire world by European powers, and sometimes by European settler populations. In effect the whole of Africa, America, Oceania, and very large parts of Asia came under European domination; and the parts of Asia which escaped this fate were often under strong indirect influence. This global conquest was, as conquests go, rather unusual. Normally, political empire is the reward of a military orientation and dedication. It is perpetrated by societies strongly committed to warfare, either because, let us say, their tribal form of life includes an automatic military training, or because they possess a leading stratum committed to it, or for some such similar reason. Moreover, the activity of conquest is arduous and takes up a large part of the energy of the conquering group.

None of this was true of the European conquest of the world. It was eventually carried out and completed by nations increasingly oriented towards industry and trade, not by a militaristic machine, nor by a swarm of temporarily cohesive tribesmen. It was achieved without any total preoccupation with the process on the part of the conqueror nations. The point made about the English, that they acquired their Empire in a state of absence of mind, can to some extent be generalized. (The English also, most laudably, lost the Empire with a similar lack of attention.) When Europe was conquering and dominating the world, it had, on the whole, other, more pressing and internal things to occupy its attention. It did not even pay the conquered nations the compliment of being specially interested in the conquest. A few untypical periods of self-conscious and vainglorious imperialism apart, and disregarding the early conquest of Latin America, which was inspired by good old-fashioned non-commercial rapacity, that was how it was. The conquest had not been planned, and was the fruit of economic and technological superiority, and not of a military orientation.

With the diffusion of this technological and economic might, the balance of power changed, and between about 1905 and 1960 the pluralistic European empire was lost or voluntarily abandoned. Once again, the specific circumstances of all this cannot be ignored; even if the core or essence of nationalism flows from the general, abstractly formulable premises which were initially laid out, nevertheless the specific forms of nationalist phenomena are obviously affected by these circumstances.

A note on the weakness of nationalism

It is customary to comment on the strength of nationalism. This is an important mistake, though readily understandable since, whenever nationalism has taken root, it has tended to prevail with ease over other modern ideologies.

Nevertheless, the clue to the understanding of nationalism is its weakness at least as much as its strength. It was the dog who failed to bark who provided the vital clue for Sherlock Holmes. The numbers of potential nationalisms which failed to bark is far, far larger than those which did, though *they* have captured all our attention.

We have already insisted on the dormant nature of this allegedly powerful monster during the pre-industrial age. But even within the age of nationalism, there is a further important sense in which nationalism remains astonishingly feeble. Nationalism has been defined, in effect, as the striving to make culture and polity congruent, to endow a culture with its own political roof, and not more than one roof at that. Culture, an elusive concept, was deliberately left undefined. But an at least provisionally acceptable criterion of culture might be language, as at least a sufficient, if not a necessary touchstone of it. Allow for a moment a difference of language to entail a difference of culture (though not necessarily the reverse).

If this is granted, at least temporarily, certain consequences follow. I have heard the number of languages on earth estimated at around 8000. The figure can no doubt be increased by counting dialects separately. If we allow the "precedent" argument, this becomes legitimate: if a kind of differential which in some places defines a nationalism is allowed to engender a "potential nationalism" wherever else a similar difference is found, then the number of potential nationalisms increases sharply. For instance, diverse Slavonic, Teutonic and Romance languages are in fact often no further apart than are the mere dialects within what are elsewhere conventionally seen as unitary languages. Slav languages, for instance, are probably closer to each other than are the various forms of colloquial Arabic, allegedly a single language.

The "precedent" argument can also generate potential nationalisms by analogies invoking factors other than language. For instance, Scottish nationalism indisputably exists. (It may indeed be held to contradict my model.) It ignores language (which would condemn some Scots to Irish nationalism, and the rest to English nationalism), invoking instead a shared historical experience. Yet if such additional links be allowed to count (as long as they don't contradict the requirement of my model, that they can serve as a base for an *eventually* homogeneous, internally mobile culture/polity with one educational machine servicing that culture under the surveillance of that polity), then the number of potential nationalisms goes up even higher.

However, let us be content with the figure of 8000, once given to me by a linguist as a rough number of languages based on what was no doubt rather an arbitrary estimate of language alone. The number of states in the world at present is some figure of the order of 200. To this figure one may add all the irredentist nationalisms, which have not yet attained their state (and perhaps never will), but which are struggling in that direction and thus have a legitimate claim to be counted among actual, and not merely potential, nationalisms. On the other hand, one must also subtract all those states which have come into being without the benefit of the blessing of nationalist endorsement, and which do not satisfy the nationalist criteria of political legitimacy, and indeed defy them; for instance, all the diverse mini-states dotted about the globe as survivals of a pre-nationalist age, and sometimes brought forth as concessions to geographical accident or political compromise. Once all these had been subtracted, the resulting figure would again, presumably, not be too far above 200. But let us, for the sake of charity, pretend that we have four times that number of reasonably effective nationalisms on earth, in other words, 800 of them. I believe this to be considerably larger than the facts would justify, but let it pass.

This rough calculation still gives us only *one* effective nationalism for *ten* potential ones! And this surprising ratio, depressing presumably for any enthusiastic pan-nationalist, if such a person exists, could be made much larger if the "precedent" argument were applied to the full to determine the number of potential nationalisms, and if the criteria of entry into the class of effective nationalisms were made at all stringent.

What is one to conclude from this? That for every single nationalism which has so far raised its ugly head, nine others are still waiting in the wings? That all the bomb-throwing, martyrdoms, exchange of populations, and worse, which have so far beset humanity, are still to be repeated tenfold?

I think not. For every effective nationalism, there are n potential ones, groups defined either by shared culture inherited from the agrarian world or by some other link (on the "precedent" principle) which *could* give hope of establishing a homogeneous industrial community, but which nevertheless do not bother to struggle, which fail to activate their potential nationalism, which do not even try.

So it seems that the urge to make mutual cultural substitutability the basis of the state is not so powerful after all. The members of *some* groups do indeed feel it, but members of most groups, with analogous claims, evidently do not.

To explain this, we must return to the accusation made against nationalism: that it insists on imposing homogeneity on the populations unfortunate enough to fall under the sway of authorities possessed by the nationalist ideology. The assumption underlying this accusation is that traditional, ideologically uninfected authorities, such as the Ottoman Turks, had kept the peace and extracted taxes, but otherwise tolerated, and been indeed profoundly indifferent to, the diversity of faiths and cultures which they governed. By contrast, their gunman successors seem incapable of resting in peace till they have imposed the nationalist principle of *cuius regio, eius lingua*. They do not want merely a fiscal surplus and obedience. They thirst after the cultural and linguistic souls of their subjects.

This accusation must be stood on its head. It is not the case that nationalism imposes homogeneity out of a wilful cultural *Machtbedürfnis*; it is the objective need for homogeneity which is reflected in nationalism. If it is the case that a modern industrial state can only function with a mobile, literate, culturally standardized, interchangeable population, as we have argued, then the illiterate, half-starved populations sucked from their erstwhile rural cultural ghettoes into the melting pots of shanty-towns yearn for incorporation into some one of those cultural pools which already has, or looks as if it might acquire, a state of its own, with the subsequent promise of full cultural citizenship, access to primary schools, employment, and all. Often, these alienated, uprooted, wandering populations may vacillate between diverse options, and they may often come to a provisional rest at one or another temporary and transitional cultural resting place.

But there are some options which they will refrain from trying to take up. They will hesitate about trying to enter cultural pools within which they know themselves to be spurned; or rather, within which they expect to *continue* to be spurned. Poor newcomers are, of course, almost always spurned. The question is whether they will continue to be slighted, and whether the same fate will await their children. This will depend on whether the newly arrived and hence least privileged stratum possesses traits which its members and their offspring cannot shed, and which will continue to identify them: genetically transmitted or deeply engrained religious-cultural habits are impossible or difficult to drop.

The alienated victims of early industrialism are unlikely to be tempted by cultural pools that are very small – a language spoken by a couple of villages offers few prospects – or very diffused or lacking in any literary traditions or personnel capable of carrying skills, and so on. They require cultural pools which are large, and/or have a good historic base, or intellectual personnel well equipped to propagate the culture in question. It is impossible to pick out any single qualification, or set of qualifications, which will either guarantee the success as a nationalist catalyst of the culture endowed with it (or them), or which on the contrary will ensure its failure. Size, historicity, reasonably compact territory, a capable and energetic intellectual class: all these will obviously help; but no single one is necessary, and it is doubtful whether any firm predictive generalization can be established in these terms. That the principle of nationalism will be operative can be predicted; just which groupings will emerge as its carriers can be only loosely indicated, for it depends on too many historic contingencies.

Nationalism as such is fated to prevail, but not any one particular nationalism. We know that reasonably homogeneous cultures, each of them with its own political roof, its own political servicing, are becoming the norm, widely implemented but for few exceptions; but we cannot predict just which cultures, with which political roofs, will be blessed by success. On the contrary, the simple calculations made above, concerning the number of cultures or potential nationalisms and concerning the room available for proper national states, clearly shows that most potential nationalisms must either fail, or, more commonly, will refrain from even trying to find political expression.

This is precisely what we do find. Most cultures or potential national groups enter the age of nationalism without even the feeblest effort to benefit from it themselves. The number of groups which in terms of the "precedent" argument could try to become nations, which could define themselves by the kind of criterion which in some other place does in fact define some real and effective nation, is legion. Yet most of them go meekly to their doom, to see their culture (though not themselves as individuals) slowly disappear, dissolving into the wider culture of some new national state. Most cultures are led to the dustheap of history by industrial civilization without offering any resistance. The linguistic distinctiveness of the Scottish Highlands within Scotland is, of course, incomparably greater than the cultural distinctiveness of Scotland within the UK; but there is no Highland nationalism. Much the same is true of Moroccan Berbers. Dialectal and cultural differences within Germany or Italy are as great as those between recognized Teutonic or Romance languages. Southern Russians differ culturally from Northern Russians, but, unlike Ukrainians, do not translate this into a sense of nationhood.

Does this show that nationalism is, after all, unimportant? Or even that it is an ideological artefact, an invention of febrile thinkers which has mysteriously captured some mysteriously susceptible nations? Not at all. To reach such a conclusion would, ironically, come close to a tacit, oblique acceptance of the nationalist ideologue's most misguided claim: namely, that the "nations" are there, in the very nature of things, only waiting to be "awakened" (a favourite nationalist expression and image) from their regrettable slumber, by the nationalist "awakener". One would be inferring from the failure of most potential nations ever to "wake up", from the lack of deep stirrings waiting for reveille, that nationalism was not important after all. Such an inference concedes the social ontology of "nations", only admitting, with some surprise perhaps, that some of them lack the vigour and vitality needed if they are to fulfil the destiny which history intended for them.

But nationalism is *not* the awakening of an old, latent, dormant force, though that is how it does indeed present itself. It is in reality the consequence of a new form of social organization, based on deeply internalized, education-dependent high cultures, each protected by its own state. It uses some of the pre-existent cultures, generally transforming them in the process, but it cannot possibly use them all. There are too many of them. A viable higher culture-sustaining modern state cannot fall below a certain minimal size (unless in effect parasitic on its neighbours); and there is only room for a limited number of such states on this earth.

The high ratio of determined slumberers, who will not rise and shine and who refuse to be woken, enables us to turn the tables on nationalism-as-seen-by-itself. Nationalism sees itself as a natural and universal ordering of the political life of mankind, only obscured by that long, persistent and mysterious somnolence. As Hegel expressed this vision: "Nations may have had a long history before they finally reach their destination – that of forming themselves into states."[3] Hegel immediately goes on to suggest that this pre-state period is really "pre-historical" (*sic*): so it would seem that on this view the real history of a nation only begins when it acquires its own state. If we invoke the sleeping-beauty nations, neither possessing a state nor feeling the lack of it, against the nationalist doctrine, we tacitly accept its social metaphysic, which sees nations as the bricks of which mankind is made up. Critics of nationalism who denounce the political movement but tacitly accept the existence of nations, do not go far enough. Nations as a natural, God-given way of classifying men, as an inherent though long-delayed political destiny, are a myth; nationalism, which sometimes takes pre-existing cultures and turns them into nations, sometimes invents them, and often obliterates pre-existing cultures: *that* is a reality, for better or worse, and in general an inescapable one. Those who are its historic agents know not what they do, but that is another matter.

But we must not accept the myth. Nations are not inscribed into the nature of things, they do not constitute a political version of the doctrine of natural kinds. Nor were national states the manifest ultimate destiny of ethnic or cultural groups. What do exist are cultures, often subtly grouped, shading into each other, overlapping, intertwined; and there exist, usually but not always, political units of all shapes and sizes. In the past the two did not generally converge. There were good reasons for their failing to do so in many cases. Their rulers established their identity by differentiating themselves downwards, and the ruled micro-communities differentiated themselves laterally from their neighbours grouped in similar units.

But nationalism is not the awakening and assertion of these mythical, supposedly natural and given units. It is, on the contrary, the crystallization of new units, suitable for the conditions now prevailing, though admittedly using as their raw material the cultural, historical and other inheritances from the pre-nationalist world. This force – the drive towards new units constructed on the principles corresponding to the new division of labour – is indeed very strong, though it is not the only force in the modern world, nor altogether irresistible. In most cases it prevails, and above all, it determines the *norm* for the legitimacy of political units in the modern world: most of them must satisfy the imperatives of nationalism, as described. It sets the accepted standard, even if it does not prevail totally and universally, and some deviant cases do succeed in defying the norm.

The ambiguity of the question – is nationalism strong or not? – arises from this: nationalism sees and presents itself as the affirmation of each and every "nationality"; and these alleged entities are supposed just to be there, like Mount Everest, since long ago, antedating the age of nationalism. So, ironically, in its own terms nationalism is astonishingly weak. Most of the potential nations, the latent differentiable communities which could claim to be nations by criteria analogous to those which somewhere else have succeeded, fail altogether even to raise their claim, let alone press it effectively and make it good. If, on the other hand, one interprets nationalism in the manner which I hold to be correct, and which indeed contradicts and offends its own self-image, then the conclusion must be that it is a very strong force, though not perhaps a unique or irresistible one.

Wild and garden cultures

One way of approaching the central issue is this. Cultures, like plants, can be divided into savage and cultivated varieties. The savage kinds are produced and reproduce themselves spontaneously, as parts of the life of men. No community is without some shared system of communication and norms, and the wild systems of this kind (in other words, cultures) reproduce themselves from generation to generation without conscious design, super-vision, surveillance or special nutrition.

Cultivated or garden cultures are different, though they have developed from the wild varieties. They possess a complexity and richness, most usually sustained by literacy and by specialized personnel, and would perish if deprived of their distinctive nourishment in the form of specialized institu-tions of learning with reasonably numerous, full-time and dedicated person-nel. During the agrarian epoch of human history the high cultures or great traditions became prominent, important, and in one sense, but one sense only, dominant. Though they could not altogether impose themselves on the totality, or even the majority of the population, nevertheless they generally succeeded in imposing themselves on it as authoritative, even if (or because) they were inaccessible and mysterious. They sometimes strengthened, and sometimes competed with, the centralized state. They could also deputize for that state, when it weakened or disintegrated during times of troubles or a dark age. A church or a ritual system could stand in for the shadow of a past or ghost empire. But the high cultures did not generally define the limits of a political unit, and there are good reasons why, in the agrarian age, they should not have been able to do so.

In the industrial age all this changes. The high cultures come to dominate in quite a new sense. The old doctrines associated with them mostly lose their authority, but the literate idioms and styles of communication they carried become far more effectively authoritative and normative, and, above all, they come to be pervasive and universal in society. In other words, virtually everyone becomes literate, and communicates in an elaborate code, in expli-cit, fairly "grammatical" (regularized) sentences, not in context-bound grunts and nods.

But the high culture, newly universalized in the population, now badly needs political support and underpinning. In the agrarian age, it sometimes had this and benefited from it, but at other times it could dispense with political protection, and that was indeed one of its strengths. In a dark age when anarchy prevailed and the king's peace was no longer kept, Christian or Buddhist monasteries, dervish *zawiyas* and Brahmin communities could survive and in some measure keep alive the high culture without benefit of protection by the sword.

Now that the task of the high culture is so much greater and so much more onerous, it cannot dispense with a political infrastructure. As a character in *No Orchids for Miss Blandish* observed, every girl ought to have a husband, preferably her own; and every high culture now wants a state, and preferably its own. Not every wild culture can become a high culture, and those without serious prospects of becoming one tend to bow out without a struggle; they do not engender a nationalism. Those which think they do have a chance –

or, if anthropomorphic talk about cultures is to be avoided, those whose human carriers credit them with good prospects – fight it out among themselves for available populations and for the available state-space. This is one kind of nationalist or ethnic conflict. Where existing political boundaries, and those of old or crystallizing high cultures with political aspirations, fail to be in harmony, another kind of conflict so highly characteristic of the age of nationalism breaks out.

Another analogy, in addition to the above botanical one, is available to describe the new situation. Agrarian man can be compared with a natural species which can survive in the natural environment. Industrial man can be compared with an artificially produced or bred species which can no longer breathe effectively in the nature-given atmosphere, but can only function effectively and survive in a new, specially blended and artificially sustained air or medium. Hence he lives in specially bounded and constructed units, a kind of giant aquarium or breathing chamber. But these chambers need to be erected and serviced. The maintenance of the life-giving and life-preserving air or liquid within each of these giant receptacles is not automatic. It requires a specialized plant. The name for this plant is a national educational and communications system. Its only effective keeper and protector is the state.

It would not in principle be impossible to have a single such cultural/ educational goldfish bowl for the entire globe, sustained by a single political authority and a single educational system. In the long run this may yet come to pass. But in the meantime, and for very good reasons yet to be discussed, the global norm is a set of discontinuous breathing chambers or aquaria, each with its own proprietary, not properly interchangeable, medium or atmosphere. They do share some general traits. The formula for the medium of the fully developed industrial goldfish bowls is fairly similar in type, though it is rich in relatively superficial, but deliberately stressed, brand-differentiating characteristics.

There are some good and obvious reasons for this new pluralism, which will be explored further. The industrial age inherited both the political units and the cultures, high and low, of the preceding age. There was no reason why they should all suddenly fuse into a single one, and there were good reasons why they should *not*: industrialism, in other words the type of production or of the division of labour which makes these homogeneous breathing tanks imperative, did not arrive simultaneously in all parts of the world, nor in the same manner. The differential timing of its arrival divided humanity into rival groups very effectively. These differences in arrival-time of industrialism in various communities became acute if they could utilize some cultural, genetic or similar differentiae, left behind by the agrarian world. The dating of "development" constitutes a crucial political diacritical mark, if it can seize upon some cultural difference inherited from the agrarian age, and use it as its token.

The process of industrialization took place in successive phases and in different conditions, and engendered various new rivalries, with new gains and losses to be made and avoided. Internationalism was often predicted by the prophets and commentators of the industrial age, both on the left and on the right, but the very opposite came to pass: the age of nationalism.

What is a Nation?

We are now at last in a position to attempt some kind of plausible answer to this question. Initially there were two especially promising candidates for the construction of a theory of nationality: will and culture. Obviously, each of them is important and relevant; but, just as obviously, neither is remotely adequate. It is instructive to consider why this is so.

No doubt will or consent contitutes an important factor in the formation of most groups, large and small. Mankind has always been organized in groups, of all kinds of shapes and sizes, sometimes sharply defined and sometimes loose, sometimes neatly nested and sometimes overlapping or intertwined. The variety of these possibilities, and of the principles on which the groups were recruited and maintained, is endless. But two generic agents or catalysts of group formation and maintenance are obviously crucial: will, voluntary adherence and identification, loyalty, solidarity, on the one hand; and fear, coercion, compulsion, on the other. These two possibilities constitute extreme poles along a kind of spectrum. A few communities may be based exclusively or very predominantly on one or the other, but they must be rare. Most persisting groups are based on a mixture of loyalty and identification (on *willed* adherence), and of extraneous incentives, positive or negative, on hopes and fears.

If we define nations as groups which *will* themselves to persist as communities,[4] the definition-net that we have cast into the sea will bring forth far too rich a catch. The haul which we shall have trawled in will indeed include the communities we may easily recognize as effective and cohesive nations: these genuine nations do in effect will themselves to be such, and their life may indeed constitute a kind of continuous, informal, ever self-reaffirming plebiscite. But (unfortunately for this definition) the same also applies to many other clubs, conspiracies, gangs, teams, parties, not to mention the many numerous communities and associations of the pre-industrial age which were not recruited and defined according to the nationalist principle and which defy it. Will, consent, identification, were not ever absent from the human scene, even though they were (and continue to be) also accompanied by calculation, fear and interest. (It is an interesting and moot question whether sheer inertia, the persistence of aggregates and combinations, is to be counted as tacit consent or as something else.)

The tacit self-identification has operated on behalf of all kinds of groupings, larger or smaller than nations, or cutting across them, or defined horizontally or in other ways. In brief, even if will were the basis of a nation (to paraphrase an idealist definition of the state), it is also the basis of so much else, that we cannot possibly define the nation in this manner. It is only because, in the modern, nationalist age, national units are the *preferred*, favoured objects of identification and willed adherence, that the definition seems tempting, because those other kinds of group are now so easily forgotten. Those who take the tacit assumptions of nationalism for granted erroneously also credit them to humanity at large, in any age. But a definition tied to the assumptions and conditions of one age (and even then constituting an exaggeration), cannot usefully be used to help to explain the *emergence* of that age.

Any definition of nations in terms of shared culture is another net which brings in far too rich a catch. Human history is and continues to be well endowed with cultural differentiations. Cultural boundaries are sometimes sharp and sometimes fuzzy; the patterns are sometimes bold and simple and sometimes tortuous and complex. For all the reasons we have stressed so much, this richness of differentiation does not, and indeed cannot, normally or generally converge either with the boundaries of political units (the jurisdictions of effective authorities) or with the boundaries of units blessed by the democratic sacraments of consent and will. The agrarian world simply could not be so neat. The industrial world tends to become so, or at least to approximate to such simplicity; but that is another matter, and there are now special factors making it so.

The establishment of pervasive high cultures (standardized, literacy- and education-based systems of communication), a process rapidly gathering pace throughout the world, has made it seem, to anyone too deeply immersed in our contemporary assumptions, that nationality may be definable in terms of shared culture. Nowadays people can live only in units defined by a shared culture, and internally mobile and fluid. Genuine cultural pluralism ceases to be viable under current conditions. But a little bit of historical awareness or sociological sophistication should dispel the illusion that this was always so. Culturally plural societies often worked well in the past: so well, in fact, that cultural plurality was sometimes invented where it was previously lacking.

If, for such cogent reasons, these two apparently promising paths towards the definition of nationality are barred, is there another way?

The great, but valid, paradox is this: nations can be defined only in terms of the age of nationalism, rather than, as you might expect, the other way round. It is not the case that the "age of nationalism" is a mere summation of the awakening and political self-assertion of this, that, or the other nation. Rather, when general social conditions make for standardized, homogeneous, centrally sustained high cultures, pervading entire populations and not just elite minorities, a situation arises in which well-defined educationally sanctioned and unified cultures constitute very nearly the only kind of unit with which men willingly and often ardently identify. The cultures now seem to be the natural repositories of political legitimacy. Only *then* does it come to appear that any defiance of their boundaries by political units constitutes a scandal.

Under these conditions, though under these conditions *only*, nations can indeed be defined in terms both of will and of culture, and indeed in terms of the convergence of them both with political units. In these conditions, men will to be politically united with all those, and only those, who share their culture. Polities then will to extend their boundaries to the limits of their cultures, and to protect and impose their culture with the boundaries of their power. The fusion of will, culture and polity becomes the norm, and one not easily or frequently defied. (Once, it had been almost universally defied, with impunity, and had indeed passed unnoticed and undiscussed.) These conditions do not define the human situation as such, but merely its industrial variant.

It is nationalism which engenders nations, and not the other way round. Admittedly, nationalism uses the pre-existing, historically inherited proliferation of cultures or cultural wealth, though it uses them very selectively, and it most often transforms them radically. Dead languages can be revived, traditions invented, quite ficitious pristine purities restored. But this culturally creative, fanciful, positively inventive aspect of nationalist ardour ought not to allow anyone to conclude, erroneously, that nationalism is a contingent, artificial, ideological invention, which might not have happened, if only those damned busy-body interfering European thinkers, not content to leave well alone, had not concocted it and fatefully injected it into the bloodstream of otherwise viable political communities. The cultural shreds and patches used by nationalism are often arbitrary historical inventions. Any old shred and patch would have served as well. But in no way does it follow that the principle of nationalism itself, as opposed to the avatars it happens to pick up for its incarnations, is itself in the least contingent and accidental.

Nothing could be further from the truth than such a supposition. Nationalism is not what it seems, and above all it is not what it seems to itself. The cultures it claims to defend and revive are often its own inventions, or are modified out of all recognition. Nonetheless the nationalist principle as such, as distinct from each of its specific forms, and from the individually distinctive nonsense which it may preach, has very very deep roots in our shared current condition, is not at all contingent, and will not easily be denied.

Durkheim taught that in religious worship society adores its own camouflaged image. In a nationalist age, societies worship themselves brazenly and openly, spurning the camouflage. At Nuremberg, Nazi Germany did not worship itself by pretending to worship God or even Wotan; it overtly worshipped itself. In milder but just as significant form, enlightened modernist theologians do not believe, or even take much interest in, the doctrines of their faith which had meant so much to their predecessors. They treat them with a kind of comic auto-functionalism, as valid simply and only as the conceptual and ritual tools by means of which a social tradition affirms its values, continuity and solidarity, and they systematically obscure and play down the difference between such a tacitly reductionist "faith", and the real thing which had preceded it and had played such a crucial part in earlier European history, a part which could never have been played by the unrecognizably diluted, watered-down current versions.

But the fact that social self-worship, whether virulent and violent or gentle and evasive, is now an openly avowed collective self-worship, rather than a means of covertly revering society through the image of God, as Durkheim insisted, does not mean that the current style is any more veridical than that of a Durkheimian age. The community may no longer be seen through the prism of the divine, but nationalism has its own amnesias and selections which, even when they may be severely secular, can be profoundly distorting and deceptive.

The basic deception and self-deception practised by nationalism is this: nationalism is, essentially, the general imposition of a high culture on society, where previously low cultures had taken up the lives of the majority, and in some cases of the totality, of the population. It means that generalized diffusion of a school-mediated, academy-supervised idiom, codified for the requirements of reasonably precise bureaucratic and technological communication. It is the establishment of an anonymous, impersonal society, with mutually substitutable atomized individuals, held together above all by a shared culture of this kind, in place of a previous complex structure of local groups, sustained by folk cultures reproduced locally and idiosyncratically by the micro-groups themselves. That is what *really* happens.

But this is the very opposite of what nationalism affirms and what nationalists fervently believe. Nationalism usually conquers in the name of a putative folk culture. Its symbolism is drawn from the healthy, pristine, vigorous life of the peasants, of the *Volk*, the *narod*. There is a certain element of truth in the nationalist self-presentation when the *narod* or *Volk* is ruled by officials of another, an alien high culture, whose oppression must be resisted first by a

cultural revival and reaffirmation, and eventually by a war of national liberation. If the nationalism prospers it eliminates the alien high culture, but it
does not then replace it by the old local low culture; it revives, or invents, a
local high (literate, specialist-transmitted) culture of its own, though admittedly one which will have some links with the earlier local folk styles and
dialects. But it was the great ladies at the Budapest Opera who really went to
town in peasant dresses, or dresses claimed to be such. At the present time in
the Soviet Union the consumers of "ethnic" gramophone records are not
the remaining ethnic rural population, but the newly urbanized, apartment-
dwelling, educated and multi-lingual population,[5] who like to express their
real or imagined sentiments and roots, and who will no doubt indulge in as
much nationalist behaviour as the political situation may allow.

So a sociological self-deception, a vision of reality through a prism of
illusion, still persists, but it is not the same as that which was analysed by
Durkheim. Society no longer worships itself through religious symbols; a
modern, streamlined, on-wheels high culture celebrates itself in song and
dance, which it borrows (stylizing it in the process) from a folk culture which
it fondly believes itself to be perpetuating, defending, and reaffirming. [...]

Notes

1   Elie Kedourie, *Nationalism*, London, 1960.
2   Personal communication from Ronald Dore.
3   G. W. F. Hegel, *Lectures on the Philosophy of World History*, tr. H. B. Nisbet,
    Cambridge, 1975, p. 134.
4   Ernest Renan, "Qu'est-ce qu'une Nation?", republished in *Ernest Renan et
    l'Allemagne*, Textes receuillis et commentés par Emile Bure, NY, 1945.
5   Yu. V. Bromley et al., *Sovremennye Etnicheskie Protessy v SSSR* (Contemporary
    Ethnic Processes in the USSR), Moscow, 1975.

32

Imagined Communities (1983)

Benedict Anderson

Benedict Anderson, ch. 3, "The Origins of National Consciousness," of *Imagined Communities* (1983) [source: Benedict Anderson, *Imagined Communities: Reflections on the Origin and Spread of Nationalism*, rev. edn. London: Verso, 1991, 37–46]

Anderson has revised the modernist theses of Kedourie and Gellner, arguing that in practice almost all forms of community are imagined in some sense, and that it would be more accurate to say that national identities are not so much fictional as created or produced. Anderson has emphasized the way certain modernist innovations – such as "print-capitalism" – allowed national community to be imagined from the start. His best-known work is *Imagined Communities*.

If the development of print-as-commodity is the key to the generation of wholly new ideas of simultaneity, still, we are simply at the point where communities of the type "horizontal-secular, transverse-time" become possible. Why, within that type, did the nation become so popular? The factors involved are obviously complex and various. But a strong case can be made for the primacy of capitalism.

As already noted, at least 20,000,000 books had already been printed by 1500,[1] signalling the onset of Benjamin's "age of mechanical reproduction." If manuscript knowledge was scarce and arcane lore, print knowledge lived by reproducibility and dissemination.[2] If, as Febvre and Martin believe, possibly as many as 200,000,000 volumes had been manufactured by 1600, it is no wonder that Francis Bacon believed that print had changed "the appearance and state of the world."[3]

One of the earlier forms of capitalist enterprise, book-publishing felt all of capitalism's restless search for markets. The early printers established branches all over Europe: "in this way a veritable 'international' of publishing houses, which ignored national [*sic*] frontiers, was created."[4] And since the years 1500–1550 were a period of exceptional European prosperity, publishing shared in the general boom. "More than at any other time" it was "a great industry under the control of wealthy capitalists."[5] Naturally, "booksellers were primarily concerned to make a profit and to sell their products, and consequently they sought out first and foremost those works which were of interest to the largest possible number of their contemporaries."[6]

The initial market was literate Europe, a wide but thin stratum of Latin-readers. Saturation of this market took about a hundred and fifty years. The determinative fact about Latin – aside from its sacrality – was that it was a language of bilinguals. Relatively few were born to speak it and even fewer, one imagines, dreamed in it. In the sixteenth century the proportion of bilinguals within the total population of Europe was quite small; very likely no larger than the proportion in the world's population today, and – proletarian internationalism notwithstanding – in the centuries to come. Then and now the bulk of mankind is monoglot. The logic of capitalism thus meant that once the elite Latin market was saturated, the potentially huge markets represented by the monoglot masses would beckon. To be sure, the Counter-Reformation encouraged a temporary resurgence of Latin-publishing, but by the mid-seventeenth century the movement was in decay, and fervently Catholic libraries replete. Meantime, a Europe-wide shortage of money made printers think more and more of peddling cheap editions in the vernaculars.[7]

The revolutionary vernacularizing thrust of capitalism was given further impetus by three extraneous factors, two of which contributed directly to the rise of national consciousness. The first, and ultimately the least important, was a change in the character of Latin itself. Thanks to the labours of the Humanists in reviving the broad literature of pre-Christian antiquity and spreading it through the print-market, a new appreciation of the sophisticated stylistic achievements of the ancients was apparent among the trans-European intelligentsia. The Latin they now aspired to write became more and more Ciceronian, and, by the same token, increasingly removed from ecclesiastical and everyday life. In this way it acquired an esoteric quality quite different from that of Church Latin in mediaeval times. For the older Latin was not arcane because of its subject matter or style, but simply because it was written at all, i.e. because of its status as *text*. Now it became arcane because of what was written, because of the language-in-itself.

Second was the impact of the Reformation, which, at the same time, owed much of its success to print-capitalism. Before the age of print, Rome easily won every war against heresy in Western Europe because it always had better internal lines of communication than its challengers. But when in 1517 Martin Luther nailed his theses to the chapel-door in Wittenberg, they were printed up in German translation, and "within 15 days [had been] seen in every part of the country."[8] In the two decades 1520–1540 three times as many books were published in German as in the period 1500–1520, an astonishing transformation to which Luther was absolutely central. His works represented no less than one third of *all* German-language books sold between 1518 and 1525. Between 1522 and 1546, a total of 430 editions (whole or partial) of his Biblical translations appeared. "We have here for the first time a truly mass readership and a popular literature within everybody's reach."[9] In effect, Luther became the first best-selling author *so known*. Or, to put it another way, the first writer who could "sell" his *new* books on the basis of his name.[10]

Where Luther led, others quickly followed, opening the colossal religious propaganda war that raged across Europe for the next century. In this titanic "battle for men's minds," Protestantism was always fundamentally on the offensive, precisely because it knew how to make use of the expanding vernacular print-market being created by capitalism, while the Counter-Reformation defended the citadel of Latin. The emblem for this is the Vatican's *Index Librorum Prohibitorum* – to which there was no Protestant counterpart – a novel catalogue made necessary by the sheer volume of printed subversion. Nothing gives a better sense of this siege mentality than François I's panicked 1535 ban on the printing of *any* books in his realm – on pain of death by hanging! The reason for both the ban and its unenforceability was that by then his realm's eastern borders were ringed with Protestant states and cities producing a massive stream of smugglable print. To take Calvin's Geneva alone: between 1533 and 1540 only 42 editions were published there, but the numbers swelled to 527 between 1550 and 1564, by which latter date no less than 40 separate printing-presses were working overtime.[11]

The coalition between Protestantism and print-capitalism, exploiting cheap popular editions, quickly created large new reading publics – not least among merchants and women, who typically knew little or no Latin – and simultaneously mobilized them for politico-religious purposes. Inevitably, it was not merely the Church that was shaken to its core. The same earthquake produced Europe's first important non-dynastic, non-city states in the Dutch Republic and the Commonwealth of the Puritans. (François I's panic was as much political as religious.)

Third was the slow, geographically uneven, spread of particular vernaculars as instruments of administrative centralization by certain well-positioned would-be absolutist monarchs. Here it is useful to remember that the universality of Latin in mediaeval Western Europe never corresponded to a universal political system. The contrast with Imperial China, where the reach of the mandarinal bureaucracy and of painted characters largely coincided, is instructive. In effect, the political fragmentation of Western Europe after the collapse of the Western Empire meant that no sovereign could monopolize Latin and make it his-and-only-his language-of-state, and thus Latin's religious authority never had a true political analogue.

The birth of administrative vernaculars predated both print and the religious upheaval of the sixteenth century, and must therefore be regarded (at least initially) as an independent factor in the erosion of the sacred imagined community. At the same time, nothing suggests that any deep-seated ideological, let alone proto-national, impulses underlay this vernacul-arization where it occurred. The case of "England" – on the northwestern periphery of Latin Europe – is here especially enlightening. Prior to the Norman Conquest, the language of the court, literary and administrative, was Anglo-Saxon. For the next century and a half virtually all royal documents were composed in Latin. Between about 1200 and 1350 this state-Latin was superseded by Norman French. In the meantime, a slow fusion between this language of a foreign ruling class and the Anglo-Saxon of the subject population produced Early English. The fusion made it possible for the new language to take its turn, after 1362, as the language of the courts – and for the opening of Parliament. Wycliffe's vernacular *manuscript* Bible followed in 1382.[12] It is essential to bear in mind that this sequence was a series of "state," not "national," languages; and that the state concerned covered at various times not only today's England and Wales, but also portions of Ireland, Scotland *and France.* Obviously, huge elements of the subject populations knew little or nothing of Latin, Norman French, or Early English.[13] Not till almost a century *after* Early English's political enthrone-ment was London's power swept out of "France".

On the Seine, a similar movement took place, if at a slower pace. As Bloch wrily puts it, "French, that is to say a language which, since it was regarded as merely a corrupt form of Latin, took several centuries to raise itself to literary dignity,"[14] only became the official language of the courts of justice in 1539, when François I issued the Edict of Villers-Cotterêts.[15] In other dynastic realms Latin survived much longer – under the Habsburgs well into the nineteenth century. In still others, "foreign" vernaculars took over: in the eighteenth century the languages of the Romanov court were French and German.[16]

In every instance, the "choice" of language appears as a gradual, unself-conscious, pragmatic, not to say haphazard development. As such, it was utterly different from the selfconscious language policies pursued by nine-teenth-century dynasts confronted with the rise of hostile popular linguistic-nationalisms. One clear sign of the difference is that the old administrative languages were *just that*: languages used by and for officialdoms for their own inner convenience. There was no idea of systematically imposing the language on the dynasts' various subject populations.[17] Nonetheless, the elevation of these vernaculars to the status of languages-of-power, where, in one sense, they were competitors with Latin (French in Paris, [Early] English in London), made its own contribution to the decline of the imagined community of Christendom.

At bottom, it is likely that the esotericization of Latin, the Reformation, and the haphazard development of administrative vernaculars are significant, in the present context, primarily in a negative sense – in their contributions to the dethronement of Latin. It is quite possible to conceive of the emergence of the new imagined national communities without any one, perhaps all, of them being present. What, in a positive sense, made the new communities imaginable was a half-fortuitous, but explosive, interaction between a system of production and productive relations (capitalism), a technology of communications (print), and the fatality of human linguistic diversity.[18]

The element of fatality is essential. For whatever superhuman feats capitalism was capable of, it found in death and languages two tenacious adversaries.[19] Particular languages can die or be wiped out, but there was and is no possibility of humankind's general linguistic unification. Yet this mutual incomprehensibility was historically of only slight importance until capitalism and print created monoglot mass reading publics.

While it is essential to keep in mind an idea of fatality, in the sense of a *general* condition of irremediable linguistic diversity, it would be a mistake to equate this fatality with that common element in nationalist ideologies which stresses the primordial fatality of *particular* languages and their association with *particular* territorial units. The essential thing is the *interplay* between fatality, technology, and capitalism. In pre-print Europe, and, of course, elsewhere in the world, the diversity of spoken languages, those languages that for their speakers were (and are) the warp and woof of their lives, was immense; so immense, indeed, that had print-capitalism sought to exploit each potential oral vernacular market, it would have remained a capitalism of petty proportions. But these varied idiolects were capable of being assembled, within definite limits, into print-languages far fewer in number. The very arbitrariness of any system of signs for sounds facilitated the assembling process.[20] (At the same time, the more ideographic the signs, the vaster the potential assembling zone. One can detect a sort of descending hierarchy here from algebra through Chinese and English, to the regular syllabaries of French or Indonesian.) Nothing served to "assemble" related vernaculars more than capitalism, which, within the limits imposed by grammars and syntaxes, created mechanically reproduced print-languages capable of dissemination through the market.[21]

These print-languages laid the bases for national consciousness in three distinct ways. First and foremost, they created unified fields of exchange and communication below Latin and above the spoken vernaculars. Speakers of the huge variety of Frenches, Englishes, or Spanishes, who might find it difficult or even impossible to understand one another in conversation, became capable of comprehending one another via print and paper. In the process, they gradually became aware of the hundreds of thousands, even millions, of people in their particular language-field, and at the same time that *only those* hundreds of thousands, or millions, so belonged. These fellow-readers, to whom they were connected through print, formed, in their secular, particular, visible invisibility, the embryo of the nationally imagined community.

Second, print-capitalism gave a new fixity to language, which in the long run helped to build that image of antiquity so central to the subjective idea of the nation. As Febvre and Martin remind us, the printed book kept a permanent form, capable of virtually infinite reproduction, temporally and spatially. It was no longer subject to the individualizing and "unconsciously modernizing" habits of monastic scribes. Thus, while twelfth-century French differed markedly from that written by Villon in the fifteenth, the rate of change slowed decisively in the sixteenth. "By the 17th century languages in Europe had generally assumed their modern forms."[22] To put it another way, for three centuries now these stabilized print-languages have been gathering a darkening varnish; the words of our seventeenth-century forebears are accessible to us in a way that to Villon his twelfth-century ancestors were not.

Third, print-capitalism created languages-of-power of a kind different from the older administrative vernaculars. Certain dialects inevitably were "closer" to each print-language and dominated their final forms. Their disadvantaged cousins, still assimilable to the emerging print-language, lost caste, above all because they were unsuccessful (or only relatively successful) in insisting on their own print-form. "Northwestern German" became Platt Deutsch, a largely spoken, thus sub-standard, German, because it was assimilable to print-German in a way that Bohemian spoken-Czech was not. High German, the King's English, and, later, Central Thai, were correspondingly elevated to a new politico-cultural eminence. (Hence the struggles in late-twentieth-century Europe by certain "sub-"nationalities to change their subordinate status by breaking firmly into print – and radio.)

It remains only to emphasize that in their origins, the fixing of print-languages and the differentiation of status between them were largely un-selfconscious processes resulting from the explosive interaction between capitalism, technology and human linguistic diversity. But as with so much else in the history of nationalism, once "there," they could become formal models to be imitated, and, where expedient, consciously exploited in a Machiavellian spirit. Today, the Thai government actively discourages attempts by foreign missionaries to provide its hill-tribe minorities with their own transcription-systems and to develop publications in their own languages: the same government is largely indifferent to what these minorities *speak*. The fate of the Turkic-speaking peoples in the zones incorporated into today's Turkey, Iran, Iraq, and the USSR is especially exemplary. A family of spoken languages, once everywhere assemblable, thus comprehensible, within an Arabic orthography, has lost that unity as a result of conscious manipulations. To heighten Turkish-Turkey's national consciousness at the expense of any wider Islamic identification, Atatürk imposed compulsory romanization.[23] The Soviet authorities followed suit, first with an anti-Islamic, anti-Persian compulsory romanization, then, in Stalin's 1930s, with a Russifying compulsory Cyrillicization.[24]

We can summarize the conclusions to be drawn from the argument thus far by saying that the convergence of capitalism and print technology on the fatal diversity of human language created the possibility of a new form of imagined community, which in its basic morphology set the stage for the modern nation. The potential stretch of these communities was inherently limited, and, at the same time, bore none but the most fortuitous relationship to existing political boundaries (which were, on the whole, the high-water marks of dynastic expansionisms).

Yet it is obvious that while today almost all modern self-conceived nations – and also nation-states – have "national print-languages," many of them have these languages in common, and in others only a tiny fraction of the population "uses" the national language in conversation or on paper. The nation-states of Spanish America or those of the "Anglo-Saxon family" are conspicuous examples of the first outcome; many ex-colonial states, particularly in Africa, of the second. In other words, the concrete formation of contemporary nation-states is by no means isomorphic with the determinate reach of particular print-languages. To account for the discontinuity-in-connectedness between print-languages, national consciousness, and nation-states, it is necessary to turn to the large cluster of new political entities that sprang up in the Western hemisphere between 1776 and 1838, all of which self-consciously defined themselves as nations, and, with the interesting exception of Brazil, as (non-dynastic) republics. For not only were they historically the first such states to emerge on the world stage, and therefore inevitably provided the first real models of what such states should "look like," but their numbers and contemporary births offer fruitful ground for comparative enquiry.

Notes

1   The population of that Europe where print was then known was about
    100,000,000. Lucien Febvre and Henri-Jean Martin, *The Coming of the Book:
    The Impact of Printing, 1450–1800* (London: New Left Books, 1976; translation
    of *L'Apparation du Livre*, Paris: Albin Michel, 1958), pp. 248–9.
2   Emblematic is Marco Polo's *Travels*, which remained largely unknown till its first
    printing in 1559. Marco Polo, *The Travels of Marco Polo*, trans. and ed. William
    Marsden (London and New York: Everyman's Library, 1946), p. xiii.
3   Quoted in Elizabeth L. Eisenstein, "Some Conjectures about the Impact of
    Printing on Western Society and Thought: A Preliminary Report," *Journal of
    Modern History*, 40: 1 (March 1968), p. 56.
4   Febvre and Martin, *The Coming of the Book*, p. 122. (The original text, however,
    speaks simply of "par-dessus les frontières." *L'Apparition*, p. 184.)
5   Ibid., p. 187. The original text speaks of "puissants" (powerful) rather than
    "wealthy" capitalists. *L'Apparition*, p. 281.
6   "Hence the introduction of printing was in this respect a stage on the road to
    our present society of mass consumption and standardisation." Ibid., pp. 259–
    60. (The original text has "une civilisation de masse et de standardisation,"
    which may be better rendered "standardized, mass civilization." *L'Apparition*,
    p. 394).
7   Ibid., p. 195.
8   Ibid., pp. 289–90.
9   Ibid., pp. 291–5.
10 From this point it was only a step to the situation in seventeenth-century France
    where Corneille, Molière, and La Fontaine could sell their manuscript tragedies
    and comedies directly to publishers, who bought them as excellent investments
    in view of their authors' market reputations. Ibid., p. 161.
11 Ibid., pp. 310–15.
12 Hugh Seton-Watson, *Nations and States: An Enquiry into the Origins of Nations
    and the Politics of Nationalism* (Boulder, CO: Westview Press, 1977), pp. 28–9;
    Marc Bloch, *Feudal Society*, trans. I. A. Manyon (Chicago: University of Chicago
    Press, 1961, 2 vols), I, p. 75.
13 We should not assume that administrative vernacular unification was immedi-
    ately or fully achieved. It is unlikely that the Guyenne ruled from London was
    ever primarily administered in Early English.
14 Bloch, *Feudal Society*, I, p. 98.
15 Seton-Watson, *Nations and States*, p. 48.
16 Ibid., p. 83.
17 An agreeable confirmation of this point is provided by François I, who, as we
    have seen, banned all printing of books in 1535 and made French the language
    of his courts four years later!
18 It was not the first "accident" of its kind. Febvre and Martin note that while a
    visible bourgeoisie already existed in Europe by the late thirteenth century, paper
    did not come into general use until the end of the fourteenth. Only paper's

smooth plane surface made the mass reproduction of texts and pictures possible – and this did not occur for still another seventy-five years. But paper was not a European invention. It floated in from another history – China's – through the Islamic world. *The Coming of the Book*, pp. 22, 30, and 45.

19 We still have no giant multinationals in the world of publishing.

20 For a useful discussion of this point, see S. H. Steinberg, *Five Hundred Years of Printing* (rev. edn.; Harmondsworth: Penguin, 1966), chapter 5. That the sign *ough* is pronounced differently in the words although, bough, lough, rough, cough, and hiccough, shows both the idiolectic variety out of which the now-standard spelling of English emerged, and the ideographic quality of the final product.

21 I say "nothing served... more than capitalism" advisedly. Both Steinberg and Eisenstein come close to theomorphizing "print" *qua* print as the genius of modern history. Febvre and Martin never forget that behind print stand printers and publishing firms. It is worth remembering in this context that although printing was invented first in China, possibly 500 years before its appearance in Europe, it had no major, let alone revolutionary impact – precisely because of the absence of capitalism there.

22 *The Coming of the Book*, p. 319. Cf. *L'Apparition*, p. 477: "Au XVIIe siècle, les langues nationales apparaissent un peu partout cristallisées."

23 Hans Kohn, *The Age of Nationalism* (New York: Harper, 1962), p. 108. It is probably only fair to add that Kemal also hoped thereby to align Turkish nationalism with the modern, romanized civilization of Western Europe.

24 Seton-Watson, *Nations and States*, p. 317.

33

The Riddle of Midnight: India, August 1987

Salman Rushdie

Salman Rushdie, "The Riddle of Midnight: India, August 1987" (1987), from *Imaginary Homelands* [source: Salman Rushdie, *Imaginary Homelands*. New York: Penguin, 1991, 26–33. Copyright © Salman Rushdie. Used by permission of Viking Penguin, a division of Penguin Putnam Inc.]

An important contemporary novelist and essayist, Rushdie has reconfigured in his novels the character of postcolonial literature, making it into a postmodern, generically hybrid, multinational form. His work has also been influential in consolidating postcolonial studies as a discipline. Rushdie has charted the vicissitudes of his own transnational and transcultural identity, as well as the task of writing about that identity, in *Imaginary Homelands*.

Forty years ago, the independent nation of India and I were born within eight weeks of one another. I came first. This gave rise to a family joke – that the departure of the British was occasioned by my arrival on the scene – and the joke, in turn, became the germ of a novel, *Midnight's Children*, in which not just one child, but one thousand and one children born in the midnight hour of freedom, the first hour of 15 August 1947, were comically and tragically connected to the birth of a nation.

(I worked out, by the way, that the Indian birth rate in August 1947 was approximately two babies per second, so my fictional figure of 1,001 per hour was, if anything, a little on the low side.)

The chain reaction continued. The novel's title became, for many Indians, a familiar catch-phrase defining that generation which was too young to remember the Empire or the liberation struggle; and when Rajiv Gandhi became Prime Minister, I found his administration being welcomed in the newspapers by such headlines as: "Enter midnight's children."

So when forty came around, it occurred to me to take a look at the state of the Indian nation that was, like me, entering its fifth decade; and to look, in particular, through the eyes of the class of '47, the country's citizen-twins, my generation. I flew to the subcontinent in search of the real-life counterparts of the imaginary beings I once made up. Midnight's real children: to meet them would be like closing a circle.

There was a riddle I wanted to try and answer, with their help: *Does India exist?* A strange, redundant sort of inquiry, on the face of it. After all, there the gigantic place manifestly is, a rough diamond two thousand miles long and more or less as wide, as large as Europe though you'd never guess it from the Mercator projection, populated by around a sixth of the human race, home of the largest film industry on earth, spawning Festivals the world over, famous as the "world's biggest democracy". Does India exist? If it doesn't, what's keeping Pakistan and Bangladesh apart?

It's when you start thinking about the political entity, the nation of India, the thing whose fortieth anniversary it is, that the question starts making sense. After all, in all the thousands of years of Indian history, there never was such a creature as a united India. Nobody ever managed to rule the whole place, not the Mughals, not the British. And then, that midnight, the thing that had never existed was suddenly "free". But what on earth was it? On what common ground (if any) did it, does it, stand?

Some countries are united by a common language; India has around fifteen major languages and numberless minor ones. Nor are its people united by race, religion or culture. These days, you can even hear some voices suggesting that the preservation of the union is not in the common interest. J. K. Galbraith's description of India as "functioning anarchy" still fits, but the stresses on the country have never been so great. Does India exist? If it doesn't, the explanation is to be found in a single word: communalism. The politics of religious hatred.

There is a medium-sized town called Ayodhya in the state of Uttar Pradesh, and in this town there is a fairly commonplace mosque named Babri Masjid. According to the *Ramayana*, however, Ayodhya was the home town of Rama himself, and according to a local legend the spot where he was born – the *Ramjanmabhoomi* – is the one on which the Muslim place of worship stands today. The site has been disputed territory ever since independence, but for most of the forty years the lid has been kept on the problem by the very Indian method of shelving the case, locking the mosque's gates, and allowing neither Hindus nor Muslims to enter.

Last year, however, the case finally came to court, and the judgement seemed to favour the Hindus. Babri Masjid became the target of the extremist Hindu fundamentalist organization, the Vishwa Hindu Parishad. Since then, Hindus and Muslims all over North India have been clashing, and in every outbreak of communal violence the Babri Masjid affair is cited as a primary cause.

When I arrived in Delhi the old Walled City was under heavy curfew because of just such an outbreak of communal violence. In the little alleys of Chandni Chowk I met a Hindu tailor, Harbans Lal, born in 1947 and as mild and gentle a man as you could wish to find. The violence terrified him. "When it started," he said, "I shut up the shop and ran away." But in spite of all his mildness, Harbans Lal was a firm supporter of the Hindu nationalist party that used to be called the Jan Sangh and is now the BJP. "I voted for Rajiv Gandhi in the election after Mrs Gandhi died," he said. "It was a big mistake. I won't do it again." I asked him what should be done about the Babri Masjid issue. Should it be locked up again as it had been for so many years? Should it be a place where both Hindus and Muslims could go to worship? "It's a Hindu shrine," he said, "It should be for the Hindus." There was no possibility, in his mind, of a compromise.

A couple of days later the Walled City was still bubbling with tension. The curfew was lifted for an hour or two every day to enable people to go out and buy food. The rest of the time, security was very tight. It was Eid, the great Muslim festival celebrating the end of the month of fasting, but the city's leading imams had said that Eid should not be celebrated. In Meerut, the mutilated corpses of Muslims floated in the river. The city's predominantly Hindu police force, the PAC, had run amok. Once again, Babri Masjid was one of the bones of contention.

I met Abdul Ghani, a Delhi Muslim who worked in a sari shop, and who, like Harbans Lal, India and me, was 1947-born. I was struck by how much like Harbans Lal he was. They were both slightly built, mild-mannered men with low, courteous voices and attractive smiles. They each earned about 1,000 rupees (100 dollars) a month, and dreamed of owning their own shops, knowing they never would. And when it came to the Hindu–Muslim communal divide, Abdul Ghani was just as unyielding as Harbans Lal had been. "What belongs to the Muslims," he said when I asked about Babri Masjid, "should be given back to the Muslims. There is nothing else to be done."

The gentleness of Harbans Lal and Abdul Ghani made their religious divisions especially telling. Nor was Babri Masjid the only issue between the faiths. At Ahmedabad, in the state of Gujarat, Hindu–Muslim violence was again centred in the old walled-city area of Manek Chowk, and had long ago acquired its own internal logic: so many families had lost members in the fighting that the cycle of revenge was unstoppable. Political forces were at work, too. At Ahmedabad hospital the doctors found that many of the knife wounds they treated were professionally inflicted. Somebody was sending trained killers into town.

All over India – Meerut, Delhi, Ahmedabad, Bombay – tension between Hindus and Muslims was rising. In Bombay, a (1947-born) journalist told me that many communal incidents took place in areas where Muslims had begun to prosper and move up the economic scale. Behind the flash-points like Ayodhya, she suggested, was Hindus' resentment of Muslim prosperity.

The Vishwa Hindu Parishad has a list of over a hundred disputed sites of the Babri Masjid type. Two are especially important. In Mathura, a Muslim shrine stands on the supposed birthplace of the god Krishna; and in Benares, a site allegedly sacred to Shiva is also in Muslim hands...

In Bombay, I found a "midnight child", a clerical worker in the docks, a Muslim named Mukadam who was such a super-citizen that he was almost too good to be true. Mukadam was absolutely dedicated to the unity of India. He believed in small families. He thought all Indians had a duty to educate themselves, and he had put himself through many evening courses. He had been named Best Worker at his dock. In his village, he claimed proudly, people of all faiths lived together in complete harmony. "That is how it should be," he said. "After all, these religions are only words. What is behind them is the same, whichever faith it is."

But when communal violence came to the Bombay docks in 1985, Mukadam's super-citizenship wasn't of much use. On the day the mob came to his dock, he was saved because he happened to be away. He didn't dare to return to work for weeks. And now, he says, he worries that it may come again at any time.

Like Mukadam, many members of Indian minority groups started out as devotees of the old, secular definition of India, and there were no Indians as patriotic as the Sikhs. Until 1984, you could say that the Sikhs were *the* Indian nationalists. Then came the storming of the Golden Temple, and the assassination of Mrs Gandhi; and everything changed.

The group of Sikh radicals led by Sant Jarnail Singh Bhindranwale, the religious leader who died in the Golden Temple storming, could not be said to represent more than a small minority of all Sikhs. The campaign for a separate Sikh state, Khalistan, had similarly found few takers among India's Sikhs – until November 1984, when Indira Gandhi died, and it became known that her assassins were Sikhs.

In Delhi, angry Hindu mobs – among whom party workers of Mrs Gandhi's Congress-I were everywhere observed – decided to hold all Sikhs responsible for the deeds of the assassins. Thus an entirely new form of communal violence – Hindu–Sikh riots – came into being, and in the next ten days the Sikh community suffered a series of traumatizing attacks from which it has not recovered, and perhaps never will.

In Block 32 of the Delhi suburb called Trilokpuri, perhaps 350 Sikhs were burned alive. I walked past streets of charred, gutted houses in some of which you could still see the bones of the dead. It was the worst place I have ever seen, not least because, in the surrounding streets, children played normally, the neighbours went on with their lives. Yet some of these neighbours were the very people who perpetrated the crime of 32 Trilokpuri, which was only one of the many massacres of Sikhs that took place that November. Many Sikh "midnight children" never reached forty at all.

I heard about many of these deaths, and will let one story stand for all. When the mob came for Hari Singh, a taxi-driver like so many Delhi Sikhs, his son fled into a nearby patch of overgrown waste land. His wife was obliged to watch as the mob literally ripped her husband's beard off his face. (This beard-ripping ritual was a feature of many of the November killings.) She managed to get hold of the beard, thinking that it was, at least, a part of him that she could keep for herself, and she ran into their house to hide it. Some members of the mob followed her in, found the beard and removed it. Then they poured kerosene over Hari Singh and set fire to him. They also chased his teenage son, found him, beat him un-conscious, and burned him, too. They knew he was a Sikh even though he had cut his hair, because when they found his father's beard they found his cut hair as well. His mother had preserved the sacred locks that identified her son.

Another taxi-driver, Pal Singh (born November 1947), told me that he had never had time for the Khalistan movement, but after 1984 he had changed his mind. "Now it will come," he said, "maybe within ten years." Sikhs were selling up their property in Delhi and buying land in the Punjab, so that if the time came when they had to flee back to the Sikh heartland they wouldn't have to leave their assets behind. "I'm doing it, too," Pal Singh said.

Almost three years after the 1984 massacres, not one person has been charged with murdering a Sikh in those fearsome days. The Congress-I, Rajiv Gandhi's party, increasingly relies on the Hindu vote, and is reluctant to alienate it.

The new element in Indian communalism is the emergence of a collective Hindu consciousness that transcends caste, and that believes Hinduism to be under threat from other Indian minorities. There is evidence that Rajiv's Congress-I is trying to ride that tiger. In Bombay, the tiger is actually in power. The ruling Shiv Sena Party, whose symbol is the tiger, is the most overtly Hindu-fundamentalist grouping ever to achieve office anywhere in India.

Its leader, Bal Thackeray, a former cartoonist, speaks openly of his belief that democracy has failed in India. He makes no secret of his open hostility towards Muslims. In the Bhiwandi riots of 1985, a few months before the Shiv Sena won the Bombay municipal elections, Shiv Sena activists were deeply involved in the anti-Muslim violence. And today, as the Sena seeks to spread its influence into the rural areas of Maharashtra (the state of which Bombay is the capital), incidents of communal violence are being reported from villages in which nothing of the sort has ever happened before.

I come from Bombay, and from a Muslim family, too. "My" India has always been based on ideas of multiplicity, pluralism, hybridity: ideas to which the ideologies of the communalists are diametrically opposed. To my mind, the defining image of India is the crowd, and a crowd is by its very nature superabundant, heterogeneous, many things at once. But the India of the communalists is none of these things.

I spent one long evening in the company of a ('47-born) Bengali intellectual, Robi Chatterjee, for whom the inadequacies of society are a cause for deep, permanent, operatic anguish. "Does India exist?" I asked him.

"What do you mean?" he cried. "Where the hell do you think this is?" I told him that I meant the idea of the nation. Forty years after a nationalist revolution, where could it be said to reside?

He said, "To the devil with all that nationalism. I am an Indian because I am born here and I live here. So is everyone else of whom that is true. What's the need for any more definitions?"

I asked, "If you do without the idea of nationalism, then what's the glue holding the country together?"

"We don't need glue," he said. "India isn't going to fall apart. All that Balkanization stuff. I reject it completely. We are simply here and we will remain here. It's this nationalism business that is the danger."

According to Robi, the idea of nationalism in India had grown more and more chauvinistic, had become narrower and narrower. The ideas of Hindu nationalism had infected it. I was struck by a remarkable paradox: that, in a country created by the Congress's nationalist campaign, the well-being of the people might now require that all nationalist rhetoric be abandoned.

Unfortunately for India, the linkage between Hindu fundamentalism and the idea of the nation shows no signs of weakening. India is increasingly defined as Hindu India, and Sikh and Muslim fundamentalism grows ever fiercer and entrenched in response. "These days," a young Hindu woman said to me, "one's religion is worn on one's sleeve." She was corrected by a Sikh friend. "It is worn," he said, "in a scabbard at the hip."

I remember that when *Midnight's Children* was first published in 1981, the most common Indian criticism of it was that it was too pessimistic about the future. It's a sad truth that nobody finds the novel's ending pessimistic any more, because what has happened in India since 1981 is so much darker than I had imagined. If anything, the book's last pages, with their suggestion of a new, more pragmatic generation rising up to take over from the midnight children, now seem absurdly, romantically optimistic.

But India regularly confounds its critics by its resilience, its survival in spite of everything. I don't believe in the Balkanization of India any more than Robi Chatterjee does. It's my guess that the old functioning anarchy will, somehow or other, keep on functioning, for another forty years, and no doubt another forty after that. But don't ask me how.

34

The Nationalist Resolution of the Women's Question (1987)

Partha Chatterjee

Partha Chatterjee, selection from "The Nationalist Resolution of the Women's Question" (1987) [source: *Recasting Women: Essays in Indian Colonial History*, eds Kumkum Sangari and Sudesh Vaid. New Brunswick, NJ: Rutgers University Press, 1990, 237–45]

Chatterjee has argued that both the primordialist and the modernist camps of Western scholarship on the nation have assumed a universal, Enlightenment perspective emphasizing historical progress and the necessary development of nation-state identities, and has criticized this assumption as an impediment to understanding non-Western national consciousness and new forms of modern community. His most influential work has been *Nationalist Thought and the Colonial World: A Derivative Discourse* (1986).

[...]

II

I have elaborated elsewhere[1] a framework for analysing the contradictory pulls on nationalist ideology in its struggle against the dominance of colonialism and the resolution it offered to these contradictions. In the main, this resolution was built around a separation of the domain of culture into two spheres – the material and the spiritual. It was in the material sphere that the claims of western civilization were the most powerful. Science, technology, rational forms of economic organization, modern methods of statecraft, these had given the European countries the strength to subjugate non-European peoples and to impose their dominance over the whole world. To overcome this domination, the colonized people must learn these superior techniques of organizing material life and incorporate them within their own cultures. This was one aspect of the nationalist project of rationalizing and reforming the "traditional" culture of their people. But this could not mean the imitation of the West in every aspect of life, for then the very distinction between the West and the East would vanish – the self-identity of national culture would itself be threatened. In fact, as Indian nationalists in the late nineteenth century argued, not only was it not desirable to imitate the West in anything other than the material aspects of life, it was not even necessary to do so, because in the spiritual domain the East was superior to the West. What was necessary was to cultivate the material techniques of modern western civilization while retaining and strengthening the distinctive spiritual essence of the national culture. This completed the formulation of the nationalist project, and as an ideological justification for the selective appropriation of western modernity it continues to hold sway to this day (*pace* Rajiv Gandhi's juvenile fascination for space-age technology).

We need not concern ourselves here with the details of how this ideological framework shaped the course of nationalist politics in India. What is important is to note that nationalism was not simply about a political struggle for power; it related the question of political independence of the nation to virtually every aspect of the material and spiritual life of the people. In every case, there was a problem of selecting what to take from the West and what to reject. And in every case, the questions were asked: is it desirable? Is it necessary? The answers to these questions are the material of the debates about social reform in the nineteenth century. To understand the self-identity of nationalist ideology in concrete terms, we must look more closely at the way in which these questions were answered.

The discourse of nationalism shows that the material/spiritual distinction was condensed into an analogous, but ideologically far more powerful, dichotomy: that between the outer and the inner. The material domain lies outside us – a mere external, which influences us, conditions us, and to which we are forced to adjust. But ultimately it is unimportant. It is the spiritual which lies within, which is our true self; it is that which is genuinely essential. It follows that as long as we take care to retain the spiritual distinctiveness of our culture, we could make all the compromises and adjustments necessary to adapt ourselves to the requirements of a modern material world without losing our true identity. This was the key which nationalism supplied for resolving the ticklish problems posed by issues of social reform in the nineteenth century.

Now apply the inner/outer distinction to the matter of concrete day-to-day living and you get a separation of the social space into *ghar* and *bahir*, the home and the world. The world is the external, the domain of the material;

the home represents our inner spiritual self, our true identity. The world is a treacherous terrain of the pursuit of material interests, where practical considerations reign supreme. It is also typically the domain of the male. The home in its essence must remain unaffected by the profane activities of the material world – and woman is its representation. And so we get an identification of social roles by gender to correspond with the separation of the social space into ghar and bahir.

Thus far we have not obtained anything that is different from the typical conception of gender roles in any "traditional" patriarchy. If we now find continuities in these social attitudes in the phase of social reforms in the nineteenth century, we are tempted to put this down as "conservatism", a mere defence of "traditional" norms. But this would be a mistake. The colonial situation, and the ideological response of nationalism, introduced an entirely new substance to these terms and effected their transformation. The material/spiritual dichotomy, to which the terms "world" and "home" corresponded, had acquired, as we have noted before, a very special significance in the nationalist mind. The world was where the European power had challenged the non-European peoples and, by virtue of its superior material culture, had subjugated them. But it had failed to colonize the inner, essential, identity of the East which lay in its distinctive, and superior, spiritual culture. That is where the East was undominated, sovereign, master of its own fate. For a colonized people, the world was a distressing constraint, forced upon it by the fact of its material weakness. It was a place of oppression and daily humiliation, a place where the norms of the colonizer had perforce to be accepted. It was also the place, as nationalists were soon to argue, where the battle would be waged for national independence. The requirement for this was for the subjugated to learn from the West the modern sciences and arts of the material world. Then their strengths would be matched and ultimately the colonizer overthrown. But in the entire phase of the national struggle, the crucial need was to protect, preserve and strengthen the inner core of the national culture, its spiritual essence. No encroachments by the colonizer must be allowed in that inner sanctum. In the world, imitation of and adaptation to western norms was a necessity; at home, they were tantamount to annihilation of one's very identity.

Once we match this new meaning of the home/world dichotomy with the identification of social roles by gender, we get the ideological framework within which nationalism answered the women's question. It would be a grave error to see in this, as we are apt to in our despair at the many marks of social conservatism in nationalist practice, a total rejection of the West. Quite the contrary. The nationalist paradigm in fact supplied an ideological principle of *selection*. It was not a dismissal of modernity; the attempt was rather to make modernity consistent with the nationalist project.

III

It is striking how much of the literature on women in the nineteenth century was concerned with the theme of the threatened westernization of Bengali women. It was taken up in virtually every form of written, oral and visual communication, from the ponderous essays of nineteenth-century moralists, to novels, farces, skits and jingles, to the paintings of the *patua* (scroll painter). Social parody was the most popular and effective medium of this ideological propagation. From Iswarchandra Gupta and the *kabiyal* (popular versifiers) of the early nineteenth century to the celebrated pioneers of modern Bengali theatre – Michael Madhusudan Dutt, Dinabandhu Mitra, Jyotirindranath Tagore, Upendranath Das, Amritalal Bose – everyone picked up the theme. To ridicule the idea of a Bengali woman trying to imitate the way of a European woman or *memsahib* (and it was very much an idea, for it is hard to find historical evidence that even in the most westernized families of Calcutta in the mid-nineteenth century there were actually any women who even remotely resembled these gross carica-tures) was a sure recipe calculated to evoke raucous laughter and moral condemnation in both male and female audiences. It was, of course, a criticism of manners: of new items of clothing such as the blouse, the petticoat and shoes (all, curiously, considered vulgar, although they clothed the body far better than the single length of fabric or sari which was customary for Bengali women, irrespective of wealth and social status, until the middle of the nineteenth century), of the use of western cosmetics and jewellery, of the reading of novels (the educated Haimabati in Jyotirin-dranath's *Alikbabu* speaks, thinks and acts like the heroines of historical romances), of needlework (considered a useless and expensive pastime), of riding in open carriages. What made the ridicule stronger was the constant suggestion that the westernized woman was fond of useless luxury and cared little for the well-being of the home. One can hardly miss in all this a criticism – reproach mixed with envy – of the wealth and luxury of the new social elite emerging around the institutions of colonial administration and trade.

This literature of parody and satire in the first half of the nineteenth century clearly contained much that was prompted by a straightforward defence of "tradition" and outright rejection of the new. The nationalist paradigm had still not emerged in clear outline. On hindsight, this – the period from Rammohun to Vidyasagar – appears as one of great social turmoil and ideological confusion among the literati. And then, drawing from various sources, a new discourse began to be formed in the second half of the century – the discourse of nationalism. Now the attempt was made to define the social and moral principles for locating the position of women in the "modern" world of the nation.

Let us take as an example one of the most clearly formulated tracts on the subject: Bhudev Mukhopadhyay's *Paribarik Prabandha* (essays on the family) published in 1882. Bhudev states the problem in his characteristic matter-of-fact style:

> Because of our hankering for the external glitter and ostentation of the English way of life . . . an upheaval is under way within our homes. The men learn English and become sahibs. The women do not learn English but nevertheless try to become bibis. In households which manage on an income of a hundred rupees, the women no longer cook, sweep or make the bed . . . everything is done by servants and maids; [the women] only read books, sew carpets and play cards. What is the result? The house and furniture get untidy, the meals poor, the health of every member of the family is ruined; children are born weak and rickety, constantly plagued by illness – they die early.
>
> Many reform movements are being conducted today; the education of women, in particular, is constantly talked about. But we rarely hear of those great arts in which women were once trained – a training which if it had still been in vogue would have enabled us to tide over this crisis caused by injudicious imitation. I suppose we will never hear of this training again.[2]

The problem is put here in the empirical terms of a positive sociology, a genre much favoured by serious Bengali writers of Bhudev's time. But the sense of crisis which he expresses was very much a reality. Bhudev is voicing the feelings of large sections of the newly emergent middle class in Bengal when he says that the very institutions of home and family were threatened under the peculiar conditions of colonial rule. A quite unprecedented external condition had been thrust upon us; we were being forced to adjust to those conditions, for which a certain degree of imitation of alien ways was unavoidable. But could this wave of imitation be allowed to enter our homes? Would that not destroy our inner identity? Yet it was clear that a mere restatement of the old norms of family life would not suffice: they were breaking down by the inexorable force of circumstance. New norms were needed, which would be more appropriate to the external conditions of the modern world and yet not a mere imitation of the West. What were the principles by which these new norms could be constructed?

Bhudev supplies the characteristic nationalist answer. In an essay on modesty entitled "Lajjasilata," he talks of the natural and social principles which provide the basis for the "feminine" virtues.[3] Modesty, or decorum in manner and conduct, he says, is a specifically human trait; it does not exist in animal nature. It is human aversion to the purely animal traits which gives rise to virtues such as modesty. In this aspect, human beings seek to cultivate in themselves, and in their civilization, spiritual or god-like qualities wholly opposed to forms of behaviour which prevail in animal nature. Further, within the human species, women cultivate and cherish these god-like qualities far more than men. Protected to a certain extent from the purely material pursuits of securing a livelihood in the external world, women express in their appearance and behaviour the spiritual qualities which are characteristic of civilized and refined human society.

The relevant dichotomies and analogues are all here. The material/spiritual dichotomy corresponds to that between animal/god-like qualities, which in turn corresponds to masculine/feminine virtues. Bhudev then invests this ideological form with its specifically nationalist content:

> In a society where men and women meet together, converse together at all times, eat and drink together, travel together, the manners of women are likely to be somewhat coarse, devoid of spiritual qualities and relatively prominent in animal traits. For this reason, I do not think the customs of such a society are free from all defect. Some argue that because of such close association with women, the characters of men acquire certain tender and spiritual qualities. Let me concede the point. But can the loss caused by coarseness and degeneration in the female character be compensated by the acquisition of a certain degree of tenderness in the male?[4]

The point is then hammered home.

> Those who laid down our religious codes discovered the inner spirituality which resides within even the most animal pursuits which humans must perform, and thus removed the animal qualities from those actions. This has not happened in Europe. Religion there is completely divorced from [material] life. Europeans do not feel inclined to regulate all aspects of their life by the norms of religion; they condemn it as clericalism.... In the Arya system there is a preponderance of spiritualism, in the European system a preponderance of material pleasure. In the Arya system, the wife is a goddess. In the European system, she is a partner and companion.[5]

The new norm for organizing family life and determining the right conduct for women in the conditions of the "modern" world could now be deduced with ease. Adjustments would have to be made in the external world of material activity, and men would bear the brunt of this task. To the extent that the family was itself entangled in wider social relations, it too could not be insulated from the influence of changes in the outside world. Consequently, the organization and ways of life at home would also have to be changed. But the crucial requirement was to retain the inner spirituality of indigenous social life. The home was the principal site for expressing the spiritual quality of the national culture, and women must take the main responsibility of protecting and nurturing this quality. No matter what the changes in the external conditions of life for women, they must not lose their essentially spiritual (i.e. feminine) virtues; they must not, in other words, become *essentially* westernized. It followed, as a simple criterion for judging the desirability of reform, that the essential distinction between the social roles of men and women in terms of material and spiritual virtues must at all times be maintained. There would have to be a marked *difference* in the degree and manner of westernization of women, as distinct from men, in the modern world of the nation.

IV

This was the central principle by which nationalism resolved the women's question in terms of its own historical project. The details were not, of course, worked out immediately. In fact, from the middle of the nineteenth century right up to the present day, there have been many controversies about the precise application of the home/world, spiritual/material, feminine/masculine dichotomies in various matters concerning the everyday life of the "modern" woman – her dress, food, manners, education, her role in organizing life at home, her role outside the home. The concrete problems arose out of the rapidly changing situation – both external and internal – in which the new middle class family found itself; the specific solutions were drawn from a variety of sources – a reconstructed "classical" tradition, modernized folk forms, the utilitarian logic of bureaucratic and industrial practices, the legal idea of equality in a liberal democratic state. The content of the resolution was neither predetermined nor unchanging, but its form had to be consistent with the system of dichotomies which shaped and contained the nationalist project.

The "new" woman defined in this way was subjected to a *new* patriarchy. In fact, the social order connecting the home and the world in which nationalism placed the new woman was contrasted not only with that of modern western society; it was explicitly distinguished from the patriarchy of indigenous tradition. Sure enough, nationalism adopted several elements from "tradition" as marks of its native cultural identity, but this was a deliberately "classicized" tradition – reformed, reconstructed. Even Gandhi said of the patriarchal rules laid down by the scriptures:

> ...it is sad to think that the *Smritis* contain texts which can command no respect from men who cherish the liberty of woman as their own and who regard her as the mother of the race... The question arises as to what to do

with the *Smritis* that contain texts . . . that are repugnant to the moral sense. I have already suggested . . . that all that is printed in the name of scriptures need not be taken as the word of God or the inspired word.[6]

The new patriarchy was also sharply distinguished from the immediate social and cultural condition in which the majority of the people lived, for the "new" woman was quite the reverse of the "common" woman who was coarse, vulgar, loud, quarrelsome, devoid of superior moral sense, sexually promiscuous, subjected to brutal physical oppression by males. Alongside the parody of the westernized woman, this other construct is repeatedly emphasized in the literature of the nineteenth century through a host of lower-class female characters who make their appearance in the social milieu of the new middle class – maidservants, washerwomen, barbers, pedlars, procuresses, prostitutes. It was precisely this degenerate condition of women which nationalism claimed it would reform, and it was through these contrasts that the new woman of nationalist ideology was accorded a status of cultural superiority to the westernized women of the wealthy parvenu families spawned by the colonial connection as well as the common women of the lower classes. Attainment by her own efforts of a superior national culture was the mark of woman's newly acquired freedom. This was the central ideological strength of the nationalist resolution of the women's question. [. . .]

Notes

1   See Partha Chatterjee, *Nationalist Thought and the Colonial World* (Delhi: Oxford University Press, 1986).
2   Bhudev Mukhopadhyay, "Grhakaryer vyavastha," in *Bhudev racanasambhar*, ed. Pramathanath Bisi (Calcutta: Mitra and Ghosh, 1969), p. 480.
3   "Lajjasilata" in ibid., pp. 445–8.
4   Ibid., p. 446.
5   Ibid., p. 447.
6   M. K. Gandhi, *Collected Works*, 64 (Delhi: Publications Division, 1970), p. 85.

35

The Origins of Nations (1989)

Anthony D. Smith

Anthony D. Smith, selection from "The Origins of Nations" (1989) [source: Anthony D. Smith, "The Origins of Nations," *Ethnic and Racial Studies* 12: 3 (1989), 341–56, 363–7 (notes and bibliography). Reprinted by permission of Taylor & Francis Ltd.]

Smith has been the leading proponent of the "primordialist" approach to understanding national identity, in that he emphasizes the way in which the ethnic rudiments of the modern nation-state are an essential, though not sufficient, component of its creation. For Smith, ethnic foundations may take different forms in new states and old states, in Western and non-Western nations; but the ethnic component is far too significant to be dismissed. Among Smith's many works on the subject, see especially *National Identity* (1991).

[...]

The "Nation" and "Nationalism"

We can begin by narrowing down our enquiry to three questions. The first concerns the relationship between abstractions and realities. The "nation" is often seen as an abstraction, something that nationalists, and élites in general, have "constructed" to serve their partisan ends. On this reading, nations lack tangibility or any "primordial" character. They constitute mere ideals, or mere legitimations and political arguments (Breuilly 1982, pp. 1–41; Hobsbawm and Ranger 1983; Sathyamurthy 1983).

Against this fashionable view, the so-called "primordialists" argued for the "reality" of nations, and the almost "natural" quality of ethnic belonging. National sentiment is no construct, it has a real, tangible, mass base. At its root is a feeling of kinship, of the extended family, that distinguishes national from every other kind of group sentiment (Connor 1978; Fishman 1980; Smith 1981, pp. 63–86; Horowitz 1985, pp. 55–92; Stack 1986, pp. 1–11).

Clearly, our investigation of the origins of nations cannot proceed far, until this fundamental question of whether the nation be viewed as construct or real historical process is resolved.

The second question is linked to the first. I have emphasized the importance, indeed the indispensability, of nations in the modern era and the modern world. The question arises whether it is fundamental in other eras and pre-modern worlds. Was there "nationalism" in antiquity? Can we find "nations" in medieval Europe or Asia? In part, of course, the answer will hinge on our definition of the nation; but equally, it will reflect our reading of the global historical process. If the "modernists" are right, if the nation is a fundamental feature only of the modern world, this will support, *prima facie*, the idea that nations are primarily abstractions and élite constructs. However, if the "perennialists" turn out to be nearer the mark, and we find nations and nationalism prior to the rise of the modern world from the sixteenth century (or the French Revolution) onwards, we may well have to change our view of the whole historical process. Nations might still be constructs, but ancient élites, or medieval ones, might be as adept at inventing them as their modern counterparts. This would inevitably devalue the importance attributed to specifically "modern" developments, like bureaucracy and capitalism, in the rise of nations, which "modernists" tend to emphasize (Nairn 1977, pp. 92–125; Anderson 1983; Gellner 1983).

The last question again concerns the nature of the concept of the nation. Should we view it as a largely political unit, or mainly a social and cultural entity? Can there be a cultural nationalism, which is not also *ipso facto* political? Or should we regard nations as operating on all these levels at once? These are important questions when it comes to looking at the political ramifications of the nation. Again, there are those who would downgrade its cultural importance for collective identity (Breuilly 1982); while others emphasize questions of cultural identity and social cohesion (Barnard 1965; Hutchinson 1987).

The answers to these three sets of questions will, I think, furnish important clues to our exploration of the processes by which nations were formed.

Let me start with a working definition of the nation. A nation is a named community of history and culture, possessing a unified territory, economy, mass education system and common legal rights. I take this definition from the ideals and blueprints of generations of nationalists and their followers. It sums up an "ideal type" of the nation that is fairly widely accepted today, even if given units of population aspiring to be full nations in this sense, lack one or other of these characteristics in lesser or greater degree. For example, in a unit of population aspiring to constitute a full nation, certain categories of the population may be excluded from the full exercise of the common legal rights. Or they may not enjoy equal access to the common system of education, or equal mobility in the territorial economy. Alternatively, they may enjoy all these attributes and rights, yet be treated by the majority as in some sense cultural aliens, standing outside the sense of history and much of the culture of the majority, as the Jews were felt to be at the time of Dreyfus, both in France and outside, or the Asians in East Africa after decolonization.

What this means is that the nation is not a once-for-all, all-or-nothing, concept; and that historical nations are ongoing processes, sometimes slow in their formation, at other times faster, often jagged and discontinuous, as some features emerge or are created, while others lag. In Europe, nations have been forming, I would argue, from the medieval period; in several other parts of the world, this process, or processes, have been more recent. It also means that both objective factors outside human control, and human will and action, go into the creation of nations. Geographical environment, and the political accidents of warfare, may provide a setting for a group to form into a nation; but, whether it will subsequently do so, may depend on how far the group, or its ruling classes, become conscious of their identity, and reinforce it through education, legal codes and administrative centralization (Tilly 1975, pp. 3–163).[1]

If this is accepted, it means in turn that nations can be seen as both constructs or visions of nationalist (or other) élites, but equally as real, historical formations that embody a number of analytically separable processes over long time-spans. It is these processes, as much as any visions, that form the object of our analysis.

Where does this leave "nationalism"? I should define nationalism as an ideological movement for attaining and maintaining the autonomy, unity and identity of an existing or potential "nation". I should also stress its often minority status as a movement. As a movement, nationalism often antedates, and seeks to create, the nation, even if it often pretends that the nation already exists (Smith 1973a; 1983, pp. 153–81).

Of course, nationalists cannot, and do not, create nations *ex nihilo*. There must be, at least, some elements in the chosen population and its social environment who favour the aspirations and activities of the nationalist visionaries. To achieve their common goals – autonomy, unity, identity – there need to be some core networks of association and culture, around which and on which nations can be "built". Language groups are usually regarded as the basic network of nations; but religious sects, like the Druse, Sikhs or Maronites may also form the starting-point for "reconstructing" the nation. So may a certain kind of historic territory, for example, the mountain fastnesses of Switzerland or Kurdistan, or island homelands like Iceland or Japan.

Besides, not all nations are the product of nationalist political endeavour. The English or Castilian nations, for example, owed more to state centralization, warfare and cultural homogeneity than to any nationalist movement. Vital for any nation is the growth and spread of a "national sentiment" outwards from the centre and usually downwards through the strata of the population. It is in and through the myths and symbols of the common past that such a national sentiment finds its expression; and these too may develop over long periods.[2]

The "Ethnic Core"

So much for initial definitions. Let us turn to the processes of nation-formation themselves.

At the turn of this century, it was quite common to argue that nations were immemorial. People talked of the ancient Greek, Persian and Egyptian nations, and even equated them with the present-day nations of those names. They certainly saw modern Bulgarian or French nations as the lineal descendants of their medieval counterparts. The familiar view was that nations were natural and perennial; people had a nationality much as they had speech or sight. Clearly, such a view of the nation is untenable. Nations are not perennial; they can be formed, and human will and effort play an important part in the process. People can also change their nationality, or at least their descendants can, over a period of time. Moreover, it is extremely doubtful, at the least, whether modern Greeks, Persians and Egyptians are lineal descendants of ancient Greeks, Persians and Egyptians. Are we not guilty here of a "retrospective nationalism" to epochs that lacked all sense of nationality (Levi 1965; Breuilly 1982)?

For these reasons, recent scholars have tended to emphasize the modernity of nations. The modernists argue that the nation is a modern construct of nationalists and other élites, and the product of peculiarly modern conditions like industrialism. They point out that ancient Egypt, and even ancient Greece, could boast no standardized, public, mass-education system, and that common legal rights, in so far as they existed, were restricted to particular classes. Because of its territorial unity, ancient Egypt did indeed enjoy more of a common economy than other ancient kingdoms, but it was unusual. In Assyria, Greece, Persia and China, local economies of different regions reflected a lack of territorial compactness of a kind unknown in the contemporary world.[3]

Clearly, in antiquity and much of the medieval era, nations in the sense that we have defined them, viz. named communities of history and culture, possessed of unified territories, economies, education systems and common legal rights, are rarely, if ever, to be found. Yet does this mean that there were no durable cultural communities in antiquity or the Middle Ages? Are we being retrospective nationalists in attributing some common history and culture to ancient Greeks and Persians or medieval Serbs and Irish? I think not. Despite the many changes that these cultures had undergone, they remained recognizably distinct to their own populations and to outsiders; and cultural differentiation was as vital a factor in social life then as now. The only difference then was that the scope and role of cultural diversity operated more at the social than the political level, but even this varied between peoples and eras.

Moreover, cultural differences, then as now, were not just a matter of outside observation. The people who possessed specific cultural attributes often formed a social network or series of networks, which over the generations became what we today designate "ethnic communities". These communities of history and culture generally display a syndrome of characteristics, by which they are usually recognized. These include:

1 a common name for the unit of population included;
2 a set of myths of common origins and descent for that population;
3 some common historical memories of things experienced together;
4 a common "historic territory" or "homeland", or an association with one;
5 one or more elements of common culture – language, customs, or religion;
6 a sense of solidarity among most members of the community.

I shall call the communities that manifest these characteristics (to a lesser or greater degree) *ethnies* (the French equivalent of the ancient Greek *ethnos*), as there is no single English-language equivalent. By no means all the cultural differences that scholars have distinguished in pre-modern or modern eras, are mirrored in such *ethnies*. Many remain as "ethnic categories"; certainly, in the past, the speakers of, say, Slovakian or Ukrainian dialects, were hardly conscious of their membership in any community. It had to wait for the rise of a romantic nationalism to build communities out of these and other differences (Brock 1976; Szporluk 1979).[4]

However, that still leaves a multitude of *ethnies* in the ancient and medieval worlds, which at first sight resemble, but are not, nations. For example, in Sassanid Persia between the third and seventh century A.D., we find a population group with a common name; a sense of a common homeland of "Iran" that the members opposed to another fabled land of enemies, "Turan"; some common historical memories and myths of descent related to Zoroaster and the Achaemenid kings; and a sense of solidarity, ever renewed by the protracted struggle with Byzantium (Frye 1966, pp. 235–62; *Cambridge History of Iran* 1983, vol. III/1, pp. 359–477).

Although it was divided, both into *poleis* and into sub-ethnic communities, ancient Greece could also be described as an *ethnie* in this sense. We find there, too, a common name, Hellas; a set of common-origin myths about the Greeks and their main divisions; common historical memories centred around the Homeric canon; common Greek dialects and a common Greek pantheon of Olympic deities; an attachment to the Greek "homeland" around the Aegean; and, above all, a shared sense of being "Greek" and not "barbarian". This did not mean that many Greeks did not intermarry, that Greek *poleis* did not fight each other most of the time, that they did not form alliances with the Persians against each other, and so on. Yet all Greeks recognized their common Greek heritage and a common Greek cultural community (Fondation Hardt 1962; Andrewes 1965; Alty 1982; Finley 1986, pp. 120–33).

Perhaps the best-known of ancient and medieval *ethnie*, the Jews, managed to retain their distinctive identity, even when most of their members were scattered in diaspora communities. A common name, common myths of origin and descent, sedulously fostered, a whole canon of historical memories centred on charismatic heroes, a common liturgical language and script, an attachment to Eretz Israel wherever they might find themselves and especially to Jerusalem, all fed a strong bond of ethnic solidarity, which outside hostility renewed with almost monotonous regularity. Again, these bonds did not prevent apostasy, intermarriage or internal class and cultural divisions, particularly between Jews of the Ashkenazi and Sephardi rite (Hirschberg 1969; Barnett 1971; Raphael 1985).

One last example, this time from medieval western Europe, must suffice to illustrate the range of *ethnies*. Apart from their fame as builders of massive castles and cathedrals in the Romanesque style, the Normans evinced a common myth of origins and descent from Duke Rollo, a common name and historical memories of warfare and colonization, common customs and adopted language, along with an attachment to the duchy in northern France that they had conquered and settled. Above all, they maintained for nearly three centuries their *esprit de corps* as a warrior community, even when they conquered Ireland and Sicily (Jones 1973, pp. 204–40; Davis 1976).

"Vertical" and "Lateral" Ethnies

What all these examples have in common is an underlying sense of historical and cultural community. This sense of community pervades and regulates their social life and culture, spilling over at times into the political and military realms. On the other hand, it rarely determines their economic conditions of existence. Generally speaking, economic localism and a subsistence economy fragment the community into a series of interlocking networks. What unites these networks, in so far as it does so, is the common fund of myths, symbols, memories and values that make up the distinctive traditions passed down the generations. Through common customs and rituals, languages, arts and liturgies, this complex of myths, symbols, values and memories ensures the survival of the sense of common ethnicity, of the sense of common descent and belonging, which characterizes a "community of fate".

Yet, the example of the Norman conquerors introduces a vital distinction. As with the Sassanid Persians, but even more so, it was really only the upper strata, especially around the Court and priesthoods that constituted the Norman *ethnie*. The myths of descent and the memories of battle clustered around the ruling house; it was their genealogies and their exploits that Dudo of St Quentin and Orderic Vitalis were called on to record and extol. At the same time, the ruling house represented a whole upper stratum of warrior-aristocrats who had founded a *regnum* in Normandy, based on common customs and myths of descent. Other classes were simply subsumed under those customs and myths; and quite often, the latter were amalgams of the heritage of the conquerors and the conquered (Reynolds 1983).

Compared, however, to the community of Greeks or Jews, that of the Norman or Sassanid Persian ruling classes was rather limited. In one sense, it was wider. The sense of common ethnicity went wherever Normans sailed, and Persian arms conquered. In another sense, it was shallower. It never really reached far down the social scale. For all Kartir's attempts to institute Zoroastrian fire-worship as a state religion, many of the Persian peasants were untouched. Although Chosroes I (A.D. 531–79) attempted to revive ancient Persian culture, he was unable to stabilize the Persian state by extending a sense of common Persian ethnicity. As McNeill puts it:

> As with other urban civilisations that lacked real roots in the countryside, the results were grand and artificial, in theology as in architecture; and Moslem conquest cut off the entire tradition in the seventh century, just as Alexander's victories had earlier disrupted the high culture of the Achaemenids. (McNeill 1963, p. 400)

This is, perhaps, going too far. A sense of specifically Persian ethnicity remained beneath Islamization, after the Sassanid armies were defeated by the Arabs at Nihavand (A.D. 642). Islam even stimulated a Persian renaissance in poetry and the arts in the tenth and eleventh centuries, a renaissance that looked back for its inspiration to Chosroes and the Sassanids (*Cambridge History of Iran* 1975, vol. IV, pp. 595–632).

Yet the basic point remains. The Persian Sassanid *ethnie*, like the Norman, the Hittite or the Philistine, was socially limited. It was an aristocratic and "lateral" *ethnie*, as territorially wide as it was lacking in social depth. In contrast to this type, with its ragged boundaries and aristocratic culture, we find communities with much more compact boundaries, a more socially diffused culture and a greater degree of popular mobilization and fervour. This type of *ethnie* we may call "vertical" and "demotic". The Armenians, Greeks and Jews are classic examples, despite their territorial dispersion, because they lived in often segregated enclaves once they had left their clearly defined homelands. Other examples of "demotic" or "vertical" *ethnies* include the Irish, Basques, Welsh, Bretons, Czechs and Serbs, as well as the Druse, Sikhs and Maronites. Such *ethnies* are as stratified as any other, but the strata all share in a common heritage and culture, and in the common defence. Hence the ethnic bond is more exclusive and intensive, and the boundaries are more marked and more strongly upheld. Thus, in contrast to the looser ties that characterized the Philistine aristocratic pentapolis, the Israelite tribal confederation was from the outset marked by a greater ethnocentric zeal and communal mobilization for war, as well as greater ritual involvement of all strata (Kitchen 1973; Seltzer 1980, pp. 7–43).[5]

The distinction between "lateral" and "vertical" types of *ethnie* is important for a number of reasons. First, because it highlights a source of conflict between pre-modern ethnic communities, as aristocratic lateral *ethnie* attempted to incorporate and subdue different demotic vertical communities. It also suggests why many *ethnies*, especially of the more demotic variety, persisted over long periods, even when they experienced "character change". The Greek *ethnie*, for example, within the Eastern Roman empire was transformed in many ways by the influx of Slav immigrants. Yet they did not basically change the cultural and religious framework of Greek ethnicity, even though they grafted their customs and mores on to an existing Hellenic culture, especially in the countryside (Campbell and Sherrard 1968, pp. 19–49; Armstrong 1982, pp. 168–200). Similarly, a tenuous sense of Egyptian identity persisted even after the Arab conquest in the seventh century A.D., especially among Copts, despite the fact that any attempts to trace "descent" back to the inhabitants of ancient Egypt were bound to run into the sands. The point is that cultural forms and frameworks may outlive their physical bearers, and even the "character change" of cultural content that new immigrants and new religious movements bring with them (Atiya 1968, pp. 79–98).

One result of ethnic survival and coexistence over the long term is a patchwork or mosaic of *ethnies* in varying relationships of status and power. Quite often we find a dominant lateral *ethnie* of landowning aristocrats like the Magyar knights or Polish *szlachta* exploiting a peasantry of different culture, Croat or Ukrainian, and so helping to preserve these cultural differences as "ethno-classes". Wherever we find lateral *ethnies* attempting to expand into territories populated by demotic, vertical communities of culture, the opportunities for a "frozen" ethnic stratification to develop are greatly increased. This has occurred, not only in Eastern Europe, but in the Middle East, southeast Asia and parts of Africa. The overall result is to preserve ethnic difference and identity right up to the onset of the age of nationalism, and afford ready-made bases for political movements of autonomy (Seton-Watson 1977, pp. 15–142; Orridge 1982).

Already certain implications of the foregoing analysis can be clarified. Only in this modern era could we expect to find unified divisions of labour, mass, public education systems and equal legal rights, all of which have come to be part and parcel of a common understanding of what we mean by the concept of the nation. Moreover, the "modernists" are right when they speak of nations being "reconstructed" (but not "invented") out of pre-existing social networks and cultural elements, often by intellectuals.

The modernist definition of the nation omits important components. Even today, a nation *qua* nation must possess a common history and culture, that is to say, common myths of origin and descent, common memories and common symbols of culture. Otherwise, we should be speaking only of territorial states. It is the conjunction, and interpenetration, of these cultural or "ethnic" elements with the political, territorial, educational and economic ones, that we may term "civic", that produce a modern nation. Today's nations are as much in need of common myths, memories and symbols, as were yesterday's *ethnies*, for it is these former that help to create and preserve the networks of solidarity that underpin and characterize nations. They also endow nations with their individuality. So that, while nations can be read as reconstructions of intellectual and other élites, they are also legitimately viewed as configurations of historical processes, which can be analysed as real trends.[6]

Because nations embody ethnic as well as civic components, they tend to form around pre-existing "ethnic cores". The fact that pre-modern eras have been characterized by different types of *ethnie* is therefore vital to our understanding of the ways in which modern nations emerged. The number, location and durability of such *ethnies* are crucial for the formation of historical nations. The relations of power and exploitation between different kinds of *ethnie* also help to determine the bases for historical nations. It is this latter circumstance that provides an essential key to the processes of nation-formation in modern times.

Bureaucratic "Incorporation"

The two basic kinds of ethnic core, the lateral and the vertical, also furnish the two main routes by which nations have been created.

Taking the lateral route first, we find that aristocratic *ethnies* have the potential for self-perpetuation, provided they can incorporate other strata of the population. A good many of these lateral *ethnies* cannot do so. Hittites, Philistines, Mycenaeans, even Assyrians, failed to do so, and they and their cultures disappeared with the demise of their states (Burney and Lang 1971, pp. 86–126; Kitchen 1973; Saggs 1984, pp. 117–21). Other lateral *ethnies* survived by "changing their character", as we saw with Persians, Egyptians and Ottoman Turks, while preserving a sense of common descent and some dim collective memories.

Still others grafted new ethnic and cultural elements on to their common fund of myths, symbols and memories, and spread them out from the core area and down through the social scale. They did so, of course, in varying degrees. The efforts of the Amhara kings, for example, were rather limited in scope; yet they managed to retain their Monophysite Abyssinian identity in their heartlands (Atiya 1968; Ullendorff 1973, pp. 54–92). That of the Castilians was more successful. They managed to form the core of a Spanish state (and empire) that expelled the Muslim rulers and almost united the Iberian peninsula. Yet, even their success pales before that of their Frankish and Norman counterparts.

In fact, the latter three efforts at "bureaucratic incorporation" were to prove of seminal historical importance. In all three cases, lower strata and outlying regions were gradually incorporated in the state, which was grounded upon a dominant ethnic core. This was achieved by administrative and fiscal means, and by the mobilization of sections of the populations for inter-state warfare, as in the Anglo-French wars (Keeney 1972). An upper-class *ethnie*, in other words, managed to evolve a relatively strong and stable administrative apparatus, which could be used to provide cultural regulation and thereby define a new and wider cultural identity (Corrigan and Sayer 1985). In practice, this meant varying degrees of accommodation between the upper-class culture and those prevalent among the lower strata and peripheral regions; yet it was the upper-class culture that set its stamp on the state and on the evolving national identity.

Perhaps the most clear-cut example is afforded by British developments. As there had been an Anglo-Saxon kingdom based originally on Wessex before the Norman Conquest, the conquered populations could not be treated simply as a servile peasantry. As a result, we find considerable intermarriage, linguistic borrowing, élite mobility and finally a fusion of linguistic culture, within a common religio-political framework.

In other words, bureaucratic incorporation of subject *ethnies* entailed a considerable measure of cultural fusion and social intermingling between Anglo-Saxon, Danish and Norman elements, especially from the thirteenth century on. By the time of Edward III and the Anglo-French and Scottish wars, linguistic fusion had stabilized into Chaucerian English and a "British" myth served to weld the disparate ethnic communities together (Seton-Watson 1977, pp. 22–31; L. Smith 1985).

I am not arguing that an English nation was fully formed by the late fourteenth century. There was little economic unity as yet, despite growing fiscal and judicial intervention by the royal state. The boundaries of the kingdom, too, both with Scotland and in France, were often in dispute. In no sense can one speak of a public, mass-education system, even for the middle classes. As for legal rights, despite the assumptions behind Magna Carta, they were common to all only in the most minimal senses. For the full development of these civic elements of nationhood, one would have to wait for the Industrial Revolution and its effects (Reynolds 1984, pp. 250–331).

The ethnic elements of the nation, on the other hand, were well developed. By the fourteenth century or slightly later, a common name and myth of descent, promulgated originally by Geoffrey of Monmouth, were widely current, as were a variety of historical memories (MacDougall 1982, pp. 7–17). These were fed by the fortunes of wars in Scotland and France. Similarly, a sense of common culture based on language and ecclesiastical organization had emerged. So had a common strong attachment to the homeland of the island kingdom, which in turn bred a sense of solidarity, despite internal class-cleavages. The bases of both the unitary state and a compact nation had been laid, and laid by a lateral Norman-origin *ethnie* that was able to develop its regnal administration to incorporate the Anglo-Saxon population. Yet the full ideology of Englishness had to wait for late-sixteenth- and seventeenth-century developments, when the old British myth gave way to a more potent middle-class "Saxon" mythology of ancient liberties (MacDougall 1982, chs 2–4).

A similar process of bureaucratic incorporation by an upper-class lateral *ethnie* can be discerned in France. Some fusion of upper-stratum Frankish with subject Romano-Gallic culture occurred under the Christianized Merovingians, but a regnal solidarity is really only apparent in northern France at the end of the twelfth century. It was in this era that earlier myths of Trojan descent, applied to the Franks, were resuscitated for all the people of northern France. At the same time, the *pays d'oc*, with its different language, customs and myths of descent, remained for some time outside the orbit of northern bureaucratic incorporation (Reynolds 1984, pp. 276–89; Bloch 1961, vol. II, pp. 431–7).

Of course, Capetian bureaucratic incorporation from Philip II onwards was able to draw on the glory and myths of the old Frankish kingdom and Charlemagne's heritage. This was partly because the kingdom of the Eastern Franks came to be known as the *regnum Teutonicorum*, with a separate identity. However, it was also due to the special link between French dynasties and the Church, notably the archbishopric of Rheims. The backing of the French clergy, and the ceremony of anointing at coronations, were probably more crucial to the prestige and survival of a French monarchy in northern France before the battle of Bouvines (1214) than the fame of the schools of Paris or even the military tenacity of the early Capetians. There was a sacred quality inhering in the dynastic *mythomoteur* of the Capetians and their territory that went back to the Papal coronation of Charlemagne and Papal legitimation of Pepin's usurpation in A.D. 754, which the Pope called a "new kingdom of David". The religious language is echoed centuries later, when at the end of the thirteenth century Pope Boniface declared: ". . . like the people of Israel . . . the kingdom of France [is] a peculiar people chosen by the Lord to carry out the orders of Heaven" (Davis 1958, pp. 298–313; Lewis 1974, pp. 57–70; Armstrong 1982, pp. 152–9).

Though there is much debate as to the "feudal" nature of the Capetian monarchy, the undoubted fact is that an originally Frankish ruling-class *ethnie* managed, after many vicissitudes, to establish a relatively efficient and centralized royal administration over north and central France (later southern France). So it became able to furnish those "civic" elements of compact territory, unified economy, and linguistic and legal standardization that from the seventeenth century onwards spurred the formation of a French nation as we know it. The process, however, was not completed until the end of the nineteenth century. Many regions retained their local character, even after the French Revolution. It required the application of Jacobin nationalism to mass education and conscription under the Third Republic to turn, in Eugen Weber's well-known phrase, "peasants into Frenchmen" (Kohn 1967; Weber 1979).[7]

An even more radical "change of character" occasioned by attempted bureaucratic incorporation by a "lateral" ethnic state is provided by Spain. Here it was the Castilian kingdom that formed the fulcrum of Christian resistance to Muslim power. Later, united with the kingdom of Aragon, it utilized religious community as an instrument of homogenization, expelling those who, like the Jews and Moriscos, could not be made to conform. Here, too, notions of *limpieza de sangre* bolstered the unity of the Spanish crown, which was beset by demands on several sides from those claiming ancient rights and manifesting ancient cultures. Quite apart from the Portuguese secession and the failed Catalan revolt, Basques, Galicians and Andalusians retained their separate identities into the modern era. The result is a less unified national community, and more polyethnic state, than either Britain or France. With the spread of ideological nationalism in the early nineteenth century, these ethnic communities felt justified in embarking on varying degrees of autonomous development, whose reverberations are still felt today. Yet, most members of these communities shared an overarching Spanish political sentiment and culture, over and beyond their often intense commitment to Basque, Catalan or Galician identity and culture (Atkinson 1960; Payne 1971; Greenwood 1977).

Historically, the formation of modern nations owes a profound legacy to the development of England, France and Spain. This is usually attributed to their possession of military and economic power at the relevant period, the period of burgeoning nationalism and nations. As the great powers of the period, they inevitably became models of the nation, the apparently success-ful format of population unit, for everyone else. Yet in the case of England and France, and to a lesser extent Spain, this was not accidental. It was the result of the early development of a particular kind of "rational" bureaucratic administration, aided by the development of merchant capital, wealthy urban centres and professional military forces and technology. The "state" formed the matrix of the new population-unit's format, the "nation". It aided the type of compact, unified, standardized and culturally homogenized unit and format that the nation exemplifies.

Some would say that the state actually "created" the nation, that royal administration, taxation and mobilization endowed the subjects within its jurisdiction with a sense of corporate loyalty and identity. Even in the West, this overstates the case. The state was certainly a necessary condition for the formation of the national loyalties we recognize today. However, its opera-tions in turn owed much to earlier assumptions about kingdoms and peoples, and to the presence of core ethnic communities around which these states were built up. The process of ethnic fusion, particularly apparent in England and France, which their lateral *ethnies* encouraged through the channels of bureaucratic incorporation, was only possible because of a relatively homo-geneous ethnic core. We are not here talking about actual descent, much less about "race", but about the *sense* of ancestry and identity that people possess. Hence the importance of myths and memories, symbols and values, embodied in customs and traditions and in artistic styles, legal codes and institutions. In *this* sense of "ethnicity", which is more about cultural perceptions than physical demography, albeit rooted perceptions and assumptions, England from an early date, and France somewhat later, came to form fairly homogeneous *ethnies*. These *ethnies* in turn facilitated the development of homogenizing states, extending the whole idea of an *ethnie* into realms and on to levels hitherto unknown, to form the relatively novel concept of the nation.

The "Rediscovery" of the "Ethnic Past"

In contrast to the route of bureaucratic incorporation by lateral *ethnies*, the process by which demotic *ethnies* may become the bases for nations is only indirectly affected by the state and its administration. This was either because they were subject communities – the usual case – or because, as in Byzantium and Russia, the state represented interests partially outside its core *ethnie*. This subdivision also produces interesting variants on the constitutive political myth, or *mythomoteur*, of vertical *ethnies*.[8]

In all these communities, the fund of cultural myths, symbols, memories and values was transmitted not only from generation to generation, but also throughout the territory occupied by the community or its enclaves, and down the social scale. The chief mechanism of this persistence and diffusion was an organized religion with a sacred text, liturgy, rites and clergy, and sometimes a specialized secret lore and script. It is the social aspects of salvation religions, in particular, that have ensured the persistence and shaped the contours of demotic *ethnies*. Among Orthodox Greeks and Russians, Monophysite Copts and Ethiopians, Gregorian Armenians, Jews, Catholic Irish and Poles, myths and symbols of descent and election, and the ritual and sacred texts in which they were embodied, helped to perpetuate the traditions and social bonds of the community.

At the same time, the very hold of an ethnic religion posed grave problems for the formation of nations from such communities. It transpired that "religion-shaped" peoples, whose ethnicity owed so much to the symbols and organization of an ancient faith, were often constrained in their efforts to become "full" nations. Or rather, their intellectuals may find it harder to break out of the conceptual mould of a religio-ethnic community. So many members of such demotic *ethnies* simply assumed that theirs was already, and indeed always had been, a nation. Indeed, according to some definitions they were. They possessed in full measure, after all, the purely ethnic components of the nation. Arabs and Jews, for example, had common names, myths of descent, memories and religious cultures, as well as attachments to an original homeland and a persisting, if sub-divided, sense of ethnic solidarity. Did this not suffice for nationhood? All that seemed to be necessary was to attain independence and a state for the community (Baron 1960, pp. 213–48; Carmichael 1967; Patai 1983).

Yet, as these examples demonstrate, matters were not so simple. Quite apart from adverse geo-political factors, social and cultural features internal to the Arab and Jewish communities made the transition from *ethnie* to nation difficult and problematic. The Arabs have been faced, of course, by their geographic extent, which flies in the face of the ideal of a "compact nation" in its clearly demarcated habitat. They have also had to contend with the varied histories of the sub-divisions of the "Arab nation", ranging from the Moroccan kingdoms to those of Egypt or Saudi Arabia. There is also the legacy of a divisive modern colonialism, which has often reinforced historical differences and shaped the modern Arab states with their varied economic patterns. Mass, public education has, in turn, like legal rights, been the product of the colonial and post-colonial states and their élites. Above all, however, the involvement of most Arabs and most Arab states with Islam, whose *umma* both underpins and challenges the circle and significance of an "Arab nation", creates an ambiguous unity and destiny, and overshadows efforts by Arab intelligentsia to rediscover an "Arab past" (Sharabi 1970; Smith 1973b).

The Jews were also faced with problems of geographic dispersion, accentuated by their lack of a recognized territory and exile from an ancient homeland. True, in the Pale of Settlement and earlier in Poland, something approaching a public religious education system and common legal rights (albeit restricted) had been encouraged by the *kahal* system and its successors. Yet, though Jews, like Armenians, were compelled to occupy certain niches in the European economy, we can hardly characterize their enclave communities as models of economic unity, let alone a territorial division of labour. Quite apart from these obstacles to national unity, there were also the ambivalent attitudes and self-definitions of Judaism and its rabbinical authorities. Only later, did some rabbis and one wing of Orthodoxy come to support Jewish nationalism and its Zionist project, despite the traditional hopes for messianic restoration to Zion of generations of the Orthodox. The concept of Jewish self-help had become alien to the medieval interpretation of Judaism; and the general notion that the Jews were a "nation in exile" actually strengthened this passivity (Hertzberg 1960; Vital 1975, pp. 3–20).

It was in these circumstances of popular resignation amid communal decline, set against Western national expansion, that a new stratum of secular intelligentsia emerged. Their fundamental role, as they came to see it, was to transform the relationship of a religious tradition to its primary bearers, the demotic *ethnies*. We must, of course, place this development in the larger context of a series of revolutions – socio-economic, political and cultural – which began in the early-modern period in the West. As we saw, the primary motor of these transformations was the formation of a new type of professionalized, bureaucratic state on the basis of a relatively homogeneous core *ethnie*. Attempts by older political formations to take over some of the dimensions of the Western "rational state" and so streamline their administrations and armies, upset the old accommodations of these empires to their constituent *ethnies*. In the Habsburg, Ottoman and Romanov empires, increasing state intervention, coupled with incipient urbanization and commerce, placed many demotic *ethnies* under renewed pressures. The spread of nationalist ideas from the late-eighteenth century on, carried with it new ideals of compact population-units, popular representation and cultural diversity, which affected the ruling classes of these empires and even more the educated stratum of their subject communities (see the essays in Sugar and Lederer 1969; more generally, Smith 1986, pp. 129–52).

For the subject vertical *ethnie*, a secularizing intelligentsia led by educator-intellectuals supplied the motor of transformation, as well as the cultural framework, which among lateral *ethnie* had been largely provided by the incorporating bureaucratic state. It was this intelligentsia that furnished the new communal self-definitions and goals. These redefinitions were not simple "inventions", or wholesale applications of Western models. Rather, they were derived from a process of "rediscovery" of the ethnic past. The process tended to reverse the religious self-view: instead of "the people" acting as a passive but chosen vessel of salvation, subordinate to the divine message, that message and its salvation ethic became the supreme expression and creation of the people's genius as it developed in history (Haim 1962; Smith 1983, pp. 230–56).[9]

At the centre of the self-appointed task of the intelligentsia stood the rediscovery and realization of the community. This entailed a moral and political revolution. In the place of a passive and subordinate minority, living precariously on the margins of the dominant ethnic society and its state, a new compact and politically active nation had to be created ("recreated" in nationalist terminology). From now on, the centre stage was to be occupied by the people, henceforth identified with "the masses", who would replace the aristocratic heroes of old. This was all part of the process of creating a unified, and preferably autarchic, community of legally equal members or "citizens", who would become the fount of legitimacy and state power. However, for this to occur, the people had to be purified of the dross of centuries – their lethargy, divisions, alien elements, ignorance and so on – and emancipate themselves. That was the primary task of the educator-intellectuals.

The transition, then, from demotic *ethnie* to civic nation carries with it several related processes and movements. These include:

1   a movement from subordinate accommodation and passivity of a peripheral minority to an active, assertive and politicized community with a unified policy;

2 a movement towards a universally recognized "homeland" for the community, a compact, clearly demarcated territory;
3 economic unification of all members of the territorially demarcated community, with control over its own resources, and movement towards economic autarchy in a competitive world of nations;
4 turning ethnic members into legal citizens by mobilizing them for political ends and conferring on each common civil, social and political rights and obligations;
5 placing the people at the centre of moral and political concern and celebrating the new role of the masses, by re-educating them in national values, myths and memories.

That traditional élites, especially the guardians of sacred texts which had so long defined the demotic *ethnie*, might resist these changes, was to be expected. This meant that the intellectuals had to undercut earlier definitions of the community by re-presenting their novel conceptions through ancient symbols and formats. These were in no sense mere manipulations (though there undoubtedly was individual manipulation, such as Tilak's use of the Kali cult in Bengal); there is no need to unmask what are so patently selective readings of an ethnic past. Yet selection can take place only within strict limits, limits set by the pre-existing myths, symbols, customs and memories of vertical *ethnies*. That still leaves considerable scope for choice of symbol or myth and understanding of history. [...]

Notes

1 Further discussions of the subjective and objective features of nations, and of their dynamic and processual character, can be found in Rustow (1967) and Nettl and Robertson (1968).
2 For a general discussion, and an example from ancient Rome, see Tudor (1972).
3 For discussions of ancient empires and their economies, see Larsen (1979, especially the essays by Lattimore, Ekholm and Friedman, and Postgate).
4 The ancient Greek term *ethnos*, like the Latin *natio*, has a connotation of common origin, and so, being alike and acting together; but the emphasis is cultural rather than biological. As always, it is what people believe, rather than objective origins, that is important.
5 In many cases, the evidence from ancient and medieval records does not allow us to infer much about the degree of social penetration of élite culture and the range of ethnic ties, as the other essays in the volume by Wiseman (1973) make clear.

6 Of course, this conclusion owes much to the definition of the nation adopted
   here. Even so, one would have to distinguish in some way(s) between the types
   of cultural community in antiquity and the Middle Ages, and the very different
   kinds prevalent in the modern world. It is therefore better to make the distinctions explicit in the definitions themselves. Though there is a "before-and-after"
   model inherent in this conception, the argument advanced here suggests that the
   earlier components are *not* simply replaced by the later, modern ones; ethnic
   components do (and must) persist, if a nation is to be formed.
7 Again, the continuity is cultural, and indirect. It remained significant into the
   nineteenth century to claim descent from "Franks" and even "Gauls" for
   political purposes; the recovery of medieval French art and history also spurred
   this sense of ethnic identification. By the later Middle Ages, the claim to Frankish
   descent could hardly be substantiated; but again, it is claims within a cultural
   framework that count.
8 These are discussed by Smith (1986, pp. 47–68); and see Armstrong (1982).
9 It is necessary to distinguish the educator-intellectuals proper from the wider
   stratum of the professional intelligentsia, on which see Gouldner (1979) and
   Smith (1981, pp. 87–107).

References

Alty, J. H. M. 1982 "Dorians and Ionians" *Journal of Hellenic Studies*, vol. 102, no.
   1, pp. 1–14.
Anderson, Benedict 1983 *Imagined Communities: Reflections on the Origin and
   Spread of Nationalism*. London: Verso.
Andrewes, Antony 1965 "The growth of the city-state", in Hugh Lloyd-Jones (ed.),
   The Greek World. Harmondsworth: Penguin, pp. 26–65.
Armstrong, John 1982 *Nations before Nationalism*. Chapel Hill: University of North
   Carolina Press.
Atiya, Aziz S. 1968 *A History of Eastern Christianity*, London: Methuen.
Atkinson, William C. 1960 *A History of Spain and Portugal*. Harmondsworth:
   Penguin.
Barnard, Frederik Mechner 1965 *Herder's Social and Political Thought*. Oxford:
   Clarendon Press.
Barnett, Richard D. (ed.) 1971 *The Sephardi Heritage: Essays on the History and
   Cultural Contribution of the Jews of Spain and Portugal*, vol. I: *The Jews in Spain
   and Portugal before and after the Expulsion of 1492*. London: Valentine, Mitchell &
   Co.
Baron, Salo W. 1960 *Modern Nationalism and Religion*. New York: Meridian Books.
Bloch, Marc 1961 *Feudal Society*, 2 vols. London: Routledge & Kegan Paul.
Breuilly, John 1982 *Nationalism and the State*. Manchester: Manchester University
   Press.
Brock, Peter 1976 *The Slovak National Awakening*. Toronto: University of Toronto
   Press.

Burney, Charles and Lang, David M. 1971 *The Peoples of the Hills: Ancient Ararat and Caucasus*. London: Weidenfeld & Nicolson.

Cambridge History of Iran 1983 Vol. III, *The Seleucid, Parthian and Sassanian Periods* (ed. Ehson Yarshater); 1975 Vol. IV, *The Period from the Arab Invasion to the Saljuqs* (ed. Richard N. Frye). Cambridge: Cambridge University Press.

Campbell, John and Sherrard, Philip 1968 *Modern Greece*. London: Benn.

Carmichael, Joel 1967 *The Shaping of the Arabs*. New York: Macmillan Company.

Connor, Walker 1978 "A Nation is a Nation, is a State, is an Ethnic Group, is a...". *Ethnic and Racial Studies* vol. 1, no. 4, pp. 377–400.

Corrigan, Philip and Sayer, Derek 1985 *The Great Arch: English State Formation as Cultural Revolution*. Oxford: Blackwell.

Davis, R. H. C. 1958 *A History of Medieval Europe*. London: Longmans, Green and Co.

——— 1976 *The Normans and Their Myth*. London: Thames & Hudson.

Finley, M. I. 1986 "The Ancient Greeks and Their Nation", in his: *The Use and Abuse of History*. London: The Hogarth Press, pp. 120–33.

Fishman, Joshua 1980 "Social Theory and Ethnography: Neglected Perspectives on Language and Ethnicity in Eastern Europe", in Peter Sugar (ed.), *Ethnic Diversity and Conflict in Eastern Europe*. Santa Barbara: ABC-Clio, pp. 69–99.

Fondation Hardt 1962 *Grecs et Barbares, Entretiens sur l'antiquité classique*, vol. VIII. Geneva.

Frye, Richard N. 1966 *The Heritage of Persia*. New York: Mentor.

Gellner, Ernest 1983 *Nations and Nationalism*. Oxford: Blackwell.

Gouldner, Alvin 1979 *The Rise of the Intellectuals and the Future of the New Class*. London: Macmillan.

Greenwood, Davydd 1977 "Continuity in Change: Spanish Basque Ethnicity as a Historical Process", in Milton Esman (ed.), *Ethnic Conflict in the Western World*. Ithaca: Cornell University Press, pp. 81–102.

Haim, Sylvia (ed.) 1962 *Arab Nationalism: An Anthology*. Berkeley: University of California Press.

Hertzberg, Arthur (ed.) 1960 *The Zionist Idea: A Reader*. New York: Meridian Books.

Hirschberg, Hayyim Ze'ev (Joachim W.) 1969 "The Oriental Jewish Communities", in Arthur J. Arberry (ed.), *Religion in the Middle East: Three Religions in Concord and Conflict*, vol. I, *Judaism and Christianity*. Cambridge: Cambridge University Press, pp. 119–225.

Hobsbawm, Eric and Ranger, Terence (eds) 1983 *The Invention of Tradition*. Cambridge: Cambridge University Press.

Horowitz, Donald L. 1985 *Ethnic Groups in Conflict*. Berkeley: University of California Press.

Hutchinson, John 1987 *The Dynamics of Cultural Nationalism: The Gaelic Revival and the Creation of the Irish Nation State*. London: Allen & Unwin.

Jones, Gwyn 1973 *A History of the Vikings*. London: Oxford University Press.

Keeney, Barnaby C. 1972 "Military Service and the Development of Nationalism in England, 1272–1327", in Leon Tipton (ed.), *Nationalism in the Middle Ages*. New York: Holt, Rinehart & Winston, pp. 87–97.

Kitchen, K. A. 1973 "The Philistines", in D. J. Wiseman (ed.), *Peoples of the Old Testament*. Oxford: Oxford University Press, pp. 53–78.

Kohn, Hans 1967 *Prelude to Nation-States: The French and German Experience, 1789–1815*. New York: Van Nostrand.

Larsen, Mogens T. (ed.) 1979 *Power and Propaganda: A Symposium on Ancient Empires*. Copenhagen: Akademisk Forlag.

Levi, Mario Attilio 1965 *Political Power in the Ancient World* (translated by J. Costello). London: Weidenfeld & Nicolson.

Lewis, Archibald 1974 *Knights and Samurai: Feudalism in Northern France and Japan*. London: Temple Smith.

MacDougall, Hugh 1982 *Racial Myth in English History: Trojans, Teutons and Anglo-Saxons*. Montreal: Harvest House.

McNeill, William H. 1963 *The Rise of the West: A History of the Human Community*. Chicago: University of Chicago Press.

Nairn, Tom 1977 *The Break-up of Britain: Crisis and Neo-nationalism*. London: New Left Books.

Nettl, J. P. and Robertson, Roland 1968 *International Systems and the Modernisation of Societies*. London: Faber.

Orridge, Andrew 1982 "Separatist and Autonomist Nationalisms: The Structure of Regional Loyalties in the Modern State", in Colin H. Williams (ed.), *National Separatism*. Cardiff: University of Wales Press, pp. 43–74.

Patai, Raphael 1983 *The Arab Mind*, rev. edn. New York: Charles Scribner's Sons.

Payne, Stanley 1971 "Catalan and Basque Nationalism". *Journal of Contemporary History*, vol. 6, no. 1, pp. 15–51.

Raphael, Chaim 1985 *The Road from Babylon*. London: Weidenfeld & Nicolson.

Reynolds, Susan 1983 "Medieval *origines gentium* and the Community of the Realm". *History*, vol. 68, pp. 375–90.

—— 1984 *Kingdoms and Communities in Western Europe, 900–1300*. Oxford: Clarendon Press.

Rustow, Dankwart 1967 *A World of Nations*. Washington, D.C.: Brookings Institution.

Saggs, Henry W. F. 1984 *The Might That Was Assyria*. London: Sidgwick & Jackson.

Sathyamurthy, T. V. 1983 *Nationalism in the Contemporary World: Political and Sociological Perspectives*. London: Frances Pinter.

Seltzer, Robert M. 1980 *Jewish People, Jewish Thought: The Jewish Experience in History*. New York: Macmillan.

Seton-Watson, Hugh 1977 *Nations and States: An Enquiry into the Origins of Nations and the Politics of Nationalism*. London: Methuen.

Sharabi, Hisham 1970 *Arab Intellectuals and the West: The Formative Years, 1875–1914*. Baltimore: Johns Hopkins Press.

Smith, Anthony D. 1973a Nationalism: A Trend Report and Annotated Bibliography. *Current Sociology*, vol. 21, no. 3. The Hague: Mouton.

—— 1973b "Nationalism and Religion: The Role of Religious Reform in the Genesis of Arab and Jewish Nationalism". *Archives de Sociologie des Religions*, vol. 35, pp. 23–43.

—— 1981a *The Ethnic Revival in the Modern World*. Cambridge: Cambridge University Press.

—— 1983a *Theories of Nationalism*, 2nd edn. London: Duckworth, and New York: Holmes & Meier.

—— 1986a *The Ethnic Origins of Nations*. Oxford: Blackwell.

Smith, Leslie (ed.) 1985 *The Making of Britain: The Middle Ages*. London: Macmillan.

Stack, John F. (ed.) 1986 *The Primordial Challenge: Ethnicity in the Contemporary World*. New York: Greenwood Press.

Sugar, Peter and Lederer, Ivo (eds) 1969 *Nationalism in Eastern Europe*. Seattle: University of Washington Press.

Szporluk, Roman 1979 *Ukraine: A Brief History*. Detroit: Ukrainian Festival Committee.

Tilly, Charles (ed.) 1975 *The Formation of National States in Western Europe*. Princeton, NJ: Princeton University Press.

Tudor, Henry 1972 *Political Myth*. London: Pall Mall Press.

Ullendorff, Edward 1973 *The Ethiopians: An Introduction to Country and People*, 3rd edn. Oxford: Oxford University Press.

Vital, David 1975 *The Origins of Zionism*. Oxford: Clarendon Press.

Weber, Eugen 1979 *Peasants into Frenchmen: The Modernization of Rural France, 1870–1914*. London: Chatto and Windus.

Wiseman, D. J. (ed.) 1973 *Peoples of the Old Testament*. Oxford: Oxford University Press.

36

A Kind of Scar: The Woman Poet in a National Tradition (1989)

Eavan Boland

Eavan Boland, selection from *A Kind of Scar* (1989) [source: Eavan Boland, *A Kind of Scar: The Woman Poet in a National Tradition*. Dublin: Attic Press, 1989, 5–6, 11–14]

Boland is a major contemporary Irish poet, and her essays have focused on the problems and challenges of writing as a woman in a male-dominated national literary tradition. She argues (perhaps thinking of Virginia Woolf) that the "intellectually seductive" path for the woman artist is "to walk away from the idea of a nation." But Boland maintains, in collections like *Object Lessons: The Life of the Woman and Poet in Our Time* (1995), that she cannot walk away, because she "is not free to": the nation, including its fragments, forms the history out of which she writes.

I

Years ago, I went to Achill for Easter. I was a student at Trinity then and I had the loan of a friend's cottage. It was a one-storey, stone building with two rooms and a view of sloping fields.

April was cold that year. The cottage was in sight of the Atlantic and at night a bitter, humid wind blew across the shore. By day there was heckling sunshine but after dark a fire was necessary. The loneliness of the place suited me. My purposes in being there were purgatorial and I had no intention of going out and about. I had done erratically, to say the least, in my first year exams. In token of the need to do better, I had brought with me a small accusing volume of the Court poets of the silver age. In other words, those sixteenth century English song writers, like Wyatt and Raleigh, whose lines appear so elegant, so off-hand yet whose poems smell of the gallows.

I was there less than a week. The cottage had no water and every evening the caretaker, an old woman who shared a cottage with her brother at the bottom of the field, would carry water up to me. I can see her still. She has a tea-towel round her waist – perhaps this is one image that has become all the images I have of her – she wears an old cardigan and her hands are blushing with cold as she puts down the bucket. Sometimes we talk inside the door of the cottage. Once, I remember, we stood there as the dark grew all around us and I could see stars beginning to curve in the stream behind us.

She was the first person to talk to me about the famine. The first person, in fact, to speak to me with any force about the terrible parish of survival and death which the event had been in those regions. She kept repeating to me that they were great people, the people in the famine. Great people. I had never heard that before. She pointed out the beauties of the place. But they themselves, I see now, were a sub-text. On the eastern side of Keel, the cliffs of Menawn rose sheer out of the water. And here was Keel itself, with its blonde strand and broken stone, where the villagers in the famine, she told me, had moved closer to the shore, the better to eat the seaweed.

Memory is treacherous. It confers meanings which are not apparent at the time. I want to say that I understood this woman as emblem and instance of everything I am about to propose. Of course I did not. Yet even then, I sensed a power in the encounter. I knew, without having words for it, that she came from a past which affected me. When she pointed out Keel to me that evening when the wind was brisk and cold and the light was going; when she gestured towards that shore which had stones as outlines and monuments of a desperate people, what was she pointing at? A history? A nation? Her memories or mine?

Those questions, once I began to write my own poetry, came back to haunt me. "I have been amazed, more than once" writes Hélène Cixous "by a description a woman gave me of a world all her own, which she had been secretly haunting since early childhood." As the years passed, my amazement grew. I would see again the spring evening, the woman talking to me. Above all, I would remember how, when I finished speaking to her I went in, lit a fire, took out my book of English court poetry and memorised all over again – with no sense of irony or omission – the cadences of power and despair.

[...]

V

Irish poetry was predominantly male. Here or there you found a small eloquence, like *After Aughrim* by Emily Lawless. Now and again, in discussion, you heard a woman's name. But the lived vocation, the craft witnessed by a human life – that was missing. And I missed it. Not in the beginning, perhaps. But later, when perceptions of womanhood began to redirect my own work, what I regretted was the absence of an expressed poetic life which would have dignified and revealed mine. The influence of absences should not be underestimated. Isolation itself can have a powerful effect in the life of a young writer. "I'm talking about real influence now" says Raymond Carver. "I'm talking about the moon and the tide."

I turned to the work of Irish male poets. After all, I thought of myself as an Irish poet. I wanted to locate myself within the Irish poetic tradition. The dangers and stresses in my own themes gave me an added incentive to discover a context for them. But what I found dismayed me.

The majority of Irish male poets depended on women as motifs in their poetry. They moved easily, deftly, as if by right among images of women in which I did not believe and of which I could not approve. The women in their poems were often passive, decorative, raised to emblematic status. This was especially true where the woman and the idea of the nation were mixed: where the nation became a woman and the woman took on a national posture.

The trouble was these images did good service as ornaments. In fact they had a wide acceptance as ornaments by readers of Irish poetry. Women in such poems were frequently referred to approvingly as mythic, emblematic. But to me these passive and simplified women seemed a corruption. Moreover, the transaction they urged on the reader, to accept them as mere decoration, seemed to compound the corruption. For they were not decorations, they were not ornaments. However distorted these images, they had their roots in a suffered truth.

What had happened? How had the women of our past – the women of a long struggle and a terrible survival – undergone such a transformation? How had they suffered Irish history and inscribed themselves in the speech and memory of the Achill woman, only to re-emerge in the Irish poetry as fictive queens and national sibyls?

The more I thought about it, the more uneasy I became. The wrath and grief of Irish history seemed to me – as it did to many – one of our true possessions. Women were part of that wrath, had endured that grief. It seemed to me a species of human insult that at the end of all, in certain

Irish poems, they should become elements of style rather than aspects of truth.

The association of the feminine and the national – and the consequent simplification of both – is not of course a monopoly of Irish poetry. "All my life" wrote Charles de Gaulle "I have thought about France in a certain way. The emotional side of me tends to imagine France like the princess in the fairytale, or the Madonna of the Frescoes." De Gaulle's words point up the power of nationhood to edit the reality of womanhood. Once the idea of a nation influences the perception of a woman then that woman is suddenly and inevitably simplified. She can no longer have complex feelings and aspirations. She becomes the passive projection of a national idea.

Irish poems simplified women most at the point of intersection between womanhood and Irishness. The further the Irish poem drew away from the idea of Ireland, the more real and persuasive became the images of women. Once the pendulum swung back the simplifications started again. The idea of the defeated nation being reborn as a triumphant woman was central to a certain kind of Irish poem. Dark Rosaleen. Cathleen Ni Houlihan. The nation as woman; the woman as national muse.

The more I looked at it, the more it seemed to me that in relation to the idea of a nation many, if not most, Irish male poets had taken the soft option. The irony was that few Irish poets were nationalists. By and large, they had eschewed the fervour and crudity of that ideal. But long after they had rejected the politics of Irish nationalism, they continued to deploy the emblems and enchantments of its culture. It was the culture, not the politics, which informed Irish poetry: not the harsh awakenings, but the old dreams.

In all of this I did not blame nationalism. Nationalism seemed to me inevitable in the Irish context; a necessary hallucination within Joyce's nightmare of history. I did blame Irish poets. Long after it was necessary, Irish poetry had continued to trade in the exhausted fictions of the nation; had allowed these fictions to edit ideas of womanhood and modes of remembrance. Some of the poetry produced by such simplifications was, of course, difficult to argue with. It was difficult to deny that something was gained by poems which used the imagery and emblem of the national muse. Something was gained, certainly; but only at an aesthetic level. While what was lost occurred at the deepest, most ethical level; and what was lost was what I valued. Not just the details of a past. Not just the hungers, the angers. These, however terrible, remain local. But the truth these details witness – human truths of survival and humiliation – these also were suppressed along with the details. Gone was the suggestion of any complicated human suffering. Instead, you had the hollow victories, the passive images, the rhyming queens.

I knew that the women of the Irish past were defeated. I knew it instinctively long before the Achill woman pointed down the hill to the Keel shoreline. What I objected to was that Irish poetry should defeat them twice.

"I have not written day after day" says Camus "because I desire the world to be covered with Greek statues and masterpieces. The man who has such a desire does exist in me. But I have written so much because I cannot keep from being drawn toward every day life, toward those, whoever they may be, who are humiliated. They need to hope and, if all keep silent, they will be forever deprived of hope and we with them."

This essay originates in some part from my own need to locate myself in a powerful literary tradition in which until then, or so it seemed to me, I had been an element of design rather than an agent of change. But even as a young poet, and certainly by the time my work confronted me with some of these questions, I had already had a vivid, human witness of the stresses which a national literature can impose on a poet. I had already seen the damage it could do. [...]

37

Narrating the Nation (1990)

Homi K. Bhabha

Homi K. Bhabha, selection from "Introduction: Narrating the Nation," of *Nation and Narration* (1990) [source: *Nation and Narration*, ed. Homi K. Bhabha. London: Routledge, 1990, 1–4]

Drawing on the work of literary theorists like Mikhail Bakhtin and Jacques Derrida, Bhabha has insisted on the irreducible hybridity of all nationalist discourse and all national identity. Difference and otherness are always present in the nation's narrative of identity, as they are in any national population. The cultural studies scholars collected in *Nation and Narration* address this theme.

Nations, like narratives, lose their origins in the myths of time and only fully realize their horizons in the mind's eye. Such an image of the nation – or narration – might seem impossibly romantic and excessively metaphorical, but it is from those traditions of political thought and literary language that the nation emerges as a powerful historical idea in the west. An idea whose cultural compulsion lies in the impossible unity of the nation as a symbolic force. This is not to deny the attempt by nationalist discourses persistently to produce the idea of the nation as a continuous narrative of national progress, the narcissism of self-generation, the primeval present of the *Volk*. Nor have such political ideas been definitively superseded by those new realities of internationalism, multinationalism, or even "late capitalism", once we acknowledge that the rhetoric of these global terms is most often underwritten in that grim prose of power that each nation can wield within its own sphere of influence. What I want to emphasize in that large and liminal image of the nation with which I began is a particular ambivalence that haunts the idea of the nation, the language of those who write of it and the lives of those who live it. It is an ambivalence that emerges from a growing awareness that, despite the certainty with which historians speak of the "origins" of nation as a sign of the "modernity" of society, the cultural temporality of the nation inscribes a much more transitional social reality. Benedict Anderson, whose *Imagined Communities* [London: Verso, 1983] significantly paved the way for this book, expresses the nation's ambivalent emergence with great clarity:

> The century of the Enlightenment, of rationalist secularism, brought with it its own modern darkness. . . . [Few] things were (are) suited to this end better than the idea of nation. If nation-states are widely considered to be "new" and "historical", the nations to which they give political expression always loom out of an immemorial past and . . . glide into a limitless future. What I am proposing is that Nationalism has to be understood, by aligning it not with self-consciously held political ideologies, but with large cultural systems that preceded it, out of which – as well as against which – it came into being. (19)

The nation's "coming into being" as a system of cultural signification, as the representation of social *life* rather than the discipline of social *polity*, emphasizes this instability of knowledge. For instance, the most interesting accounts of the national idea, whether they come from the Tory Right, the Liberal high ground, or the New Left, seem to concur on the ambivalent tension that defines the "society" of the nation. Michael Oakeshott's "Character of a modern European state" is perhaps the most brilliant conservative account of the equivocal nature of the modern nation. The national space is, in his view, constituted from competing dispositions of human association as *societas* (the acknowledgement of moral rules and conventions of conduct) and *universitas* (the acknowledgement of common purpose and substantive end). In the absence of their merging into a new identity they have survived as competing dogmas – *societas cum universitate* – "impos[ing] a particular ambivalence upon all the institutions of a modern state and a specific ambiguity upon its vocabulary of discourse".[1] In Hannah Arendt's view, the society of the nation in the modern world is "that curiously hybrid realm where private interests assume public significance" and the two realms flow unceasingly and uncertainly into each other "like waves in the never-ending stream of the life-process itself".[2] No less certain is Tom Nairn, in naming the nation "the modern Janus", that the "uneven development" of capitalism inscribes both progression and regression, political rationality and irrationality in the very genetic code of the nation. This is a structural fact to which there are no exceptions and "in this sense, it is an exact (not a rhetorical) statement about nationalism to say that it is by nature ambivalent".[3]

It is the cultural representation of this ambivalence of modern society that is explored in this book. If the ambivalent figure of the nation is a problem of its transitional history, its conceptual indeterminacy, its wavering between vocabularies, then what effect does this have on narratives and discourses that signify a sense of "nationness": the *heimlich* pleasures of the hearth, the *unheimlich* terror of the space or race of the Other; the comfort of social belonging, the hidden injuries of class; the customs of taste, the powers of political affiliation; the sense of social order, the sensibility of sexuality; the blindness of bureaucracy, the strait insight of institutions; the quality of justice, the common sense of injustice; the *langue* of the law and the *parole* of the people.

The emergence of the political "rationality" of the nation as a form of narrative – textual strategies, metaphoric displacements, sub-texts and figurative strategems – has its own history.[4] It is suggested in Benedict Anderson's view of the space and time of the modern nation as embodied in the narrative culture of the realist novel, and explored in Tom Nairn's reading of Enoch Powell's post-imperial racism which is based on the "symbol-fetishism" that infests his febrile, neo-romantic poetry. To encounter the nation *as it is written* displays a temporality of culture and social consciousness more in tune with the partial, overdetermined process by which textual meaning is produced through the articulation of difference in language; more in keeping with the problem of closure which plays enigmatically in the discourse of the sign. Such an approach contests the traditional authority of those national objects of knowledge – Tradition, People, the Reason of State, High Culture, for instance – whose pedagogical value often relies on their representation as holistic concepts located within an evolutionary narrative of historical continuity. Traditional histories do not take the nation at its own word, but, for the most part, they do assume that the problem lies with the interpretation of "events" that have a certain transparency or privileged visibility.

To study the nation through its narrative address does not merely draw attention to its language and rhetoric; it also attempts to alter the conceptual object itself. If the problematic "closure" of textuality questions the "totalization" of national culture, then its positive value lies in displaying the wide dissemination through which we construct the field of meanings and symbols associated with national life. This is a project that has a certain currency within those forms of critique associated with "cultural studies". Despite the considerable advance this represents, there is a tendency to read the Nation rather restrictively; either, as the ideological apparatus of state power, somewhat redefined by a hasty, functionalist reading of Foucault or Bakhtin; or, in a more utopian inversion, as the incipient or emergent expression of the "national-popular" sentiment preserved in a radical memory. These approaches are valuable in drawing our attention to those easily obscured, but highly significant, recesses of the national culture from which alternative constituencies of peoples and oppositional analytic capacities may emerge – youth, the everyday, nostalgia, new "ethnicities", new social movements, "the politics of difference". They assign new meanings and different directions to the process of historical change. The most progressive development from such positions take "a *discursive* conception of ideology – ideology (like language) is conceptualised in terms of the articulation of elements. As Volosinov said, the ideological sign is always multi-accentual and Janus-faced".[5] But in the heat of political argument the "doubling" of the sign can often be stilled. The Janus face of ideology is taken at face value and its meaning fixed, in the last instance, on one side of the divide between ideology and "material conditions".

It is the project of *Nation and Narration* to explore the Janus-faced ambivalence of language itself in the construction of the Janus-faced discourse of the nation. This turns the familiar two-faced god into a figure of prodigious doubling that investigates the nation-space in the *process* of the articulation of elements: where meanings may be partial because they are *in medias res*, and history may be half-made because it is in the process of being made; and the image of cultural authority may be ambivalent because it is caught, uncertainly, in the act of "composing" its powerful image. Without such an understanding of the performativity of language in the narratives of the nation, it would be difficult to understand why Edward Said prescribes a kind of "analytic pluralism" as the *form* of critical attention appropriate to the cultural effects of the nation. For the nation, as a form of cultural *elaboration* (in the Gramscian sense), is an agency of *ambivalent* narration that holds culture at its most productive position, as a force for "subordination, fracturing, diffusing, reproducing, as much as producing, creating, forcing, guiding".[6]

I wrote to my contributors with a growing, if unfamiliar, sense of the nation as one of the major structures of ideological ambivalence within the cultural representations of "modernity". My intention was that we should develop, in a nice collaborative tension, a range of readings that engaged the insights of poststructuralist theories of narrative knowledge – textuality, discourse, enunciation, *écriture*, "the unconscious as a language" to name only a few strategies – in order to evoke this ambivalent margin of the nation-space. To reveal such a margin is, in the first instance, to contest claims to cultural supremacy, whether these are made from the "old" post-imperialist metropolitan nations, or on behalf of the "new" independent nations of the periphery. The marginal or "minority" is not the space of a celebratory, or utopian, self-marginalization. It is a much more substantial intervention into those justifications of modernity – progress, homogeneity, cultural organicism, the deep nation, the long past – that rationalize the authoritarian, "normalizing" tendencies within cultures in the name of the national interest or the ethnic prerogative. In this sense, then, the ambivalent, antagonistic perspective of nation as narration will establish the cultural boundaries of the nation so that they may be acknowledged as "containing" thresholds of meaning that must be crossed, erased, and translated in the process of cultural production.

The "locality" of national culture is neither unified nor unitary in relation to itself, nor must it be seen simply as "other" in relation to what is outside or beyond it. The boundary is Janus-faced and the problem of outside/inside must always itself be a process of hybridity, incorporating new "people" in relation to the body politic, generating other sites of meaning and, inevitably, in the political process, producing unmanned sites of political antagonism and unpredictable forces for political representation. The address to nation as narration stresses the insistence of political power and cultural authority in what Derrida describes as the "irreducible excess of the syntactic over the semantic".[7] What emerges as an effect of such "incomplete signification" is a turning of boundaries and limits into the *in-between* spaces through which the meanings of cultural and political authority are negotiated. It is from such narrative positions between cultures and nations, theories and texts, the political, the poetic and the painterly, the past and the present, that *Nation and Narration* seeks to affirm and extend Frantz Fanon's revolutionary credo: "National consciousness, which is not nationalism, is the only thing that will give us an international dimension".[8] It is this *inter*national dimension both within the margins of the nation-space and in the boundaries *in-between* nations and peoples that the authors of this book have sought to represent in their essays. The representative emblem of this book might be a chiasmatic "figure" of cultural difference whereby the anti-nationalist, ambivalent nation-space becomes the crossroads to a new transnational culture. The "other" is never outside or beyond us; it emerges forcefully, within cultural discourse, when we *think* we speak most intimately and indigenously "between ourselves". [. . .]

Notes

1 Michael Oakeshott, *On Human Conduct* (Oxford: Oxford University Press, 1975), p. 201.
2 Hannah Arendt, *The Human Condition* (Chicago: University of Chicago Press, 1958), pp. 33–5 *et passim*.
3 Tom Nairn, *The Break-up of Britain* (London: Verso, 1985), p. 348.
4 Patrick Wright's *On Living in an Old Country* (London: Verso, 1985) and Paul Gilroy's *There Ain't No Black in the Union Jack* (London: Hutchinson, 1987) are significant recent contributions to such an approach.
5 Stuart Hall, *The Hard Road to Renewal* (London: Verso, 1988), p. 9.
6 Edward Said, *The World, the Text, and the Critic* (Cambridge, MA: Harvard University Press, 1983), p. 171.
7 Jacques Derrida, *Dissemination* (Chicago: University of Chicago Press, 1981), p. 221.
8 Frantz Fanon, *The Wretched of the Earth* (Harmondsworth: Penguin, 1967), p. 199.

38

Culture and Imperialism (1993)

Edward W. Said

Edward W. Said, selection from *Culture and Imperialism* (1993) [source: Edward W. Said, *Culture and Imperialism*. New York: Alfred A. Knopf, 1993, 215–20.]

A literary scholar and defender of Palestinian rights, Said has emphasized the fundamental relation between national cultures in the West and imperialism. His most influential work, *Orientalism* (1978), argued that, from the ancient Greeks to the contemporary period, the West produced a "knowledge" of the Orient that helped to determine the course of its dominance. The postcolonial nation must thus rebuild its culture while avoiding isolation and chauvinism.

[. . .] Three great topics emerge in decolonizing cultural resistance, separated for analytical purposes, but all related. One, of course, is the insistence on the right to see the community's history whole, coherently, integrally. Restore the imprisoned nation to itself. (Benedict Anderson connects this in Europe to "print-capitalism," which "gave a new fixity to language" and "created unified fields of exchange and communications below Latin and above the spoken vernaculars.")[1] The concept of the national language is central, but without the practice of a national culture – from slogans to pamphlets and newspapers, from folktales and heroes to epic poetry, novels, and drama – the language is inert; national culture organizes and sustains communal memory, as when early defeats in African resistance stories are resumed ("they took our weapons in 1903; now we are taking them back"); it reinhabits the landscape using restored ways of life, heroes, heroines, and exploits; it formulates expressions and emotions of pride as well as defiance, which in turn form the backbone of the principal national independence parties. Local slave narratives, spiritual autobiographies, prison memoirs form a counterpoint to the Western powers' monumental histories, official discourses, and panoptic quasi-scientific viewpoint. In Egypt, for example, the historical novels of Girgi Zaydan bring together for the first time a specifically Arab narrative (rather the way Walter Scott did a century before). In Spanish America, according to Anderson, *creole* communities "produced creoles who consciously redefined these [mixed] populations as fellow nationals."[2] Both Anderson and Hannah Arendt note the widespread global movement to "achieve solidarities on an essentially imagined basis."[3]

Second is the idea that resistance, far from being merely a reaction to imperialism, is an alternative way of conceiving human history. It is particularly important to see how much this alternative reconception is based on breaking down the barriers between cultures. Certainly, as the title of a fascinating book has it, *writing back* to the metropolitan cultures, disrupting the European narratives of the Orient and Africa, replacing them with either a more playful or a more powerful new narrative style is a major component in the process.[4] Salman Rushdie's novel *Midnight's Children* is a brilliant work based on the liberating imagination of independence itself, with all its anomalies and contradictions working themselves out. The conscious effort to enter into the discourse of Europe and the West, to mix with it, transform it, to make it acknowledge marginalized or suppressed or forgotten histories is of particular interest in Rushdie's work, and in an earlier generation of resistance writing. This kind of work was carried out by dozens of scholars, critics, and intellectuals in the peripheral world; I call this effort *the voyage in*.

Third is a noticeable pull away from separatist nationalism toward a more integrative view of human community and human liberation. I want to be very clear about this. No one needs to be reminded that throughout the imperial world during the decolonizing period, protest, resistance, and independence movements were fuelled by one or another nationalism. Debates today about Third World nationalism have been increasing in volume and interest, not least because to many scholars and observers in the West, this reappearance of nationalism revived several anachronistic attitudes; Elie Kedourie, for example, considers non-Western nationalism essentially condemnable, a negative reaction to a demonstrated cultural and social inferiority, an imitation of "Western" political behavior that brought little that was good; others, like Eric Hobsbawm and Ernest Gellner, consider nationalism as a form of political behavior that has been gradually superseded by new trans-national realities of modern economies, electronic communications, and superpower military projection.[5] In all these views, I believe, there is a marked (and, in my opinion, ahistorical) discomfort with non-Western societies acquiring national independence, which is believed to be "foreign" to their ethos. Hence the repeated insistence on the *Western* provenance of nationalist philosophies that are therefore ill-suited to, and likely to be abused by Arabs, Zulus, Indonesians, Irish, or Jamaicans.

This, I think, is a criticism of newly independent peoples that carries with it a broadly *cultural* opposition (from the Left as well as from the Right) to the proposition that the formerly subject peoples are entitled to the same kind of nationalism as, say, the more developed, hence more deserving, Germans or Italians. A confused and limiting notion of priority allows that only the original proponents of an idea can understand and use it. But the history of all cultures is the history of cultural borrowings. Cultures are not impermeable; just as Western science borrowed from Arabs, they had borrowed from India and Greece. Culture is never just a matter of ownership, of borrowing and lending with absolute debtors and creditors, but rather of appropriations, common experiences, and interdependencies of all kinds among different cultures. This is a universal norm. Who has yet determined how much the domination of others contributed to the enormous wealth of the English and French states?

A more interesting critique of non-Western nationalism comes from the Indian scholar and theoretician Partha Chatterjee (a member of the *Subaltern Studies* group). Much nationalist thought in India, he says, depends upon the realities of colonial power, either in totally opposing it or in affirming a patriotic consciousness. This "leads inevitably to an elitism of the intelligentsia, rooted in the vision of a radical regeneration of national culture."[6] To *restore* the nation in such a situation is basically to dream a romantically utopian ideal, which is undercut by the political reality. According to Chatterjee, the radical milestone in nationalism was reached in Gandhi's opposition to modern civilization entirely: influenced by anti-modern thinkers like Ruskin and Tolstoi, Gandhi stands epistemically outside the thematic of post-Enlightenment thought.[7] Nehru's accomplishment was to take the Indian nation as liberated from modernity by Gandhi and deposit it entirely within the concept of the state. "The world of the concrete, the world of differences, of conflict, of the struggle between classes, of history and politics, now finds its unity in the life of the state."[8]

Chatterjee shows that successful anti-imperialist nationalism has a history of evasion and avoidance, and that nationalism can become a panacea for *not* dealing with economic disparities, social injustice, and the capture of the newly independent state by a nationalist elite. But he does not emphasize enough, I think, that the culture's contribution to statism is often the result of a separatist, even chauvinist and authoritarian conception of nationalism. There is also, however, a consistent intellectual trend within the nationalist consensus that is vitally critical, that refuses the short-term blandishments of separatist and triumphalist slogans in favor of the larger, more generous human realities of community *among* cultures, peoples, and societies. This community is the real human liberation portended by the resistance to imperialism. Basil Davidson makes roughly the same point in his magisterial book *Africa in Modern History: The Search for a New Society.*[9]

I do not want to be misunderstood as advocating a simple anti-nationalist position. It is historical fact that nationalism – restoration of community, assertion of identity, emergence of new cultural practices – as a mobilized political force instigated and then advanced the struggle against Western domination everywhere in the non-European world. It is no more useful to oppose that than to oppose Newton's discovery of gravity. Whether it was the Philippines, or any number of African territories, or the Indian subcontinent, the Arab world, or the Caribbean and much of Latin America, China or Japan, natives banded together in independence and nationalist groupings that were based on a sense of identity which was ethnic, religious, or communal, and was opposed to further Western encroachment. That happened from the beginning. It became a global reality in the twentieth century because it was so widespread a reaction to the Western incursion, which had also become extraordinarily widespread; with few exceptions people banded together in asserting their resistance to what they perceived was an unjust practice against them, mainly for being what they were, i.e., non-Western. Certainly it was the case that these groupings were at times fiercely exclusivist, as many historians of nationalism have shown. But we must also focus on the intellectual and cultural argument within the nationalist resistance that once independence was gained new and imaginative reconceptions of society and culture were required in order to avoid the old orthodoxies and injustices.

The women's movement is central here. For as primary resistance gets under way, to be followed by fully fledged nationalist parties, unfair male practices like concubinage, polygamy, foot-binding, *sati*, and virtual enslavement become the focal points of women's resistance. In Egypt, Turkey, Indonesia, China, and Ceylon the early-twentieth-century struggle for the emancipation of women is organically related to nationalist agitation. Raja Ramuhan Roy, an early-nineteenth-century nationalist influenced by Mary Wollstonecraft, mobilized the early campaign for Indian women's rights, a common pattern in the colonized world, where the first intellectual stirrings against injustice included attention to the abused rights of all oppressed classes. Later women writers and intellectuals – often from privileged classes and often in alliance with Western apostles of women's rights like Annie Besant – came to the forefront of agitation for women's education. Kumari Jayawardena's central work *Feminism and Nationalism in the Third World* describes the efforts of Indian reformers like Tora Dutt, D. K. Karve, and Cornelia Sorabjee, and of militants such as Pundita Ramabai. Their counterparts in the Philippines, Egypt (Huda Shaarawi), Indonesia (Raden Kartini) broadened the stream of what became feminism, which after independence became one of the main liberationist tendencies.[10]

This larger search for liberation was most in evidence where the nationalist accomplishment had been either checked or greatly delayed – in Algeria, Guinea, Palestine, sections of the Islamic and Arab world, and South Africa. Students of post-colonial politics have not, I think, looked enough at the ideas that minimize orthodoxy and authoritarian or patriarchal thought, that take a severe view of the coercive nature of identity politics. Perhaps this is because the Idi Amins and Saddam Husseins of the Third World have hijacked nationalism so completely and in so ghastly a manner. That many nationalists are sometimes more coercive or more intellectually self-critical than others is clear, but my own thesis is that, at its best, nationalist resistance to imperialism was always critical of itself. An attentive reading of towering figures within the nationalist ranks – writers like C. L. R. James, Neruda, Tagore himself, Fanon, Cabral, and others – discriminates among the various forces vying for ascendancy within the anti-imperialist, nationalist camp. James is a perfect case in point. Long a champion of Black nationalism, he always tempered his advocacy with disclaimers and reminders that assertions of ethnic particularity were not enough, just as solidarity without criticism was not enough. There is a great deal of hope to be derived from this if only because, far from being at the end of history, we are in a position to do something about our own present and future history, whether we live inside or outside the metropolitan world.

In sum, decolonization is a very complex battle over the course of different political destinies, different histories and geographies, and it is replete with works of the imagination, scholarship and counter-scholarship. The struggle took the form of strikes, marches, violent attack, retribution and counter-retribution. Its fabric is also made up of novelists and colonial officials writing about the nature of the Indian mentality, for example, of the land rent schemes of Bengal, of the structure of Indian society; and, in response, of Indians writing novels about a greater share in their rule, intellectuals and orators appealing to the masses for greater commitments to and mobilization for independence.

One cannot put timetables or fixed dates on this. India followed one course, Burma another, West Africa another, Algeria still another, Egypt, Syria, and Senegal still others. But in all cases one sees the gradually more and more perceptible divisions between the massive national blocks: the West – France, Britain, Holland, Belgium, Germany, etc. – on one side, most of the natives on the other. Generally speaking therefore anti-imperialist resistance builds gradually from sporadic and often unsuccessful revolts until after World War One it erupts variously in major parties, movements, and person-alities all over the empire; for three decades after World War Two, it becomes more militantly independence-minded and yields up the new states in Africa and Asia. In the process it permanently changes the internal situation of the

Western powers, which divided into opponents and supporters of the imperial policy. [...]

Notes

1 Benedict Anderson, *Imagined Communities: Reflections on the Origin and Spread of Nationalism* (London: New Left, 1983), p. 47.
2 Ibid., p. 52.
3 Ibid., p. 74.
4 Bill Ashcroft, Gareth Griffiths, and Helen Tiffin, *The Empire Writes Back: Theory and Practice in Post-Colonial Literature* (London and New York: Routledge, 1989).
5 Eric Hobsbawm, *Nations and Nationalism Since 1780: Programme, Myth, Reality* (Cambridge: Cambridge University Press, 1990); Ernest Gellner, *Nations and Nationalism* (Ithaca: Cornell University Press, 1983).
6 Partha Chatterjee, *Nationalist Thought and the Colonial World: A Derivative Discourse* (London: Zed, 1986), p. 79. See also Rajat K. Ray, "Three Interpretations of Indian Nationalism," in *Essays in Modern India*, ed. B. Q. Nanda (Delhi: Oxford University Press, 1980), pp. 1–41.
7 Chatterjee, *Nationalist Thought*, p. 100.
8 Ibid., p. 161.
9 Basil Davidson, *Africa in Modern History: The Search for a New Society* (London: Allen Lane, 1978), especially p. 204. See also *General History of Africa*, ed. A. Adu Boaher, vol. 7, *Africa Under Colonial Domination, 1880–1935* (Berkeley, Paris, and London: University of California Press, UNESCO, James Currey, 1990), and *The Colonial Moment in Africa: Essays on the Movement of Minds and Materials, 1900–1940*, ed. Andrew Roberts (Cambridge: Cambridge University Press, 1990).
10 Kumari Jayawardena, *Feminism and Nationalism in the Third World* (London: Zed, 1986), especially pp. 43–56, 73–108, 137–54 *et passim*. For emancipatory perspectives on feminism and imperialism, see also Laura Nader, "Orientalism, Occidentalism and the Control of Women," *Cultural Dynamics* 2, No. 3 (1989), 323–55; Maria Mies, *Patriarchy and Accumulation on a World Scale: Women in the International Division of Labour* (London: Zed, 1986). See also Helen Callaway, *Gender, Culture and Empire: European Women in Colonial Nigeria* (Urbana: University of Illinois Press, 1987), and Nupur Chandur and Margaret Strobel, eds, *Western Women and Imperialism: Complicity and Resistance* (Bloomington: Indiana University Press, 1992).

Index